Troubleshooting Java
Second Edition

Laurenţiu Spilcă

Foreword by Ben Evans

M
MANNING
Shelter Island

brief contents

contents

foreword

You may already be familiar with Laurențiu Spilcă from his books *Spring Security in Action* and *Spring Start Here*, but if not, *Troubleshooting Java* provides a great introduction to his unique style of writing and pervasive humor. If you're a newcomer to Java development, you may well find his careful coverage of concepts extremely useful, especially when combined with thorough coverage of the available (free) tools and how to use them. In addition, the book includes many examples and demonstrations of what can go wrong, to help you build experience and confidence in using the tools.

Part 1 focuses on debuggers and covers common tools like the IntelliJ CE debugger—both their capabilities and their limitations. Unlike many other resources, Laurențiu covers several debugger techniques that go well beyond the basics, such as conditional breakpoints and nonpausing breakpoints. There's also solid coverage of the basics of troubleshooting Java applications using logs.

In part 2, the key topic of resource consumption and its central role in troubleshooting is front and center. The free VisualVM tool serves as a primary means of understanding this area and its related concepts. There is in-depth coverage of important topics such as CPU sampling and instrumentation and how to use the tools effectively. One essential, but often overlooked, area—the handling of external dependencies—is neatly showcased via the example of an SQL database using Hibernate. The subject of multithreaded programming, and especially troubleshooting locks, follows naturally from CPU profiling.

Part 3 is devoted to memory-related issues, including tracking down memory leaks with sampling and profiling techniques, as well as creating and navigating heap dumps. Practical techniques, such as filtering out JDK types and using the capabilities of VisualVM to consider live objects, are also covered, as well as the use of OQL to query heap dumps. Just as in part 1, the use of logs (in this case, GC logs) forms the subject of the last chapter in part 3.

To conclude, Laurențiu takes us on a quick tour through larger-scale systems, starting with an introduction to distributed tracing as a key technique, before tying it all together by discussing distributed transactions across heterogeneous systems. Throughout the book, Laurențiu makes careful and tactical use of AI tools, stressing the lack of magic bullets and focusing on practical use cases. While these tools cannot replace a human user, they can make a proficient engineer more productive and able to concentrate on the higher-level concerns. The end result is a book that is suitable for newcomers but is also forward-looking and recognizes how modern tooling can complement and enhance the intuition, experience, and problem-solving insight of working software engineers.

—BEN EVANS
JAVA CHAMPION AND AUTHOR OF
The Well-Grounded Java Developer

preface

preface

What does a software developer do for a living? "Implement software" is most likely the answer many would give. But what does implementing software really mean? Is it only writing code? Not quite. While the code is the visible result of a developer's work, the activity of writing it takes only a small fraction of the time. Most of a developer's day is spent designing solutions, reading existing code to understand how it behaves, and learning new concepts. Writing code is simply the outcome of successfully doing all of these.

That's why programmers often spend far more time reading code than writing it. Clean coding as a discipline grew out of this realization: it is more efficient to write solutions from the start in a way that makes them easier to read later. Still, not all code is clean, and not all systems are simple. You will always face situations where you need to dig into an unfamiliar solution and uncover how code really works.

The truth is, a software developer spends much of their career investigating how applications behave. We trace through our own code and third-party dependencies to understand why something doesn't work as expected. Sometimes, we do it to fix problems and other times just to learn. Often, reading code isn't enough. We need to go deeper—using debugging, profiling, or log analysis—to understand what is happening inside the JVM or how the environment affects the application. Knowing the right techniques, and when to apply them, can save enormous amounts of time. Optimizing this investigative activity is one of skills with the greatest strategic effect a developer can build.

The goal of this book is to help you optimize the way you investigate software systems. You will find relevant techniques illustrated with practical examples—debugging, profiling, log analysis, and how to combine them effectively. Along the way, I share tips and practices that will help you become faster and more confident in tackling difficult problems.

In this second edition, we also explore a new and increasingly important partner in troubleshooting: artificial intelligence. AI tools have become part of the developer's daily toolkit, capable of analyzing logs, suggesting hypotheses, or even pointing out suspicious code paths. They can accelerate investigation dramatically. But AI does not replace your judgment. Just like a detective uses assistants and tools but still solves the case, you remain the expert who interprets the evidence and makes the decisions. Used wisely, AI can help you focus on the most meaningful parts of the investigation and reach insights faster.

My goal remains the same: to make you more efficient as a developer. But in today's landscape, efficiency also means knowing how to use AI without becoming dependent on it. With the techniques and mindset in this book, you will be better equipped to find root causes quickly, learn continuously, and solve even the toughest problems with confidence.

I hope this edition brings you both practical value and inspiration for your daily work.

acknowledgments

This book wouldn't be possible without the large number of smart, professional, and friendly people who helped me out throughout its development process.

A heartful thank you goes to my wife Daniela, who was there for me, helped with valuable opinions, and continuously supported and encouraged me.

I'd like to thank the entire Manning team for their huge help in making this a valuable resource. I specifically want to mention Marina Michels and Nick Watts for being incredibly supportive and professional. Their advice brought great value to this book.

I also thank my friend Ioana Gôz for the drawings she created for the book. She did a great job turning my thoughts into the cartoons you'll discover here and there in the book.

Next, I thank everyone who reviewed the manuscript and provided useful feedback. To Alok Ranjan, Andrew Oswald, Becky Huett, Burkhard Nestmann, Chris Allan, Curtis Krauskopf, Faiz Gouri, Frank Beutelschiess, German Gonzalez-Morris, Jason Clark, Jitender Jain, Lars Opitz, Max Loukianov, Mebin Jacob, Naga Rishyendar Panguluri, Nancy Al Kalach, Nicolas Bievre, Prashant Gupta, Purushotham Krishnegowda, Ravi Laudya, Sachin Handiekar, Sanjay Belaturu Krishnegowda, Sathiesh Veera, Sumit Bhatnagar, Vamsi Kavuri, William Brawner, Heinz Kabuz, and Vlad Mihalcea, your feedback helped me improve the content of this book.

Finally, thanks to Ben Evans for taking the time to review the book and write its foreword.

about this book

Because you opened this book, I assume you are a developer working with a JVM language. You might use Java, but you could just as well be coding in Kotlin or Scala. Regardless of the JVM language, you will find the content valuable. This book teaches practical investigation techniques that help you identify the root causes of problems and also learn new technologies more effectively.

As a software developer, you've probably noticed how much of your time is spent understanding what your application actually does. Whether you are reading code, debugging, analyzing logs, or checking performance, chances are you spend far more time on these activities than on writing new code. That's why becoming more efficient at investigating and analyzing application behavior pays off so quickly—it helps you solve problems faster and with greater confidence.

This second edition also includes a new dimension: how to take advantage of AI as a partner in troubleshooting. AI can process large volumes of logs, highlight unusual patterns, or suggest possible causes. It won't replace your skills, but it can accelerate your work and allow you to focus on the insights that matter.

This book discusses and illustrates through examples topics such as

- Simple and advanced debugging techniques
- Efficient use of logs to understand application behavior
- Profiling CPU and memory resource consumption
- Profiling to locate executing code
- Profiling to understand how an app interacts with persisted data
- Analyzing communication between services

- Monitoring system events
- Using AI to assist in log analysis, root-cause identification, and knowledge discovery

Who should read this book?

This book is for any developer working with Java or another JVM language such as Kotlin or Scala. Regardless of your level of experience, you will find value—whether you are learning investigation techniques for the first time or refreshing skills you already use. Beginners and intermediate developers are likely to benefit the most, but even seasoned engineers may discover new tips, tools, or perspectives to sharpen their troubleshooting practice.

While the book is written with JVM developers in mind, many of the techniques—such as debugging strategies, log analysis, and profiling—apply broadly to software development in other languages as well. This edition also introduces ways to incorporate AI into troubleshooting, which is useful for any developer looking to work more efficiently in modern environments.

The only prerequisite for this book is a basic understanding of the Java language. All examples are presented in Java (for consistency), but the ideas can be applied in any JVM language. If you are comfortable with fundamental concepts such as classes, methods, variables, and basic control flow (loops and conditionals), you will have no difficulty following the discussions.

How this book is organized: A road map

This book is divided into four parts, each with its own focus. Think of them as stages in your journey from local detective work to system-wide investigations. You don't have to read them in order (though that's how I recommend it), but the sequence is designed to build your skills step by step.

- *Part 1*—We start at the beginning: the everyday techniques you'll use most often. Debugging and logging are your bread and butter as a developer. Here you'll learn not just how to set a breakpoint, but how to use advanced debugging tricks (such as conditional and nonblocking breakpoints) and how to make logs work for you instead of against you. This part is about building your investigative reflexes—the same way a detective first learns how to look for fingerprints.
- *Part 2*—In this part, we move to profiling. Profiling sounds fancy, but it's really just asking, What's eating my CPU? What's this app actually doing when I'm not looking? You'll learn how to track resource consumption, find hidden performance bottlenecks, and even spot suspicious SQL queries. We'll also use these chapters to introduce AI assistance—because sometimes you really do want a sidekick who can sift through mountains of data while you focus on the bigger picture.
- *Part 3*—Memory is where things get subtle (and sometimes sneaky). Here we dive into heap dumps, GC logs, and techniques for finding leaks or tuning memory

usage. It's not always glamorous but knowing how to read the JVM's diary of what happened inside memory can save you from days of head-scratching.

- *Part 4*—Finally, we zoom out. Real-world systems are rarely just one app; they're networks of services talking to each other. In this part we explore systemic problems: failed communication between services, data inconsistencies, cascading failures, retry storms, and all the other fun surprises of distributed computing. If part 1 was about using a magnifying glass, part 4 is about climbing a hill and seeing the whole landscape.

Each chapter stands on its own, so if you're currently battling memory leaks, go straight to part 3. If distributed tracing is your headache today, jump to part 4. But if you follow the road map in order, you'll gradually develop a complete troubleshooting toolkit— from quick debugging to understanding system-level chaos.

About the code

This book provides about 20 projects. We use them to study various investigation techniques throughout the book. You are not expected to write these projects yourself but can run and use them to test specific techniques discussed. Even if the Java technologies we employ here are less relevant for the techniques I teach, I chose to use the latest long-term supported Java version (Java 17) and Spring, one of the most used Java application frameworks today.

Each project is built with Maven, making it easy to be imported in any IDE. I have used IntelliJ IDEA to write the projects, but you can choose to run them in Eclipse, Netbeans, or any other tool of your choice. Appendix A includes an overview of the recommended tools.

This book contains many examples of source code, both in numbered listings and in line with normal text. In both cases, source code is formatted in a `fixed-width font like this` to separate it from ordinary text. Sometimes code is also in bold to highlight code that has changed from previous steps in the chapter, such as when a new feature adds to an existing line of code. In many cases, the original source code has been reformatted; we've added line breaks and reworked indentation to accommodate the available page space in the book. In rare cases, even this was not enough, and listings include line-continuation markers ( ). Additionally, comments in the source code have often been removed from the listings when the code is described in the text. Code annotations accompany many of the listings, highlighting important concepts.

You can get executable snippets of code from the liveBook (online) version of this book at https://livebook.manning.com/book/troubleshooting-java-second-edition. The complete code for the examples in the book is available for download from the Manning website at www.manning.com/books/troubleshooting-java-second-edition.

liveBook discussion forum

Purchase of *Troubleshooting Java, Second Edition* includes free access to liveBook, Manning's online reading platform. Using liveBook's exclusive discussion features, you can attach comments to the book globally or to specific sections or paragraphs. It's a snap to make notes for yourself, ask and answer technical questions, and receive help from the author and other users. To access the forum, go to https://livebook.manning .com/book/troubleshooting-java-second-edition.

Manning's commitment to our readers is to provide a venue where a meaningful dialogue between individual readers and between readers and the author can take place. It is not a commitment to any specific amount of participation on the part of the author, whose contribution to the forum remains voluntary (and unpaid). We suggest you try asking the author some challenging questions lest their interest stray! The forum and the archives of previous discussions will be accessible from the publisher's website for as long as the book is in print.

about the author

LAURENŢIU SPILCĂ is a dedicated development lead and trainer at Endava, and a Java Champion. He has experience with dozens of projects that employed various technologies of the Java ecosystem. Laurenţiu believes it's important to not only deliver high-quality software but also share knowledge and help others to up-skill, which has driven him to design and teach courses related to Java technologies, and deliver various presentations and workshops.

- Twitter handle @laurspilca
- YouTube handle @laurspilca

about the cover illustration

The figure on the cover of *Troubleshooting Java, Second Edition* is "Homme de l'Istrie," or "Man from Istria," taken from a collection by Jacques Grasset de Saint-Sauveur, published in 1797. Each illustration is finely drawn and colored by hand.

In those days, it was easy to identify where people lived and what their trade or station in life was just by their dress. Manning celebrates the inventiveness and initiative of the computer business with book covers based on the rich diversity of regional culture centuries ago, brought back to life by pictures from collections such as this one.

Part 1

Revisiting the foundation for code investigation

The ability to investigate code is one of the most important skills a developer can have. Whether you're fixing a bug, adding a new feature, or just trying to understand how things work, knowing how to read and explore your app's behavior is key.

In this part of the book, we go back to the basics—debugging and logging—but with a fresh twist. These classic tools have helped developers for decades. Debugging lets you pause and step through code, while logs give you a record of what happened. But today, there is something changing the game—artificial intelligence.

What if you could ask an AI to pick the best place to set a breakpoint? Or to read your logs and explain what went wrong? Or to summarize a messy piece of code so you can understand it faster?

This is no longer science fiction. In the pages ahead, you'll learn how traditional tools and AI work together to make troubleshooting easier, faster, and even a bit more fun.

Chapter 1 explains why code investigation matters. Chapters 2–4 dive into techniques—both familiar and new—that will help you solve problems with more confidence.

Starting to know your apps

This chapter covers
- Troubleshooting and why you should learn it
- The definition of a code investigation technique
- Code investigation techniques used to understand Java apps

Software developers have various responsibilities. Most of these responsibilities depend on how they understand the code they are working with. They also spend a significant amount of time analyzing code to identify and resolve problems, implement new capabilities, and learn new technologies. Because time is precious, developers need efficient investigation techniques to be productive. Learning how to be efficient in understanding your (or others') code and how your apps execute it is the main topic of this book.

I recall a quote from Robert C. Martin's book, *Clean Code: A Handbook of Agile Software Craftsmanship* (Pearson, 2008). He said, "Indeed, the ratio of time spent reading versus writing is well over 10 to 1. We are constantly reading old code as part of the effort to write new code. . . . [Therefore,] making it easy to read makes it easier to write." Well, I believe there is much more to add here besides reading the code. The real deal is to investigate the code, and we combine several techniques to do that.

NOTE Software developers generally spend more time understanding how the software works than writing code to implement new features or correct errors.

Troubleshooting is one of the most valuable skills a developer can master. Regardless of whether you're writing brand-new code or maintaining a complex system in production, things will go wrong. Maybe a service starts timing out. Maybe the app works on your machine but crashes in QA. Maybe everything looks fine, but users still report incorrect results. Troubleshooting is the skill that helps you make sense of these situations. It's about investigation, not guesswork.

At its core, troubleshooting means understanding how a system behaves, comparing that to how it should behave, and then identifying what's different. It's a combination of logic, observation, and sometimes a bit of intuition. Unlike fixing a syntax error or a failed unit test, real troubleshooting usually begins when you don't know yet what's wrong. And that's where many developers get stuck.

DEFINITION   *Troubleshooting* means understanding how a system behaves, comparing that to how it should behave, and then identifying what's different.

Learning to troubleshoot effectively makes you faster, more confident, and more independent. It gives you the tools to work on unfamiliar codebases, solve production problems, and even spot design flaws before they become outages. It's a skill that sets senior engineers apart, not because they know all the answers, but because they know how to investigate.

But let's turn our heads toward something of the same importance—the era we live in today. AI has become a powerful assistant for developers, and troubleshooting is one of the areas where it can truly shine. Whether you're inspecting a stack trace, asking for a regex fix, or trying to understand a cryptic configuration error, an AI assistant can help you move faster.

But make no mistake: AI won't do the job for you. It can point you in the right direction, summarize logs, or suggest solutions. However, it won't understand your system's business rules, history, or architectural decisions. It won't recognize that a seemingly minor inconsistency is the key to the whole mystery.

Think of it as of investigating a crime scene—the AI is a capable partner, helping process evidence and suggesting leads, but you are the detective. You ask the right questions. You connect the dots. And when you know what you're doing, AI can make you faster and more effective than ever. But if you don't have a solid foundation in trouble-shooting, no AI will save you from chasing red herrings.

> **TIP** Use AI to learn, upskill, and solve things yourself with its help. Be the puppeteer, not the puppet. This approach will maximize your efficiency.

There is another aspect I want to clarify before we dig in. Often, software developers use the word *debugging* for any investigation techniques; however, this is only one of the various tools available for examining logic implemented as code. While debugging should mean "finding problems and solving them," developers use it to describe different purposes for analyzing how code works:

- Learning a new framework
- Finding the root cause of a problem
- Understanding existing logic to extend it with new capabilities

1.1 How to more easily understand your app

First, it is essential to understand what investigating code and app execution are and how developers do it. This section looks at several commonly encountered scenarios in which you can apply the techniques you'll learn from this book.

I define *investigating code* as being the process of analyzing a software capability's specific behavior. You might wonder, "Why such a generic definition? What is the investigation's purpose?" Early in the history of software development, looking through code had one precise purpose: finding and correcting software errors (i.e., *bugs*). For this reason, many developers still use the term *debugging* for these techniques. Look at the way the word *debug* is formed:

de-bug = take out bugs, eliminate errors

In many cases today, we still debug apps to find and correct errors. But unlike the early days of software development, apps are more complex now. In many cases, developers find themselves investigating how a particular software capability works to learn a specific technology or library. Debugging is no longer only about finding a particular problem; it is also about correctly understanding its behavior (figure 1.1; see also http://mng.bz/M012).

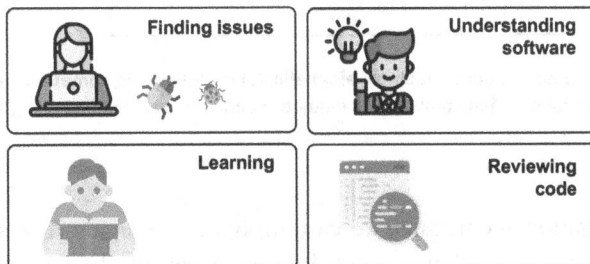

Finding issues

Understanding software

Learning

Reviewing code

Figure 1.1 Code investigation is not only about finding problems in software. Today, apps are complex. We often use investigation techniques to understand an app's behavior or simply learn new technologies.

We analyze code in apps for the following reasons:

- To find a particular problem
- To understand how a particular software capability works so we can enhance it
- To review code for correctness
- To learn a specific technology or library
- To optimize performance
- To eliminate vulnerabilities and improve security
- To enhance maintainability

Many developers also investigate code for enjoyment, because exploring how code works is fun. It can sometimes become frustrating as well, but nothing compares to the feeling of finding the root cause of a problem or finally understanding how things work (figure 1.2).

Figure 1.2   Investigating code doesn't require much physical effort, but debugging sometimes makes you feel like Lara Croft or Indiana Jones. Many developers enjoy the unique sensation of solving the puzzle of software problems.

There are various investigation techniques we can apply to investigate how software behaves. As discussed later in the chapter, developers (especially beginners) often wrongly consider debugging equivalent to using a debugger tool. The debugger (or a debugging tool) is a software program you can use to read and more easily understand the source code of an application, usually by pausing the execution on specific instructions and running the code step by step. It is a common way to investigate software behavior (and usually the first one a developer learns). But it is not the only technique you can use, and it doesn't help you in every scenario. We'll discuss both standard and more advanced ways of using a debugger in chapters 2 and 3.

Modern investigation techniques can be significantly enhanced through collaboration with AI. In this book, we explore various AI tools to elevate the way we analyze code and track application executions. By integrating AI, we augment traditional troubleshooting methods, making our work more efficient and less stressful. This approach allows us to identify problems faster and more accurately. Figure 1.3 illustrates the diverse investigation techniques you'll learn throughout the book.

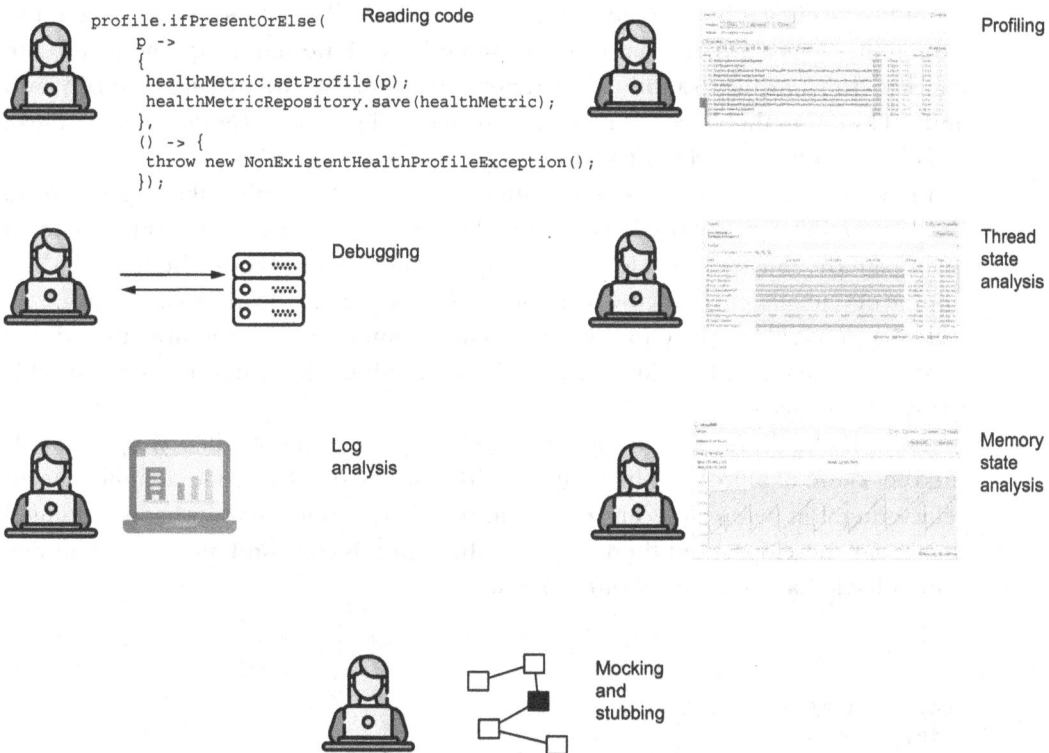

Figure 1.3 Code investigation techniques. Depending on the case, a developer can choose from one or more of these techniques to understand how a certain capability works.

When a developer fixes a bug, they spend most of their time understanding a particular feature rather than making the correction. The changes they make sometimes reduce the problem to a single line of code. This correction can be a missing condition, an instruction, or a misused operator. It's not writing the code but rather understanding how the app works, which occupies most of a developer's time.

> **NOTE** In many situations, I've seen developers advised to improve their coding speed to become more efficient. While that's excellent advice, I strongly believe that improving your troubleshooting skills should come first. Most of a developer's time isn't spent writing new code but reading existing code, understanding how the application behaves, and figuring out why things don't work as expected. That means sharpening your ability to investigate and reason through problems will make you faster and more effective much sooner than focusing solely on typing speed or code generation. Troubleshooting well is a force multiplier that saves time not just when something breaks, but also when you're trying to extend or refactor existing logic.

In some cases, simply reading the code is enough to understand it, but reading code is not like reading a book. When we read code, we don't read nice short paragraphs written in a logical order from top to bottom. Instead, we step from one method to another, from one file to another; we sometimes feel like we advance in a vast labyrinth and get lost. (On this subject, I recommend an excellent book, *The Programmer's Brain*, by Felienne Hermans [Manning, 2021]).

In many cases, the source code is written in a way that doesn't make it easy to read. Yes, I know what you are thinking: it should be. And I agree with you. Today, we learn many patterns and principles for code design and how to avoid code smells, but let's be honest: developers still don't use these principles properly in too many cases. Moreover, legacy apps usually don't follow these principles, simply because the principles didn't exist many years ago when those capabilities were written. But you still need to be able to investigate such code.

Take a look at listing 1.1. Suppose you find this piece of code while trying to identify the root cause of a problem in an app you're working on. This code definitely needs refactoring. But before you can refactor it, you need to understand what it is doing. I know some developers out there can read through this code and immediately understand what it does, but I'm not one of them.

Listing 1.1 Hard-to-read logic that requires use of a debugger

```java
public int m(int f, int g) {
  try {
    int[] far = new int[f];
    far[g] = 1;
    return f;
  } catch(NegativeArraySizeException e) {
    f = -f;
    g = -g;
    return (-m(f, g) == -f) ? -g : -f;
  } catch(IndexOutOfBoundsException e) {
```

```
    return (m(g, 0) == 0) ? f : g;
  }
}
```

To easily understand the logic in listing 1.1, I use a debugger, a tool that allows me to pause the execution on specific lines and manually run each instruction while observing how the data changes, to go through each line to observe how it works with the given input, as discussed in detail in chapter 2. With a bit of experience and some tricks mentioned in chapters 2 and 3, by parsing this code a few times, you will find that it calculates the maximum between the given inputs. This code is part of the project da-ch1-ex1 provided with the book.

As discussed, you can use AI assistants to help you understand the easier parts of your code. But remember that your purpose is to learn how it works and not that it's given to you what it does. So never use a prompt where you ask directly for the final result, such as

(LS) What does this code do?
.°.°. provided code .°.°.

Instead, prefer prompts that help you understand what's going on:

(LS) Explain this piece of code step by step so that I understand what it does:
.°.°. provided code .°.°.

If you go with the option of getting straight away with what the code does, several things might happen that will not help you either short or long term:

- The answer might be wrong. Remember, AI can make mistakes and sometimes hallucinate. Don't just take what it says for granted.
- If the answer is not right but looks right, you might in fact spend more time figuring out how that particular piece of code affects the execution.
- Even if the answer is the right one, you might not understand how code does what it does, which might not help you get its purpose into the whole context.

But some scenarios don't even allow you to navigate through the code, or they make navigating more challenging. Today, most apps rely on dependencies such as libraries or frameworks. In most cases, it's still difficult to follow the source code that defines a framework's logic, even when you have access to the source code (when you use an open source dependency). Usually, frameworks and libraries tend to have certain layers of abstraction that make them extensible and easy to configure. However, this aspect can add complexity when investigating code functionality.

In many cases, you don't even know where to start, and you must use different techniques to understand the app. For example, you could use a profiling tool (as you'll learn in chapters 5 through 8) to identify what code executes before deciding where to start the investigation.

NOTE Troubleshooting is particularly more complicated when you need to work with source code that doesn't belong to your application. In many cases, you have to deal with libraries' or frameworks' implementations.

In situations where an application crashes and is no longer running, traditional debugging methods are no longer viable. This situation leads us to the concept of postmortem investigation. For example, if a production service crashes due to an unexpected memory error, developers must perform a postmortem investigation to determine the cause and implement a fix.

Postmortem investigation refers to the process of troubleshooting an application after it has crashed. This type of investigation is necessary when the app is no longer running, such as after a crash in a production environment. The goal is to quickly identify the root cause of the crash using data collected during or after the event, such as logs, heap dumps, or thread dumps. These tools, explored in chapters 8 to 11, are essential for diagnosing problems and preventing future crashes.

Tools commonly used in postmortem investigations include

- *Output*—The result or outcome produced by the app after execution (if applicable)
- *Logs*—Capture application activity up to the point of failure
- *Heap dumps*—Provide a snapshot of the application's memory
- *Thread dumps*—Show the state of all threads at a particular moment

DEFINITION *Postmortem investigation* means troubleshooting a situation or behavior that caused an app crash after the event took place. Since the app is no longer running, a postmortem investigation limits you to only part of the techniques you can use and is usually more difficult to troubleshoot than other situations.

1.2   *Typical scenarios for using investigation techniques*

Let's discuss some common scenarios for using code investigation approaches. We must look at some typical cases from real-world apps and analyze them to emphasize the importance of this book's subject matter:

- To understand why a particular piece of code or software capability provides a different result than expected
- To learn how the technologies the app uses as dependencies work
- To identify causes for performance problems such as app slowness
- To find root causes for cases in which an app suddenly stops

For each presented case, you'll find one or more techniques helpful in investigating the app's logic. Later, we'll dive into these techniques and demonstrate with examples how to use them.

1.2.1 Demystifying the unexpected output

The most frequent scenario in which you'll need to analyze code is when some logic ends up with an output that is different than expected. This might sound simple, but it isn't necessarily easy to solve.

First, let's define *output*. This term might have many definitions for an app. Output could be some text in the app's console, or it could be some records changed in a database. We can consider output that an HTTP request the app sends to a different system or some data sent in the HTTP response to a client's request.

> **DEFINITION** *Output* is any result of executing a piece of logic that might result in data change, the exchange of information, or action against a different component or system.

How do we investigate a case in which a specific part of the app doesn't have the expected execution result? We do so by choosing the proper technique based on the expected output. Let's look at some examples.

SCENARIO 1: THE SIMPLE CASE

Suppose an app should insert some records into a database. Yet, the app adds only part of the records. That is, you expected to find more data in the database than the app actually produces.

The simplest way to begin analyzing this problem is using a debugging tool to follow the code execution and understand how it works (figure 1.4). You'll learn about the main features of a debugger in chapters 2 and 3. With the debugger, you add a marker (named breakpoint) at a specific line of code of your choosing to pause the app execution at that line. Then, the debugger allows you to continue the execution manually. You run code instructions one by one to observe how the variables' values change and then evaluate expressions on the fly.

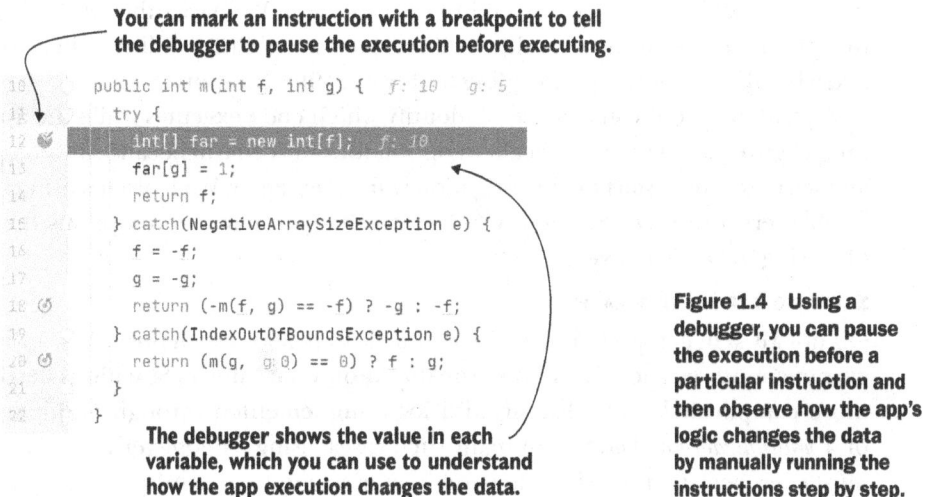

You can mark an instruction with a breakpoint to tell the debugger to pause the execution before executing.

```
10    public int m(int f, int g) {    f: 10    g: 5
11      try {
12        int[] far = new int[f];    f: 10
13        far[g] = 1;
14        return f;
15      } catch(NegativeArraySizeException e) {
16        f = -f;
17        g = -g;
18        return (-m(f, g) == -f) ? -g : -f;
19      } catch(IndexOutOfBoundsException e) {
20        return (m(g, g-0) == 0) ? f : g;
21      }
22    }
```

The debugger shows the value in each variable, which you can use to understand how the app execution changes the data.

Figure 1.4 Using a debugger, you can pause the execution before a particular instruction and then observe how the app's logic changes the data by manually running the instructions step by step.

This scenario is the simplest, and by learning how to use all the relevant debugger features properly, you can find solutions to such problems in no time. Unfortunately, other cases are more complex, and a debugger tool isn't always enough to solve the puzzle and find the cause of the problem.

> **TIP** In many cases, one investigative technique isn't enough to understand the app's behavior. You'll need to combine various approaches to understand more complex behavior faster.

SCENARIO 2: THE WHERE-SHOULD-I-START-DEBUGGING CASE?

Sometimes, you won't be able to use a debugger simply because you don't know what to debug (i.e., what part of the code). Suppose your app is a complex service with many lines of code. You investigate a problem where the app doesn't store the expected records in a database. It's definitely an output problem, but out of the thousands of lines of code defining your app, you don't know what part implements the capability you need to fix.

I remember a colleague who was investigating such a problem. Stressed from being unable to find where to start the debugging from, he exclaimed: "I wish debuggers had a way for you to add a breakpoint on all the lines of an app so you could see what it actually hits."

My colleague's statement was funny, and he was obviously joking, because having such a feature in a debugger wouldn't be a solution. We have other ways to approach this problem. You would most likely narrow the possibilities of lines where you could add a breakpoint by using a profiling tool (or profiler for short).

A *profiler* is a tool you can use to identify which code executes while the app is running (figure 1.5). This is an excellent option for our scenario because it would give you an idea of where to start the investigation with a debugger. We'll discuss using a profiler in chapters 5 through 8, where you'll learn that you have more options than simply observing the code in execution.

SCENARIO 3: A MULTITHREADED APP

Oh no! My skin gets goosebumps every time I think about such problems, and if you've ever encountered such cases, you probably know what I mean. Situations become even more complicated when dealing with logic implemented through multiple threads, or a *multithreaded architecture*. In many such cases, using a debugger is not an option in most cases because multithreaded architectures tend to be sensitive to interference.

The sampling capability of a profiling tool
shows the code in execution.

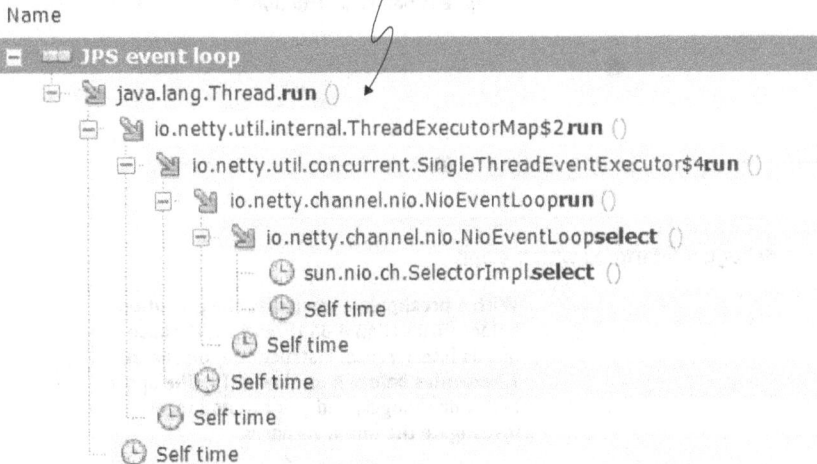

Name

- JPS event loop
  - java.lang.Thread.**run** ()
    - io.netty.util.internal.ThreadExecutorMap$2 **run** ()
      - io.netty.util.concurrent.SingleThreadEventExecutor$4 **run** ()
        - io.netty.channel.nio.NioEventLoop **run** ()
          - io.netty.channel.nio.NioEventLoop **select** ()
            - sun.nio.ch.SelectorImpl.**select** ()
            - Self time
          - Self time
        - Self time
      - Self time
    - Self time
  - Self time

Figure 1.5   Identifying code in execution with a profiler. If you don't know where to start debugging, the profiler can help you to identify the code that is running and give you an idea of where you can use the debugger.

In other words, the way the app behaves is different when you use the debugger. Developers call this characteristic a *Heisenberg execution* or *Heisenbug* (figure 1.6). The name comes from the twentieth-century physicist Werner Heisenberg, who formulated the uncertainty principle, which states that once you interfere with a particle, it behaves differently, so you cannot accurately predict both its velocity and position simultaneously. If you are a modern physics fan, you might know what I mean and enjoy the following article; if not, don't worry about it (https://plato.stanford.edu/entries/qt-uncertainty/). A multithreaded architecture might change its behavior if you interfere with it, just the way quantum mechanics particles behave differently if you interfere with them.

Multithreaded functionality presents a wide range of complex scenarios, which, in my opinion, makes it one of the most challenging aspects to test. While profilers can sometimes help, they may interfere with the app's execution, potentially skewing the results. An alternative approach is to implement logging within the app (covered in chapter 4). For certain problems, you can simplify the debugging process by reducing the number of active threads to one, allowing for more straightforward investigation using a debugger.

SCENARIO 4: SENDING THE WRONG CALLS TO A GIVEN SERVICE

You may need to investigate a scenario where the app doesn't correctly interact with another system component or an external system. Suppose your app sends HTTP

When nothing interferes with the app

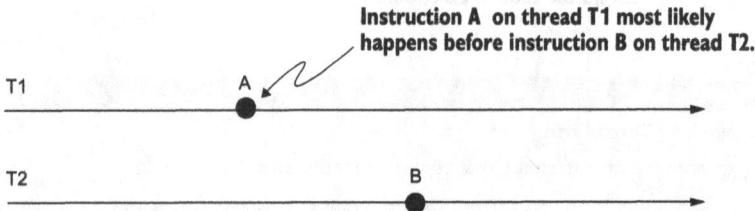

Instruction A on thread T1 most likely happens before instruction B on thread T2.

T1 ——————————— A ———————————————→

T2 ——————————————— B ————————————→

When a debugger interferes with the app

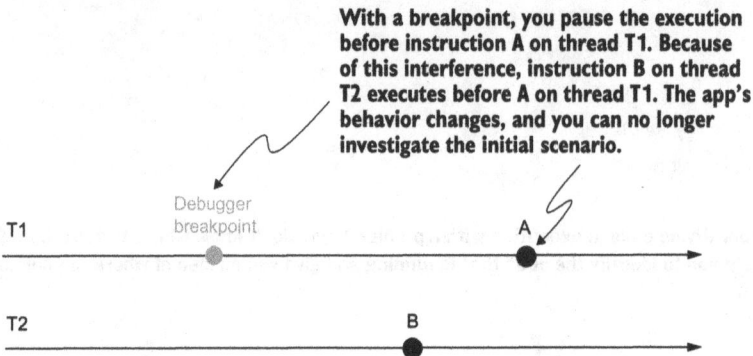

With a breakpoint, you pause the execution before instruction A on thread T1. Because of this interference, instruction B on thread T2 executes before A on thread T1. The app's behavior changes, and you can no longer investigate the initial scenario.

Debugger
breakpoint

T1 ———————○——————————— A ————————→

T2 ——————————————— B ————————————→

Figure 1.6   A Heisenberg execution. In a multithreaded app, when a debugger interferes with the app's execution, it might change how the app behaves. This change doesn't allow you to correctly investigate the initial app behavior that you wanted to research.

requests to another app. You get notified by the maintainers of the second app that the HTTP requests don't have the right format (maybe a header is missing, or the request body contains wrong data). Figure 1.7 illustrates this case.

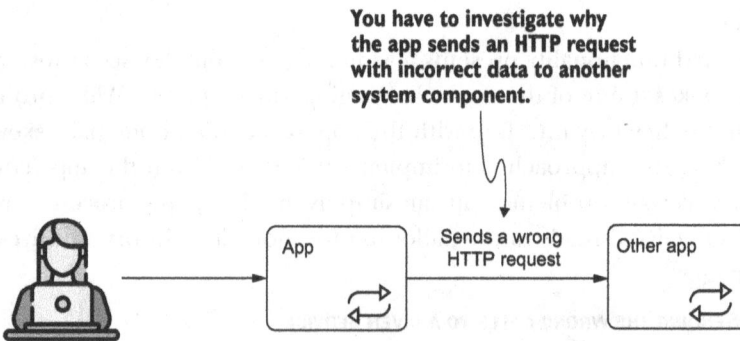

You have to investigate why the app sends an HTTP request with incorrect data to another system component.

App   Sends a wrong
HTTP request   Other app

Figure 1.7   A wrong output can be your app sending erroneous requests to another system component. You may be asked to investigate such behavior and find its root cause.

This is a *wrong output* scenario. How could you approach it? First, identify what part of the code sends the requests. If you already know, you can use a debugger to investigate how the app creates the request and determine what is going wrong. If you need to find what part of the app sends a request, you may need to use a profiler, as you'll learn in chapters 5 through 8. You can use a profiler to determine what code acts at a given time in the execution process.

Here's a trick I always use when dealing with a complex case such as this one, in which I can't straightforwardly identify where the app sends the request to/from: I replace the other app (the one my app wrongly sends requests to) with a stub.

DEFINITION   A *stub* is a fake application that can be controlled to help identify the problem.

For example, to determine what part of the code sends the requests, I can make my stub block the request, so my app indefinitely waits for a response. Then, I use a profiler to determine what code is being stuck by the stub. Figure 1.8 shows the usage of a stub. Compare this figure to figure 1.7 to understand how the stub replaced the real app.

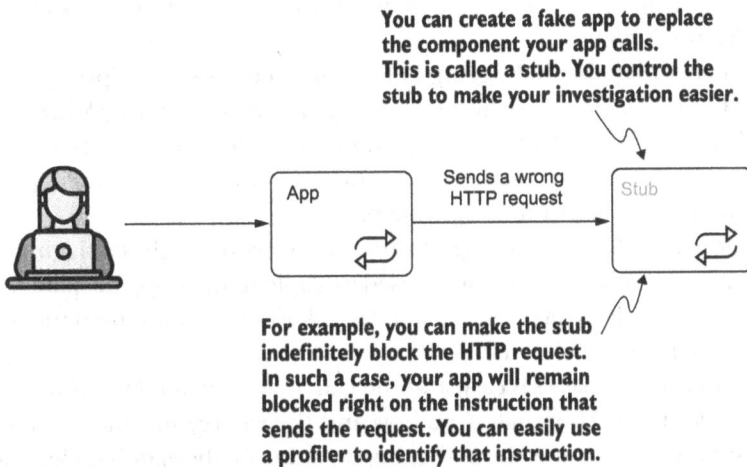

Figure 1.8   You can replace the system component your app calls with a stub. You control the stub to determine where your app sends the request from quickly. You can also use the stub to test your solution after you correct the problem.

1.2.2   Getting familiar with your external libraries

Another use of investigative techniques for analyzing code (one which I absolutely love and wish more developers would try) is learning how certain technologies work. Some developers joke that 6 hours of debugging can save 5 minutes of reading the documentation. While it's true that reading documentation is also essential when learning something new, some technologies are too complex to learn just from reading books or the specifications. I always advise my students and colleagues to dive deeper into a specific framework or library to understand it properly.

TIP For any technology (framework or library) you learn, spend some time reviewing the code you write. Always try to go deeper and debug the framework's code.

I'll start with my favorite, Spring Security. At first glance, Spring Security may seem trivial. It's just implementing authentication and authorization, isn't it? In fact, it is—until you discover various ways to configure these two capabilities into your app. You mix them wrong, and you may get in trouble. When things don't work, you must deal with what isn't working, and the best choice to deal with what isn't working is by investigating Spring Security's code.

More than anything else, debugging helped me to understand Spring Security. To help others, I put my experience and knowledge into a book, *Spring Security in Action*, second edition (Manning, 2023). In it, I provide more than 70 projects for you to not only re-create and run, but also to debug. I invite you to debug all examples provided in the books you read to learn various technologies.

The second example of technology I learned mostly through debugging is Hibernate. Hibernate is a high-level framework used to implement an app's capability to work with an SQL database. Hibernate is one of the best-known and most-used frameworks in the Java world, so it's a must-learn for any Java developer.

Learning Hibernate's basics is easy, and you can do this by simply reading books. But in the real world, using Hibernate (the how and the where) includes so much more than the basics. And for me, without digging deep into Hibernate's code, I definitely wouldn't have learned as much about this framework as I know today.

My advice for you is simple: for any technology (framework or library) you learn, spend some time reviewing the code you write. Always try to go deeper and debug the framework's code. This will make you a better developer.

1.2.3   *Clarifying slowness*

Performance problems occur occasionally in apps, and like any other problem, you need to investigate it before you know how to solve it. Learning to properly use different debugging techniques to identify the causes of performance problems is vital.

In my experience, the most frequent performance problems that occur in apps are related to how quickly an app responds. However, even if most developers consider slowness and performance equal, that's not the case. Slowness problems (situations in which an app responds slowly to a given trigger) are just one kind of performance problems.

For example, I once had to debug a mobile app that was consuming the device's battery too quickly. I had an Android app using a library that connected to an external device via Bluetooth. For some reason, the library was creating lots of threads without closing them. These threads, which remain open and run without purpose, are called *zombie threads* and typically cause performance and memory problems. They are also usually challenging to investigate.

However, this type of problem, in which the battery is being consumed too fast, is also an app performance problem. An app using too much network bandwidth while transferring data over the network is another good example.

Let's stick to slowness problems, which are encountered the most. Many developers fear this type of problem. Usually, that's not because they are complex to identify, but because they can be challenging to solve. Finding the cause of a performance problem is usually an easy job with a profiler, as you'll learn in chapters 5 through 8. In addition to identifying which code executes, as discussed in section 1.2.1, a profiler also displays the time the app spends on each instruction (figure 1.9).

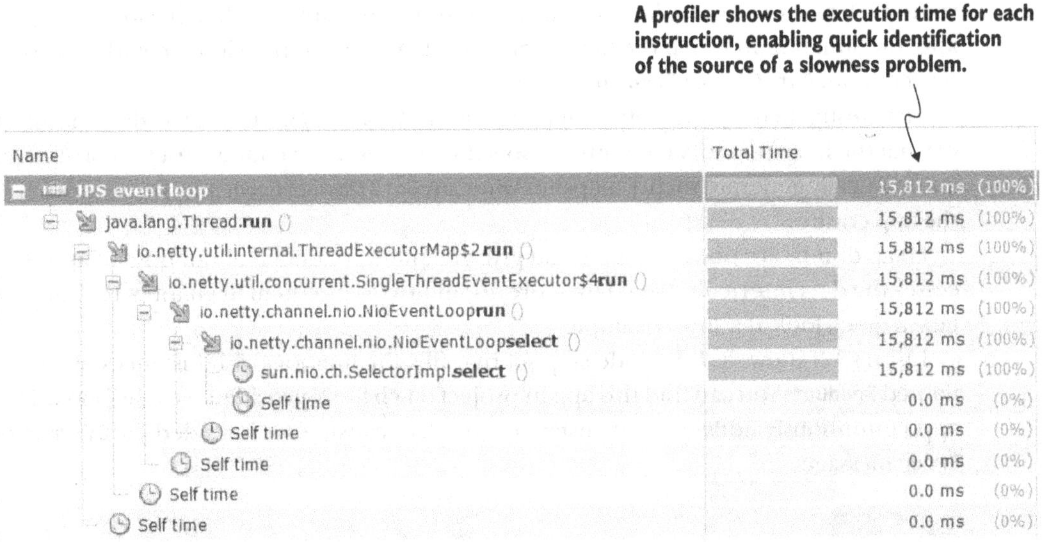

A profiler shows the execution time for each instruction, enabling quick identification of the source of a slowness problem.

Name	Total Time	
JPS event loop	15,812 ms	(100%)
java.lang.Thread.**run** ()	15,812 ms	(100%)
io.netty.util.internal.ThreadExecutorMap$2 **run** ()	15,812 ms	(100%)
io.netty.util.concurrent.SingleThreadEventExecutor$4**run** ()	15,812 ms	(100%)
io.netty.channel.nio.NioEventLoop**run** ()	15,812 ms	(100%)
io.netty.channel.nio.NioEventLoop**select** ()	15,812 ms	(100%)
sun.nio.ch.SelectorImpl**select** ()	15,812 ms	(100%)
Self time	0.0 ms	(0%)
Self time	0.0 ms	(0%)
Self time	0.0 ms	(0%)
Self time	0.0 ms	(0%)
Self time	0.0 ms	(0%)

Figure 1.9 **Investigating slowness problems with a profiler. The profiler shows you the time spent on each instruction during code execution. This profiler feature is excellent for identifying the root causes of performance problems.**

In many cases, slowness problems are caused by I/O calls, such as reading or writing from a file or a database or sending data over the network. For this reason, developers often act empirically to find the cause of the problem. If you know what capability is affected, you can focus on the I/O calls that capability executes. This approach also helps in minimizing the scope of the problem, but you usually still need a tool to identify its exact location.

1.2.4 *Understanding app crashes*

Sometimes apps completely stop responding for various reasons. These kinds of problems are usually considered more challenging to investigate. In many cases, app crashes occur only under specific conditions, so you can't reproduce (make the problem happen on purpose) them in the local environment.

Every time you investigate a problem, you should first try to reproduce it in an environment where you can study the problem. This approach gives your investigation more flexibility and helps you to confirm your solution. However, we're not always lucky enough to be able to reproduce a problem. And app crashes are usually not easy to reproduce.

We find app crash scenarios in two main flavors:

- The app completely stops.
- The app still runs but doesn't respond to requests.

When the app stops completely, it's usually because it encountered an error that prevented it from recovering. Most often, a memory error causes such behavior. For a Java app, the situation in which the heap memory fills and the app no longer works is represented by an OutOfMemoryError message.

To investigate heap memory problems, we use *heap dumps*, which provide a snapshot of what the heap memory contains at a specific time. You can configure a Java process to automatically generate such a snapshot when an OutOfMemoryError message occurs and the app crashes.

Heap dumps are powerful tools that give you plenty of details about how an app processes the data internally. We'll talk more about how to use them in chapter 10. But let's take a quick look at a short example.

Listing 1.2 shows a short code snippet that fills the memory with instances of a class named Product. You can find this app in project da-ch1-ex2 provided with the book. The app continuously adds Product instances to a list, causing an intended OutOfMemory-Error message.

Listing 1.2 An app example causing an OutOfMemoryError message

```
public class Main {

  private static List<Product> products =      ◄──  Declares a list that stores
    new ArrayList<>();                               references of Product objects

  public static void main(String[] args) {
    while (true) {                                    Adds Product instances
      products.add(                          ◄──      continuously to the list until the
                                                       heap memory completely fills
```

```
            new Product(UUID.randomUUID().toString()));
    }
  }
}
```

> **Each Product instance has a String attribute. We use a unique random identifier as its value.**

Figure 1.10 shows a heap dump created for one execution of this app. You can easily see that Product and String instances fill most of the heap memory. A heap dump is like a map of the memory. It gives you many details, including the relationships between instances, as well as values. For example, even if you don't see the code, you can still notice a connection between the Product and the String instances based on how close the numbers of these instances are. Don't worry if these aspects look complex. We'll discuss in detail everything you need to know about using heap dumps in chapter 10.

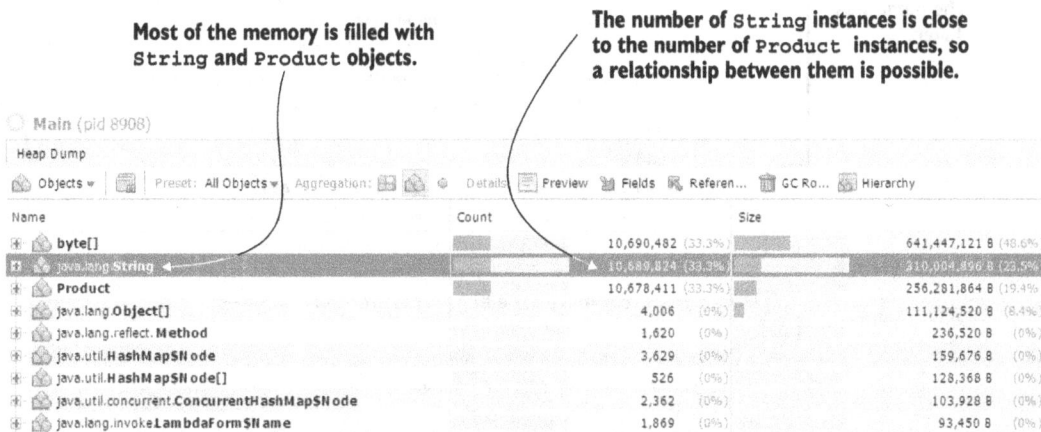

> **Most of the memory is filled with String and Product objects.**

> **The number of String instances is close to the number of Product instances, so a relationship between them is possible.**

Main (pid 8908)

Heap Dump

Objects ▾   Preset: All Objects ▾   Aggregation: ▦ ▦ ◉   Details ▤ Preview ▦ Fields ▦ Referen... ▦ GC Ro... ▦ Hierarchy

Name	Count		Size	
byte[]	10,690,482	(33.3%)	641,447,121 B	(48.6%)
java.lang.String	10,689,824	(33.3%)	310,004,896 B	(23.5%)
Product	10,678,411	(33.3%)	256,281,864 B	(19.4%)
java.lang.Object[]	4,006	(0%)	111,124,520 B	(8.4%)
java.lang.reflect.Method	1,620	(0%)	236,520 B	(0%)
java.util.HashMap$Node	3,629	(0%)	159,676 B	(0%)
java.util.HashMap$Node[]	526	(0%)	128,368 B	(0%)
java.util.concurrent.ConcurrentHashMap$Node	2,362	(0%)	103,928 B	(0%)
java.lang.invoke.LambdaForm$Name	1,869	(0%)	93,450 B	(0%)

Figure 1.10 A heap dump is like a map of the heap memory. If you learn how to read it, it gives you invaluable clues about how the app internally processes data. A heap dump helps you investigate memory or performance problems. In this example, you can easily find which object fills most of the app's memory and that the Product and String instances are related.

If the app still runs but stops responding to requests, then a *thread dump* is the best tool to analyze a thread dump is the best tool for analyzing what is happening. Figure 1.11 shows an example of a thread dump and some of the details this tool provides. Chapter 8 discusses generating and analyzing thread dumps to investigate code.

1.3 *AI as a game changer in troubleshooting apps*

We've recently entered a new era in software development—the artificial intelligence (AI) era. AI has revolutionized many aspects of software development, and troubleshooting is no exception. By employing AI tools, developers can diagnose problems faster, automate repetitive tasks, and gain deeper insights into complex problems. This

A thread dump clearly
shows the state of each
thread.

Name

⊟ 🖵 "main" prio=5 tid=1 RUNNABLE ◄
　　at sun.security.provider.SHA2**implCompressCheck** (SHA2.java:209)
⊞　at sun.security.provider.SHA2**implCompress** (SHA2.java:198)
⊞　at sun.security.provider.SHA2**implDigest** (SHA2.java:111)
⊞　at sun.security.provider.DigestBase.**engineDigest** (DigestBase.java:210)
⊞　at sun.security.provider.DigestBase.**engineDigest** (DigestBase.java:189)
　　at java.security.MessageDigest$Delegate.**engineDigest** (MessageDigest.java:639)
⊞　at java.security.MessageDigest.**digest** (MessageDigest.java:385)
⊞　at sun.security.provider.HashDrbg.**generateAlgorithm** (HashDrbg.java:224)
　　at sun.security.provider.AbstractDrbg.**engineNextBytes** (AbstractDrbg.java:394)
　　at sun.security.provider.AbstractDrbg.**engineNextBytes** (AbstractDrbg.java:334)
　　at sun.security.provider.DRBG.**engineNextBytes** (DRBG.java:233)
　　at java.security.SecureRandom.**nextBytes** (SecureRandom.java:751)
⊞　at java.util.UUID.**randomUUID** (UUID.java:150)
⊞　at Main.**main** (Main.java:11)

⊟ 🖵 "Reference Handler" daemon prio=10 tid=2 RUNNABLE ◄
　　at java.lang.ref.Reference.**waitForReferencePendingList** (Native Method)
　　at java.lang.ref.Reference.**processPendingReferences** (Reference.java:241)
⊞　at java.lang.ref.Reference$ReferenceHandler.**run** (Reference.java:213)

⊟ 🖵 "Finalizer" daemon prio=8 tid=3 WAITING ◄
　　at java.lang.Object.**wait** (Native Method)
⊞　at java.lang.ref.ReferenceQueue.**remove** (ReferenceQueue.java:155)
⊞　at java.lang.ref.ReferenceQueue.**remove** (ReferenceQueue.java:176)
⊞　at java.lang.ref.Finalizer$FinalizerThread.**run** (Finalizer.java:120)

🖵 "Signal Dispatcher" daemon prio=9 tid=4 RUNNABLE ◄

You can also
easily see
what the thread
was doing when
the dump was
taken.

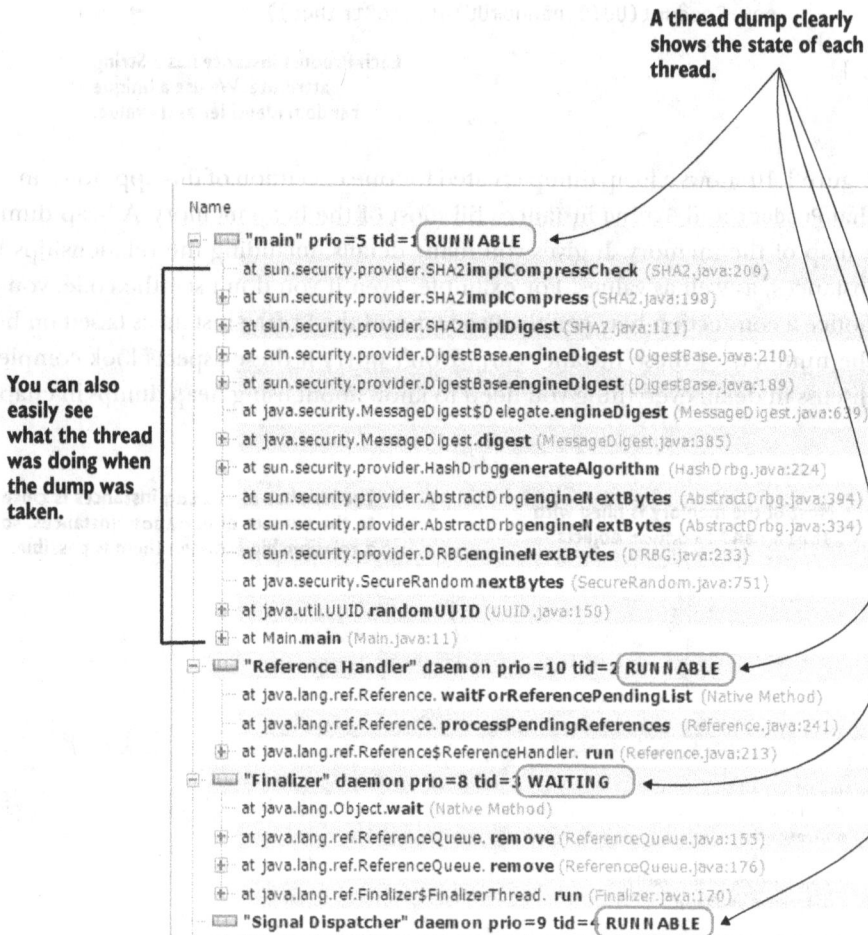

Figure 1.11　A thread dump provides details about the threads that were running when the dump was taken. It includes thread states and stack traces, which tell you what the threads were executing or what blocked them. These details are valuable for investigating why an app is stuck or is having performance problems.

section explores how AI, including tools such as ChatGPT, can enhance the debugging and troubleshooting process in Java applications.

Some may argue, "Why AI? Isn't this just hype?" Well, do you still find developers often using Notepad, vi, or a similar text editor to write code? No. Today, we all use IDEs that integrate in one place and provide us with several capabilities to make our lives easier with reading and writing code. We always transition to better tools and techniques to make our job easier, and that's why, in the future, AI tools will be part of what we'll commonly use.

NOTE　Start using and adapt quickly to the new AI tools. Failing to adapt and rejecting their evolution will only drag you behind.

Let me provide an initial use case of AI in troubleshooting. Section 1.2 described several types of troubleshooting situations. In this book, we'll focus on identifying which situation you're in and how to start troubleshooting. This experience will help you better understand the problems and how to deal with them over time. Remember that AI tools may prove extremely helpful in such situations.

The first tip is to use an AI prompt to get some ideas about where to start. For example, you can use ChatGPT or a similar tool to describe your problem and identify some starting points. I have tried this since these tools became popular and have made a habit of using them. Overall, I feel they have helped me improve the speed of understanding the capabilities I learn or the behavior I investigate. Let me tell you a story.

The mystery of a legacy bug

It was a typical Monday morning at the software development firm. The office was buzzing with the usual chatter of developers, product managers, and designers, all discussing their weekend escapades and gearing up for another busy week. In the corner of the office, Sarah, a seasoned Java developer, was already hard at work, her brow furrowed in concentration as she stared at lines of code on her screen.

Sarah had been assigned to work on a legacy Java application that the company had maintained for years. The application was critical to their business, serving thousands of customers daily. However, over the past week, the app had started behaving erratically—occasionally crashing without any clear reason. The logs were sparse, and traditional debugging methods had yielded no clues. Sarah knew she was dealing with an elusive bug, the kind that seemed to lurk in the shadows, striking without warning. She tried various troubleshooting techniques, but nothing worked, and her frustration was growing.

Just then, Michael, a junior developer, walked by her desk. Noticing her frustration, he paused and asked, "Hey, Sarah, everything okay?"

Sarah gave a weary smile. "Just wrestling with this legacy bug. I've tried everything—breakpoints, code reviews, even a profiler. Nothing. It's like the bug doesn't want to be found."

Michael nodded sympathetically. "Have you tried using ChatGPT? I heard it can help suggest possible causes for bugs based on the problem description."

Sarah was skeptical. She had heard about AI tools like ChatGPT but never considered them seriously for debugging. However, at this point, she was willing to try anything. "Why not," she thought. "It can't hurt to give it a shot."

She opened ChatGPT and began typing a detailed description of the problem.

"I'm working on a legacy Java application that's been crashing intermittently with no clear pattern. The logs are sparse, and traditional debugging methods haven't been helpful. The app uses older versions of Hibernate and Spring, and it interfaces with an Oracle database. Error messages are inconsistent, and the crash seems to occur after a series of complex transactions."

(continued)

Within seconds, ChatGPT responded:

"It sounds like you might be dealing with a memory leak or a race condition. Given that the application is using older versions of Hibernate and Spring, it's possible there could be a configuration issue or a hidden bug in those libraries. Have you checked for any misconfigured session factories or potential infinite loops in transaction handling?"

Sarah's eyes widened. The suggestion about the session factory misconfiguration struck a chord. She hadn't considered that angle. Excited, she dove back into the code, focusing on the Hibernate configuration files. As she combed through the files, she noticed something peculiar—a session factory was set to open a new session for every transaction, without properly closing the previous ones. This configuration could easily lead to memory problems and random crashes.

"Could it really be that simple?" she muttered to herself.

She quickly adjusted the configuration, making sure each session was properly closed after use. Then, she redeployed the application and waited, her heart racing. Minutes passed. Then an hour. The app continued running smoothly, with no crashes in sight.

Michael, noticing her excitement, walked over. "Did it work?"

Sarah nodded, grinning from ear to ear. "I think it did! It looks like the issue was a misconfigured session factory, just like ChatGPT suggested. I can't believe I didn't think of it earlier!"

Michael smiled. "Sometimes, it takes a fresh perspective. Even if it comes from an AI."

Even if Sarah's story is fictitious, I made it similar to several situations I've been through or witnessed since AI tools became a thing. And I advise you to try it yourself. In fact, we'll analyze different ideas further in this book. I will start with just a few helpful points (which we'll also detail more later in the following chapters) when using an AI prompt to help you identify the kind of problem you are solving and how to begin investigating it:

- *Always be as descriptive as possible when creating the prompt.* Give as many details as you can. I shortened Sarah's prompt in our story, but assume she gave even more details about her specific case.

- *Be careful with the details you provide.* Remember never to share sensitive information in the prompt, even if you want to be as descriptive as possible. Sensitive details might be related to the company you work for (like package names, which may contain the company name in some cases) or private details such as keys and passwords. Imagine Sarah might have also copied and pasted some code. She should be careful with what exactly she puts in the prompt to avoid any sensitive details. You should also review the policies of the company you're working for, as some may have stricter guidelines regarding the use of certain AI tools. It's important to exercise caution and ensure that you always comply with the company's internal regulations.

- *Use AI-generated responses as a guide but never rely on them blindly.* AI tools can sometimes produce incorrect or misleading information, a phenomenon known as *AI hallucination.* This means the AI might fabricate details that seem plausible but are not grounded in reality. Additionally, the accuracy of the output depends heavily on the input quality (i.e., your prompt). Always verify the information and cross-check it with reliable sources to ensure accuracy.

- *Use multiple prompts to fill in gaps according to the response you get.* Even if I made the story short in this case, don't be discouraged if the solution doesn't enlighten from the start. Sometimes, you need to continue the discussion and get more involved.

1.4   *What you will learn in this book*

This book is designed for Java developers with varying experience levels, ranging from beginners to experts. You'll learn various code investigation techniques, the best scenarios in which to apply them, and how to apply them to save you troubleshooting and investigation time.

If you are a junior developer, you'll most likely learn many things from this book. Some developers master all these techniques only after years of experience; others never master them. Even if you are an expert, you may find familiar concepts, but there's still a good chance you'll discover new and exciting approaches.

When you finish the book, you will have learned the following skills:

- Applying different approaches to using a debugger to understand an app's logic or find a problem
- Correctly choosing which app investigation techniques to use to make your investigation faster and utilize AI tools to help you get on the fastest track from the beginning
- Investigating hidden functionality with a profiler to better understand how your app or a specific dependency of your app works
- Analyzing code techniques to determine whether your app or one of its dependencies causes a particular problem
- Investigating data in an app's memory snapshot to identify potential problems with how the app processes data
- Using logging to identify problems in an app's behavior or security breaches
- Analyzing logs and large data for troubleshooting purposes using AI tools

Summary

- You can use various investigation techniques to analyze software behavior.

- Depending on your situation, one investigation technique may work better than another. You need to know how to choose the correct approach to make your investigation more efficient. AI tools can be extremely helpful in determining where to start and which troubleshooting techniques to apply.

- For some scenarios, using a combination of techniques can help identify a problem faster. Learning how each analyzing technique works gives you an excellent advantage in dealing with complex problems.

- In many cases, developers use investigation techniques to learn new things rather than solve problems. When learning complex frameworks such as Spring Security or Hibernate, simply reading books or the documentation isn't enough. An excellent way to accelerate your learning is to debug examples that use the technology you want to understand better.

- A situation is easier to investigate if you can reproduce it in an environment where you can study it. Reproducing a problem not only helps you find its root cause more easily, but it also helps you verify that a solution works when applied.

Understanding your app's logic through debugging techniques

Not long ago, during one of my piano lessons, I shared the sheet music of a song I wanted to learn with my piano teacher. I was so impressed when he just played the song while reading the music sheet for the first time. "How cool is that?" I thought. "How does someone gain this skill?"

Then, I remembered that some years ago, I was in a peer-programming session with one of the newly hired juniors in the company I was working for. It was my turn at the keyboard, and we were investigating a relatively large and complex piece of code using a debugger. I started navigating through the code, pressing relatively quickly the keyboard keys that allowed me to step over, into, and out of specific lines of code. I was focused on the code but was quite calm and relaxed, almost forgetting

I had someone near me (which was rude). I heard this person say, "Wow, stop a bit. You're too fast. Can you even read that code?"

I realized that situation resembled my experience with my piano teacher. How can you acquire this skill? The answer is easier than you think: work hard and gain experience. While practicing is invaluable and takes a lot of time, I have some tips to share that will help you improve your technique much faster. This chapter discusses one of the most important tools used in understanding code—the debugger.

DEFINITION A *debugger* is a tool that allows you to pause the execution on specific lines and manually execute each instruction, while observing how the data changes.

Using a debugger is like navigating with Google Maps: it helps you find your way through complex logic implemented in your code. It's also the most used tool for understanding code.

A debugger is usually the first tool developers learn to use to help them understand what code does. Fortunately, all IDEs come with a debugger, so you don't have to do anything special to have one. In this book, I use IntelliJ IDEA Community in my examples, but any other IDE is quite similar and offers (sometimes with a different look) the same options we'll discuss. Although a debugger seems to be a tool most developers know how to use, you may find (in this chapter and in chapter 3) some new techniques.

Section 2.1 discusses how developers read code and why. In many cases, simply reading the code isn't enough to understand it. Enter the debugger or a profiler (which we'll talk about later, in chapters 5–8). In section 2.2, we continue the discussion by applying the simplest techniques for using a debugger with an example.

If you are an experienced developer, you might already know these techniques. But you may still find it useful to read through the chapter as a refresher, or you could go straight to the more advanced techniques for using a debugger discussed in chapter 3.

OK! Let's see!

2.1 *When analyzing code is not enough*

Let's start by discussing how to read code and why sometimes reading just the logic isn't enough to understand it. In this section, I'll explain how reading code works and how it is different from reading something else, like a story or a poem. To observe this difference and understand what causes the complexity in deciphering code, we'll use a code snippet that implements a short piece of logic. Understanding what's behind the way our brain interprets code will clarify the need for tools such as a debugger.

Any code investigation scene starts with reading the code. But reading code is different from reading poetry. When reading a verse, you move through the text line by line in a given linear order, letting your brain assemble and picture the meaning. If you read the same verse twice, you might understand different things.

With code, however, it's the opposite. First, code is not linear. When reading code, you don't simply go line by line. Instead, you jump in and out of instructions to understand how they affect the data being processed. Reading code is more like a maze than a straight road. And, if you're not attentive, you might get lost and forget where you started. Second, unlike a poem, the code always means the same thing for everyone. That meaning is the objective of your investigation.

Just like you'd use a compass to find your path, a debugger helps you identify more easily what your code does. As an example, we'll use the decode(List<Integer> input) method. You can find this code in project da-ch2-ex1 provided with the book.

Listing 2.1 An example of a method to debug

```java
public class Decoder {

  public Integer decode(List<String> input) {
    int total = 0;
    for (String s : input) {
      var digits = new StringDigitExtractor(s).extractDigits();
      total += digits.stream().collect(Collectors.summingInt(i -> i));
    }

    return total;
  }
}
```

If you read from the top to the bottom line, you must assume how some things work to understand the code. Are those instructions really doing what you think they're doing? When you are not sure, you must dive deeper and observe what the code actually does—you have to analyze the logic behind it. Figure 2.1 points out two uncertainties in the given code snippet:

- What does the StringDigitExtractor() constructor do? It might just create an object, or it might also do something else. It could be that it somehow changes the value of the given parameter.

- What is the result of calling the `extractDigits()` method? Does it return a list of digits? Does it also change the parameter inside the object we used when creating the `StringDigitsExtractor` constructor?

Does this constructor only create an object, or does it also do something else?

```
public class Decoder {

  public Integer decode(List<String> input) {
    int total = 0;
    for (String s : input) {
      var digits = new StringDigitExtractor(s).extractDigits();
      total += digits.stream().collect(Collectors.summingInt(i -> i));
    }

    return total;
  }
}
```

What does this method really do? Does it use the `String` parameter value?

Figure 2.1   When reading a piece of code, you often need to figure out what happens behind the scenes in some of the instructions composing that logic. The method names are not always suggestive enough, and you can't totally rely on them. Instead, you need to go deeper into what these methods do.

Even with a small piece of code, you may have to dive deeper into the instructions. Each new code instruction you examine creates a new investigation plan and adds to its cognitive complexity (figures 2.2 and 2.3). The deeper you go into the logic and the more plans you open, the more complex the process becomes.

You take a piece of stone,
chisel it with blood,
grind it with Homer's eye,
burnish it with beams
until the cube comes out perfect.

Next you endlessly kiss the cube
with your mouth, with others' mouths,
and, most important,
with infanta's mouth.

Then you take a hammer
and suddenly knock a corner off.

All, indeed absolutely all will say
what a perfect cube
this would have been
if not for the broken corner.

("A Lecture on the Cube," N. Stanescu)

Reading poetry is linear.
You read each verse one
by one, from top to bottom.

Figure 2.2   Compare how you read poetry with how you read code. You read poetry line by line, but when you read code, you jump around.

Reading code is not linear. Any instruction
might create a separate cognitive plan.
Sometimes you need to dive into those plans
to understand the full picture.

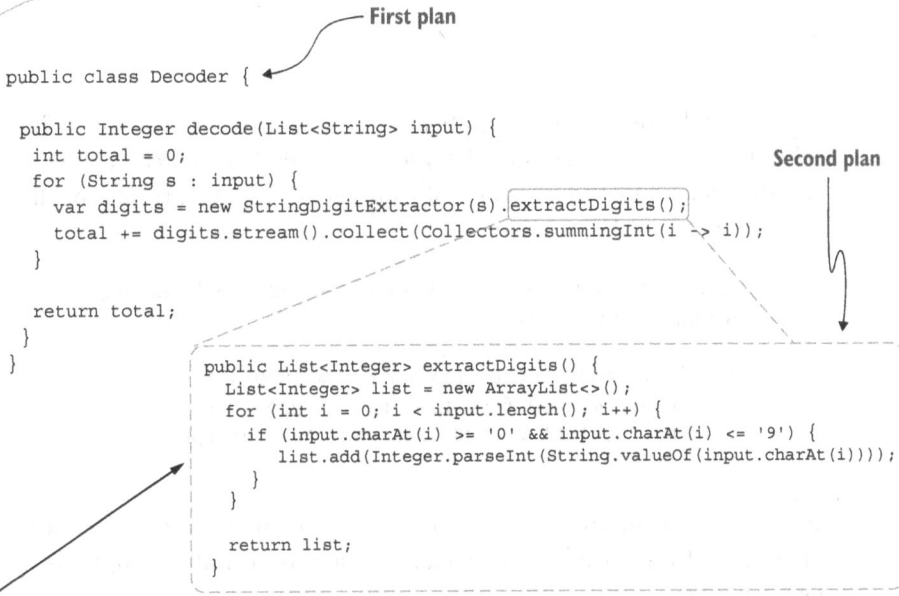

First plan

```java
public class Decoder {

    public Integer decode(List<String> input) {
        int total = 0;
        for (String s : input) {
            var digits = new StringDigitExtractor(s).extractDigits();
            total += digits.stream().collect(Collectors.summingInt(i -> i));
        }

        return total;
    }
}
```

Second plan

```java
public List<Integer> extractDigits() {
    List<Integer> list = new ArrayList<>();
    for (int i = 0; i < input.length(); i++) {
        if (input.charAt(i) >= '0' && input.charAt(i) <= '9') {
            list.add(Integer.parseInt(String.valueOf(input.charAt(i))));
        }
    }

    return list;
}
```

Figure 2.3 Reading code is different from reading poetry and is much more complex. You can imagine reading code as reading in two dimensions. One dimension is reading a piece of code top to bottom. The second dimension is going into a specific instruction to understand it in detail. Trying to remember how things work for each plan and how it assembles makes understanding code just by reading it very difficult.

Reading poetry always has one path. Code analysis, however, creates many paths instead through the same piece of logic. Did I say two plans earlier (figure 2.3)? Well, every time you go deeper, you leave one plan behind. So when you look at a particular piece of code, you see the current plan, and you know the method you see hides its own plan. But each time you jump into a method, you also leave behind one plan. The more you jump into methods, the more plans you open.

The more plans you open, the more complex the debugging process is. And the opposite is also true: the fewer new plans you open, the less complex the process is. You must choose between skipping over a certain instruction, making the overall investigation process simpler, or going into detail to understand each individual instruction better and raise the process complexity.

TIP Always try to shorten the reading path by minimizing the number of plans you open for investigation. Use a debugger to help you more easily navigate the code, keep track of where you are, and observe how the app changes the data while executing.

Reading code today can be significantly enhanced using AI tools such as ChatGPT or other large language model (LLM) tools. Remember, you can always use a prompt to get ideas about a code snippet. For example, you may start by providing a prompt as given in the following snippet.

Can you help me understand what this method does? Please provide me step-by-step explanation of the code?

```
public Integer decode(List<String> input) {
  // whole method from Listing 2.1 provided
  // but content erased from here to save space
}
```

Your LLM tool should give you an answer containing a detailed description of the method and the assumptions made. The summary and assumptions made may look like as follows:

The decode method

- Takes a list of strings as input.
- Iterates through each string in the list.
- For each string, extracts all numeric digits using `StringDigitExtractor` `.extractDigits()`.
- Sums up the extracted digits for each string.
- Accumulates these sums into a total.
- Returns the total sum of all digits extracted from all the strings.

Assumptions

To fully understand how this method works, we need to make a few assumptions about the `StringDigitExtractor` class and its `extractDigits()` method, as they are not defined in the code you provided:

- `StringDigitExtractor` is a class that takes a string as an argument in its constructor.
- `extractDigits()` is a method in `StringDigitExtractor` that returns a collection of numeric digits (likely as integers or numeric strings) found within the input string.

With these assumptions, the method effectively calculates the sum of all digits found in the entire list of strings.

Observe that the LLM tool correctly intuited the purpose of the decode() method. However, because you have only provided the first cognitive plan, the LLM tool made some assumptions and also provided you with the list of assumptions.

In my experience, the tool will always deliver a list of assumptions if it makes any assumptions. In case it doesn't, but you believe it might have, you can continue the conversation with a prompt asking for possible assumptions that have been made.

If the result doesn't satisfy your expectations, the casual flow is to continue the conversation by providing more information from the next cognitive plans until you reach a conclusion.

> **TIP** Remember that the majority of LLM tools can easily extract text from an image. If you cannot easily copy and paste the code but can extract it in an image (presumably with a screen capture), you can provide that image instead to obtain the same result.

2.2 Investigating code with a debugger

This section discusses a tool that can help you to minimize the cognitive effort of reading code to understand how it works—a debugger. All IDEs provide a debugger, and even if the interface might look slightly different from one IDE to another, the options are generally the same. I'll use IntelliJ IDEA Community in this book, but I encourage you to use your favorite IDE and compare it with the examples. You'll find they are pretty similar.

A debugger simplifies the investigation process by

- Providing you with a means to pause the execution at a particular step and execute each instruction manually at your own pace.
- Showing you where you are and where you came from in the code's reading path; this way, the debugger works as a map you can use, rather than trying to remember all the details.
- Showing you the values that variables hold, which makes the investigation easier to visualize and process.
- Allowing you to try things on the fly by using watchers and evaluating expressions.

Let's take the example in project da-ch2-ex1 again and use the most straightforward debugger capabilities to understand the code.

Listing 2.2 A piece of code we want to understand

```
public class Decoder {

  public Integer decode(List<String> input) {
    int total = 0;
    for (String s : input) {
```

```
        var digits = new StringDigitExtractor(s).extractDigits();
        total += digits.stream().collect(Collectors.summingInt(i -> i));
    }

    return total;
  }
}
```

I'm sure you're wondering, "How do I know when to use a debugger?" This is a fair question I want to answer before we continue. The main prerequisite is *knowing what piece of logic you want to investigate.* As you'll learn in this section, the first step in using a debugger is selecting an instruction where you want the execution to pause.

> **NOTE** Unless you already know which instruction you need to start your investigation from, you can't use a debugger.

In the real world, you'll find cases in which you don't know up front the specific piece of logic you want to investigate. In this case, before you can use a debugger, you must apply other techniques to find the part of the code you want to explore using the debugger (addressed in later chapters). In chapters 2 and 3, we focus only on using the debugger, so we'll assume you somehow found the piece of code you want to understand.

Going back to our example, where do we start? First, we need to read the code and figure out what we do and don't understand. Once we identify where the logic becomes unclear, we can execute the app and tell the debugger to pause the execution. We can pause the execution on those lines of code that are not clear to observe how they change the data. To tell the debugger where to pause the app's execution, we use *breakpoints.*

> **DEFINITION** A *breakpoint* is a marker used on lines where we want the debugger to pause the execution so we can investigate the implemented logic. The debugger will pause the execution before executing the line marked with the breakpoint.

In figure 2.4, I shaded the code that is pretty easy to understand (considering you know the language fundamentals). As you can see, this code takes a list as an input, parses it, processes each item in it, and somehow calculates an integer that the method returns in the end. Moreover, the process the method implements is easy to ascertain without a debugger.

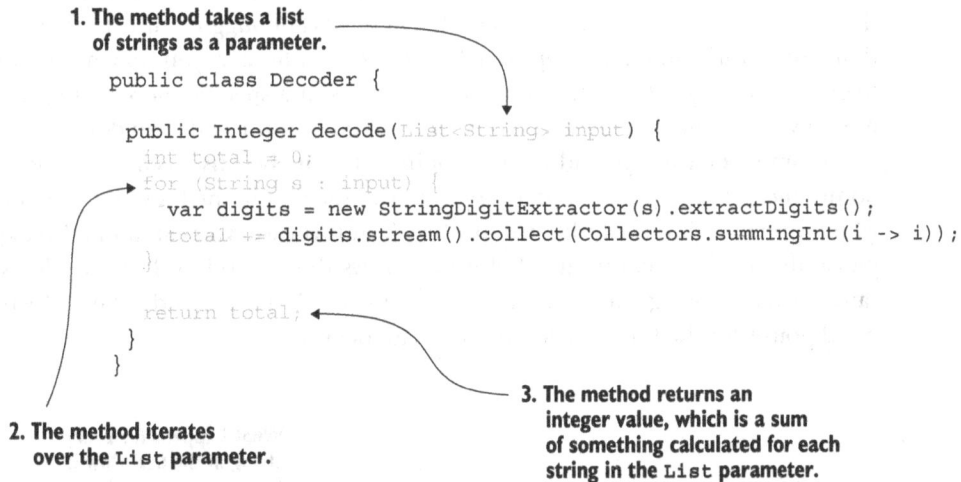

1. The method takes a list of strings as a parameter.

```
public class Decoder {

  public Integer decode(List<String> input) {
    int total = 0;
    for (String s : input) {
      var digits = new StringDigitExtractor(s).extractDigits();
      total += digits.stream().collect(Collectors.summingInt(i -> i));
    }

    return total;
  }
}
```

2. The method iterates over the List parameter.

3. The method returns an integer value, which is a sum of something calculated for each string in the List parameter.

Figure 2.4   Assuming you know the language fundamentals, you can easily see that this code takes a collection as an input and parses the collection to calculate an integer.

In figure 2.5, I shaded the lines that usually cause difficulties in understanding what the method does. These lines of code are more challenging to decipher because they hide their own implemented logic. You may recognize digits.stream().collect (Collectors.summingInt(i -> i)) as it's been part of the Stream API provided with the JDK since Java 8. But we can't say the same thing about new StringDigitExtractor(s) .extractDigits(). Because this is part of the app's codebase we are investigating, this instruction might do anything.

The way a developer writes the code may also add additional complexity. For example, starting with Java 10, developers can infer the type of a local variable using var. Inferring the variable type is not always a wise choice because it can make the code even more difficult to read (figure 2.5), adding another scenario in which using the debugger would be beneficial.

TIP When investigating code with a debugger, start from the first line of code that you can't figure out.

While training junior developers and students over the many years, I have observed that they often start debugging on the first line of a specific code block. Although this method is acceptable, it's more efficient if you first read the code without the debugger and try to figure out whether you can understand it. Remember, you can use AI help for this purpose, as discussed in section 2.1. Then, start debugging directly from the point that causes difficulties. This approach will save you time as you may notice you don't need the debugger to understand what happens in a specific piece of logic. After all, even if you use the debugger, you only need to go over the code you don't understand.

In some scenarios, you add a breakpoint on a line because its intent is not obvious. Sometimes, your app throws an exception; you see that in the logs, but you don't know which previous line is causing the problem. In this case, you can add a breakpoint to pause the app's execution just before it throws the exception. But the idea stays the same: avoid pausing the execution of the instructions you understand. Instead, use breakpoints for the lines of code you want to focus on.

> **What happens for every string in the list? How is the `String` turned into a number?**

```
public class Decoder {

  public Integer decode(List<String> input) {
    int total = 0;
    for (String s : input) {
      var digits = new StringDigitExtractor(s).extractDigits();
      total += digits.stream().collect(Collectors.summingInt(i -> i));
    }

    return total;
  }
}
```

Figure 2.5 In this piece of code, I shaded the lines that are more difficult to understand. When you use a debugger, add the first breakpoint on the first line that makes the code more challenging to understand.

A useful strategy is to reduce the number of variables displayed in the IDE's scope to focus only on the ones that are relevant. An LLM can analyze your code and help identify variables relevant to the debugging process, suggesting the removal of those that aren't necessary. Focusing on essential variables only simplifies debugging by removing irrelevant data, which lets you concentrate on what's important.

For this example, we start by adding a breakpoint on line 11, presented in figure 2.6:

```
var digits = new StringDigitExtractor(s).extractDigits();
```

Generally, to add a breakpoint on a line in any IDE, you click on or near the line number (or even better, use a keyboard shortcut; for IntelliJ, you can use Ctrl-F8 for

Windows/Linux, or Command-F8 for macOS). The breakpoint will be displayed with a circle, as presented in figure 2.6. Make sure you run your application with the debugger. In IntelliJ, look for a small bug icon near the one you use to start the app. You can also right-click the main class file and use the Debug button in the context menu. When the execution reaches the line you marked with a breakpoint, it pauses, allowing you to navigate further manually.

1. Add a breakpoint on the line where you want the debugger to stop the execution. This line should be the first instruction that creates concerns.

2. Run the app with the debugger.

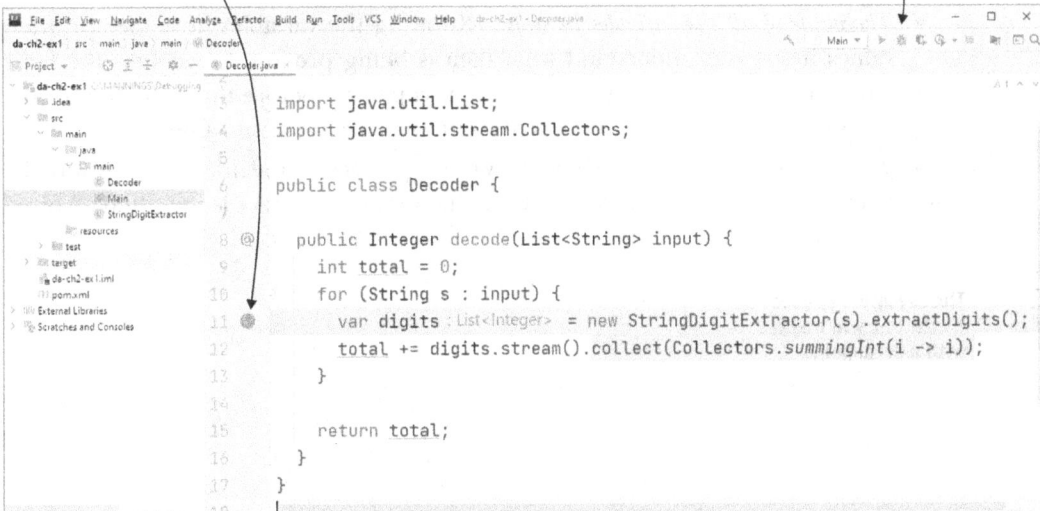

```
import java.util.List;
import java.util.stream.Collectors;

public class Decoder {

    public Integer decode(List<String> input) {
        int total = 0;
        for (String s : input) {
            var digits : List<Integer> = new StringDigitExtractor(s).extractDigits();
            total += digits.stream().collect(Collectors.summingInt(i -> i));
        }

        return total;
    }
}
```

Figure 2.6 Click near the line number to add a breakpoint on a specific line. The area where the IDE displays the breakpoint is also called the "gutter." Then, run the app with the debugger. The execution pauses on the line you marked with a breakpoint and allows you to control it manually.

Since the shortcuts can change and differ depending on the operating system you use (some developers even prefer to customize them), I'm not going to discuss them here. However, I advise you to check your IDE's manual and learn to use the keyboard shortcuts.

NOTE Remember, you must execute the app using the Debug option to have an active debugger. If you use the Run option, the breakpoints won't be considered since the IDE doesn't attach the debugger to the running process. Some IDEs may run your app by default and attach the debugger, but if that's not the case (like for IntelliJ or Eclipse), then the app execution won't pause at the breakpoints you define.

Attaching a debugger in Java (locally) means that your IDE connects to your running Java program to control and inspect it. Behind the scenes, when you run your app in debug mode, the JVM starts with special settings that allow it to accept debugger connections (through a local port). When the IDE attaches, it connects to this port and uses the Java Debug Wire Protocol (JDWP) to communicate. This approach lets you pause the program, step through code, inspect variables, and set breakpoints.

DEFINITION   Attaching a debugger means the IDE connects to the JVM in a special way to let you watch and control how your code runs.

When the debugger pauses the code execution on a specific instruction from the line you mark with a breakpoint, you can use the valuable information the IDE displays. Figure 2.7 shows that my IDE displays two essential pieces of information:

- *The value of all the variables in scope*—Knowing the variables in scope and their values helps you understand what data is being processed and how the logic affects it. Remember that the execution is paused before the execution of the line marked with a breakpoint, so the data state remains the same.

- *The execution stack trace*—It shows how the app executes the line of code where the debugger paused the execution. Each line in the stack trace is a method involved

The execution paused
on the line you marked
with a breakpoint.

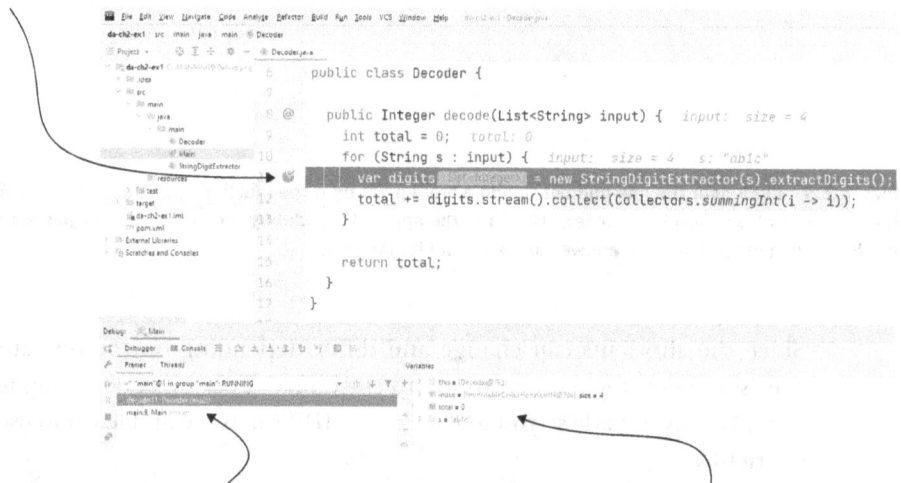

The debugger also shows the stack trace, which displays the execution path so that you can easily see who called the method you are investigating.

When the debugger pauses the app execution on a specific line, you can see the values of all the variables in the scope.

Figure 2.7   When the execution is paused on a given line of code, you can see all the variables in scope and their values. You can also use the execution stack trace to remember where you are as you navigate through the lines of code.

in the calling chain. The execution stack trace helps visualize the execution path, without needing to remember how you got to a specific instruction when using the debugger to navigate through code.

TIP You can add as many breakpoints as you want, but it is best to use a limited number at a time and focus only on those lines of code. I usually use no more than three breakpoints at the same time. I often see developers add too many breakpoints, forget them, and get lost in the investigated code.

Generally, observing the values of the variables in scope is easily understandable. But, depending on your experience, you may or may not be aware of what the execution stack trace is. Section 2.2.1 addresses the execution stack trace and why this tool is essential. We'll then discuss navigating the code using essential operations such as step over, step into, and step out. You can skip section 2.2.1 and go directly to 2.2.2 if you are already familiar with the execution stack trace.

2.2.1 What is the execution stack trace, and how do I use it?

The *execution stack trace* is a valuable tool you use to understand the code while debugging it. Just like a map, the execution stack trace shows the execution's path to the specific line of code where the debugger paused it, helping you decide where to navigate further.

Figure 2.8 shows a comparison of the execution stack trace and the execution in a tree format. The stack trace shows how methods called one another up to the point where the debugger paused the execution. In the stack trace, you can find the method names, the class names, and the lines that caused the calls.

NOTE In our examples, you'll notice that the main() method consistently appears as the first line in the execution stack. However, in real-world applications, multiple threads often run concurrently, each maintaining its own execution stack (see appendixes D and E for more details). For instance, in a typical thread-per-request web application, a new thread is spawned for each incoming HTTP request. Therefore, the starting point of an execution stack varies depending on which thread is executing the specific piece of code you're analyzing. In our examples, you always see the main() method as the first line of the execution stack. Remember that a real-world app has multiple threads executing, and each thread has their own stack (also see appendixes D and E). For example, a standard thread-per-request web app will create a new thread for each HTTP request. So, the starting point of an execution stack depends on which thread executes the piece of code you investigate.

We read the execution stack from bottom to top.
The bottom layer in the stack is the first layer.
The first layer is the one where the execution began.
The top layer (the last layer) is the method where
the execution is currently paused.

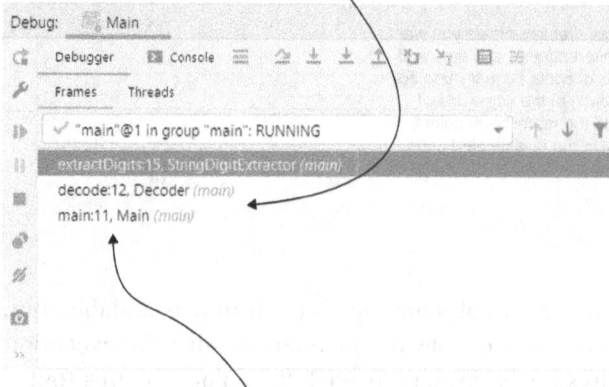

This is a tree representation of the
execution stack trace. Method `main()`
in class `Main` calls method `decode()` in
class `Decoder`. Further, method `decode()`
calls method `extractDigits()` in class
`StringDigitsExtractor`. The execution
is paused in method `extractDigits()`.

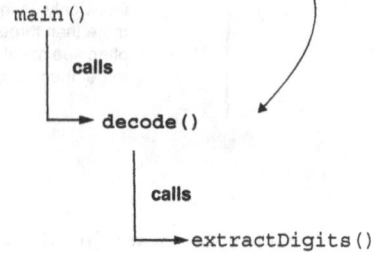

The execution stack trace shows the class names
and the line in the file where the method was called.

Execution paused in method `extractDigits()`

Figure 2.8   The top layer of the execution stack trace is where the debugger paused the execution. All other
layers in the execution stack trace are where the methods represented by the above layers were called. The
bottom layer of the stack trace (the first layer) is where the execution of the current thread began.

One of my favorite uses of the execution stack trace is finding hidden logic in the execution path. In most cases, developers simply use the execution stack trace to understand who calls a particular method. But you also need to consider that apps that use frameworks (such as Spring, Hibernate, etc.) sometimes alter the execution chain of the method.

> **DEFINITION**   The *execution stack trace* is a breadcrumb trail of method calls that tells you how your program got to where it is.

For example, Spring apps often use code that is decoupled in what we call *aspects* (in Java/Jakarta EE terminology, we call them *interceptors*). These aspects implement logic that the framework uses to augment the execution of specific methods in certain conditions. Unfortunately, such logic is often difficult to observe since you can't see the aspect code directly in the call chain when reading the code (figure 2.9). This characteristic makes it challenging to investigate a given capability.

Let's take a code example to examine this behavior and how the execution stack trace is helpful in such cases. You can find this example in project da-ch2-ex2 provided with the book (appendix B provides a refresher for opening the project and starting the app). The project is a small Spring app that prints the parameter's value in the console.

The apparent flow of method execution

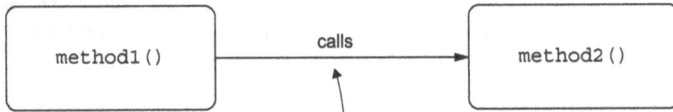

It looks like method 1 directly calls method 2.

How the code really executes

Instead, method 1 calls the logic implemented by an aspect. The aspect might further call the second method.

Figure 2.9 An aspect logic is completely decoupled from the code. For this reason, when reading the code, it is difficult to see that there's more logic that will execute. Such cases of hidden logic executing can be confusing when investigating a certain capability.

Listings 2.3, 2.4, and 2.5 show the implementation of these three classes. As presented in listing 2.3, the main() method calls ProductController's saveProduct() method, sending the parameter value "Beer".

Listing 2.3 The main class calls the ProductController's saveProduct() method

```
public class Main {

  public static void main(String[] args) {
    try (var c =
      new AnnotationConfigApplicationContext(ProjectConfig.class)) {
      c.getBean(ProductController.class).saveProduct("Beer");
    }
  }
}
```

Calling the saveProduct() method with the parameter value "Beer"

In listing 2.4, you can see that ProductController's saveProduct() method simply calls the ProductService's saveProduct() method with the received parameter value.

Listing 2.4 ProductController calling ProductService

```
@Component
public class ProductController {

  private final ProductService productService;

  public ProductController(ProductService productService) {
    this.productService = productService;
```

```
  }

  public void saveProduct(String name) {
    productService.saveProduct(name);
  }
}
```

ProductController calls the service and sends the parameter value.

Listing 2.5 shows the ProductService's saveProduct() method that prints the parameter value in the console.

Listing 2.5   ProductService printing the value of the parameter

```
@Component
public class ProductService {

  public void saveProduct(String name) {
    System.out.println("Saving product " + name);
  }
}
```

Prints the parameter value in the console

As presented in figure 2.10, the flow is quite simple:

1   The main() method calls the saveProduct() method of a bean named Product-Controller, sending the value "Beer" as a parameter.

2   Then, the ProductController's saveProduct() method calls the saveProduct() method of another bean, ProductService.

3   The ProductService bean prints the value of the parameter in the console.

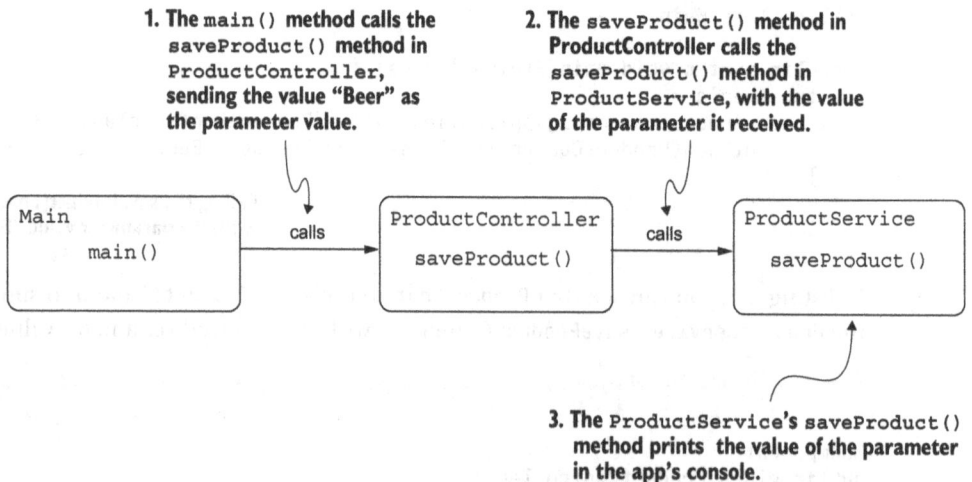

1. The main() method calls the saveProduct() method in ProductController, sending the value "Beer" as the parameter value.

2. The saveProduct() method in ProductController calls the saveProduct() method in ProductService, with the value of the parameter it received.

```
Main              calls    ProductController    calls    ProductService
    main()          →          saveProduct()      →          saveProduct()
```

3. The ProductService's saveProduct() method prints the value of the parameter in the app's console.

Figure 2.10   The main() method calls saveProduct() of bean ProductController, sending the value "Beer" as the parameter value. The ProductController's saveProduct() method calls the ProductService bean, sending the same parameter value as the one it receives. The Product-Service bean prints the parameter value in the console. The expectation is that "Beer" will be printed in the console.

Naturally, you would assume the following message is printed when you run the app:

```
Saving product Beer
```

However, when you run the project, the message is different:

```
Saving product Chocolate
```

How is that possible? To answer this question, the first thing to do is use the execution stack trace to find out who changed the parameter value. Add a breakpoint on the line that prints a different value than you expect, run the app with the debugger, and observe the execution stack trace (figure 2.11). Instead of having the Product-Service's saveProduct() method from the ProductController bean, you find that an aspect alters the execution. If you review the aspect class, you will, indeed, see that the aspect is responsible for replacing "Beer" with "Chocolate" (see listing 2.6).

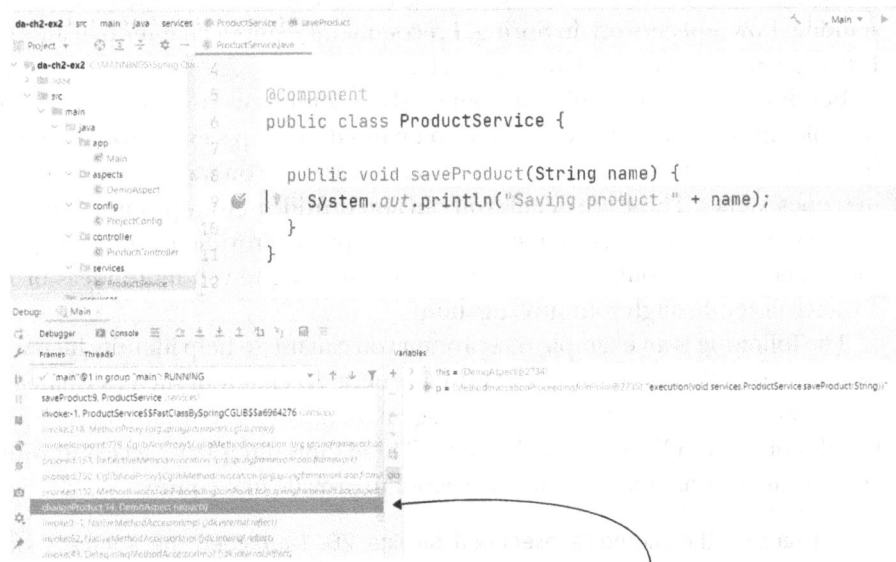

The execution stack trace is much larger than you would expect when reading the code. It clearly shows that ProductService's saveProduct() method is not called directly from ProductController. Somehow, an aspect executes in between the two methods.

Figure 2.11 The execution stack trace shows that an aspect has altered the execution. This aspect is the reason that the parameter value changes. Without using the stack trace, finding why the app has a different behavior than expected would be more difficult.

Listing 2.6 shows the aspect that alters the execution by replacing the value Product-Controller sends to ProductService.

Listing 2.6   The aspect logic that alters the execution

```
@Aspect
@Component
public class DemoAspect {

  @Around("execution(* services.ProductService.saveProduct(..))")
  public void changeProduct(ProceedingJoinPoint p) throws Throwable {
    p.proceed(new Object[] {"Chocolate"});
  }
}
```

Aspects are quite a fascinating and useful feature in Java application frameworks today. But if you don't use them properly, they can make apps difficult to understand and maintain. Of course, in this book, we are discussing relevant techniques that can help you to identify and understand code even in such cases. But, trust me, if you need to use this technique for an application, it means the application is not easily maintainable. A clean-coded app (without technical debt) is always a better choice than an app in which you must invest effort to debug later. If you're interested in better understanding how aspects work in Spring, I recommend reading chapter 6 of another book I wrote, *Spring Start Here* (Manning, 2021).

Besides the code, remember that an LLM can understand execution stack traces and variables in scope as well. So, assume you paused the app's execution on a given line, but you can't understand the execution stack trace, or you want to check the variable-in-scopes' values. These are details you can also provide in your prompt. Most likely, the easiest way to provide these details is a screen capture. Provide the screen captures with the details in the prompt, asking questions that can give you more ideas or help you advance faster through your investigation.

The following is an example of a prompt you can use to help identify inconsistencies in your code. While you can use it with a general AI chat tool such as ChatGPT, it will usually work more effectively with an AI agent integrated into your IDE, such as GitHub Copilot or the IntelliJ IDEA AI Assistant. These tools often have access to your source code context automatically or make it easier to provide that context.

I paused the method's execution on line 26. I attached the source code for the current class and a print screen of the variables' values. Do you expect these are correct values for the variable in scope I provided in the attached screen capture? If there's any inconsistency, please help me understand where and why.

An answer to such a prompt, if there were any problems, could look like the following:

Thanks for the information. Based on the source code you provided for `UserService` and the variable values in the screenshot, here's what I observe:

You're paused at line 26 inside the `createAccount` method. At this point, the user object has the following values:

You're clearly creating a new user, so `user.getId()` being null is expected—good.

However, the value of `user.getEmail()` looks suspicious. Earlier in the method, I see you're calling `user.setEmail(input.getEmail().trim().toLowerCase());`, but `input.getEmail()` is `"Admin@Company.Com"` (as seen in your screenshot).

That means after `.trim()` and `.toLowerCase()`, the expected value should be `"admin@company.com"`, which does match the value in your current variable. So from that point of view, it seems consistent.

That said, there's a subtle risk: you're directly using `input.getEmail()` without checking if it's null. If the input were missing or malformed, this could lead to a `NullPointerException`.

Now your job is to follow the logic and verify whether the AI assistant's explanation is correct. Keep in mind that the AI can be wrong, often due to missing context. It's your responsibility to recognize when that happens and supply the missing information.

The key idea to remember is that you're not using the AI to solve the case for you—you're using it to help you understand parts that seem confusing or complex. In the end, you're the one solving the problem.

Here's another example of prompt you could use with the details a debugger provides.

> I expected the console to display X, but it displayed Y. Can you help me figure out why? I attached a screenshot of the execution stack trace.

Remember to provide as much context as needed for the AI to be helpful. Of course, you won't always be able to share the entire source code, and that's okay. Just include whatever parts you believe are relevant.

The good news is that you don't have to rely solely on copy-pasting. You can upload files that contain the necessary information or even share screenshots. For example, most IDEs make it easy to save the execution stack trace to a file, which is especially useful when the trace is too large to copy and paste. In such cases, simply save the stack trace and upload the file instead.

2.2.2 Navigating code with the debugger

This section, discusses the basic ways you navigate code with a debugger. You'll learn how to use three fundamental navigation operations:

- *Step over*—Continue executing the next line of code in the same method.
- *Step into*—Continue the execution inside one of the methods called on the current line.
- *Step out*—Return the execution to the method that called the one you are investigating.

To start the investigation process, you must identify the first line of code where you want the debugger to pause the execution. To understand the logic, you need to navigate through the lines of code and observe how the data changes when different instructions execute.

Navigation operations can be used in any IDE through buttons on the GUI or keyboard shortcuts. Figure 2.12 shows how these buttons appear in the IntelliJ IDEA Community GUI, the IDE I use.

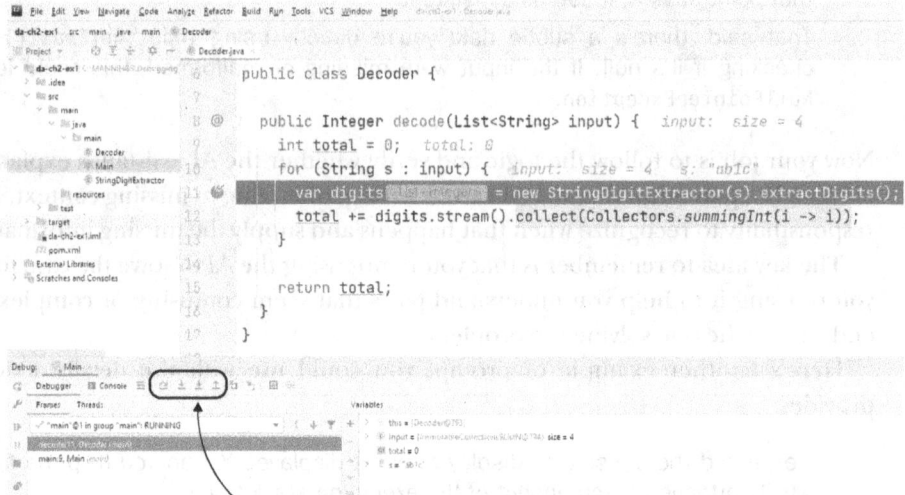

Use the navigation instructions to tell the debugger to continue the execution. The most essential navigation instructions are step over, step in, and step out.

Figure 2.12 The navigation operations help you walk through the app logic in a controlled way to identify how the code works. To navigate through code, you can use the buttons on the IDE's GUI or use the keyboard shortcuts associated with these operations.

TIP Even if at the beginning you find it easier to use the buttons on the IDE's GUI, I recommend you use the keyboard shortcuts instead. Once you get comfortable using the keyboard shortcuts, you'll see they are much faster than a mouse.

Figure 2.13 depicts the navigation operations. You can use the step over operation to go to the next line in the same method. Generally, this is the most commonly used navigation operation.

Sometimes you need to better understand what happens with a particular instruction. In our example, you may need to enter the extractDigits() method to clearly

Step over allows you to continue the execution in the same method with the next line of code without entering any details from the current line.

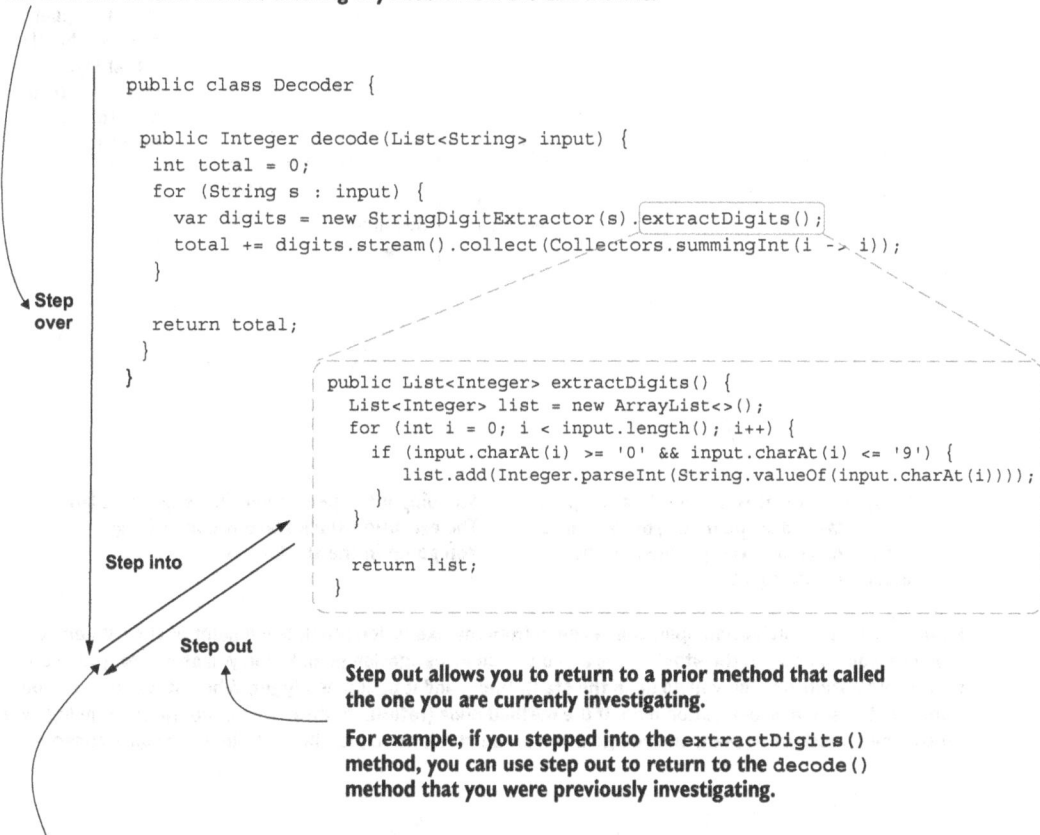

```java
public class Decoder {

    public Integer decode(List<String> input) {
        int total = 0;
        for (String s : input) {
            var digits = new StringDigitExtractor(s).extractDigits();
            total += digits.stream().collect(Collectors.summingInt(i -> i));
        }

        return total;
    }
}
```

Step over

```java
public List<Integer> extractDigits() {
    List<Integer> list = new ArrayList<>();
    for (int i = 0; i < input.length(); i++) {
        if (input.charAt(i) >= '0' && input.charAt(i) <= '9') {
            list.add(Integer.parseInt(String.valueOf(input.charAt(i))));
        }
    }

    return list;
}
```

Step into

Step out

Step out allows you to return to a prior method that called the one you are currently investigating.

For example, if you stepped into the `extractDigits()` method, you can use step out to return to the `decode()` method that you were previously investigating.

Step into allows you to enter the instruction on which the execution is currently stopped. For example, you may step into the `extractDigits()` method to understand what happens behind that method call.

Figure 2.13   Navigation operations. Stepping over allows you to go to the next instruction in the same method. When you want to start a new investigation plan and go into detail in a specific instruction, you can use the step into operation. You can go back to the previous investigation plan with the step out operation.

understand what it does. In such a case, you use the step into operation. When you want to return to the decode() method, you can use step out.

You can also visualize the operations on the execution stack trace, as presented in figure 2.14.

Ideally, you start with using the step over operation as much as possible when trying to understand how a piece of code works. The more you step into, the more investigation plans you open, and thus the more complex the investigation process becomes (figure 2.15). In many cases, you can deduce what a specific line of code does only by stepping over it and observing the output.

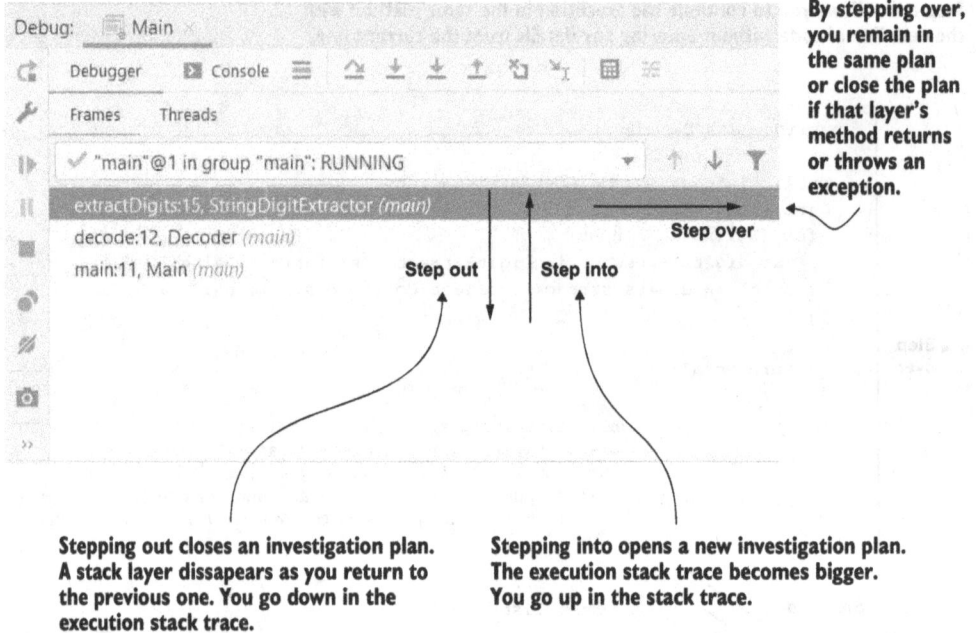

By stepping over, you remain in the same plan or close the plan if that layer's method returns or throws an exception.

Step over

Step out   Step into

Stepping out closes an investigation plan. A stack layer dissapears as you return to the previous one. You go down in the execution stack trace.

Stepping into opens a new investigation plan. The execution stack trace becomes bigger. You go up in the stack trace.

Figure 2.14   The navigation operation as seen from the execution stack trace point of view. When you step out, you go down in the stack trace and close an investigation plan. When you step into, you open a new investigation plan, so you go up in the stack trace, and it becomes bigger. When stepping over, you remain in the same investigation plan. If the method ends (returns or throws an exception), stepping over closes the investigation plan, and you go down in the stack trace just like you did when you stepped out.

I TOLD YOU TO STOP DEEPLY DEBUGGING MANY LAYERS AT ONCE!

Figure 2.15
The movie *Inception* (2010) portrays the idea of dreaming in a dream. The more layers your dream has, the longer you stay there. You can compare this idea with stepping into a method and opening a new investigation layer. The deeper you step in, the more time you'll spend investigating the code.

Figure 2.16 shows the result of using the step over navigation operation. The execution pauses on line 12, one line below where we initially paused the debugger with the breakpoint. The `digits` variable is now initialized as well, so you can see its value.

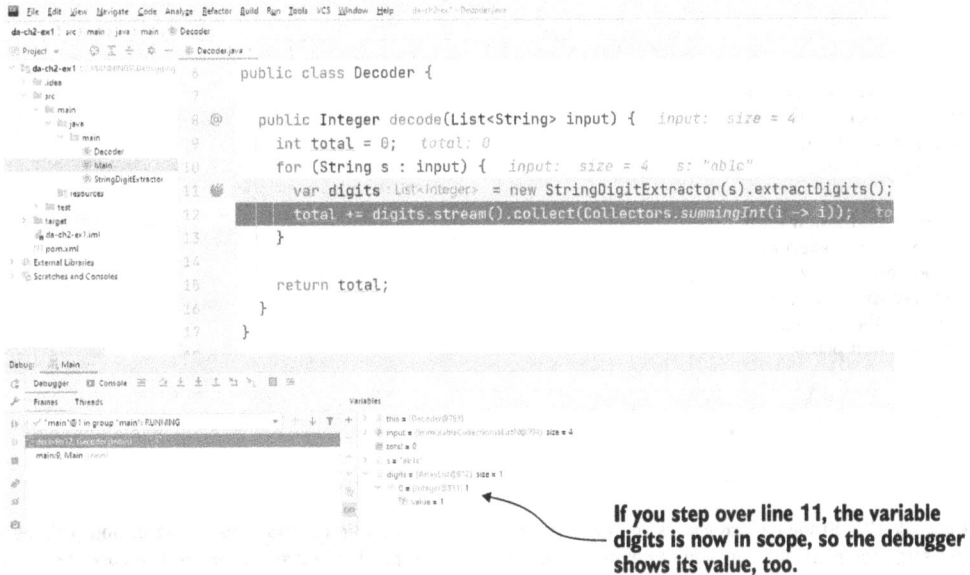

If you step over line 11, the variable digits is now in scope, so the debugger shows its value, too.

Figure 2.16 When you step over a line, the execution continues in the same method. In our case, the execution paused on line 12, and you can see the value of the `digits` variable that was initialized by line 11. You can use this value to deduce what line 11 does without having to go into more detail.

Try continuing the execution multiple times. You'll observe that, on line 11, for each string input, the result is a list that contains all the digits in the given string. Often, the logic is easy enough to understand simply by analyzing the outputs for a few executions. But what if you can't figure out what a line does just by executing it?

If you don't understand what happens, you need to go into more detail on that line. This should be your last option since it requires that you open a new investigation plan, which complicates your process. But, when you have no other choice, you can step into an instruction to get more details on what the code does. Figure 2.17 shows the result of stepping into line 11 of the `Decoder` class:

```
var digits = new StringDigitExtractor(s).extractDigits();
```

If you stepped into an instruction, take the time to first read what's behind that code line. In many cases, looking at the code is enough to spot what happens, and then you can go back to where you were before stepping into. I often observe students rushing into debugging the method they stepped into without first taking a breath and reading that piece of code. Why is it important to read the code first? Because stepping into a

When stepping into a line, the execution continues in the method called on that specific line. ───

Observe that a new level appears in the execution stack. You can always use the execution stack as a map of the opened investigation plans.

Figure 2.17 Stepping into allows you to observe the entire execution of the current instruction. This opens a new investigation plan, allowing you to parse the logic behind that particular instruction. You can use the execution stack trace to retrace the execution flow.

method opens another investigation plan, so if you want to be efficient, you have to redo the investigation steps:

1 Read the method and find the first line of code you don't understand.

2 Add a breakpoint on that line of code, and start the investigation from there.

Often, if you stop and read the code, you'll find that you don't need to continue that investigation plan. If you already understand what happens, you simply need to return to where you were previously. And you can do this using the step out operation. Figure 2.18 shows what happens when using step out from the `extractDigits()` method: the execution returns to the previous investigation plan in the `decode(List <String> input)` method.

TIP The step out operation can save you time. When entering a new investigation plan (by stepping into a code line), first read the new piece of code. Step out of the new investigation plan once you understand what the code does.

When you step out of the `extractDigits()` method, the execution returns to the previous investigation plan.

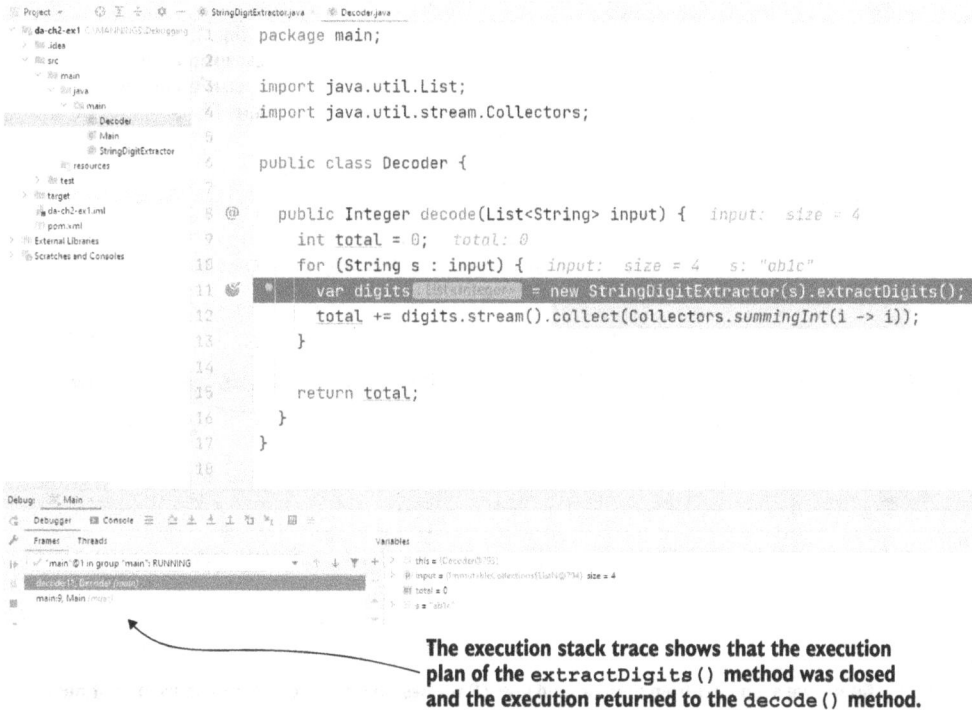

The execution stack trace shows that the execution plan of the `extractDigits()` method was closed and the execution returned to the `decode()` method.

Figure 2.18 The step out operation allows you to close an investigation plan and return to the previous one in the execution stack trace. Using step out is helpful to save time since you don't have to step over each instruction until the current execution plan closes by itself. Stepping out offers a shortcut to return to the previous execution plan you were investigating.

Why is the next execution line not always the next line in the method?

When discussing code navigation with a debugger, I often talk about the "next execution line." I want to make sure I'm clear about the difference between the "next line" and the "next execution line."

The next execution line is the line of code the app executes next. When we say the debugger paused the execution on line 12, the *next line* is always line 13, but the *next execution line* can be different. For example, if line 12 doesn't throw an exception, as shown in the following figure, the next execution line will be 13, but if line 12 throws an exception, the next execution line is line 18. This example is available in project da-ch2-ex3.

When using the step over operation, the execution will continue to the *next execution line*.

(continued)

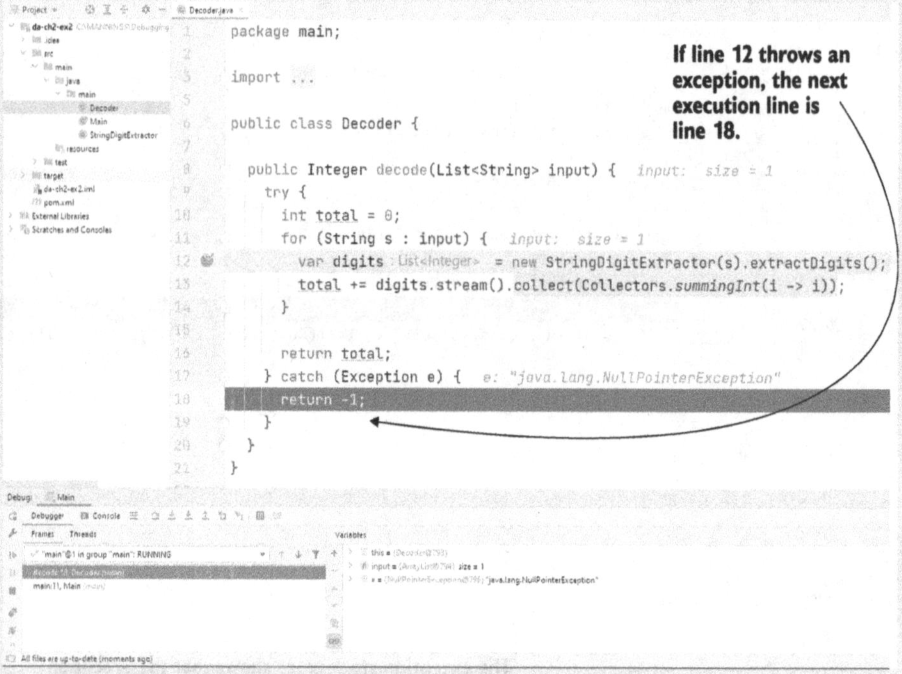

```
package main;

import ...

public class Decoder {

    public Integer decode(List<String> input) {   input:  size = 1
        try {
            int total = 0;
            for (String s : input) {   input:  size = 1
                var digits : List<Integer> = new StringDigitExtractor(s).extractDigits();
                total += digits.stream().collect(Collectors.summingInt(i -> i));
            }

            return total;
        } catch (Exception e) {   e: "java.lang.NullPointerException"
            return -1;
        }
    }
}
```

If line 12 throws an exception, the next execution line is line 18.

In this figure, we step over from line 12, and line 12 throws an exception; the execution continues on line 18, which is the next execution line. In other words, the next execution line is not always the next line.

2.3   When using the debugger might not be enough

The debugger is an excellent tool that can help you analyze code by navigating through the code to understand how it works with data. But not all code can be investigated with a debugger. This section discusses some scenarios in which using a debugger is not possible or not enough. You need to be aware of these cases so that you don't waste time using a debugger.

Here are some of the most often encountered investigation scenarios when using a debugger (or only a debugger) is not the right approach:

- Investigating output problems when you don't know which part of the code creates the output
- Investigating performance problems
- Investigating crashes where the entire app fails
- Investigating multithreaded implementations
- Investigating time-sensitive operations

TIP Remember that a critical prerequisite for using a debugger is knowing where to pause the execution.

Before you start debugging, you need to find the part of the code that is generating the wrong output. Depending on the app, it may be easier to find where something happens in the implemented logic. If the app has a clean class design, it is relatively easy to find the part of the app responsible for the output. If the app lacks a class design, it may be more challenging to discover where things happen and thus where to use the debugger. In the upcoming chapters, you'll learn several other techniques. Some of these techniques, such as profiling the app or using stubs, will help you to identify where to start the investigation with a debugger.

Performance problems are a particular set of difficulties you usually can't investigate with a debugger. Slow applications or those that freeze completely are frequent performance problems. In most cases, profiling and logging techniques (discussed in chapters 4–8) will help you troubleshoot such scenarios. For the particular instances in which the app blocks entirely, getting and analyzing a thread dump is usually the most straightforward investigation path. We'll talk about analyzing thread dumps in chapter 8.

If the app encountered a problem and the execution stopped (the app crashed), you cannot use a debugger on the code. A debugger allows you to observe the app in execution. If the application no longer executes, a debugger clearly won't help. Depending on what happened, you might need to audit logs, as we'll discuss in chapter 4, or investigate thread or heap dumps, which you'll learn about in chapters 8 and 10.

Most developers find *multithreaded implementations* the most challenging to investigate. Such implementations can be easily influenced by your interference with tools such as a debugger. This interference creates a Heisenberg effect (discussed in chapter 1): the app behaves differently when you use the debugger than when you don't interfere with it. As you'll learn, you can sometimes isolate the investigation to one thread and use the debugger. But in most cases, you'll have to apply a set of techniques that include debugging, mocking and stubbing, and profiling to understand the app's behavior in the most complex scenarios.

Time-sensitive operations can sometimes be tricky to investigate using a debugger. By time-sensitive operations, I mean code executions where behavior may change depending on how long the code takes to run—particularly when you're stepping through it with a debugger. Here are a few examples:

- An access token that expires after a certain period. If you spend too much time in the debugger, the token might expire before you complete your investigation.
- A timer set to trigger a specific use case after a predefined interval.

- A short-lived session with another application or system that may expire if you pause execution for too long.

Debugging is typically an activity where you want to give yourself ample time to analyze and think through what you're observing. As I mentioned earlier, allow yourself the mental space to pause, reflect, and treat each new hypothesis as a fresh start.

For this reason, time-sensitive operations often don't play well with traditional step-by-step debugging. They require either a different strategy (e.g., logging or simulation) or extra care when pausing execution.

Summary

- Every time you open a new piece of logic (e.g., entering a new method that defines its own logic), you open a new investigation plan.
- Unlike a text paragraph, reading code is not linear. Each instruction might create a new plan you need to investigate. The more complex the logic you explore, the more plans you need to open. The more plans you open, the more complex the process becomes. One trick to speeding up a code investigation process is to open as few plans as possible.
- A debugger is a tool that allows you to pause the app's execution on a specific line so that you can observe the app's execution, step by step, and the way it manages data. Using a debugger can help you to reduce some of the cognitive load of reading code.
- You can use breakpoints to mark the specific lines of code where you want the debugger to pause an app's execution so you can evaluate the values of all the variables in the scope.
- You can step over a line, which means continuing to the next execution line in the same plan, or step into a line, which means going into detail on the instruction on which the debugger paused the execution. You should minimize the number of times you step into a line and rely more on stepping over. Every time you step into a line, the investigation path gets longer and the process more time-consuming.
- Even though using the mouse and the IDE's GUI to navigate through the code is initially more comfortable, learning to use the keyboard shortcuts for these operations will help you debug faster. I recommend learning the keyboard shortcuts of your favorite IDE and use them instead of triggering the navigation with the mouse.
- After stepping into a line, first read the code and try to understand it. If you can figure out what happens, use the step out operation to return to the previous investigation plan. If you don't understand what happens, identify the first unclear instruction, add a breakpoint, and start debugging from there.

Finding problem root causes using advanced debugging techniques

This chapter covers

- Using conditional breakpoints to investigate specific scenarios
- Using breakpoints to log debug messages in the console
- Modifying data during debugging to simulate specific app behavior
- Rerunning part of the code during debugging

Chapter 2 discussed the most common ways to use a debugger. When debugging a piece of implemented logic, developers often use code navigation operations such as stepping over, into, and out of an instruction. Knowing how to properly use these operations helps investigate a piece of code to better understand or find a problem.

However, many developers underestimate just how powerful a debugger can be. Developers sometimes struggle when debugging code, using only the basic navigation, whereas they could save a lot of time if they used some of the other, less known approaches a debugger offers.

In this chapter, you'll learn how to get the most out of the features such as

- Conditional breakpoints
- Breakpoints as log events
- Modifying in-memory data
- Dropping execution frames

We'll discuss some beyond-basic ways to navigate the code you are investigating, and you'll learn how and when to use these approaches. We'll also use code examples to discuss these investigation approaches so that you learn how to use them to save time and when to avoid them.

3.1 Minimizing investigation time with conditional breakpoints

This section discusses the use of *conditional breakpoints* to pause the app's execution on a line of code under specific conditions.

> **DEFINITION** A *conditional breakpoint* is a breakpoint you associate with a condition so that the debugger pauses the execution only if the condition is fulfilled. Conditional breakpoints are helpful in investigation scenarios when you are only interested in how a part of the code works with given values; using conditional breakpoints where appropriate saves you time and facilitates your understanding of how your app works.

Let's look at an example to understand how conditional breakpoints work and typical cases in which you'll want to use them. Listing 3.1 presents a method that returns the sum of the digits in a list of String values. You might already be familiar with this method from chapter 2. We'll use the same piece of code here as well to discuss conditional breakpoints. Next, we'll compare this simplified example with similar situations you may encounter in real world. The example is available in project da-ch3-ex1 provided with the book.

Listing 3.1   Using conditional breakpoints for investigation

```
public class Decoder {

  public Integer decode(List<String> input) {
    try {
      int total = 0;
      for (String s : input) {
        var digits = new StringDigitExtractor(s).extractDigits();
        var sum = digits.stream().collect(Collectors.summingInt(i -> i));
        total += sum;
      }

      return total;
    } catch (Exception e) {
```

```
        return -1;
      }
    }
}
```

When debugging a piece of code, we are often only interested in how logic works for specific values. For example, say you suspect the implemented logic doesn't work well in a given case (e.g., some variable has a certain value), and you want to prove it. Or you simply want to understand what happens in a given situation to have a better overview of the entire functionality.

Suppose that, in this case, you only want to investigate why the variable sum is sometimes zero. How can you work only on this specific case? You could use the step over operation to navigate the code until you observe that the method returns zero. This approach is likely acceptable in a demo example such as this one (small enough). But in a real-world case, you may have to step over a lot of times until you reach the case you expect. In fact, in a real-world scenario, you may not even know when the specific case you want to investigate appears.

Using conditional breakpoints is more efficient than navigating through code until you get to the conditions you want to research. Figure 3.1 illustrates how to apply a condition to a breakpoint in IntelliJ IDEA. Right-click the breakpoint you want to add the condition for and write the condition to which the breakpoint applies. The condition

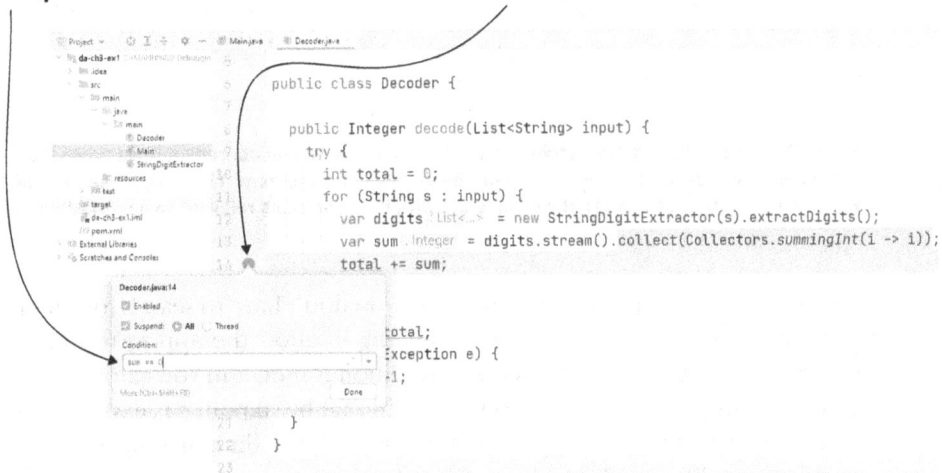

In IntelliJ, right-click on the breakpoint to define its condition. In this example, the debugger stops only on this breakpoint when the variable sum is zero.

You can add a condition on certain breakpoints. The debugger considers these breakpoints only if their condition evaluates to true.

Figure 3.1 Using a conditional breakpoint to pause the execution just for specific cases. In this case, we want to pause the execution on line 14 only if sum is zero. We can apply a condition on the breakpoint that instructs the debugger to consider that breakpoint only if the given state is true. This helps you more quickly get to a scenario you want to investigate.

needs to be a Boolean expression (it should be something that can be evaluated as true or false). Using the sum == 0 condition on the breakpoint, you tell the debugger to consider that breakpoint and pause the execution only when it reaches a case where the variable sum is zero.

When you run the app with the debugger, the execution pauses only when the loop first iterates on a string that contains no digits, as shown in figure 3.2. This situation causes the variable sum to be zero, and the condition on the breakpoint is thus evaluated as true.

When you run the app with the debugger, it pauses the execution for the first element in the parameter list that doesn't contain digits (for which the variable sum will be zero).

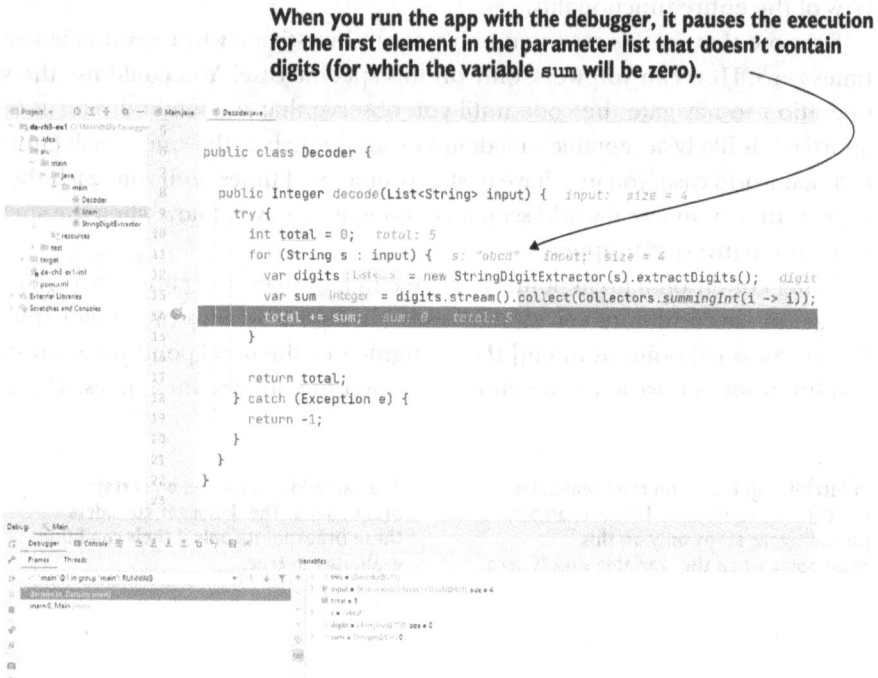

Figure 3.2   A conditional breakpoint. Line 14 in the figure was executed multiple times, but the debugger only paused the execution when the variable sum was zero. This way, we skipped all the cases we were not interested in so that we can start with the conditions relevant to our investigation.

A conditional breakpoint saves time since you don't have to search for the specific case you want to investigate. Rather than halting it, allow the app to run. The debugger pauses the execution when a certain condition is met, and you can begin your investigation at this point. Although using conditional breakpoints is easy, many developers seem to forget about this approach and waste a lot of time investigating scenarios that could be simplified with conditional breakpoints.

DEFINITION   A *conditional breakpoint* is a special type of breakpoint that only pauses the program when a certain condition is true. It lets you pause the execution only when a specific variable has a certain value or when a set custom rule is met.

To further optimize your debugging process, AI-powered tools can significantly assist in the effective use of conditional breakpoints. These tools integrate with your development environment to provide intelligent suggestions and automate parts of the debugging workflow, making it more efficient and less error prone.

One way AI tools can help is by analyzing your code and suggesting optimal breakpoint conditions. For instance, giving them the piece of code you investigate, they can identify variables that frequently lead to exceptions or anomalous behavior and recommend conditions based on those insights.

Take a look at figure 3.3. In this example, I intentionally introduced a minor error in the if clause condition. To investigate the problem, I used GitHub Copilot as my AI assistant. I highlighted the code snippet I wanted to troubleshoot and asked Copilot for guidance on where to place the breakpoints.

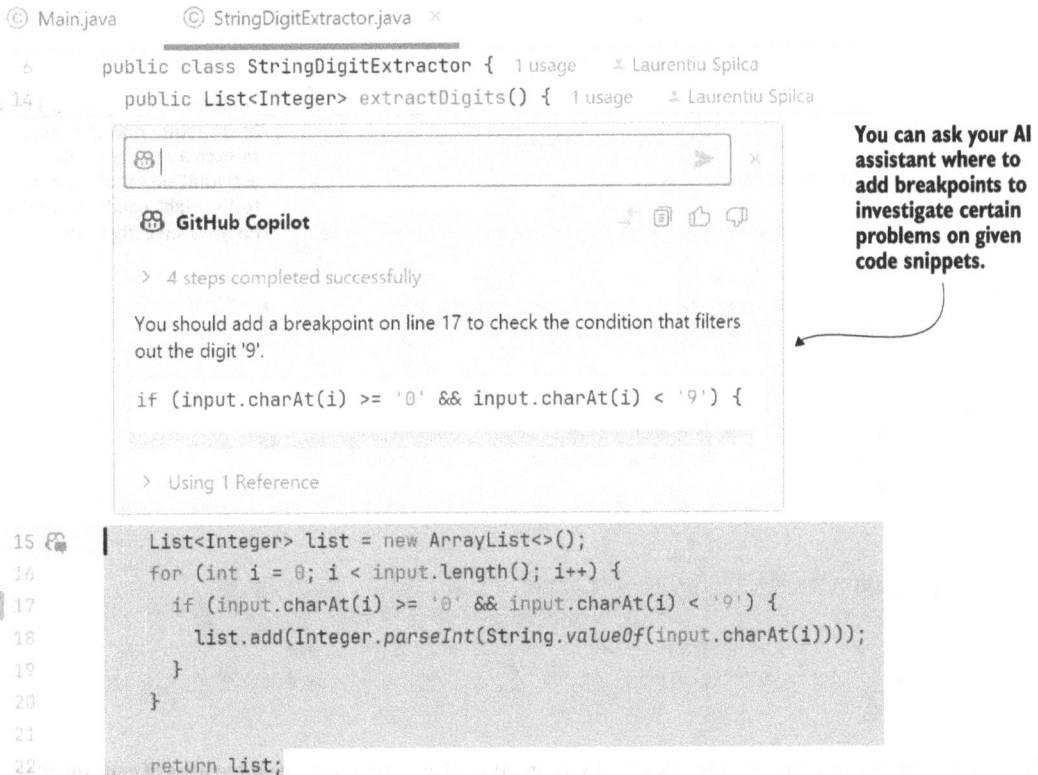

Figure 3.3 AI assistants such as GitHub Copilot can help you better understand a code snippet or assist in selecting the appropriate troubleshooting technique. In this example, I asked Copilot for guidance on where to place breakpoints to easily identify the source of the problem in my code.

In some cases, the AI assistant may suggest using conditional breakpoints. If you believe that conditional breakpoints could enhance your debugging efficiency, you can explicitly request this guidance, even if the AI assistant didn't initially recommend it. Additionally, you can save time by asking the AI assistant for the appropriate condition to use. Figure 3.4 demonstrates how my AI assistant helped me identify the line for adding a conditional breakpoint and provided the necessary condition to continue my investigation.

However, I want to caution you against relying exclusively on AI to generate conditions for your breakpoints or to decide where to place them every time. As someone wisely put it, you need to keep training that muscle yourself. AI should serve as a helpful assistant, not a crutch. The goal is to build your own diagnostic instincts and sharpen your debugging skills—with AI as a supportive tool, not the primary driver.

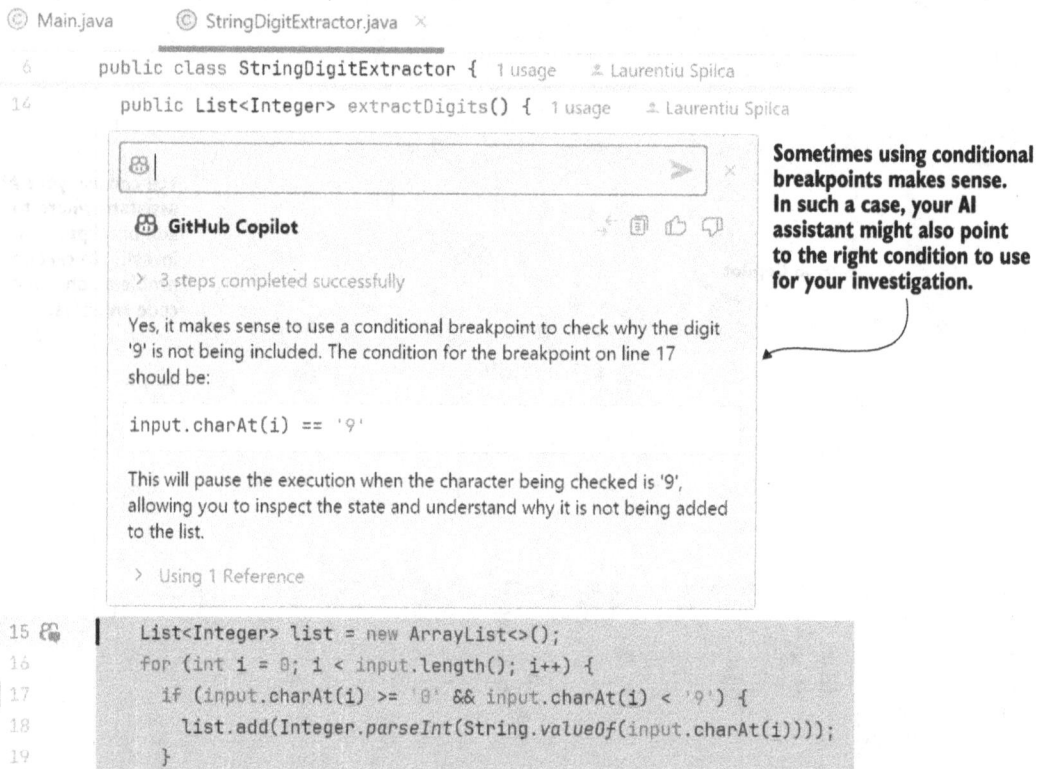

Figure 3.4   You can speed up your investigation by asking your AI assistant to suggest the lines of code for adding conditional breakpoints and the right condition to use for them.

Assistants such as GitHub Copilot, integrated with your IDE, are convenient to use in situations like the one shown here because they have direct access to the context they need. However, you can also use a chat-based AI tool, such as ChatGPT, successfully.

Figure 3.5 shows how I used ChatGPT for the same task. When provided with the necessary context, ChatGPT was able to offer advice and even a solution to the problem.

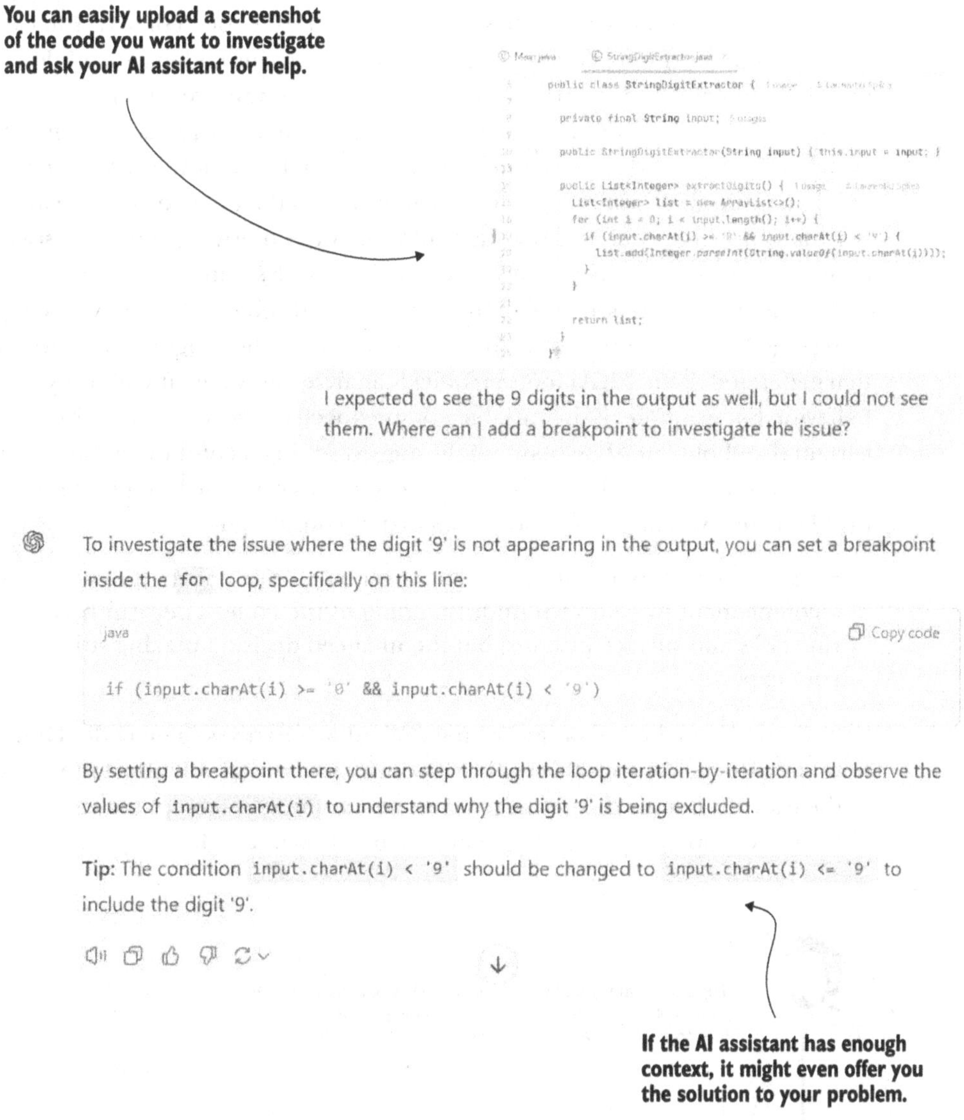

You can easily upload a screenshot of the code you want to investigate and ask your AI assitant for help.

```
ⓒ Main.java      ⓒ StringDigitExtractor.java

      public class StringDigitExtractor {

          private final String input;

          public StringDigitExtractor(String input) { this.input = input; }

          public List<Integer> extractDigits() {
              List<Integer> list = new ArrayList<>();
              for (int i = 0; i < input.length(); i++) {
                  if (input.charAt(i) >= '0' && input.charAt(i) < '9') {
                      list.add(Integer.parseInt(String.valueOf(input.charAt(i))));
                  }
              }

              return list;
          }
      }
```

I expected to see the 9 digits in the output as well, but I could not see them. Where can I add a breakpoint to investigate the issue?

To investigate the issue where the digit '9' is not appearing in the output, you can set a breakpoint inside the `for` loop, specifically on this line:

```java
if (input.charAt(i) >= '0' && input.charAt(i) < '9')
```
⎘ Copy code

By setting a breakpoint there, you can step through the loop iteration-by-iteration and observe the values of `input.charAt(i)` to understand why the digit '9' is being excluded.

Tip: The condition `input.charAt(i) < '9'` should be changed to `input.charAt(i) <= '9'` to include the digit '9'.

If the AI assistant has enough context, it might even offer you the solution to your problem.

Figure 3.5 Tools such as ChatGPT, Gemini, or similar AI-powered chatbots can also assist with your code investigation. In some cases, if they have enough context, they may even provide a complete solution.

Of course, since this is a simple example, ChatGPT could easily solve the problem rather than just guide the investigation. In a real-world scenario, you may not be able to give ChatGPT all the needed context, but it could still offer helpful advice on how to proceed. You can use AI assistants to gradually move forward in your investigation (while learning) by asking for advice and sharing observations within the same chat.

Usually, an IDE-integrated tool has an advantage over AI-powered chatbots such as ChatGPT or Gemini because it has direct access to your code context. You can see this in the current example: GitHub Copilot has access to my codebase, so I don't need to provide a screenshot for it to suggest where to place the breakpoint. With ChatGPT, however, I had to carefully include the line numbers in the screenshot to give it the necessary context. Without those line numbers, ChatGPT wouldn't have known that the line in question was number 17. This is attention to the context you provide. Remember that you need to provide enough information; otherwise, your AI assistant would either not be able to help you, or worse—hallucinate a solution.

Another method is to combine this approach with what we'll discuss in chapter 4 on using logs. You can provide your AI assistant with execution logs together with the code that generated them. An AI tool can quickly analyze many logs and identify unexpected behavior. For example, if the variable sum unexpectedly becomes negative or exceeds a certain threshold, an AI assistant might suggest setting a conditional breakpoint when sum < 0 or sum > 1000. This proactive approach saves you time by highlighting potential problem areas you might not have immediately considered.

> **NOTE** While AI tools offer these enhancements, it's important to use them as a complement to your own understanding of the code. They can handle routine tasks and surface insights, but the nuanced decision-making still relies on your expertise.

Setting conditional breakpoints is an excellent way to investigate code. However, they have their downside. Conditional breakpoints can dramatically affect the performance of the execution since the debugger must continuously intercept the values of the variables in the scope you use and evaluate the breakpoint conditions.

> **TIP** Use a small number of conditional breakpoints. Preferably, use only one conditional breakpoint at a time to avoid slowing down the execution too much.

Conditional breakpoints can also be used to log specific execution details such as various expression values and stack traces for particular conditions (figure 3.6). We'll continue with this topic in section 3.2.

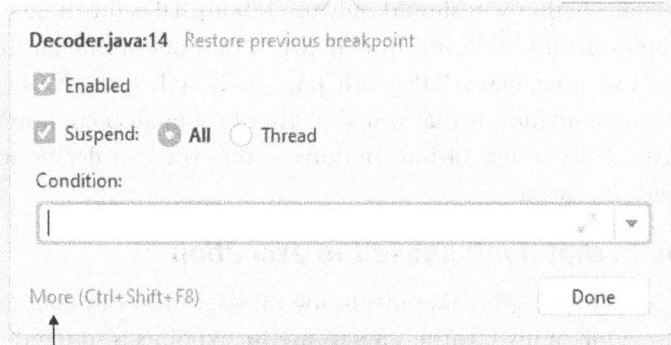

Figure 3.6
To apply advanced configuration on the breakpoint in IntelliJ, you can click the More button.

Click on More to define more advanced configurations for the conditional breakpoint.

Unfortunately, this feature only works in certain IDEs. For example, even though you can use conditional breakpoints in Eclipse in the same way as described here, Eclipse does not allow you to use breakpoints just for logging execution details (figure 3.7).

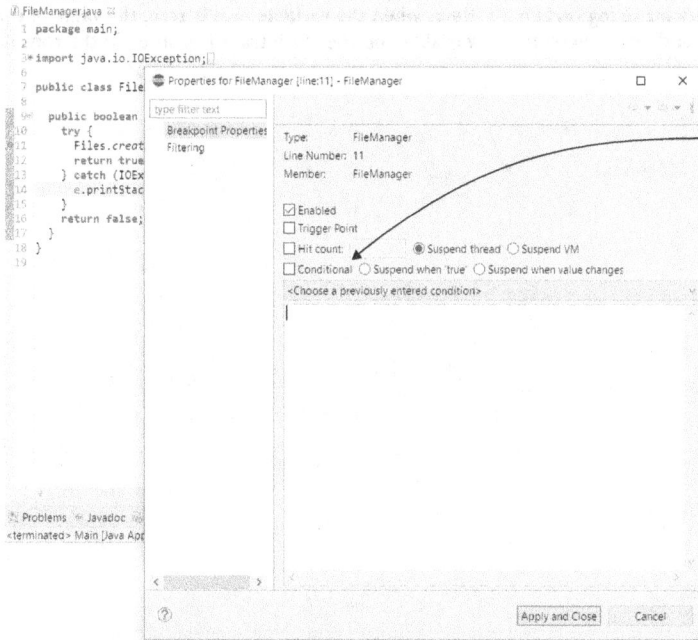

In Eclipse, you can define a conditional breakpoint. However, you can't log specific execution details instead of suspending the thread.

Figure 3.7 Not all IDEs offer the same debugging tools. All IDEs give you the basic operations, but some features, such as logging the execution details instead of pausing the execution, may be missing. In Eclipse, you can define conditional breakpoints, but you can't use the logging feature.

You might ask yourself whether you should only use IntelliJ IDEA for these examples. Even if most examples in this book use IntelliJ IDEA, that doesn't mean this IDE is better than others. I've used many IDEs with Java, such as Eclipse, Netbeans, and JDeveloper. My recommendation is that you shouldn't become too comfortable with using one IDE. Instead, try to use various options so that you can decide which is a better fit for you and your team.

3.2   *Using breakpoints that don't pause the execution*

In this section, we discuss using breakpoints to log messages you can later employ to investigate the code. One of my favorite ways to use breakpoints is to log details that can help me to understand what happened during the app's execution without pausing it. As you'll learn in chapter 4, logging is an excellent investigation practice in some cases. Many developers struggle with adding log instructions when they could have simply used a conditional breakpoint.

Figure 3.8 shows how to configure a conditional breakpoint that doesn't pause the execution. Instead, the debugger logs a message every time the line marked with the breakpoint is reached. In this case, the debugger logs the value of the digits variable and the execution stack trace.

You can use a breakpoint to log certain details without suspending the execution.   **Here, when the variable sum is zero, the value of the digits variable and the stack trace is printed in the console.**

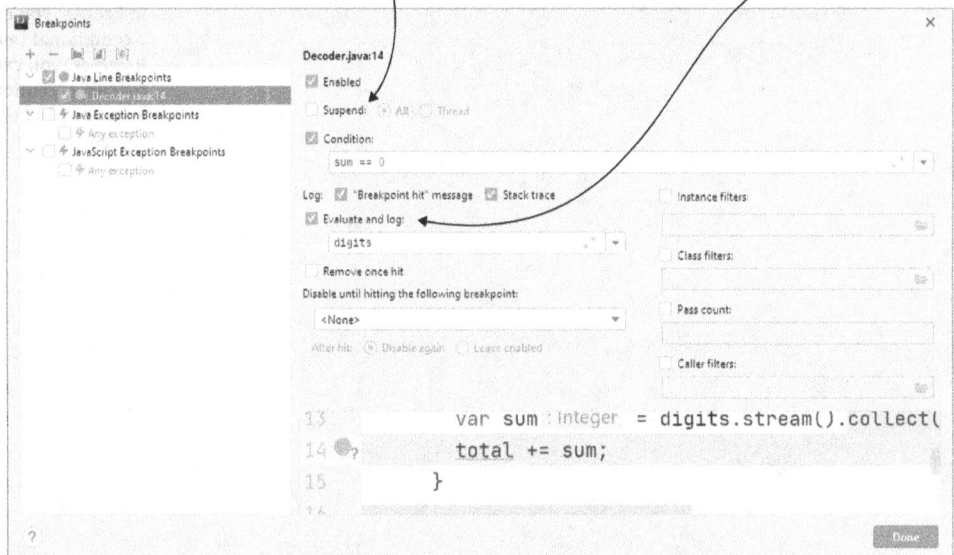

Figure 3.8 Conditional breakpoint advanced configuration. In addition to specifying a condition for the breakpoint, you can instruct the debugger to not suspend the execution for the given breakpoint. Instead, you can simply log the data you need to understand your case.

Figure 3.9 shows the result of running the app with the conditional breakpoint configured. Notice that the debugger logged the execution stack trace in the console, and the value of the `digits` variable is an empty list: []. This kind of information can help solve the puzzles of the code you investigate in real-world scenarios.

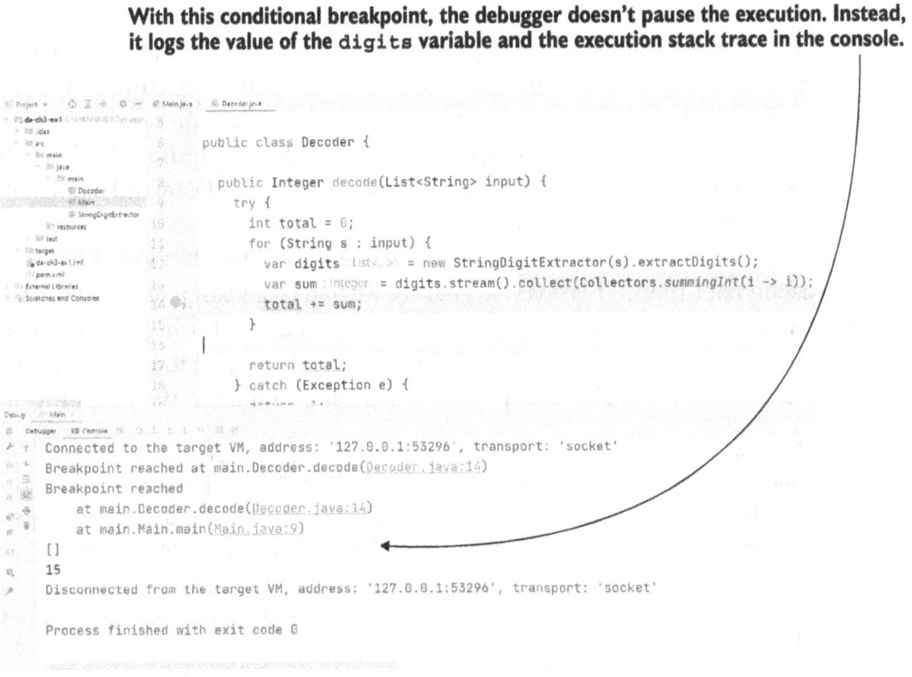

With this conditional breakpoint, the debugger doesn't pause the execution. Instead, it logs the value of the `digits` variable and the execution stack trace in the console.

Figure 3.9 Using breakpoints without pausing the execution. Instead, the debugger logs a message when the line has been reached. The debugger also logs the value of the `digits` variable and the execution stack trace.

> **DEFINITION** A *non-blocking breakpoint* is a type of breakpoint that logs information (like a message or variable value) when it's hit, but it does not pause the program's execution. It lets you see what's happening at a certain point in the code without pausing the program.

Furthermore, this technique can be combined with the approach discussed in section 3.1. By using non-blocking breakpoints, you can capture log messages without interrupting the execution flow or modifying the code. For lengthy processes that generate extensive logs, you can employ an AI assistant to efficiently analyze the output and extract meaningful insights (as discussed in chapter 4).

I remember working on an app years ago with a large, messy codebase. There were several long-running scheduled processes responsible for generating settlements and invoices, but every so often, the data in some of the invoices didn't meet expectations—a frustrating output problem. Initially, I thought the problem was specific to those invoices. However, every time I tried to isolate the problem by running the process to generate only the faulty invoices, they would be generated correctly. Yet, rerunning the full process would sometimes result in errors with other documents, making it tricky to pinpoint the cause.

Since I could execute the process locally, I decided to use non-blocking breakpoints to log messages without altering the code itself. This approach was particularly valuable because it allowed me to compare the exact same lines of code from different environments. Had I added manual logging statements, the line numbers would have changed, complicating any side-by-side comparisons. Through this method, I eventually uncovered some irregularities caused by a few conditions in the Date and Time APIs, which introduced randomness into the output.

Although I was able to solve the problem, I couldn't help but wish I had access to an AI assistant back then. This was years before we had large language models (LLMs) and other modern AI tools at our disposal, but I'm certain that using an AI to analyze and compare the log messages would have significantly shortened the investigation process.

I would now solve it a lot easier by using a prompt similar to the following:

> The two files I attached contain logs provided by the execution of the same scheduled process in two different environments. The fist file named prod.txt contains the logs from the environment where the output is not the one expected, while the other file names local.txt contain logs generated in the environment where the output is the one expected.
>
> <<Included here would be a detailed description of what is excepted to happen and doesn't in the first environment>>
>
> Can you please analyze and compare the logs and identify context differences that could indicate where the issue comes from?

Execution stack trace: Visual vs. text representation

Notice the way the stack trace is printed in the console. You'll often find the execution stack trace in a text format rather than a visual one. The advantage of the text representation is that it can be stored in any text format output, such as the console or a log file.

The following figure shows a comparison between the visual representation of the execution stack trace provided by the debugger and its textual representation. In both cases, the debugger provides the same essential details that can help you understand how a specific line of code was executed.

In this particular case, the stack trace tells us that the execution started from the main() method of the Main class. Remember that the first layer of the stack trace is the bottom one. On line 9, the main() method called the decode() method in the Decoder class (layer 2), which then called the line we marked with the breakpoint.

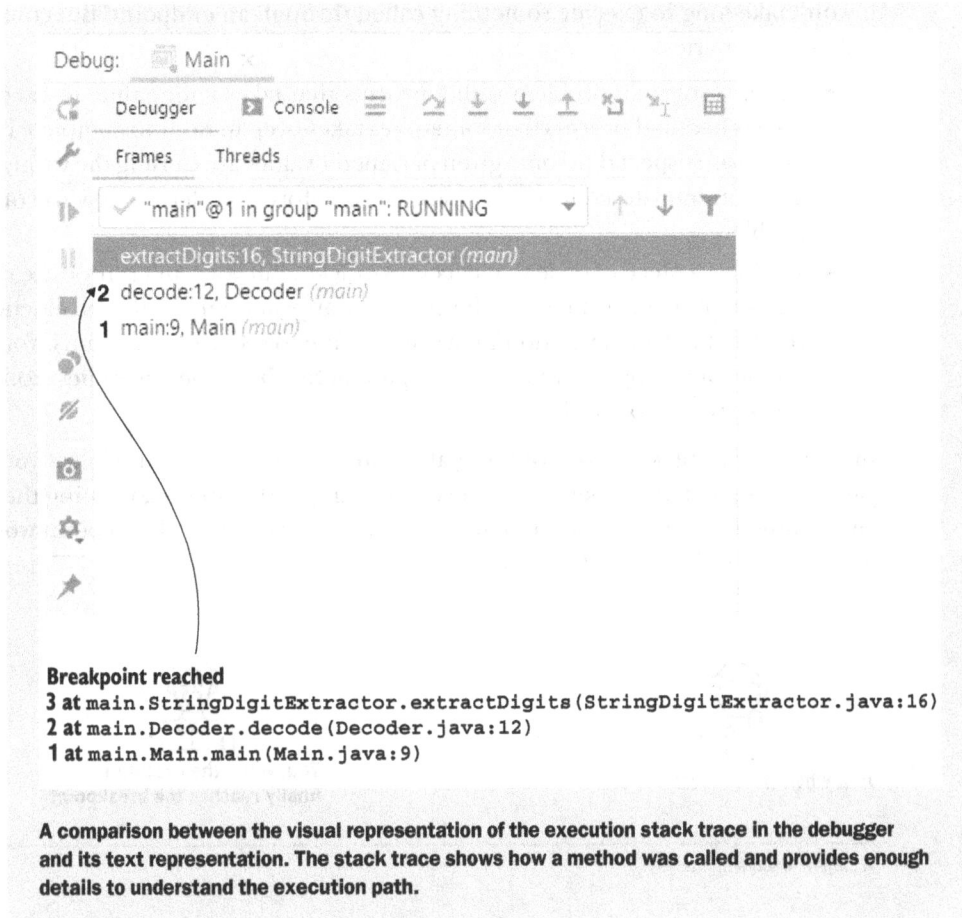

Debug: Main

Debugger | Console

Frames | Threads

✓ "main"@1 in group "main": RUNNING

extractDigits:16, StringDigitExtractor *(main)*
2 decode:12, Decoder *(main)*
1 main:9, Main *(main)*

Breakpoint reached
3 at `main.StringDigitExtractor.extractDigits(StringDigitExtractor.java:16)`
2 at `main.Decoder.decode(Decoder.java:12)`
1 at `main.Main.main(Main.java:9)`

A comparison between the visual representation of the execution stack trace in the debugger and its text representation. The stack trace shows how a method was called and provides enough details to understand the execution path.

3.3 Dynamically altering the investigation scenario

In this section, you'll learn another valuable technique that will make your code investigations easier: changing the values of the variables in scope while debugging. In some cases, this approach can save a significant amount of time. We'll begin by discussing the scenarios in which changing variables' values on the fly is the most effective approach. Then, I will demonstrate how to use this approach with an example.

Earlier in this chapter, we talked about conditional breakpoints. Conditional breakpoints allow you to tell the debugger to pause the execution under specific conditions (e.g., when a given variable has a certain value). Often, we investigate logic that executes in a short time, and using conditional breakpoints is enough. For cases such as debugging a piece of logic called through a REST endpoint (especially if you have the right data to reproduce a problem in your environment), you would simply use a conditional breakpoint to pause the execution when appropriate. That's because you know it won't take long to execute something called through an endpoint. But consider the following scenarios:

- You investigate a problem with a process that takes a long time to execute. Say it's a scheduled process that sometimes takes over an hour to complete its execution. You suspect that some given parameter values are causing the wrong output, and you want to confirm your suspicion before you decide how to correct the problem.

- You have a piece of code that executes quickly, but you can't reproduce the problem in your environment. The problem appears only in the production environment to which you don't have access due to security constraints. You believe the problem appears when certain parameters have specific values. You want to prove your theory is right.

In scenario 1, breakpoints (conditional or not) aren't so helpful. Unless you investigate some logic that happens at the very beginning of the process, running the process and waiting for the execution to pause on a line marked with a breakpoint would take too much time (figure 3.10).

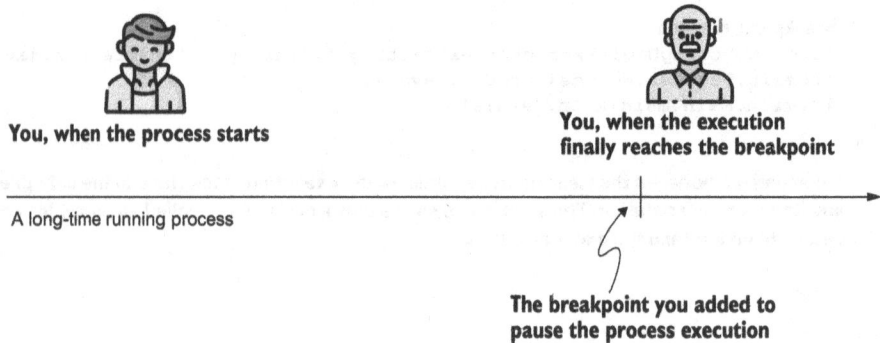

You, when the process starts

You, when the execution finally reaches the breakpoint

A long-time running process

The breakpoint you added to pause the process execution

Figure 3.10   Usually, when investigating problems in a long-running process, using breakpoints is not really an option. It can take a long time for the execution to reach the part of code you are investigating, and if you must rerun the process several times, you will definitely spend too much time on it.

Figure 3.11 shows how to change the data in one of the variables in the scope when the debugger pauses the execution. In IntelliJ IDEA, right-click the variable which value you want to change. You complete this action in the frame where the debugger shows the current values of the variables in scope. Let's go back to our previous example, da-ch3-ex1.

Once you select the variable you want to change, set the value as presented in figure 3.12. Remember that you must use a value according to the variable's type. That means that if you change a `String` variable, you still need to use a `String` value; you cannot use a `long` or a `Boolean` value.

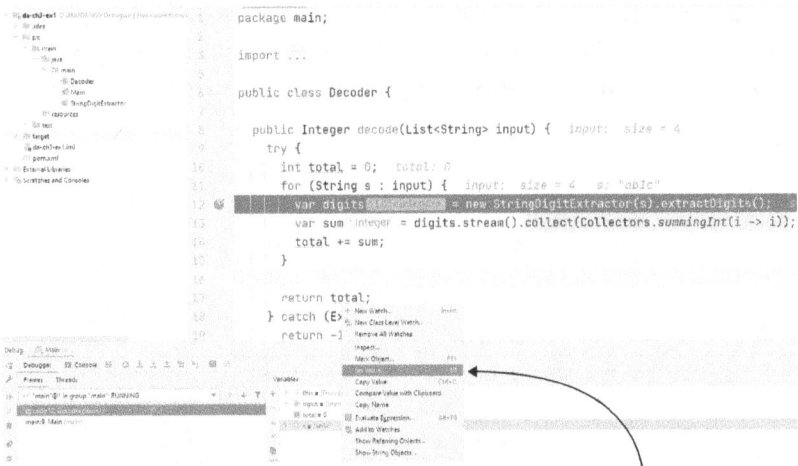

When the debugger pauses the execution on a line, you can set values in the variables in scope. This way, you can create you own investigation scenario with the conditions you need in this case.

Figure 3.11 Setting a new value in a variable in scope. The debugger shows the values for the variables in scope when it pauses the execution on a given line. You can also change the values to create a new investigation case. In some cases, this approach can help you validate your suspicions about what the code does.

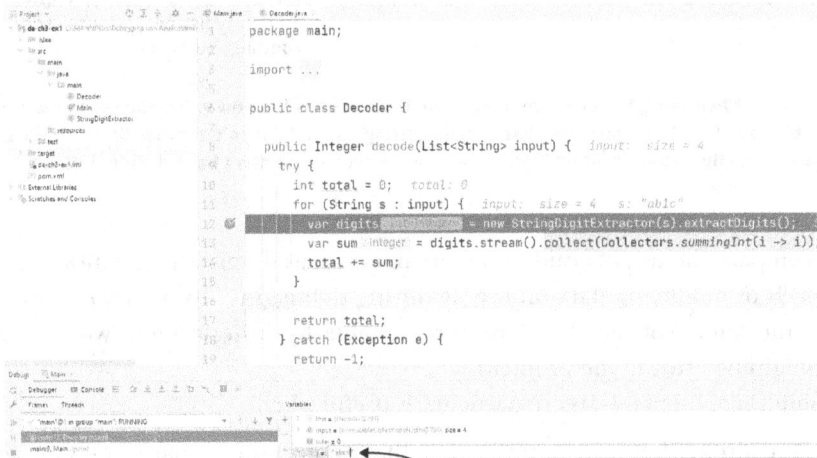

You can set any value in a variable in the scope, but you must retain its type. In this example, we change the value of s from "ab1c" to "abcd".

Figure 3.12 Change the variable's value to observe how the app's execution behaves in different conditions.

When you continue the execution, as presented in figure 3.13, the app now uses the new value. Instead of calling `extractDigits()` for value `"ab1c"`, the app used the value `"abcd"`. The list the method returns is empty because the string `"abcd"` doesn't contain digits.

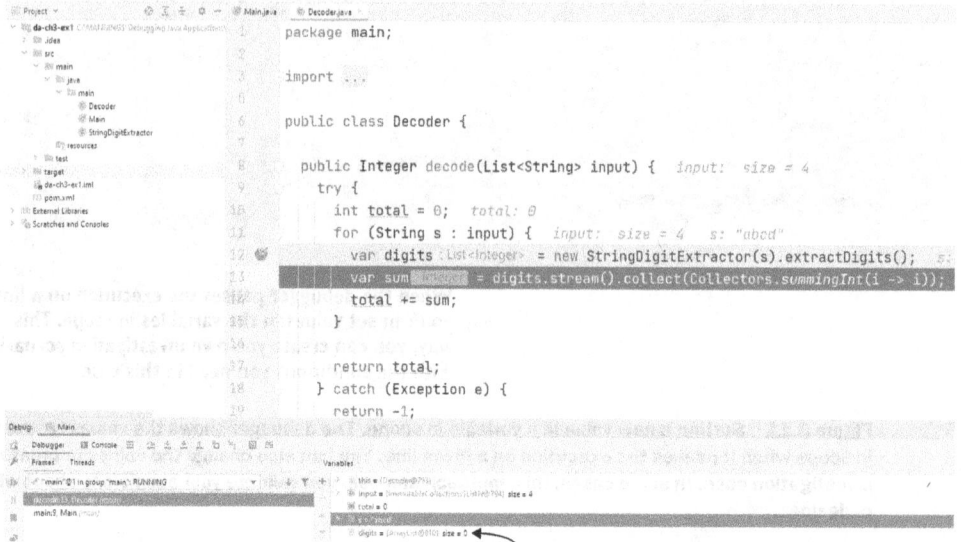

The app will now use the new value you set in the variable. When stepping over, the `extractDigits()` method returns an empty list because the string `"abcd"` contains no digits.

Figure 3.13   When using the step over operation, the app uses the new value you set to the s variable. `extractDigits()` returns an empty list because string `"abcd"` doesn't contain digits. Setting values in variables on the fly enables testing different scenarios even if you don't have the input data you need.

Let's compare the use of conditional breakpoints, as discussed in section 3.1, with the approach of modifying data on the fly during debugging. In both scenarios, the first step is the same: you need to have a reasonable hypothesis about which part of the code might be causing the problem.

Conditional breakpoints are particularly useful when

- You already have access to the data that triggers the scenario you want to investigate. For example, in our earlier case, you needed to know the specific value that would match an entry in the list and trigger the behavior you're interested in.
- The code under investigation doesn't take too long to execute. If, for instance, you're dealing with a large list and processing each element takes several seconds, hitting the right condition might become time-consuming. In such cases,

relying solely on conditional breakpoints could significantly slow down your investigation.

You can use the approach of changing a variable's value if

- You don't have the data necessary to cause the scenario you want to investigate.
- Executing the code takes too long.

I know what you are thinking now: Why are we using conditional breakpoints at all? It might look like you should avoid using conditional breakpoints entirely since you can create any environment you need to investigate simply by changing the variables' values on the fly.

Both techniques come with their own advantages and disadvantages. Modifying variable values directly can be an effective approach when you only need to adjust a few values (two at most in my opinion). However, as the changes grow in scope, the complexity of managing the scenario can escalate quickly. Additionally, when altering data in-memory, it's usually because you have a hypothesis about the problem and want to confirm it. In contrast, there are situations where you have no clear understanding of what's going wrong. In such cases, using breakpoints can be invaluable to observe how the logic manipulates the data, helping you gain insights into the underlying problem and guiding your investigation.

Moreover, remember that we sometimes deal with cases involving immutability. In such situations, the IDE won't be able to modify the value of a final variable during debugging. Java records, introduced as a preview feature in Java 14 and officially added in Java 16, are a great way to strengthen immutability in your model layer. However, one drawback is that their attributes are implicitly final, which means you won't be able to modify their values on the fly while debugging.

3.4 Rewinding the investigation case

We can't go back in time. However, with debugging, rewinding the investigation is sometimes possible. This section discusses when and how we can "go back in time" while investigating code with a debugger. We call this approach *dropping frames, dropping execution frames*, or *quitting execution frames*.

We'll look an example using IntelliJ IDEA. We'll compare this approach with the ones we discussed previously in this chapter, and then we'll also determine when this technique can't be used.

Dropping an execution frame is, in fact, going back one layer in the execution stack trace. For example, suppose you stepped into a method and want to go back; you can drop the execution frame to return to where the method was called.

Many developers confuse dropping a frame with stepping out, most likely because the current investigation plan closes in both cases, and the execution goes back to where the method is called. However, there's a big difference. When you step out of a method, the execution continues in the current plan until the method returns or throws an exception. Then, the debugger pauses the execution right after the current method exits.

> **DEFINITION**   Dropping execution frames means going back to an earlier point in the call stack and re-running a method from that point. It lets you rewind the program a bit and try running part of the code again, without restarting the whole case.

Figure 3.14 shows how stepping out works using the example in project da-ch3-ex1. You are in the `extractDigits()` method, which, as you can see from the execution stack trace, has been called from the `decode()` method in the `Decoder` class. If you use the step out operation, the execution continues in the method that called `extract-Digits()`until the method returns. Then, the debugger pauses the execution in the `decode()` method. In other words, stepping out is like fast-forwarding this execution plan to close it and return to the previous one.

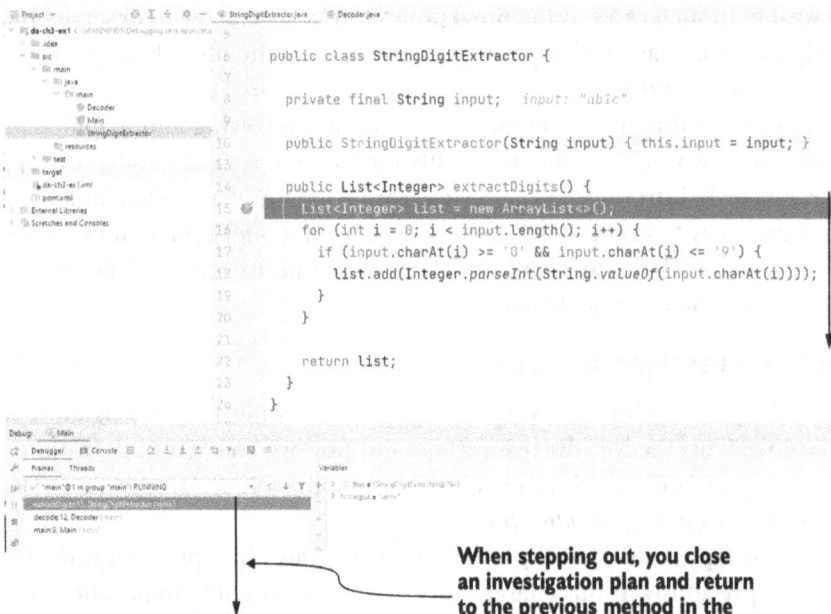

When you step out, you let the current method execute. You return to the previous method one line after the one that created the current investigation plan.

When stepping out, you close an investigation plan and return to the previous method in the execution stack trace.

Figure 3.14   Stepping out closes the current investigation plan by executing the method and then pausing the execution right after the method call. This operation allows you to continue the execution and return one layer in the execution stack.

When you drop an execution frame, the execution returns in the previous plan before the method is called, unlike stepping out. This way, you can replay the call. If the step out operation is like fast-forwarding, dropping an execution frame (figure 3.15) is like rewinding.

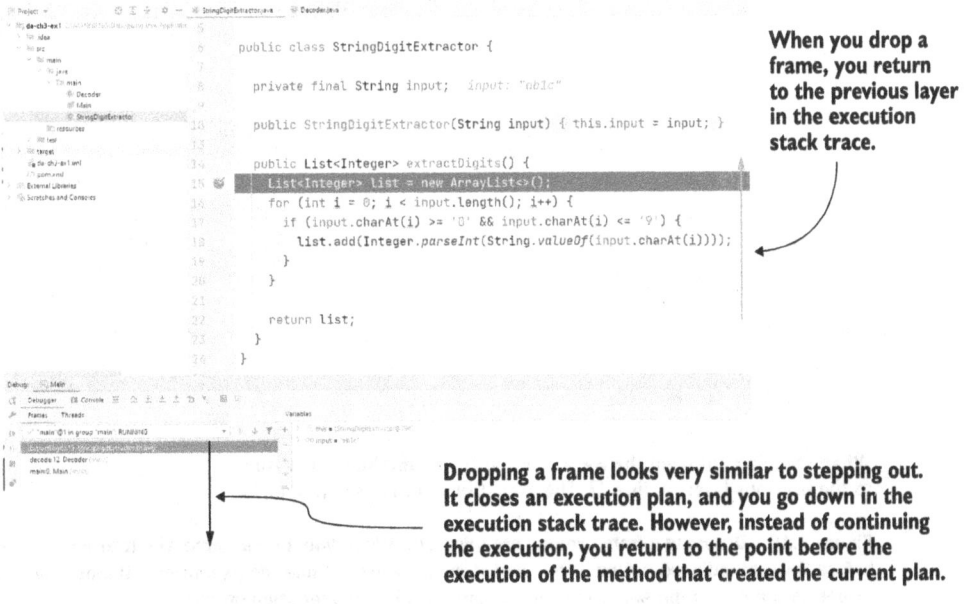

When you drop a frame, you return to the previous layer in the execution stack trace.

Dropping a frame looks very similar to stepping out. It closes an execution plan, and you go down in the execution stack trace. However, instead of continuing the execution, you return to the point before the execution of the method that created the current plan.

Figure 3.15 When you drop a frame, you return to the previous layer in the execution stack trace before the method call. This way, you can replay the method execution either by stepping into it again or stepping over it.

Figure 3.16 shows (relative to our example) a comparison between stepping out from the extractDigits() method and dropping the frame created by the extractDigits() method. If you step out, you'll go back to line 12 in the decode() method, from where extractDigits() is called, and the next line the debugger will execute is line 13. If you drop the frame, the debugger goes back to the decode() method, but the next line that will execute is line 12. Basically, the debugger returns to the line before the execution of the extractDigits() method.

Figure 3.17 shows how to use the drop frame functionality in IntelliJ IDEA. To drop the current execution frame, right-click the method's layer in the execution stack trace and select Drop Frame.

Why is the drop frame useful, and how does it help save time? Whether you use an endpoint to find a specific case you want to investigate or create one by changing the values of the variables, as discussed in section 3.3, you'll still sometimes find it useful to repeat the same execution several times. Understanding a certain piece of code is not always trivial, even if you use the debugger to pause the execution and take it step by step. But going back now and then to review the steps and how specific code instructions change the data may help you understand what's going on.

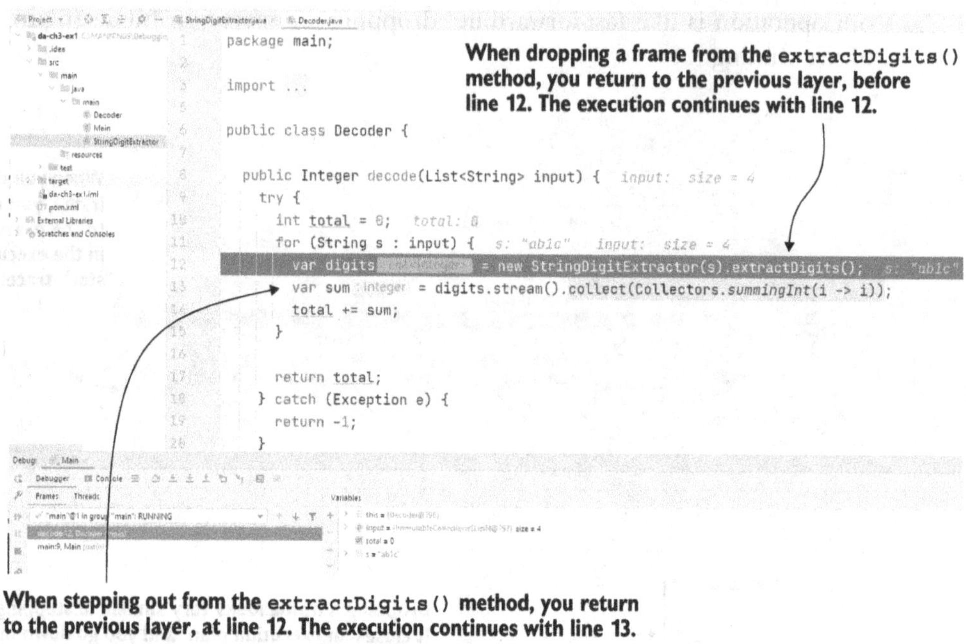

When dropping a frame from the `extractDigits()` method, you return to the previous layer, before line 12. The execution continues with line 12.

```java
package main;

import ...

public class Decoder {

    public Integer decode(List<String> input) {   input:  size = 4
        try {
            int total = 0;   total: 0
            for (String s : input) {   s: "abic"   input:  size = 4
                var digits            = new StringDigitExtractor(s).extractDigits();   s: "abic"
                var sum : Integer = digits.stream().collect(Collectors.summingInt(i -> i));
                total += sum;
            }

            return total;
        } catch (Exception e) {
            return -1;
        }
```

When stepping out from the `extractDigits()` method, you return to the previous layer, at line 12. The execution continues with line 13.

Figure 3.16 Dropping a frame versus stepping out. When you drop a frame, you return to the line before the method's execution. When you step out, you continue the execution but close the current investigation plan (represented by the current layer in the execution stack).

```java
    public List<Integer> extractDigits() {
        List<Integer> list = new ArrayList<>();
        for (int i = 0; i < input.length(); i++) {
            if (input.charAt(i) >= '0' && input.charAt(i) <= '9') {
                list.add(Integer.parseInt(String.valueOf(input.charAt(i
            }
        }
```

To drop the execution frame and return to the line before the current method execution, right-click the method's layer in the execution stack. Then, select Drop Frame.

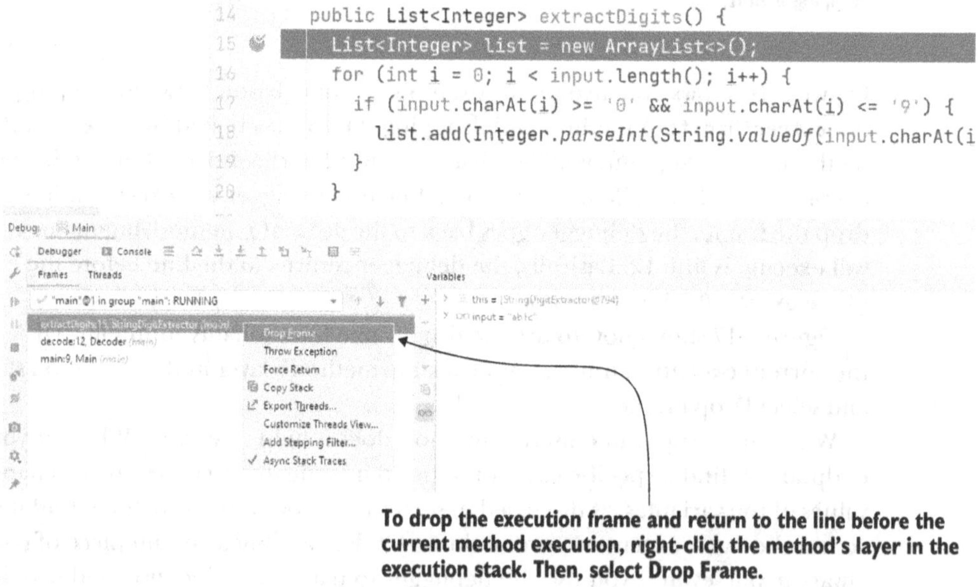

Figure 3.17 When using IntelliJ IDEA, you can drop a frame by right-clicking the method's layer in the execution stack trace and then selecting Drop Frame.

You also need to pay attention when you decide to repeat particular instructions by dropping the frame. This approach can sometimes be more confusing than helpful. Remember that if you run any instruction that changes values outside of the app's internal memory, you can't undo that change by dropping the frame. Examples of such cases are (figure 3.18)

- Modifying data in a database (insert, update, or delete)
- Changing the filesystem (creating, removing, or changing files)
- Calling another app, which changes the data for that app
- Adding a message into a queue that is read by a different app, which changes data for that app
- Sending an email message

You can drop a frame that results in committing a transaction that changes data in a database, but going back to a previous instruction won't undo the changes made by the transaction. If the app calls an endpoint that posts something into a different service, the changes resulting from the endpoint call cannot be undone by dropping the frame. If the app sends an email message, dropping the frame cannot take back the message, and so on.

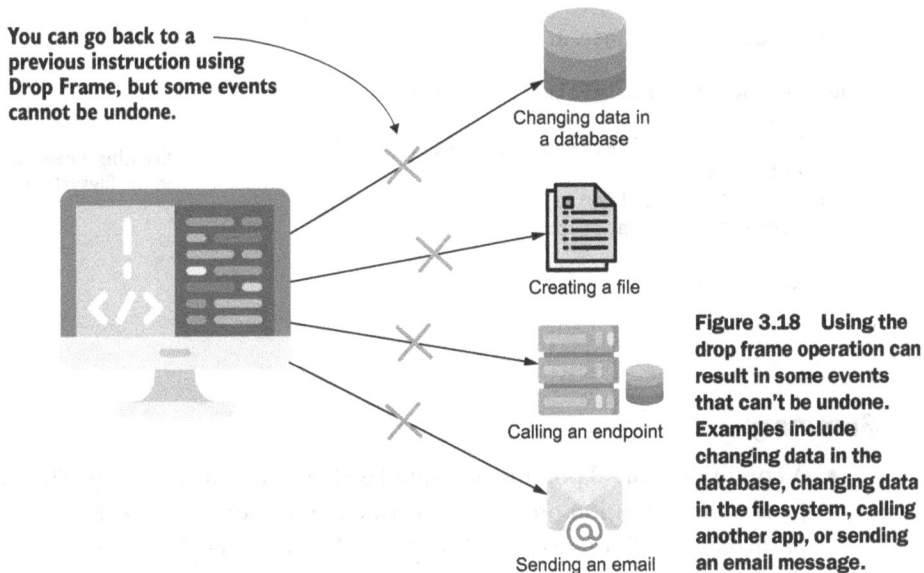

You can go back to a previous instruction using Drop Frame, but some events cannot be undone.

Changing data in a database

Creating a file

Calling an endpoint

Sending an email

Figure 3.18 Using the drop frame operation can result in some events that can't be undone. Examples include changing data in the database, changing data in the filesystem, calling another app, or sending an email message.

You need to be careful when data is changed outside the app, as sometimes repeating the same code won't have the same result. Take as an example a simple piece of code (listing 3.2, which you can find in project da-ch3-ex2). What happens if you drop the frame after the execution of the line that creates a file?

```
Files.createFile(Paths.get("File " + i));
```

The created file remains in the filesystem, and after the second time you execute the code after dropping the frame, you get an exception (because the file already exists). This is a simple example of when going back in time while debugging is not helpful. The worst part is that, in real-world cases, it's not this obvious. My recommendation is to avoid repeating the execution of large pieces of code and, before deciding to use this approach, make sure that part of the logic doesn't make external changes.

If you notice differences that seem unusual after running a dropped frame again, it may be because the code changed something externally. Often in large apps, observing such behavior is not straightforward. For example, your app may use a cache or log data accessing a certain library to observe or execute code that is completely decoupled through interceptors (aspects).

NOTE   Dropping a frame is not equivalent to an undo operation.

Calling the `Files.createFile()` method creates a new file in the filesystem. If you drop the frame after running this line, you'll return to the line before the `createFile()` method is called. However, this doesn't undo the file creation.

Listing 3.2   A method that makes changes outside the app when executing

```
public class FileManager {

  public boolean createFile(int i) {
    try {
      Files.createFile(Paths.get("File " + i));    ◄─── Creating a new file
      return true;                                       in the filesystem
    } catch (IOException e) {
      e.printStackTrace();
    }
    return false;
  }
}
```

Summary

- A conditional breakpoint is associated with a Boolean condition. The debugger pauses the execution only if the provided condition is true—that is, only when particular conditions apply. This approach eliminates the need to step through the code line by line just to reach your starting point.
- You can use breakpoints to log the values of certain variables in the console that don't suspend the app's execution. This approach is quite helpful because you can add log messages without changing the code.
- Moreover, you can use AI assistants to analyze large amounts of log messages to discover anomalies and guide your next steps in the troubleshooting process.

- When the debugger pauses the execution on specific lines of code, you can alter the data on the fly to create custom scenarios based on what you want to investigate. This way, you don't have to wait until the execution gets to a conditional breakpoint. In some cases, when you don't have an appropriate environment, modifying data during debugging eliminates the need to preconfigure it in the environment, saving valuable time.

- Changing variables' values to create a custom investigation scenario can be an efficient technique when trying to understand just a piece of the logic of a long-running process or when you don't have the desired data in the environment where you run the app. However, changing more than one or two variable values at a time may add considerable complexity and make your investigation more challenging.

- You can step out of an investigation plan and return to the point before the method was called. This is termed dropping a frame, but it can sometimes introduce an unwanted side effect. If the app changed anything externally (e.g., committed a transaction and changed some database records, changed a file in the filesystem, or made a RESTful call to another app), returning to a previous execution step won't undo these changes.

Making the most of
logs: Auditing an
app's behavior

This chapter covers

- Using log messages to understand an app's behavior
- Correctly implementing log capabilities in your app
- Using AI assistants to investigate large log files
- Avoiding problems caused by logs

This chapter discusses using log messages recorded by an app. The concept of logging didn't appear with software. For centuries, people used logs to understand past events and processes better. In fact, people have used logging since writing was invented, and we still use it today. All ships have logbooks. Sailors record decisions (direction, speed increase or decrease, etc.) and given or received orders, along with any encountered event (figure 4.1). If something happens to the onboard equipment, they can use the logbook notes to understand where they are and navigate to the nearest shore. If an accident happens, the logbook notes can be used in the investigation to determine how the unfortunate event could have been avoided.

Figure 4.1   Sailors store events in logs that they can use to determine their route or analyze the crew's response to a given event. In the same way, apps store log messages so that developers can later analyze a potential problem or discover breaches in the app.

If you've ever watched a chess game, you've probably seen players jot down each move. Why? These logs help them re-create the entire game afterward. They analyze their own and their opponent's decisions to uncover mistakes or vulnerabilities. Similarly, applications log messages so that developers can trace what happened during execution. Reading these messages is like reconstructing a game of chess or like studying a ship's logbook to understand a voyage.

Some logs track routine steps (e.g., debug logs), others record unexpected events (e.g., error or warning logs), and some might highlight potential threats (e.g., security logs). Each type serves a different purpose. But as with any log, they don't capture everything, and they're only as useful as the information they contain. Still, logs remain one of our most important tools when investigating strange behavior or uncovering subtle problems in an application.

I'm sure you already know what logs look like. You've seen log messages, at least when running your app with an IDE (figure 4.2). All IDEs have a *log console*. It's one of the first things all software developers learn. But an app doesn't just display log messages in the IDE's console. Real-world apps store logs to allow developers to investigate a specific app behavior at a given time.

Figure 4.3 shows the anatomy of a standard-formatted log message. A log message is just a string, so theoretically, it can be any sentence. However, clean and easy-to-use

When running an app on your local system using the IDE, you find the log messages in the console.
2021-07-25 16:10:59.943 INFO 76928 --- [main] : Starting DemoApplicatio
2021-07-25 16:10:59.948 INFO 76928 --- [main] : No active profile set,
2021-07-25 16:11:01.006 INFO 76928 --- [main] : Tomcat initialized with
2021-07-25 16:11:01.015 INFO 76928 --- [main] : Starting service [Tomca
2021-07-25 16:11:01.015 INFO 76928 --- [main] : Starting Servlet engine
2021-07-25 16:11:01.091 INFO 76928 --- [main] : Initializing Spring emb
2021-07-25 16:11:01.092 INFO 76928 --- [main] : Root WebApplicationCont
2021-07-25 16:11:01.434 INFO 76928 --- [main] : Tomcat started on port(
2021-07-25 16:11:01.447 INFO 76928 --- [main] : Started DemoApplication

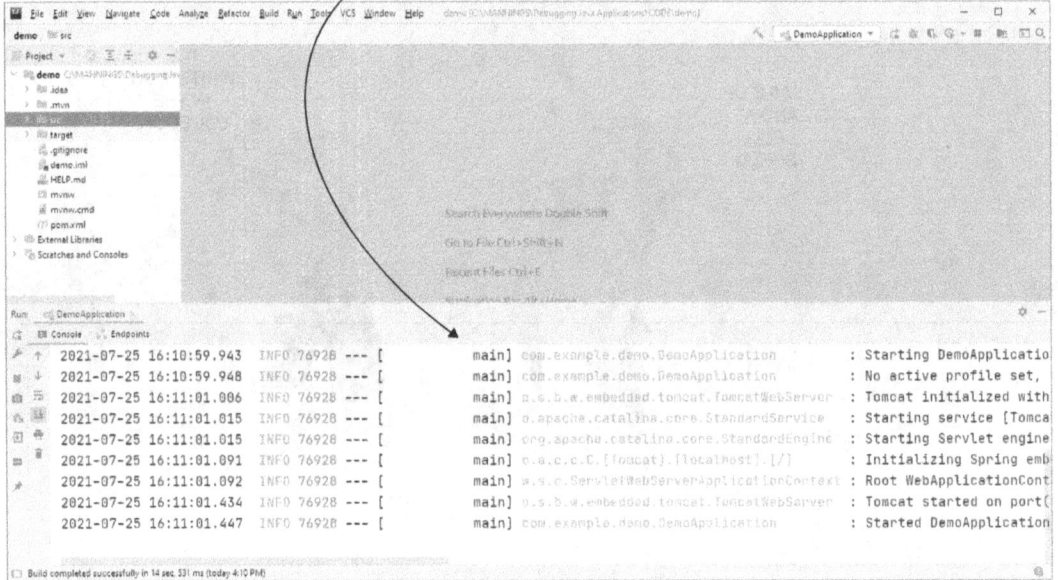

Figure 4.2 IDE log console. All IDEs have a log console. While logging messages in the console is useful when running the app locally, real-world apps also store logs needed to understand how the app behaved at a given time.

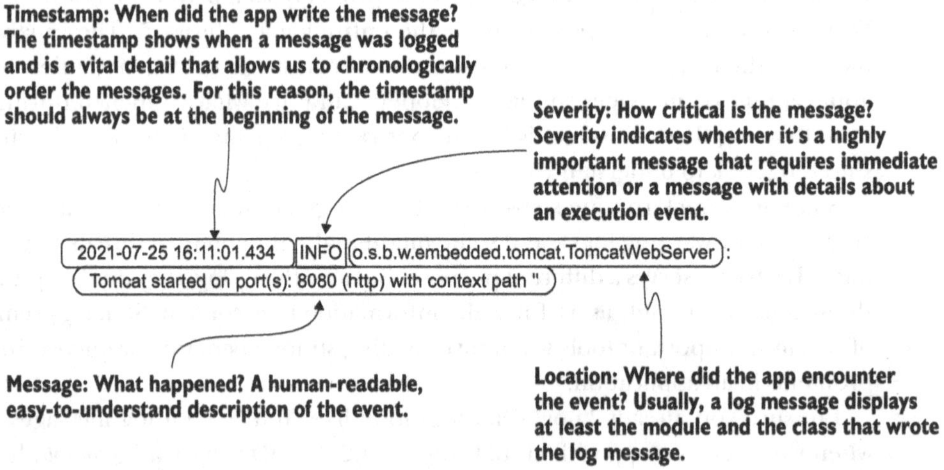

Timestamp: When did the app write the message? The timestamp shows when a message was logged and is a vital detail that allows us to chronologically order the messages. For this reason, the timestamp should always be at the beginning of the message.
Severity: How critical is the message? Severity indicates whether it's a highly important message that requires immediate attention or a message with details about an execution event.
2021-07-25 16:11:01.434
INFO
o.s.b.w.embedded.tomcat.TomcatWebServer
:
Tomcat started on port(s): 8080 (http) with context path ''
Message: What happened? A human-readable, easy-to-understand description of the event.
Location: Where did the app encounter the event? Usually, a log message displays at least the module and the class that wrote the log message.

Figure 4.3 The anatomy of a well-formatted log message. In addition to describing a situation or an event, a log message should also contain several other relevant details: the timestamp of when the app logged the message, the event's severity, and where the message was written. Reviewing the log details makes problem investigation much easier.

logs need to follow some best practices (that you'll learn throughout this chapter). For example, in addition to a description, a log message contains a timestamp of when the app wrote the message, a description of the severity, and a notation for the part of the app that wrote the message (figure 4.3).

Moreover, in many modern systems, logs are aggregated in a centralized location, such as a log management platform or observability stack. In these setups, it's crucial that each log entry includes the name (or identifier) of the application that generated it—otherwise, you won't be able to trace each message back to its source component.

In many cases, logs are an efficient way to investigate an app's behavior. Some examples include

- Investigating an event or a timeline of events that already happened
- Investigating problems where interfering with the app changes the app's behavior (Heisenbugs)
- Understanding the app's behavior over the long term
- Raising alarms for critical events that require immediate attention

These details are essential for providing you (and your AI assistant, as we'll discuss in this chapter) with the necessary context to investigate problems, proactively identify vulnerabilities, or detect other potential problems in your app's execution. Although we haven't discussed investigation techniques yet, I want to emphasize that there are steps you can take in advance with your app's logs to make future investigations easier when necessary. I strongly believe that when it comes to using logs, the way you initially design them is crucial for making your life easier later.

We generally don't use just one technique when investigating how a particular app capability behaves. Depending on the scenario, a developer may combine several techniques to understand a particular behavior. In some cases, you'll use the debugger with logs, as well as other techniques (discussed in the following chapters) to figure out why something works the way it does.

I always recommend that developers check the logs before doing anything else when investigating a problem (figure 4.4). Logs often allow you to immediately identify

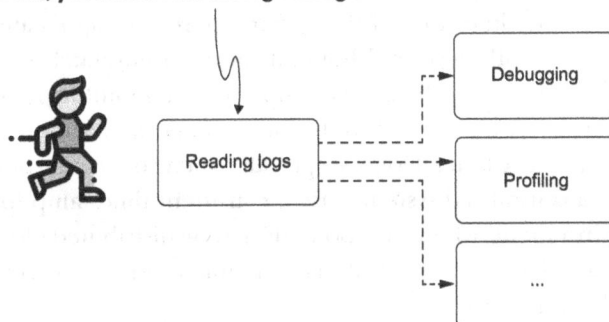

Figure 4.4   Whenever you investigate a problem, the first thing you should always do is read the app's logs. In many cases, the log messages give you a starting point or offer valuable hints on what you should do next to solve the problem.

strange behavior that helps pinpoint where to begin your investigation. The logs won't necessarily answer all your questions, but having a starting point is extremely important. If the log messages show you where to begin, you've already saved a lot of time!

In my opinion, logs are not just extremely valuable; they are, in fact, indispensable for any application. The next section discusses how to use logs and learn the typical investigation scenarios in which logs are essential. Among these are

- Using logs to identify exceptions
- Identifying who's calling a method with exception stack traces
- Measuring the execution time of a piece of logic

In section 4.2, you'll learn how to properly implement logging capabilities in your app. We'll discuss using logging levels to help you filter events and problems caused by logs more easily.

I also recommend reading part 4 of *Logging in Action* by Phil Wilkins (Manning, 2022). This chapter focuses more on investigation techniques with logs, while *Logging in Action* dives more deeply into logs' technicalities. You'll also find logging demonstrated using a different language than Java (Python).

4.1   *Investigating issues with logs*

Like any other investigation technique, using logs makes sense in some situations and doesn't in others. In this section, we examine various scenarios in which using logs facilitates our understanding of software's behavior. We'll begin by discussing several key points of log messages and then analyze how these characteristics assist developers in their investigation of app problems.

One of the biggest advantages of log messages is that they allow you to visualize the execution of a certain piece of code at a given time. When you use a debugger, as discussed in chapters 2 and 3, your attention is mainly on the present. You look at how the data looks while the debugger pauses the execution on a specific line of code. A debugger doesn't give you many details on the execution history. You can use the execution stack trace to identify the execution path, but everything else is focused on the present.

In contrast, logs focus on the app's execution over a past period (figure 4.5). Log messages have a strong relationship with time.

Always pay attention to the time zone of the system where your application is running. Log timestamps can be off by several hours if there's a mismatch between the system's time zone and the one used by the developer or the monitoring tools. This discrepancy can quickly become a source of confusion during troubleshooting.

To avoid this situation, ensure that all logs—especially when collected from multiple services or regions into a centralized system—use a consistent timestamp format and time zone. In cloud environments where components may be distributed globally, standardizing on a single time zone (such as UTC) makes it much easier to correlate events across systems and track down problems accurately.

Debugging

With debugging, you focus on the present state of the app's execution.

Past   Future

Investigating with logs

When investigating with logs, you focus on a past time period.

Past   Future

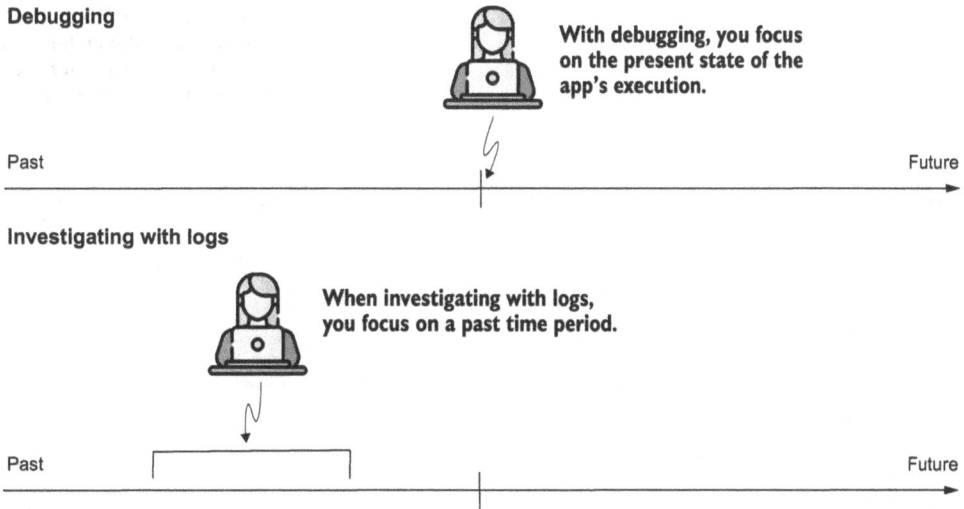

Figure 4.5   When investigating a problem with the debugger, you focus on the present. When you use log messages, you focus on a given period in the past. This difference can help you select an approach.

Today, AI assistants are immensely beneficial, especially when investigating large volumes of log messages. My primary advice for using logs in troubleshooting is to remember that AI can assist in understanding complex logged messages, making your work more efficient. With sufficient context, an AI assistant can even suggest solutions or point you toward the potential root cause of a problem.

NOTE Always include the timestamp in a log message. You'll use the timestamp to easily identify the order in which messages were logged, which will give you an idea of when the app wrote a certain message. I recommend the timestamp be in the first part (at the beginning) of the message.

For instance, assistants integrated into IDEs, such as GitHub Copilot or IntelliJ IDEA AI Assistant, can be particularly straightforward to use. These tools typically have access to the entire or most of the codebase, as well as the IDE console, thus allowing them to provide more comprehensive assistance. Figure 4.6, shows an example where I intentionally caused an exception in the logs and then asked my AI assistant for a potential solution. In this case, I used the IntelliJ IDEA AI Assistant.

Depending on its configuration, your IDE-integrated AI companion might have direct access to specific files and locations. For example, you could simply ask, "Please check the logs and determine where the issue comes from." This capability makes

You can ask your AI assistant to give you a solution for a given problem in the log or for the current log messages in the console.

AI Assistant   All Chats   New Chat   ⋮ ⸱⸱

> **Me**   ⋮
>
> Can you provide me a solution to the exception in the logs?
>
> Exception in thread "main" java.lang.NullPointerException: Cannot invoke "java.util.List.add(Object)" because "list" is null
> at main.StringDigitExtractor.extractDigits(StringDigitExtractor.java:27)
> at main.Decoder.decode(Decoder.java:11)
> at main.Main.main(Main.java:9)

AI Assistant   👍 👎 ↻

Certainly! The `NullPointerException` occurs when attempting to invoke a method on an object that hasn't been initialized. Based on the exception message, it seems the `list` object in your `StringDigitExtractor` class is null when you call the `add` method.

Here's an example of what might be happening and how you can fix it:

Share your feedback ↗

Ask AI Assistant. Use # for mentions and / for commands

🗇 #   ▷

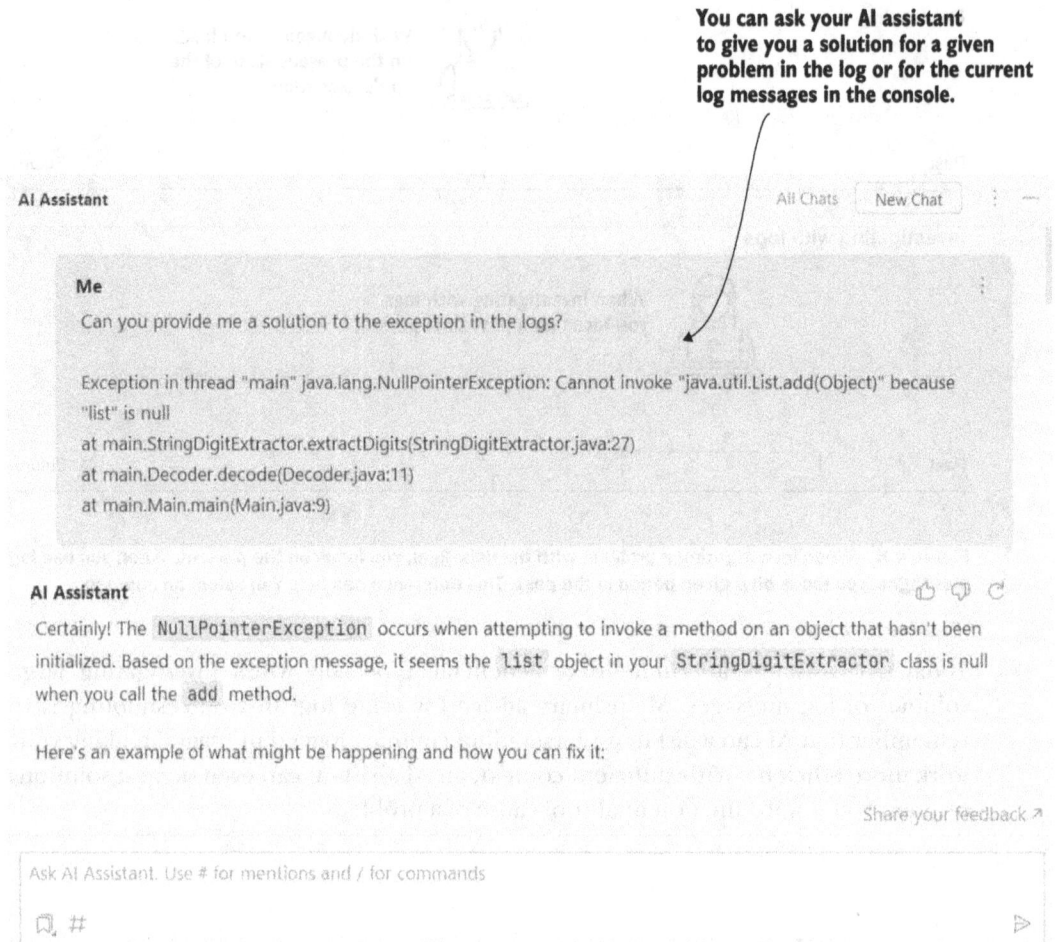

Figure 4.6   When you encounter an exception or a console message that isn't immediately clear, you can quickly ask your AI companion for a concise analysis.

IDE-integrated assistants particularly convenient to use, as they already have much of the context needed to analyze specific cases and provide accurate solutions.

If an IDE-integrated companion isn't available, you can still use a chat-driven AI. While a chat-driven AI might be less convenient since you may not be able to provide it with all the necessary context, it can still guide you in the right direction in most cases. In figure 4.7, I'm using Google Gemini to get insights into a potential problem hidden in the exception stack trace in my console.

If you think your AI could provide a clearer answer, continue to incrementally add context within the same chat. In a real-world scenario, providing all the context may be impossible, but you can still form a good understanding of the problem before investing too much time.

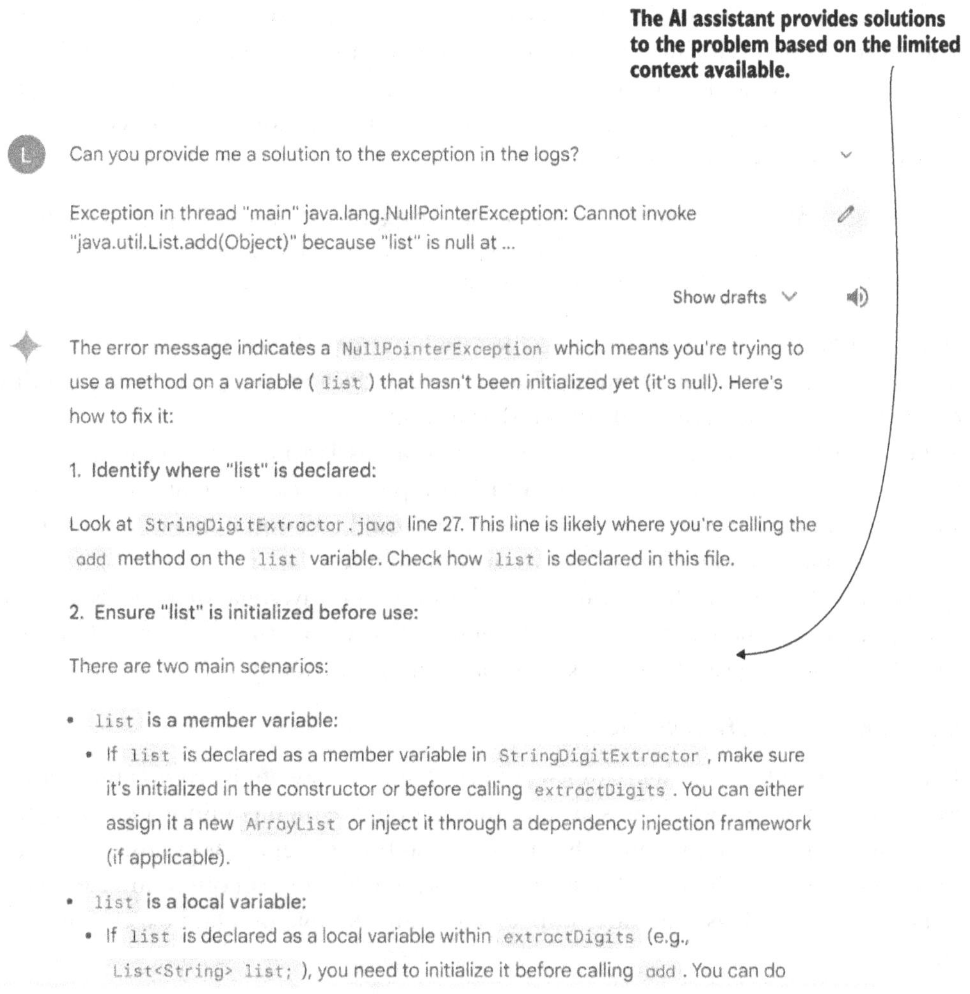

**The AI assistant provides solutions
to the problem based on the limited
context available.**

L Can you provide me a solution to the exception in the logs?   ∨

Exception in thread "main" java.lang.NullPointerException: Cannot invoke   ✎
"java.util.List.add(Object)" because "list" is null at ...

                                                                        Show drafts ∨   ◀))

✦ The error message indicates a `NullPointerException` which means you're trying to
use a method on a variable (`list`) that hasn't been initialized yet (it's null). Here's
how to fix it:

1. Identify where "list" is declared:

Look at `StringDigitExtractor.java` line 27. This line is likely where you're calling the
`add` method on the `list` variable. Check how `list` is declared in this file.

2. Ensure "list" is initialized before use:

There are two main scenarios:

- `list` is a member variable:
  - If `list` is declared as a member variable in `StringDigitExtractor` , make sure
    it's initialized in the constructor or before calling `extractDigits` . You can either
    assign it a new `ArrayList` or inject it through a dependency injection framework
    (if applicable).
- `list` is a local variable:
  - If `list` is declared as a local variable within `extractDigits` (e.g.,
    `List<String> list;`), you need to initialize it before calling `add` . You can do

**Figure 4.7   When an IDE-integrated AI companion isn't an option, you can use a chat-based AI. Even without
complete context, a chat-based AI can still provide useful suggestions on how to continue your investigation.**

If you feel you're spending too much time without getting an answer, you may want to
consider other investigative techniques. Depending on the problem you're troubleshooting, you could try debugging—as discussed in chapters 2 and 3—or profiling,
which we'll cover later.

Another way to use chat-based AI assistants for log analysis is by providing them
with a complete log file and asking for help in extracting details related to a specific problem, if there is any. Unlike humans, AI assistants don't get bored looking
through a massive amount of log messages. They can easily pinpoint log entries that
might reference a problem or at least significantly reduce the amount of data you
need to review.

For example, when conducting a post-mortem investigation—analyzing a problem that caused a process to fail after the app stopped working—I often need to identify relevant log messages to determine the root cause. This typically involves sifting through a large volume of logs produced by the application over many hours, even days.

An example of a prompt could look like

> Please find in the attached log file all the exceptions that are related to locks in the database. Please group them by queries that thrown them or by the methods in the code that apparently caused the exception.

Doing this kind of work manually on a file with hundreds of thousands of log lines can be exhausting and time-consuming. Fortunately, perfect accuracy isn't critical in this case, which makes it a great task for an AI assistant.

For example, if the AI misses a few log entries or misclassifies some, it's usually not a problem. The goal, such as identifying which component is causing database locks, can still be achieved. The real benefit is speed: what could take you hours or even days to analyze manually can now be done in seconds or minutes.

Recently, AI assistants have dramatically improved my investigation process. By providing them with the extracted log messages, I've been able to collaborate effectively with the AI to analyze and identify key problems more efficiently.

4.1.1   Using logs to identify exceptions

Logs help identify a problem after it occurred and investigate its root cause. Often, we use logs to decide where to start an investigation. We then continue exploring the problem using other tools and techniques, such as the debugger (as discussed in chapters 2 and 3) or a profiler (as discussed in chapters 5–8). You can often find exception stack traces in the logs. The next snippet shows an example of a Java exception stack trace:

```
java.lang.NullPointerException
at java.base/java.util.concurrent.ThreadPoolExecutor
  runWorker(ThreadPoolExecutor.java:1128) ~[na:na]
at java.base/java.util.concurrent.ThreadPoolExecutor$Worker
  run(ThreadPoolExecutor.java:628) ~[na:na]
at org.apache.tomcat.util.threads.TaskThread$WrappingRunnable
  run(TaskThread.java:61) ~[tomcat-embed-core-9.0.26.jar:9.0.26]
at java.base/java.lang.Thread.run(Thread.java:830) ~[na:na]
```

Seeing this exception stack trace, or something similar, in the application's log tells you that something potentially went wrong with a given feature. Each exception has its own meaning that helps identify where the app encountered a problem. For example, a NullPointerException tells you that, somehow, an instruction referred to an attribute or a method through a variable that didn't contain a reference to an object instance (figure 4.8).

If the app throws a `NullPointerException` on this line, it means that the invoice variable doesn't hold an object reference. In other words, the invoice variable is null.

```
var invoice = getLastIssuedInvoice();

if (client.isOverdue()) {
  invoice.pay();
}
```

Figure 4.8 A `NullPointerException` indicates the app execution encountered a behavior that was called without the behaving instance. But that doesn't mean that the line that produced the exception is also the cause of the problem. The exception could be a consequence of the root cause. You should always look for the root cause instead of locally treating a problem.

NOTE Remember that the location where an exception occurs is not necessarily the root cause of the problem. An exception tells you where something went wrong, but the exception itself can be a consequence of a problem elsewhere. It is not necessarily the problem itself. Don't make a decision about solving the exception locally by adding a `try-catch-finally` block or an `if-else` statement too quickly. First, make sure you understand the root cause of the problem before looking for a solution to solve it.

I often find that this concept confuses beginners. Let's take a simple `NullPointer-Exception`, which is probably the first exception any Java developer encounters and one of the simplest to understand. However, when you find a `NullPointerException` in the logs, you need first to ask yourself, "Why is that reference missing?" It could be because a particular instruction that the app executed earlier didn't work as expected (figure 4.9).

A developer should first understand why the `getLastIssuedInvoice()` returns null in this case.

```
var invoice = getLastIssuedInvoice();

if (client.isOverdue()) {
  if (invoice != null) {
    invoice.pay();
  }
}
```

A beginner would be tempted to simply check for a null here, but this is sweeping the problem under the rug.

Figure 4.9 Locally solving the problem is in many cases equivalent to sweeping it under the rug. If the root cause remains, more problems can appear later. Remember that an exception in the logs doesn't necessarily indicate the root cause.

4.1.2   *Using exception stack traces to identify what calls a method*

One of the techniques developers consider unusual, but that I find advantageous in practice, is logging an exception stack trace to identify what calls a specific method. Since starting my career as a software developer, I've worked with messy codebases of (usually) large applications. One of the difficulties I frequently encounter is figuring out who calls a given method when an app is running in a remote environment. If you just read the app's code, you will discover hundreds of ways that method could've been called.

Exceptions in Java have a capability that is often disregarded: they keep track of the execution stack trace. When discussing exceptions, we often call the execution stack trace an *exception* stack trace. But they are, in the end, the same thing. The exception stack trace displays the chain of method calls that cause a specific exception, and you have access to this information even without throwing that exception. In code, it's enough to use the exception:

```
new Exception().printStackTrace();
```

Consider the method in listing 4.1. If you don't have a debugger, you can simply print the exception stack trace, like I did in this example, as the first line in the method to find the execution stack trace. Keep in mind that this code only prints the stack trace and doesn't throw the exception, so it doesn't interfere with the executed logic. This example is in project da-ch4-ex1.

Listing 4.1   Printing the execution stack trace in logs using an exception

```
public List<Integer> extractDigits() {
  new Exception().printStackTrace();        ◀——— Prints the exception
  List<Integer> list = new ArrayList<>();            stack trace
  for (int i = 0; i < input.length(); i++) {
    if (input.charAt(i) >= '0' && input.charAt(i) <= '9') {
      list.add(Integer.parseInt(String.valueOf(input.charAt(i))));
    }
  }

  return list;
}
```

The next snippet shows how the app prints the exception stack trace in the console. In a real-world scenario, the stack trace helps you to immediately identify the execution flow, which leads to the call you want to investigate, as we discussed in chapters 2 and 3. In this example, you can see from the logs that the extractDigits() method was called on line 11 of the Decoder class from within the decode() method:

```
java.lang.Exception at main.StringDigitExtractor
  extractDigits(StringDigitExtractor.java:15)
    at main.Decoder.decode(Decoder.java:11)
    at main.Main.main(Main.java:9)
```

4.1.3   *Measuring time spent to execute a given instruction*

Log messages are an easy way to measure the time a given set of instructions takes to execute. You can always log the difference between the timestamp before and after a given line of code. Suppose you are investigating a performance problem in which some given capability takes too long to execute. You suspect that the cause is a query the app executes to retrieve data from the database. For some parameter values, the query is slow, which is decreasing the app's overall performance.

To find which parameter is causing the problem, you can write the query and the query execution time in logs. Once you identify the troublesome parameter values, you can start looking for a solution. Maybe you need to add one more index to a table in the database, or perhaps you can rewrite the query to make it faster.

Listing 4.2 shows how to log the time spent by the execution of a specific piece of code. For example, let's figure out how much time it takes the app to run the operation of finding all the products from the database. Yes, I know, we have no parameters here; I simplified the example to allow you to focus on the discussed syntax. But in a real-world app, you would most likely investigate a more complex operation.

> **Listing 4.2   Logging the execution time for a certain line of code**

```
public TotalCostResponse getTotalCosts() {
  TotalCostResponse response = new TotalCostResponse();

  long timeBefore = System.currentTimeMillis();        ← Logs the timestamp before the method's execution
  var products = productRepository.findAll();           ← Executes the method for which we want to calculate the execution time
  long spentTimeInMillis =
    System.currentTimeMillis() - timeBefore;            ← Calculates the time spent between the timestamp after execution and the timestamp before the execution

  log.info("Execution time: " + spentTimeInMillis);     ← Prints the execution time

  var costs = products.stream().collect(
      Collectors.toMap(
          Product::getName,
          p -> p.getPrice()
            .multiply(new BigDecimal(p.getQuantity()))));

  response.setTotalCosts(costs);

  return response;
}
```

Precisely measuring how much time an app spends executing a given instruction is a simple but effective technique. However, I would only use this technique temporarily when investigating a problem. I don't recommend keeping such logs in the code for long since they most likely will not be needed later, and they make the code more difficult to read. Once you've solved the problem and no longer need to know the execution time for that line of code, you can remove the logs.

4.1.4 Investigating problems in multithreaded architectures

A multithreaded architecture is a type of capability that uses multiple threads to execute its functionality and is often sensitive to external interference (figure 4.10).

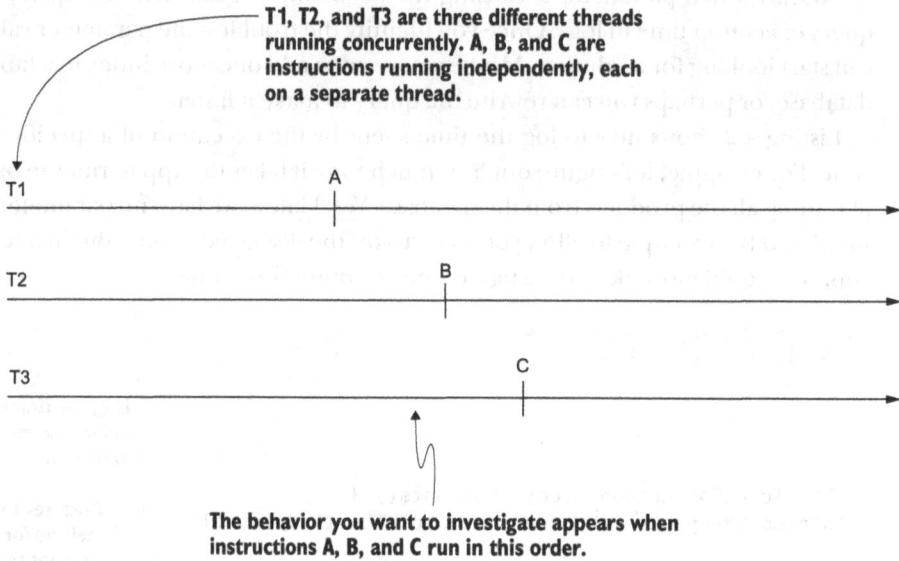

T1, T2, and T3 are three different threads
running concurrently. A, B, and C are
instructions running independently, each
on a separate thread.

T1 ———————————————— A ————————————————→

T2 ————————————————————— B ————————————————→

T3 ——————————————————————————— C ————————————————→

The behavior you want to investigate appears when
instructions A, B, and C run in this order.

Figure 4.10 A multithreaded architecture. An app with the capability to use multiple threads running concurrently to process data is a multithreaded app. Unless explicitly synchronized, instructions running on independent threads (A, B, and C) can run in any order.

For example, if you use a debugger or a profiler (tools that interfere with the app's execution), the app's behavior may change (figure 4.11).

However, if you use logs, there's a smaller chance the app will be affected while running. Logs can also sometimes interfere in multithreaded apps, but they don't have an effect big enough on the execution to change the app's flow. Thus, they can be a solution for retrieving data needed for your investigation.

Since log messages contain a timestamp (as discussed earlier in the chapter), you can order the log messages to find the sequence in which the operations execute. In a Java app, it is sometimes helpful to log the thread's name that executes a certain instruction. You can get the name of the current thread in execution using the following instruction:

```
String threadName = Thread.currentThread().getName();
```

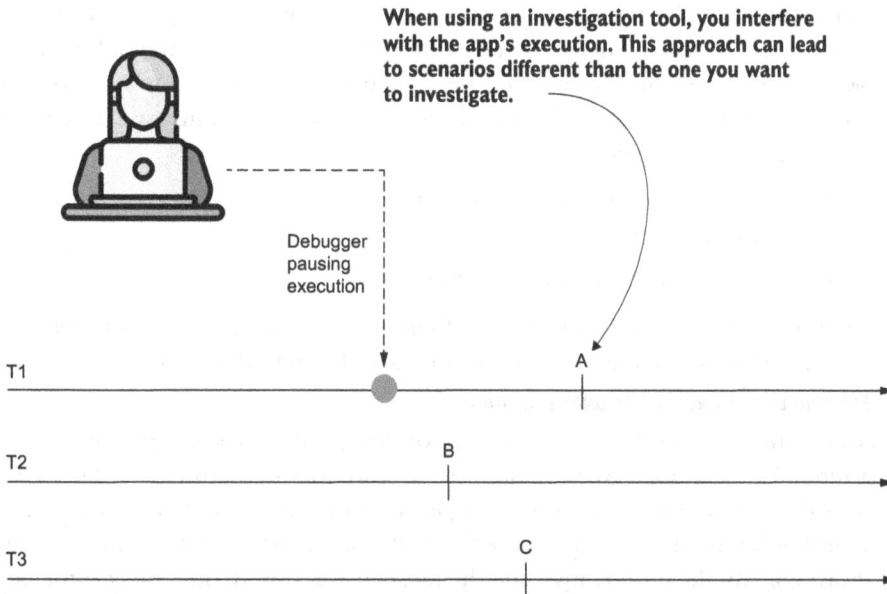

When using an investigation tool, you interfere with the app's execution. This approach can lead to scenarios different than the one you want to investigate.

Debugger pausing execution

T1

A

T2

B

T3

C

Figure 4.11   Using a tool such as a debugger or a profiler interferes with the execution, making some (or all) threads slower. Because of this, the execution often changes, and some instructions may execute in a different order than the scenario you wanted to investigate. In such a case, the tool is no longer useful since you can't research the behavior you're interested in.

In Java apps, all threads have a name. The developer can name them, or the JVM will identify the threads using a name with the pattern Thread-x, where x is an incremented number. For example, the first thread created will be named Thread-0; the next one, Thread-1; and so on. As we'll discuss in chapter 10 when we address thread dumps, naming your app's threads is good practice so that you can identify them easier when investigating a case.

4.2   Implementing logging

This section discusses best practices for implementing logging capabilities in apps. To make your app's log messages ready for investigations and avoid causing trouble with the app's execution, you need to take care of some implementation details.

We'll start by discussing how apps persist logs in section 4.2.1—specifically the advantages and disadvantages of these practices. In section 4.2.2, you'll learn how to use the log messages more efficiently by classifying them based on severity and thus make the app perform better. In section 4.2.3, we'll discuss the problems log messages can cause and how to avoid them.

4.2.1   Persisting logs

Persistence is one of the essential characteristics of log messages. As discussed earlier in this chapter, logging is different from other investigation techniques because it focuses more on the past than the present. We read logs to understand something that happened. Therefore, the app needs to store them so that we can read them later. How log messages are stored can affect the logs' usability and the app's performance. I've worked with many apps and have had the chance to see various ways developers implement log message persistence:

- Storing logs in nonrelational databases
- Storing logs in files
- Storing logs in relational databases

These can all be good choices, depending on what your app does. Let's look at some of the main things you need to consider to make the right decision.

STORING LOGS IN NONRELATIONAL DATABASES

Nonrelational (NoSQL) databases help you compromise between performance and consistency. You can use a NoSQL database to store logs in a more performant way, which gives the database a chance to miss log messages or not store them in the exact chronological order in which the app wrote them. But, as discussed earlier, a log message should always contain the timestamp when the message was stored, preferably at the beginning.

Storing log messages in NoSQL databases is common. In most cases, apps use a complete engine that stores the logs and has the capability to retrieve, search, and analyze the log messages. Today's two most-used engines are the ELK stack (https://www.elastic .co/what-is/elk-stack) and Splunk (https://www.splunk.com/).

STORING LOGS IN FILES

In the past, apps stored logs in files. You may still find older applications that write log messages directly in files, but this approach is less common today because it is generally slower, and searching for logged data is more difficult. I bring this to your attention because you'll find many tutorials and examples in which apps store their logs in files, but with more current apps, you should avoid this.

STORING LOGS IN RELATIONAL DATABASES

We rarely use relational databases to store log messages. A relational database mainly guarantees data consistency, which ensures log messages are not lost. Once they are stored, you can retrieve them. But consistency comes with a compromise in performance.

In most apps, losing a log message is not a big deal, and performance is generally preferred over consistency. But, as always, in real-world apps, there are exceptions. For example, governments worldwide impose log message regulations for financial apps, especially for payment capabilities. Such capabilities should generally have specific log messages that the app isn't allowed to lose. Failure to comply with these regulations can result in sanctions and fines.

4.2.2   Defining logging levels and using logging frameworks

In this section, we discuss logging levels and properly implementing logging in an app using logging frameworks. We'll start by examining why logging levels are essential and then implement an example.

Logging levels, also called *severities*, are a way to classify log messages based on their importance to your investigation. An app usually produces a large number of log messages while running. However, you often don't need all the details in all the log messages. Some of the messages are more important to your investigation than others; some represent critical events that always require attention.

The most common log levels (severities) are

- *Error*—A critical issue. The app should always log such events. Usually, unhandled exceptions in Java apps are logged as errors.

- *Warn*—An event that is potentially an error, but the application handles it. For example, if a connection to a third-party system initially fails but the app manages to send the call on a second try, the problem should be logged as a warning.

- *Info*—"Common" log messages. These messages represent the main app execution events that help you to understand the app's behavior in most situations.

- *Debug*—Fine-grained details that you should enable only when info messages are not enough.

> **NOTE** Different libraries may use more than, or different names for, these four severity levels. For example, in some cases, apps or frameworks may use the severity levels *fatal* (more critical than error) and *trace* (less critical than debug). In this chapter, I focus only on the most encountered severities and terminologies in real-world apps.

Classifying the log messages based on severity allows you to minimize the number of log messages your app stores. You should only allow your app to log the most relevant details and enable more logging only when you need more details.

Look at figure 4.12, which presents the log severity pyramid:

- An app logs a small number of critical problems, but these have high importance, so they always need to be logged.

- The closer you get to the bottom of the pyramid, the more log messages the app writes, but they become less critical and less frequently needed in investigations.

For most investigation cases, you won't need the messages classified as debug. Plus, because of their large number, they make your research more challenging. For this reason, debug messages are generally disabled, and you should enable them only when you face a problem for which you need more details.

When you started learning Java, you were taught how to print something in the console using `System.out` or `System.err`. Eventually, you learned to use `printStackTrace()` to log an exception message, as I used in section 4.1.2. But these ways of working with

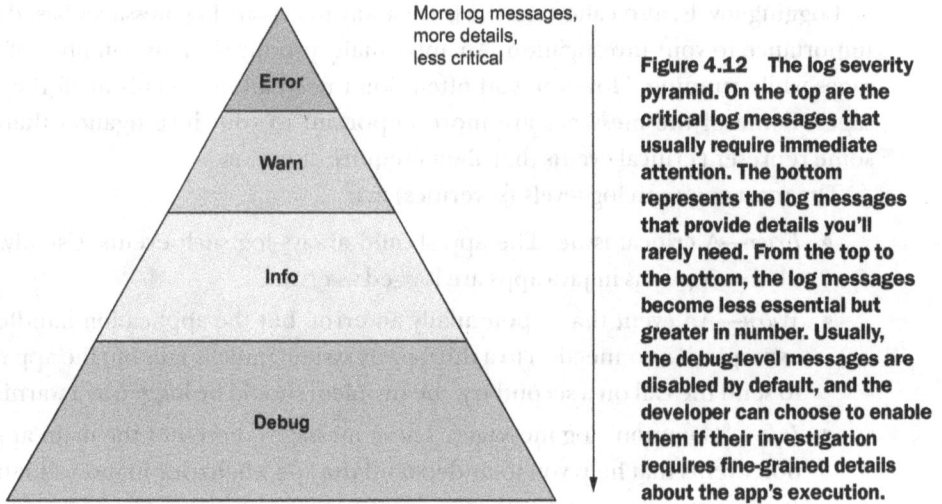

More log messages, more details, less critical

Error

Warn

Info

Debug

Figure 4.12   The log severity pyramid. On the top are the critical log messages that usually require immediate attention. The bottom represents the log messages that provide details you'll rarely need. From the top to the bottom, the log messages become less essential but greater in number. Usually, the debug-level messages are disabled by default, and the developer can choose to enable them if their investigation requires fine-grained details about the app's execution.

logs in Java apps don't give enough flexibility for configuration. So, instead of using them in real-world apps, I recommend you use a logging framework.

Implementing the logging levels is simple. Today, the Java ecosystem offers various logging framework options such as Logback, Log4j, and the Java Logging API. These frameworks are similar, and using them is straightforward.

Let's take an example and implement logging with Log4j. This example is in project da-ch4-ex2. To implement the logging capabilities with Log4j, you first need to add the Log4j dependency. In our Maven project, you must change the pom.xml and add the Log4j dependency.

Listing 4.3   Dependencies you need to add in the pom.xml file to use Log4j

```
<dependencies>
   <dependency>
      <groupId>org.apache.logging.log4j</groupId>
      <artifactId>log4j-api</artifactId>
      <version>2.14.1</version>
   </dependency>
   <dependency>
      <groupId>org.apache.logging.log4j</groupId>
      <artifactId>log4j-core</artifactId>
      <version>2.14.1</version>
   </dependency>
</dependencies>
```

Once you have the dependency in the project, you can declare a `Logger` instance in any class where you want to write log messages. With Log4j, the simplest way to create a `Logger` instance is by using the `LogManager.getLogger()` method, as presented in listing 4.4. This method allows writing log messages that are named the same as the severity of the event they represent. For example, if you want to log a message with the info severity level, you'll use the `info()` method. If you want to log a message with the debug severity level, you'll use the `debug()` method, and so on.

Listing 4.4 Writing the log messages with different severities

```
public class StringDigitExtractor {

  private static Logger log = LogManager.getLogger();    ◄──  Declares a logger
                                                              instance for the
  private final String input;                                current class to
                                                              write log messages
  public StringDigitExtractor(String input) {
    this.input = input;
  }

  public List<Integer> extractDigits() {                        Writes a message
    log.info("Extracting digits for input {}", input);   ◄──   with the info severity
    List<Integer> list = new ArrayList<>();
    for (int i = 0; i < input.length(); i++) {               Writes a message
      log.debug("Parsing character {} of input {}",     ◄──  with the debug severity
          input.charAt(i), input);
      if (input.charAt(i) >= '0' && input.charAt(i) <= '9') {
        list.add(Integer.parseInt(String.valueOf(input.charAt(i))));
      }
    }

    log.info("Extract digits result for input {} is {}", input, list);
    return list;
  }
}
```

Once you've decided which messages to log and used the `Logger` instance to write them, you need to configure Log4j to tell the app how and where to write these messages. We'll use an XML file that we name log4j2.xml to configure Log4j. This XML file must be in the app's class path, so we'll add it to the resources folder of our Maven project. We need to define three things (figure 4.13):

- *A logger*—Tells Log4j which messages are to be written to which appender
- *An appender*—Tells Log4j where to write the log messages
- *A formatter*—Tells Log4j how to print the messages

The logger defines which messages the app logs. In this example, we use `Root` to write the messages from any part of the app. Its attribute level, which has the value info, means only the messages with a severity of info and higher are logged. The logger can also decide to log only messages from specific app parts. For example, when using a framework, you are rarely interested in the log messages the framework prints, but you are often interested in your app's log messages, so you can define a logger that excludes the framework's log messages and only prints those coming from your app.

The logger decides which log messages are printed. For example, it can decide to log only messages with the severity level info and above or that come from a specific package in the app.

An appender decides where to log the messages. For example, one appender can write messages in the system console, and another can write them in a database.

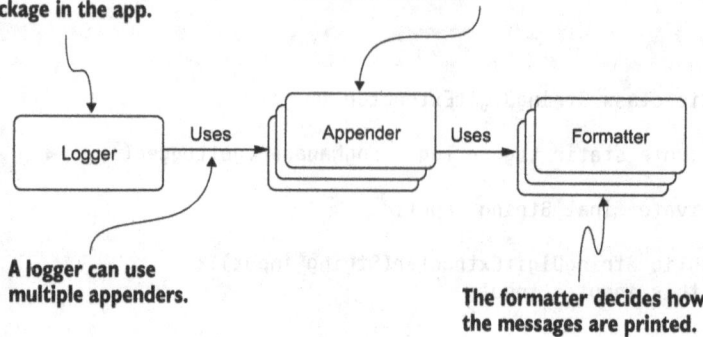

Logger — Uses → Appender — Uses → Formatter

A logger can use multiple appenders.

The formatter decides how the messages are printed.

Figure 4.13   The relationship between the appender, logger, and formatter. A logger uses one or more appenders. The logger decides what to write (e.g., only log messages printed by objects in the package). The logger gives the messages to be written to one or more appenders. Each appender then implements a certain way to store the messages. The appender uses formatters to shape the messages before storing them.

Remember that you want to write only essential log messages. Otherwise, an investigation can become unnecessarily more challenging since you must then filter out the nonessential log messages.

In a real-world app, you can define multiple appenders, which will most likely be configured to store the messages in different sources, like a database or files in the filesystem. In section 4.2.1, we discussed multiple ways apps can retain log messages. Appenders are simply implementations that take care of storing the log messages in a given way.

The appender also uses a formatter that defines the format of the message. For this example, the formatter specifies that the messages should include the timestamp and the severity level, so the app only needs to send the description.

Listing 4.5 shows the configuration that defines both an appender and a logger. In this example, we define just one appender, which tells Log4j to log the messages in the standard output stream of the system (the console).

Listing 4.5   Configuring the appender and the logger in the log4j2.xml file

```xml
<?xml version="1.0" encoding="UTF-8"?>
<Configuration status="WARN">                          Defines an appender
    <Appenders>
        <Console name="Console" target="SYSTEM_OUT">
            <PatternLayout pattern="%d{yy-MM-dd HH:mm:ss.SSS} [%t]
                %-5level %logger{36} - %msg%n"/>
        </Console>
```

```
    </Appenders>
    <Loggers>
      <Root level="info">
        <AppenderRef ref="Console"/>
      </Root>
    </Loggers>
</Configuration>
```

Defines a logger configuration

Figure 4.14 shows the link between the XML configuration in listing 4.5 and the three components it defines: the logger, appender, and formatter.

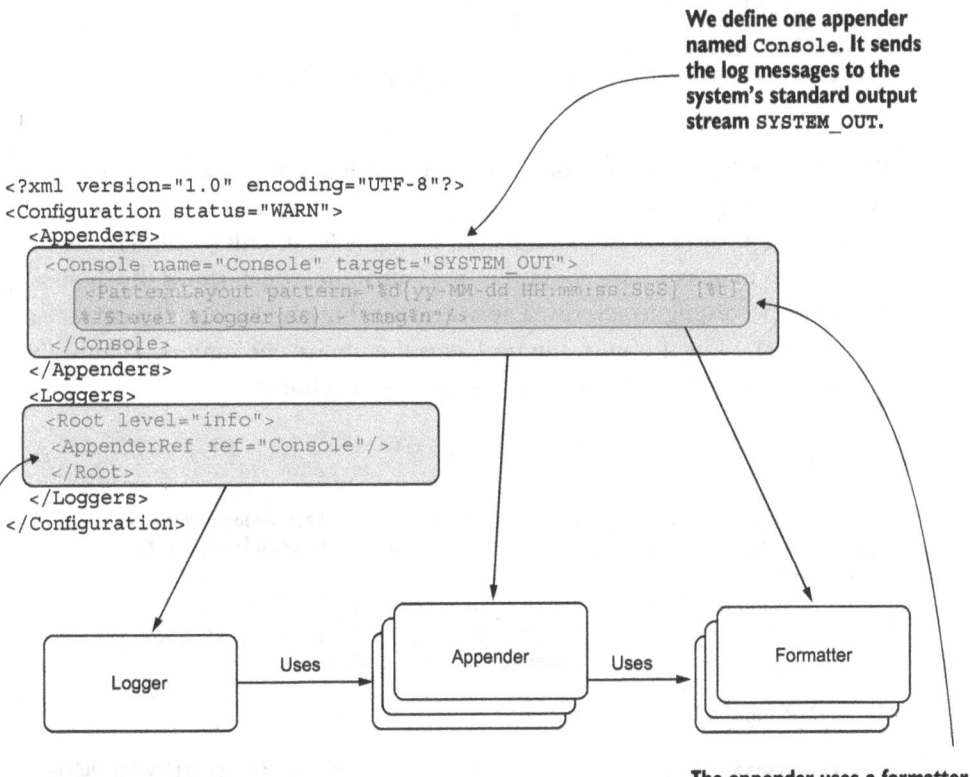

We define one appender named Console. It sends the log messages to the system's standard output stream SYSTEM_OUT.

```
<?xml version="1.0" encoding="UTF-8"?>
<Configuration status="WARN">
  <Appenders>
    <Console name="Console" target="SYSTEM_OUT">
      <PatternLayout pattern="%d{yy-MM-dd HH:mm:ss.SSS} [%t]
      %-5level %logger{36} - %msg%n"/>
    </Console>
  </Appenders>
  <Loggers>
    <Root level="info">
    <AppenderRef ref="Console"/>
    </Root>
  </Loggers>
</Configuration>
```

Logger **Uses** Appender **Uses** Formatter

We configure a logger that takes all the messages with the severity level info and sends them to the appender named Console.

The appender uses a formatter that defines how the messages will look. Using a pattern, we configure the formatter to attach the timestamp and severity to each message.

Figure 4.14 The configuration components. The logger Root takes all the log messages with severity level info that the app writes. The logger sends the messages to the appender named Console. The appender Console is configured to send the messages to the system terminal. It uses a formatter to attach the timestamp and the severity level to the message before writing it.

The next snippet shows a section of the logs printed when the example runs. Note that debug messages aren't logged since they are lower in severity than info (line 10 in listing 4.5).

```
21-07-28 13:17:39.915 [main] INFO
main.StringDigitExtractor
Extracting digits for input ab1c
21-07-28 13:17:39.932 [main] INFO
main.StringDigitExtractor
Extract digits result for input ab1c is [1]
21-07-28 13:17:39.943 [main] INFO
main.StringDigitExtractor
Extracting digits for input a112c
21-07-28 13:17:39.944 [main] INFO
main.StringDigitExtractor
Extract digits result for input a112c is [1, 1, 2]
...
```

If we wanted the app to also log the messages with the debug severity, we would have to change the logger definition.

In listing 4.6, you can see a status and a logging level. This usually creates confusion. Most of the time, you care about the `level` attribute, which shows which messages will be logged according to severity. The `status` attribute in the `<Configuration>` tag is the severity of the Log4J events, the problems the library encounters. That is, the `status` attribute is the logging configuration of the logging library.

Listing 4.6   Using a different severity configuration

```
<?xml version="1.0" encoding="UTF-8"?>           | Sets the logging level for
<Configuration status="WARN">          ◀────── | internal Log4j events
  <Appenders>
      <Console name="Console" target="SYSTEM_OUT">
          <PatternLayout pattern="%d{yy-MM-dd HH:mm:ss.SSS} [%t]
            %-5level %logger{36} - %msg%n"/>
      </Console>
  </Appenders>

  <Loggers>                                  | Changes the logging level to debug
      <Root level="debug">        ◀──────
          <AppenderRef ref="Console"/>
      </Root>
  </Loggers>
</Configuration>
```

We can change the logger in listing 4.6 to also write the messages with the priority:

```
21-07-28 13:18:36.164 [main ] INFO
main.StringDigitExtractor
Extracting digits for input ab1c
```

```
21-07-28 13:18:36.175 [main] DEBUG
 main.StringDigitExtractor
 Parsing character a of input ab1c
21-07-28 13:18:36.176 [main] DEBUG
 main.StringDigitExtractor
 Parsing character b of input ab1c
21-07-28 13:18:36.176 [main] DEBUG
 main.StringDigitExtractor
 Parsing character 1 of input ab1c
21-07-28 13:18:36.176 [main] DEBUG
 main.StringDigitExtractor
 Parsing character c of input ab1c
21-07-28 13:18:36.177 [main] INFO
 main.StringDigitExtractor
 Extract digits result for input ab1c is [1]
21-07-28 13:18:36.181 [main] INFO
 main.StringDigitExtractor
 Extracting digits for input a112c
 ...
```

A logger library gives you the flexibility to log only what you need. Writing the minimum number of log messages necessary to investigate a certain problem is good practice as it can help you understand the logs more easily and keep the app performing well and maintainable. A logging library also gives you the capability of configuring the logs without needing to recompile the app.

4.2.3 Problems caused by logging and how to avoid them

We store log messages so that we can use them to understand how an app behaved at a certain point in time or over time. Logs are necessary and extremely helpful in many cases, but they can also become malicious if mishandled. In this section, we discuss three main problems logs can cause and how to avoid them (figure 4.15):

- *Security and privacy problems*—Caused by log messages exposing private data
- *Performance problems*—Caused by the app storing too many or too-large log messages
- *Maintainability problems*—Caused by log instructions that make the source code more difficult to read

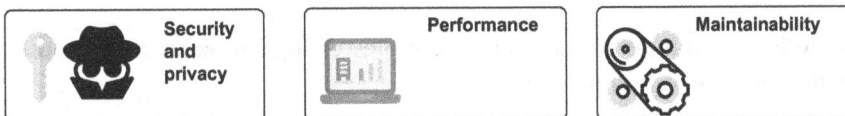

Figure 4.15 Small details can cause big problems. Developers sometimes consider an app's logging capability harmless by default and disregard the problems logging can introduce. Logging, however, like all the other software capabilities, deals with the data, and wrongly implemented, it can affect the app's functionality and maintainability.

SECURITY AND PRIVACY ISSUES

Security is one of my favorite topics and one of the most important subjects a developer needs to consider when they implement an app. One of the books I wrote concerns security, and if you implement apps using the Spring Framework and want to learn more about securing them, I recommend you read it: *Spring Security in Action, second edition* (Manning, 2023).

Surprisingly, logs can sometimes cause vulnerabilities in applications, and in most cases, these problems happen because developers are not attentive to the details they expose. Remember that logs make specific details visible to anyone who can access them. You always need to think about whether the data you log should be visible to those who can access the logs (figure 4.16).

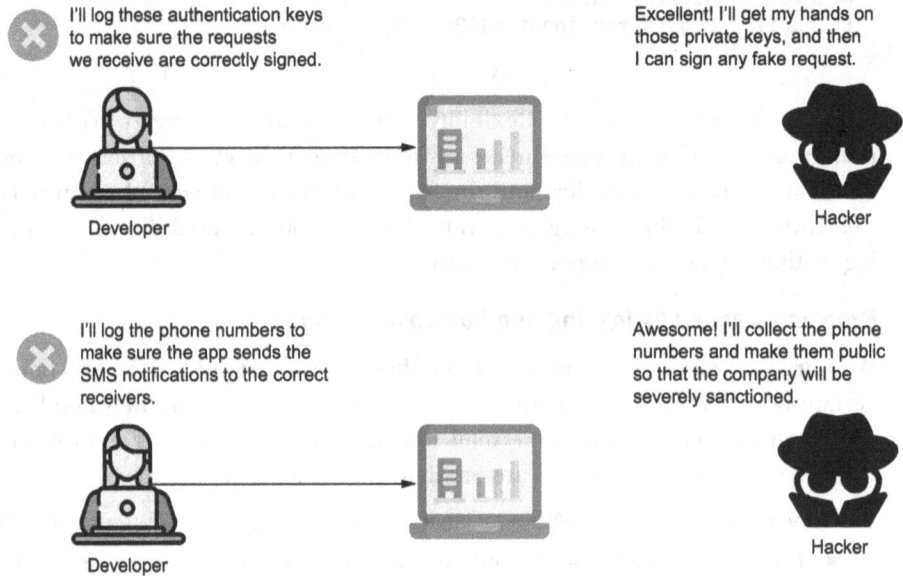

I'll log these authentication keys to make sure the requests we receive are correctly signed.

Developer

Excellent! I'll get my hands on those private keys, and then I can sign any fake request.

Hacker

I'll log the phone numbers to make sure the app sends the SMS notifications to the correct receivers.

Developer

Awesome! I'll collect the phone numbers and make them public so that the company will be severely sanctioned.

Hacker

Figure 4.16   Log messages should not contain secret or private details. No one working on the app or the infrastructure where the app is deployed should access such data. Exposing sensitive details in logs can help a malicious person (hacker) to find easier ways to break the system or create security-related problems.

The following snippet shows some examples of log messages that expose sensitive details and cause vulnerabilities:

```
Successful login.
User bob logged in with password RwjBaWIs66

Failed authentication.
The token is unsigned.
```

```
The token should have a signature with IVL4KiKMfz.

A new notification was sent to
  the following phone number +1233...
```

What's wrong with the logs presented here? The first two log messages expose private details. You should never log passwords or private keys that are used to sign tokens, or any other exchanged information. A password is something only its owner should know. For this reason, no app should store any passwords in clear text (whether in a log or a database). Private keys and similar secret details should be stored in a secrets vault to protect them from being stolen. If someone gets the value of such a key, they can impersonate an application or a user.

The third log message example exposes a phone number. A phone number is considered a personal detail, and around the world, specific regulations restrict the use of such details. For example, the European Union implemented the General Data Protection Regulation (GDPR) in May 2018. An application with users in any European Union state must comply with these regulations to avoid severe sanctions. The regulations allow any user to request all their personal data an app uses and to request immediate deletion of the data. Storing information such as phone numbers in logs exposes these private details and makes retrieving and deleting them more difficult.

NOTE Even if this information is not directly related to troubleshooting, you may encounter these cases when investigating certain problems. Make sure to treat them as important and resolve these problems as soon as possible when they arise. Keep in mind that today's logs can persist in large databases for extended periods. If you encounter a situation where sensitive data is exposed, it is important to report the problem promptly. Additionally, determine whether any previously stored data needs to be erased or obscured to protect privacy.

PERFORMANCE PROBLEMS

Writing logs entails sending details (usually as strings) through an I/O stream somewhere outside the app. We can simply send this information to the app's console (terminal), or we can store it in files or even a database, as discussed in section 4.2.1. Either way, you need to remember that logging a message is also an instruction that takes time; adding too many log messages can dramatically decrease an app's performance.

I remember an issue my team investigated some years ago. A customer in Asia reported a problem with the application we were implementing in factories for inventory purposes. The problem wasn't causing much trouble, but we found it challenging to get to the root cause, so we decided to add more log messages. After delivering a patch with the small change, the system became very slow, almost unresponsive sometimes, which ultimately caused a production standstill, and we had to quickly revert our change. We somehow managed to change a mosquito into an elephant.

Ugly problem! Did it end well?

Our client was definitely not happy, but we managed to revert fast enough to avoid really bad consequences.

The point is, learn from me and don't make the same mistake. Learning from your mistakes is good; learning from others' mistakes is best.

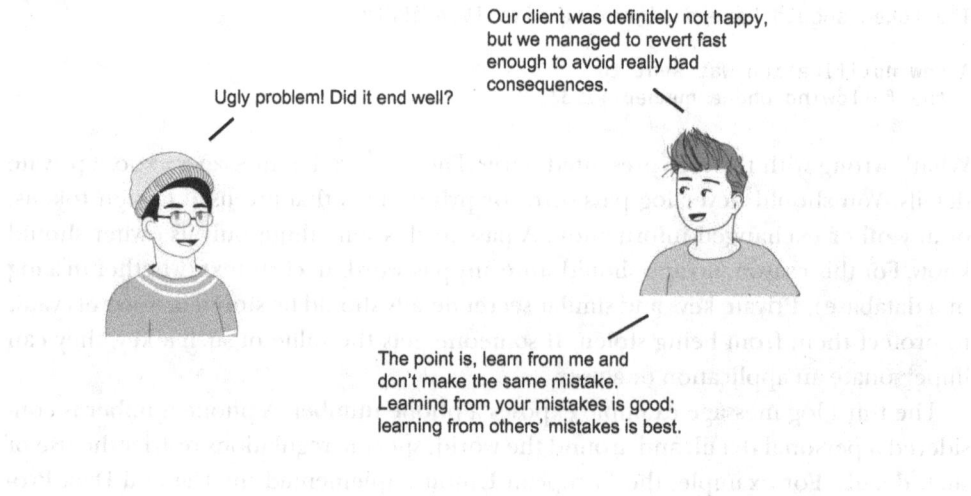

But how could some simple log messages cause such big trouble? The logs were configured to send the messages to a separate server in the network, where they persisted. Not only was the network extremely slow in that factory, but also the log message added to a loop that was iterating over a significant number of items, making the app extremely slow.

In the end, we learned some things that helped us be more careful and avoid repeating the same mistake:

- Make sure you understand how the app logs the messages. Remember that even for the same app different deployments can have different configurations (see section 4.2.2).

- Avoid logging too many messages. Don't log messages in loops iterating over a large number of elements. Logging too many messages will also make reading the logs complicated. If you need to log messages in a large loop, use a condition to narrow the number of iterations for which the message is logged.

- Make sure that the app stores a given log message only when that's really needed. You limit the number of log messages you store by using logging levels, as discussed in section 4.2.2.

- Implement the logging mechanism in such a way that you enable and disable it without needing to restart the service. This will allow you to change to a finer-grained logging level, get your needed details, and then make your logging less sensitive again.

MAINTAINABILITY

Log messages can also negatively affect an app's maintainability. If you add log messages too frequently, they can make the app's logic more difficult to understand. Let's look at an example: try reading listings 4.7 and 4.8. Which code is easier to understand?

Listing 4.7 A method implementing a simple piece of logic

```java
public List<Integer> extractDigits() {
  List<Integer> list = new ArrayList<>();
  for (int i = 0; i < input.length(); i++) {
    if (input.charAt(i) >= '0' && input.charAt(i) <= '9') {
      list.add(Integer.parseInt(String.valueOf(input.charAt(i))));
    }
  }

  return list;
}
```

Listing 4.8 A method implementing a simple piece of logic crowded with log messages

```java
public List<Integer> extractDigits() {
  log.info("Creating a new list to store the result.");
  List<Integer> list = new ArrayList<>();
  log.info("Iterating through the input string " + input);
  for (int i = 0; i < input.length(); i++) {
    log.info("Processing character " + i + " of the string");
    if (input.charAt(i) >= '0' && input.charAt(i) <= '9') {
      log.info("Character " + i +
               " is digit. Character: " +
               input.charAt(i))
      log.info("Adding character" + input.charAt(i) + " to the list");
      list.add(Integer.parseInt(String.valueOf(input.charAt(i))));
    }
  }

  Log.info("Returning the result " + list);
  return list;
}
```

Both show the same piece of implemented logic. But in listing 4.8, I added numerous log messages, which make the method's logic more challenging to read.

How do we avoid affecting an app's maintainability?

- You don't necessarily need to add a log message for each instruction in the code. Identify those instructions that provide the most relevant details. Remember, you can add extra logging later if the existing log messages are not enough.

- Keep the methods small enough so that you only need to log the parameters' values and the value the method returned after the execution.

- Some frameworks allow you to decouple part of the code from the method. For example, in Spring, you can use custom aspects to log the result of a method's execution (including the parameters' values and the value the method returned after the execution).

Summary

- Always check the app's logs when you start investigating a problem. The logs may indicate what's wrong or at least give you a starting point for your investigation.

- All log messages should include a timestamp. Remember that in most cases a system doesn't guarantee the order in which the logs are stored. The timestamp will help you to order the log messages chronologically.

- AI assistants can be highly effective in analyzing large volumes of log messages, making the investigation process more efficient and reducing the amount of data required to manually sift through.

- IDE-integrated AI companions, such as GitHub Copilot or IntelliJ IDEA AI Assistant, can provide comprehensive assistance by having access to the codebase and IDE console, helping to solve problems faster.

- If an IDE-integrated AI isn't available, a chat-based AI (such as ChatGPT or Gemini) can still be helpful in identifying potential root causes by providing incremental context and insights into complex logs.

- An exception in the logs is not necessarily the root of the problem. It could be a consequence of a problem. Research what caused the exception before treating it locally.

- You can use exception stack traces to figure out what called a given method. In large, messy, and difficult-to-understand codebases, this approach can be very helpful and save you time.

- Never write sensitive details (e.g., passwords, private keys, or personal details) in a log message. Logging passwords or private keys introduces security vulnerabilities since anyone with access to the logs can see and use them. Writing personal details such as names, addresses, or phone numbers also may not comply with various government regulations.

Part 2

Deep diagnosing an app's execution

In the first part of this book, we focused on problems that can be caught by reading the code, stepping through it with a debugger, or checking well-written tests. But some problems only reveal themselves when the application is running under real conditions.

This part is about tracking down problems in execution—specifically, those tied to CPU usage and multithreading behavior. These are the kinds of problems that cause slow responses, uneven performance, or sudden bottlenecks even when the code looks fine. You won't find them just by reading source files—you need profiling tools that show exactly what the CPU is busy doing and where time is being spent.

We'll explore techniques for identifying excessive CPU consumption, spotting inefficient code paths, and uncovering hidden synchronization problems. You'll also learn how to investigate blocked threads, lock contention, and deadlocks—problems that can quietly grind an application to a halt.

By the end of this part, you'll be able to diagnose and fix CPU-related execution problems with confidence, using the right tools to see what's really happening behind the scenes.

Part 2

Deep diagnosing
an app's execution

Identifying resource consumption problems using profiling techniques

This chapter covers

- Evaluating resource consumption
- Identifying problems with resource consumption
- Installing and configuring a profiling tool
- Simplifying profiling techniques with AI assistance

"And for you, Frodo Baggins, I give you the light of Eärendil, our most beloved star. May it be a light to you in dark places when all other lights go out."

—Galadriel (*The Fellowship of the Ring*, by J.R.R. Tolkien)

This chapter introduces a profiling tool, and we'll continue the discussion in chapter 6. A profiling tool (or profiler) may not be as powerful as the light of Eärendil, but it is definitely a source of light in dark cases when all the other lights go out. A *profiler* is a powerful tool that has helped me understand the root cause of an app's strange behavior in many difficult situations. I consider learning to use a profiler a must for all developers, as it can guide you to the cause of a seemingly hopeless problem. As you'll learn in this chapter, the profiler intercepts the executing JVM processes and offers extremely useful details, such as:

- How the app consumes resources such as the CPU and memory
- The threads in execution and their current status
- The code in execution and the resources spent by a given piece of code (e.g., the duration of each method's execution)

In section 5.1, some scenarios will be analyzed to show how the details provided by a profiler can be useful and why they are so important. In section 5.2, we discuss using a profiler to solve the scenarios in section 5.1. We'll start by installing and configuring a profiler in section 5.2.1. Then, in section 5.2.2., we'll analyze how an app consumes system resources, and in section 5.2.3, we'll learn how to identify when an app is having problems with managing the used memory. Later, in chapter 6, you'll learn how to identify the code in execution and the performance problems related to it.

I use the VisualVM profiler for the examples in this chapter. VisualVM is a free profiler and an excellent tool I've successfully used for many years. You can download VisualVM here: https://visualvm.github.io/download.html. VisualVM is not the only profiling tool for Java apps. Some other well-known profiling tools are Java Mission Control (http://mng.bz/AVQE) and JProfiler (http://mng.bz/Zplj).

5.1   Where would a profiler be useful?

In this section, we look at three ways a profiling tool can save the day:

- *Catching resource hogs*—Is your app slowing down for no reason? A profiling tool can find those parts of your program that are using way too much memory or CPU, like a guest who eats all the snacks at a party.
- *Finding lazy code*—Not sure which parts of your code are doing the work and which parts are just hanging out? Profiling tools show you exactly which pieces are running and which need a push.
- *Fixing slow apps*—If your app is crawling instead of running, profiling tools help you find out where it's getting stuck so you can speed things up before users start complaining (or sometimes after, depending on how lucky you are).

5.1.1   Identifying abnormal usage of resources

A profiler is commonly used to determine how an app consumes CPU and memory, which helps you to understand the app's specific problems. Thus, it is the first step in investigating such problems. Observing how the app consumes resources will usually lead you to two categories of problems:

- *Thread-related problems*—Usually concurrency problems caused by a lack of or improper synchronization
- *Memory leaks*—Situations in which the app fails to remove unnecessary data from memory, causing slowness in execution and potentially a complete failure

I've encountered both types of problems in real-world apps more than I would have liked. The effects of resource usage problems are very diverse. In some cases, they just cause sluggishness in the app; in other cases, they may cause the app to fail entirely.

My "favorite" thread-related problem I have had to solve using a profiler was causing battery problems on a mobile device. Slowness wasn't the biggest problem. Users complained that their device's battery was consumed unnaturally fast when they used this Android-based app. This behavior definitely required investigation. After spending some time observing the app's behavior, I discovered that one of the libraries the app used sometimes created threads that remained in execution and did nothing but consume the system's resources. In a mobile app, CPU resource use is often reflected in the battery's consumption.

Once you discover the potential problem, you can investigate it further with a thread dump, as you'll learn in chapter 8. Generally, the root cause of such problems is a faulty synchronization of the threads.

I also occasionally find memory leaks in apps. In most cases, the final result of a memory leak is an OutOfMemoryError that leads to an app crash. So, when I hear about an app crashing, I usually suspect a memory problem.

TIP Whenever you encounter an app that is randomly crashing, you should consider a memory leak.

The root cause of abnormal resource use is often an error in coding that allows object references to exist even after the objects are no longer needed. Remember that although the JVM has an automatic mechanism that releases unneeded data from memory (we call this mechanism the *garbage collector* [GC]), it's still the developer's responsibility to remove all references to unnecessary data.

If we implement code that retains references to objects, the GC doesn't know they are no longer used and won't remove them. We call this situation a *memory leak*. In section 5.2.3, you'll learn to use the profiler to identify when such a problem exists; then, in chapter 10, you'll learn to research its root cause using a heap dump.

5.1.2 Finding out what code executes

As a developer and consultant, I've had my fair share of wrestling with large, complex, and downright messy codebases. More than once, I've been thrown into situations where I needed to investigate a specific app feature. Sure, I could reproduce the problem, but figuring out which part of the code was to blame? Not a clue.

One memorable case involved a legacy app running some critical processes. The company's management had made the brilliant decision to let a single developer handle the entire codebase. No backups, no team collaboration—just one person. Naturally, when that developer left (without leaving behind a single line of documentation or even a friendly sticky note), I was called in to figure out what was going wrong.

My first glance at the code was unsettling. There was no class design to speak of, and it was a chaotic mix of Java and Scala, sprinkled with some Java reflection for that extra layer of confusion. It felt like opening a closet and having random languages and frameworks tumble out. At that moment, I seriously considered starting a support group for developers abandoned by documentation.

So, how do you even begin to figure out which part of the code to investigate in a situation like this? Luckily, that's where a profiler steps in like a detective with a magnifying glass. Profilers can sample the running code—basically, they sneak a peek at what's actually being executed. The tool intercepts methods and visually shows what's happening behind the scenes, giving you just enough breadcrumbs to start following the trail.

Once you spot the code in action, you can dive in, read through it, and eventually bring in the big guns—a debugger (covered in chapters 2 and 3).

The beauty of a profiler is that it reveals what's running without forcing you to dig through mountains of confusing code. This feature, called *sampling*, is a lifesaver when the code is so tangled and messy that you can't even tell which functions are being triggered. It's like having X-ray vision for spaghetti code.

5.1.3   *Identifying slowness in an app's execution*

In many situations, you'll need to tackle performance problems. The key question in these cases is, "What is causing the delay in execution?" Developers often start by suspecting parts of the code related to I/O operations.

Actions such as calling a web service, connecting to a database, or writing data to a file are common sources of latency in applications. However, I/O operations aren't always causing slow performance. Even when they are, identifying the exact problem can be challenging—especially if you're not deeply familiar with the codebase (which is rarely the case).

Fortunately, a profiler can make this task much easier. It can intercept running code and measure the resources each part of the program is using, helping you pinpoint performance bottlenecks. We'll explore these powerful profiling capabilities in detail in chapter 6.

5.2   *Using a profiler*

This section explores how to effectively use a profiler to tackle the types of problems discussed in section 5.1. We start by walking through the installation and configuration of VisualVM in section 5.2.1, laying the foundation for effective profiling. From there, we dive into the profiler's powerful investigative features, giving you the tools designed to uncover hidden performance problems.

To make these concepts practical, I'll demonstrate each technique using a sample app—simple enough to keep the focus on the topic but complex enough to reflect real-world challenges.

Section 5.2.2 analyzes system resource consumption, and you are going to learn how to detect if your app is overusing resources. Then, in section 5.2.3, we'll dive into common memory problems that can affect performance and how to identify them before they escalate.

By the end of this section, you'll have a solid understanding of how to employ a profiler to diagnose and resolve performance bottlenecks with confidence.

5.2.1 Installing and configuring VisualVM

Let's start by getting VisualVM up and running. Before you can unleash the power of a profiler, you need to make sure it's properly installed and configured. Once that's done, you can dive into the examples provided with this book to test each of the profiler's features covered in this chapter.

If you're working on a real-world project, I highly recommend applying these techniques to your own app. After all, there's no better way to learn than by hunting down performance bugs in code you actually care about. Plus, it's far more satisfying than just watching a demo app behave perfectly (because when does that ever happen in real life?).

Installing VisualVM is straightforward. Once you download the version based on your operating system from the official site (https://visualvm.github.io/download .html), the only thing you need to do is make sure the location of the JDK you want VisualVM to use is configured correctly. In the configuration file, which you can find at the `etc/visualvm.config` location in the VisualVM folder, define the location of the JDK in your system. You need to assign the JDK path to the `visualvm_jdkhome` variable and uncomment the line (remove the # in front of it), as presented in the next snippet. VisualVM works with Java 8 or above:

```
visualvm_jdkhome="C:\Program Files\Java\openjdk-17\jdk-17"
```

Once you configure the JDK location, you can run VisualVM using the executable code in the bin folder where you installed the app. If you correctly configured the JDK location, the app will start, and you'll see an interface similar to the one presented in figure 5.1.

Let's start a Java app. You can use the project da-ch5-ex1 provided with this book. You can either start the app using the IDE or from the console directly. The way the app is started does not affect profiling a Java process.

Once you start the app, VisualVM displays the process on the left side. Usually, if you didn't explicitly give a particular name to the process, VisualVM displays the main class name, as presented in figure 5.2.

All the Java processes running locally

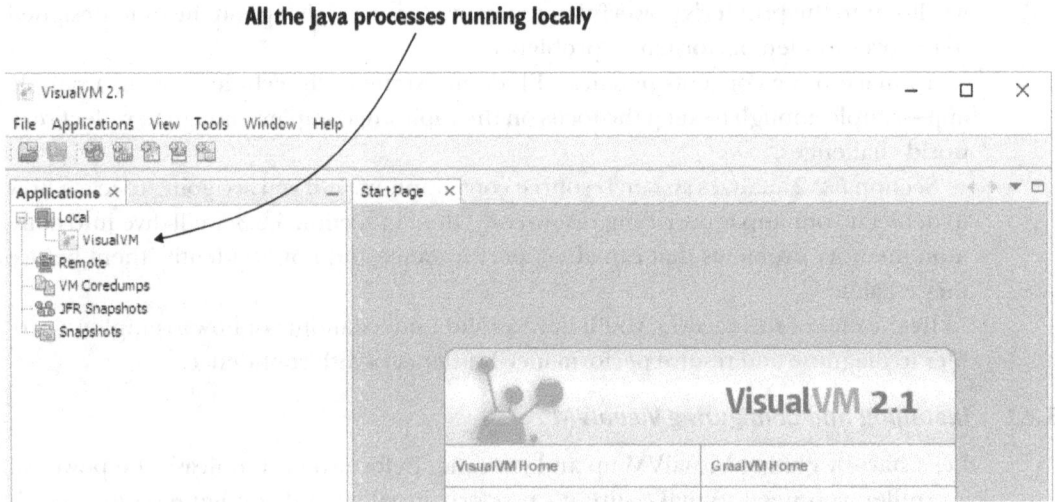

Figure 5.1   VisualVM welcome screen. Once you configure and start VisualVM, you find that the tool has a simple and easy-to-learn GUI. On the left of the welcome screen are the processes running locally that you can investigate with the tool.

Once you start your app, you will also see its process on the left side of the VisualVM frame. Since we gave no particular name to our process, VisualVM displays the `main` class name.

Double-click the process name, and VisualVM displays the Details tab for the process.

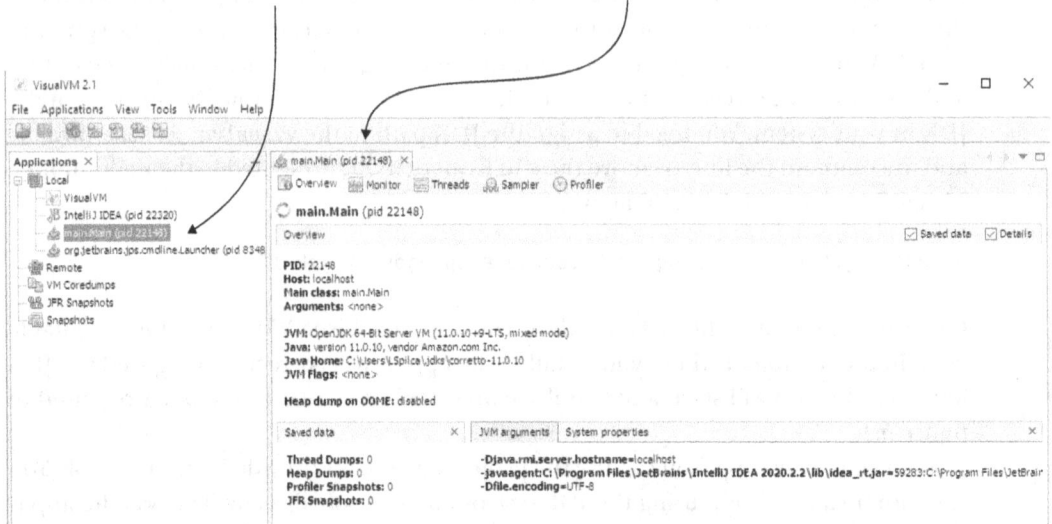

Figure 5.2   Double-click a process name to start using VisualVM to investigate that process, and a new tab will appear. In this tab are all the needed capabilities VisualVM provides for exploring that particular process.

Generally, starting the app should be enough. However, in some cases, VisualVM doesn't know how to connect to a local process because of various problems, as presented in figure 5.3. In such a case, the first thing to try is explicitly specifying the domain name using a VM argument when starting the application you want to profile:

```
-Djava.rmi.server.hostname=localhost
```

A similar problem can also be caused by using a JVM version that VisualVM doesn't support. If adding the `-Djava.rmi.server.hostname=localhost` argument doesn't solve your problem, check that the JVM distribution you configured is among those VisualVM supports (according to the download section on its website: https://visualvm .github.io/download.html).

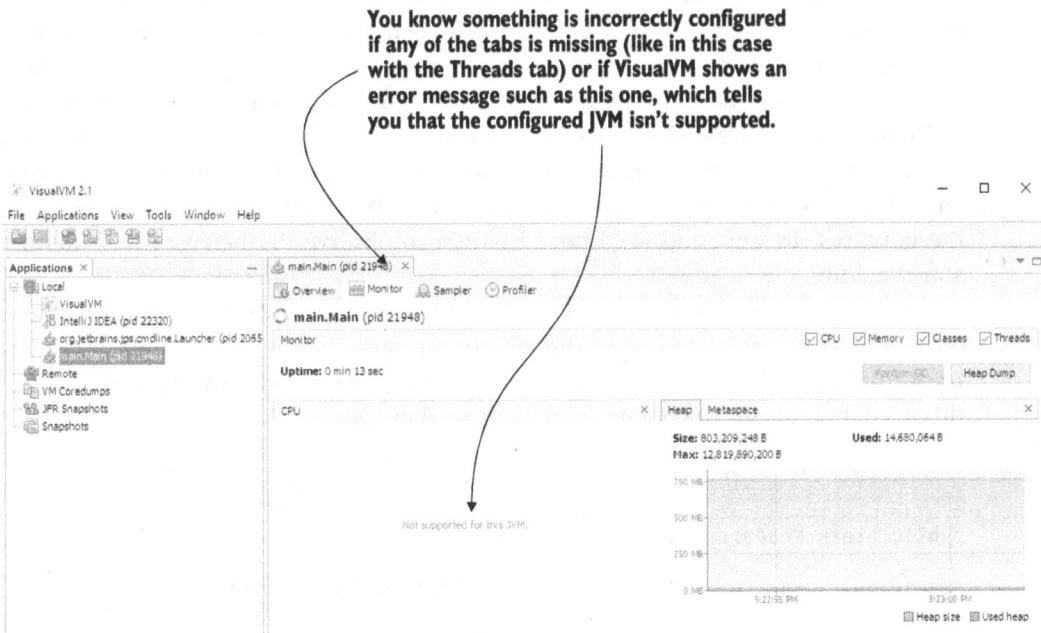

Figure 5.3 If the tool doesn't seem to be working properly, you need to check how it is configured. Such problems can occur when the configured JVM distribution is not among those VisualVM supports. Sometimes, the tool can't connect to the local process you want to investigate. In such cases, use a different JVM distribution that complies with the tool's requirements or review how the process you want to investigate was started.

5.2.2 Observing the CPU and memory usage

One of the most straightforward yet powerful ways to use a profiler is to monitor how your app consumes system resources. This insight allows you to quickly detect problems such as memory leaks quietly draining your system or zombie threads lurking in the background that are wasting valuable CPU power. By keeping an eye on resource usage, you can catch these problems early—before they turn into full-blown performance nightmares.

> **DEFINITION** A *memory leak* is when your app doesn't deallocate unneeded data. Over time, there will be no more free memory. This is a problem.

In this section, you'll discover how a profiler can visually confirm when your app isn't playing nice. Take zombie threads, for example—these are threads that refuse to die, endlessly running in the background and quietly draining your app's resources. With VisualVM, spotting these resource-hungry culprits becomes much easier, allowing you to identify and address performance problems before they spiral out of control. I prepared some projects to demonstrate how to use a profiler to identify app problems that cause abnormal resource consumption. We'll run the apps provided with the book one by one, and we'll use VisualVM to observe the behavior and identify abnormalities.

Let's start with app da-ch5-ex1. The idea of the app is simple: two threads continuously add values, while two other threads continuously remove (consume) the values from this list. We often call this implementation a *producer-consumer approach*, a multithreaded design pattern commonly encountered in apps.

Listing 5.1   The producer thread adding values to a list

```java
public class Producer extends Thread {

    private Logger log = Logger.getLogger(Producer.class.getName());

    @Override
    public void run() {
        Random r = new Random();
        while (true) {
            if (Main.list.size() < 100) {          // Sets a maximum number
                int x = r.nextInt();                //  of values for the list
                Main.list.add(x);                   // Adds a random value in the list
                log.info("Producer " + Thread.currentThread().getName() +
                        " added value " + x);
            }
        }
    }

}
```

The following code shows the implementation of the consumer thread.

Listing 5.2 The consumer thread removing values from the list

```java
public class Consumer extends Thread {

  private Logger log = Logger.getLogger(Consumer.class.getName());

  @Override
  public void run() {
    while (true) {
      if (Main.list.size() > 0) {          // Checks whether the list contains any value
        int x = Main.list.get(0);          // If the list contains values, removes the first value from the list
        Main.list.remove(0);
        log.info("Consumer " + Thread.currentThread().getName() +
                " removed value " + x);
      }
    }
  }
}
```

The Main class creates and starts two instances of the producer thread and two instances of the consumer thread.

Listing 5.3 The Main class creating and starting the producer and consumer threads

```java
public class Main {

  public static List<Integer> list = new ArrayList<>();   // Creates a list to store the random values the producer generates

  public static void main(String[] args) {
    new Producer().start();
    new Producer().start();
    new Consumer().start();   // Starts the consumer and produces threads
    new Consumer().start();
  }
}
```

This application wrongly implements a multithreaded architecture. More precisely, multiple threads concurrently access and change a list of type ArrayList. Because ArrayList is not a concurrent collection implementation in Java, it doesn't manage the threads' access itself. Multiple threads accessing this collection potentially enter a *race condition*. A race condition happens when multiple threads compete to access the same resource. That is, they are in a race to access the same resource.

In project da-ch5-ex1, the implementation lacks thread synchronization. When you run the app, some threads stop after a short time because of exceptions caused by the race condition, while others remain alive forever, doing nothing (zombie threads). We'll use VisualVM to identify all these problems. Then, we'll run project da-ch5-ex2, which applies a correction to the app synchronizing the threads that access the list.

We'll compare the results displayed by VisualVM for the first example to the second example to identify the difference between a normal and a problematic app.

The app will run quickly and then stop (potentially showing an exception stack trace in the console). The next code snippet shows what the log messages the app prints in the console look like:

```
Aug 26, 2021 5:22:42 PM main.Producer run
INFO: Producer Thread-0 added value -361561777
Aug 26, 2021 5:22:42 PM main.Producer run
INFO: Producer Thread-1 added value -500676534
Aug 26, 2021 5:22:42 PM main.Producer run
INFO: Producer Thread-0 added value 112520480
```

You may think that, because this app only has three classes, you don't need a profiler to spot the problem—reading the code is enough here. Indeed, with only three classes, you may be able to spot the problem without using a separate tool. That's because the apps we use are simplified examples so you can focus on using the profiler. But in the real world, apps are more complex, and problems are much more challenging to spot without an appropriate tool.

Even if the app appears to be paused, VisualVM can reveal some surprising activity happening behind the scenes. To uncover the cause of this unexpected behavior, follow these steps:

1 *Check the process CPU usage.* This step helps you determine whether the app is silently consuming CPU power, thus indicating a hidden loop or an inefficient process running in the background.

2 *Check the process memory usage.* Monitoring memory usage can reveal memory leaks or excessive allocation that may be causing the app to slow down or freeze.

3 *Visually investigate the executing threads.* This step allows you to spot stuck, blocked, or zombie threads that could be preventing the app from responding properly.

The process is consuming a lot of CPU resources, so somehow, it seems to still be alive. To observe its resource consumption, use the Monitor tab in VisualVM after double-clicking the process name in the left panel. One of the widgets on this tab shows you the CPU usage (figure 5.4).

The consumer and producer threads seem to have entered a continuous running state where they consume the system's resources even if they don't correctly fulfill their tasks. In this case, the state is a consequence of race conditions because the threads try to access and change a nonconcurrent collection. But we already know there's something wrong with the app. We want to observe the symptoms such problems cause so that we will know our app encountered the same problem in other similar situations.

This widget also shows the amount of CPU resources the Garbage Collector (GC) uses. The GC is the JVM mechanism for removing data the app no longer needs from

You can use the CPU usage widget to check
CPU consumption. Note that in this case,
the process spends about 50% of the system's
processing power.

Another interesting fact is how much
the GC is responsible for CPU consumption.
In this case, the GC spends no resources.

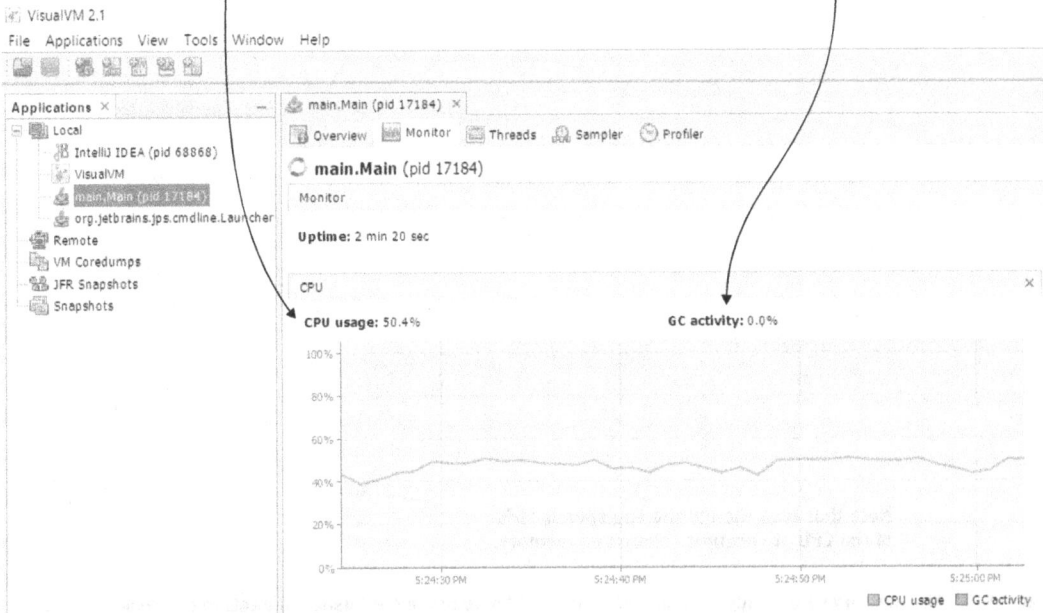

Figure 5.4   Using VisualVM to observe the use of CPU resources. The widget in the Monitor tab shows how much CPU the process uses and how much of the usage is caused by the GC. This information helps you to understand whether the app has execution problems and is excellent guidance for the next steps in your investigation. In this particular example, the process spends about 50% CPU. The GC doesn't affect this value. These signs are often indicators of zombie threads that are usually generated by concurrency problems.

memory. The information on GC CPU usage is valuable because it can indicate that the app has a problem with memory allocation. If the GC spends a lot of CPU resources, it can signify that the app has a memory leak problem.

In this case, the GC doesn't spend any CPU resources. This is not a good sign either. In other words, the app is spending a lot of processing power but not processing anything. These signs usually indicate zombie threads, which are generally a consequence of concurrency problems.

The next step is to look at the widget showing memory consumption. This widget is strategically placed near the one showing the CPU consumption, as presented in figure 5.5. We'll discuss this widget in more detail in section 5.2.3, but for now, notice that the app spends almost no memory. This behavior is, again, not a good sign as it is equivalent to saying, "The app does nothing." We can conclude that we are most likely facing a concurrency problem by using just these two widgets.

On the right side of the CPU usage widget, you find another widget that displays the memory consumption.

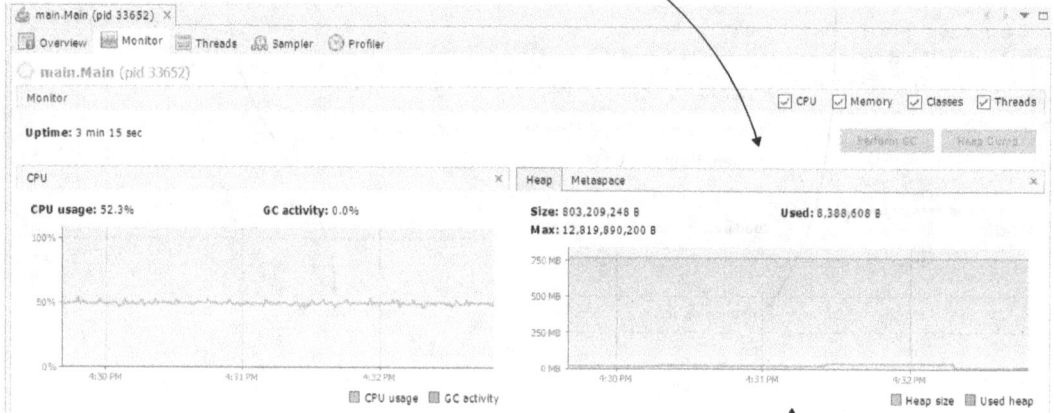

Note that even though the app spends 50% of the CPU, it consumes almost no memory.

Figure 5.5   The memory usage widget is placed on the right side of the CPU usage widget. In this example, the app uses almost no memory. This is also why the GC activity is zero. An app not consuming any memory means the app isn't doing anything.

We'll discuss using thread dumps in chapter 8. For now, we focus only on the high-level widgets the profile offers and compare the results these widgets provide for a healthy and an unhealthy app.

> Before going into a detailed investigation of the threads in execution, I prefer to use VisualVM to visually observe how the threads execute. In most cases, doing so gives me some clues about which threads I need to pay attention to. Once I get this info, I use a thread dump to find the concurrency problem and learn how to fix it.

Figure 5.6 shows the Threads tab, located near the Monitor tab. The Threads tab offers a visual representation of the threads in execution and their states. In this example, all four threads the app started are executing and are in a running state.

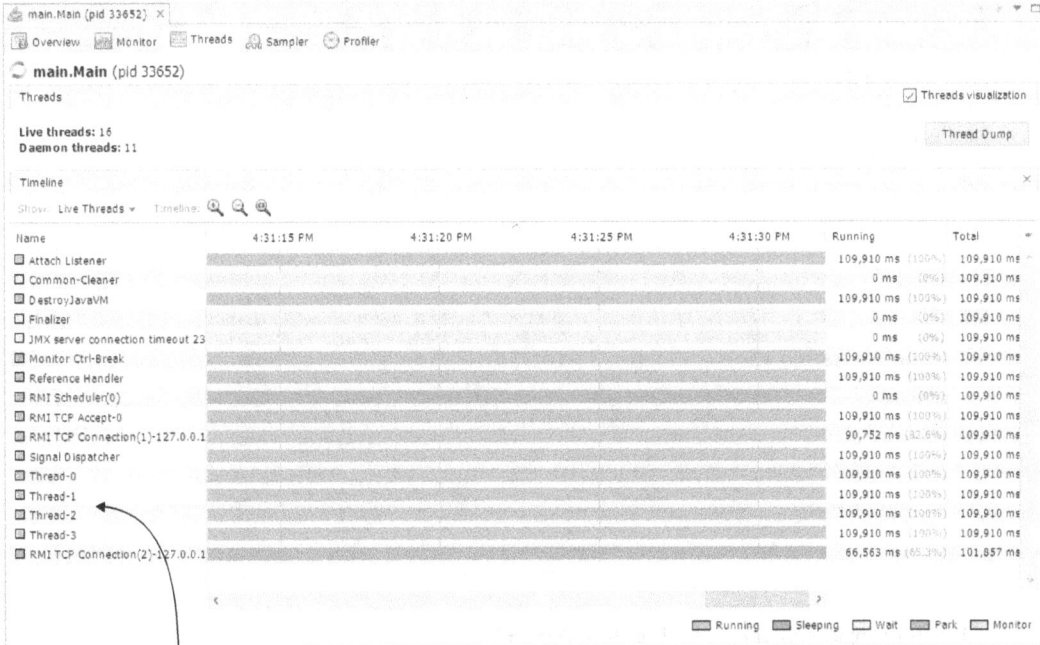

Even if the app doesn't seem to do anything, the four threads it created are continuously running. These running threads that do nothing but stay alive are called zombie threads. The only thing they do is consume CPU resources.

Figure 5.6 The Threads tab offers a visual representation of the threads that are alive and their status. The widget shows all the process threads, including those started by the JVM, which helps you easily identify the threads you should pay attention to and eventually investigate deeper using a thread dump.

Concurrency problems can have different results. Not necessarily all the threads will remain alive, for example. Sometimes, concurrent access can cause exceptions that interrupt some or all the threads entirely. The next snippet shows an example of such an exception that can occur during an app's execution:

```
Exception in thread "Thread-1"
java.lang.ArrayIndexOutOfBoundsException:
Index -1 out of bounds for length 109
    at java.base/java.util.ArrayList.add(ArrayList.java:487)
    at java.base/java.util.ArrayList.add(ArrayList.java:499)
    at main.Producer.run(Producer.java:16)
```

If such an exception happens, then some threads may be stopped, and the Threads tab won't display them. Figure 5.7 shows a case in which the app threw an exception and only one of the threads stayed alive.

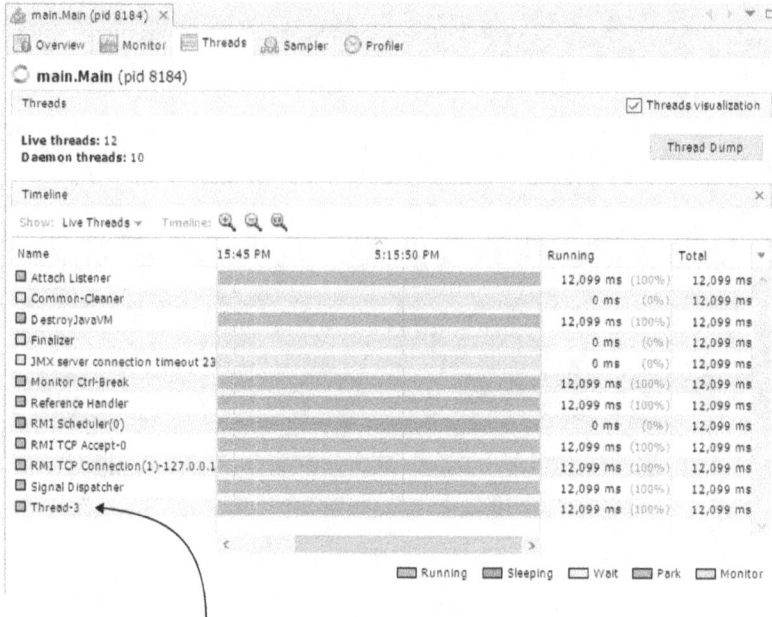

In this example, only one of the threads is alive and became a zombie thread. The other threads encountered exceptions caused by the race conditions and stopped.

Figure 5.7   **If exceptions occur during an app's execution, some threads may be stopped. This figure shows a case in which the concurrent access caused exceptions in three threads and stopped them. Only one thread remained alive. Remember, concurrency problems in multithreaded apps can cause different unexpected results.**

In this example, we focus only on discovering a resource consumption problem. The next step is to use a thread dump to determine the exact cause of the concurrency problem. We'll cover everything about thread dumps in chapter 8, but for now, let's remain focused on identifying resource consumption problems. We will run the same verifications on a healthy app and compare it to the unhealthy one. This way, you'll know how to immediately recognize correct and incorrect app behavior.

The example in project da-ch5-ex2 is the corrected version of the same app we just looked at. I added some synchronized blocks to avoid concurrent thread access and eliminate race condition problems. I used the list instance as the thread monitor for the synchronized code blocks for both consumers and producers.

Listing 5.4   Synchronizing access for the consumer

```
public class Consumer extends Thread {

    private Logger log = Logger.getLogger(Consumer.class.getName());

    public Consumer(String name) {
```

```
      super(name);
    }

    @Override
    public void run() {
      while (true) {
        synchronized (Main.list) {        ◄─── Synchronizes the access on the list, using
          if (Main.list.size() > 0) {            the list instance as a thread monitor
            int x = Main.list.get(0);
            Main.list.remove(0);
            log.info("Consumer " +
                Thread.currentThread().getName() +
                " removed value " + x);
          }
        }
      }
    }
}
```

The following code shows the synchronization applied to the Producer class.

Listing 5.5 Synchronizing access for the producer

```
public class Producer extends Thread {

  private Logger log = Logger.getLogger(Producer.class.getName());

  public Producer(String name) {
    super(name);
  }

  @Override
  public void run() {
    Random r = new Random();
    while (true) {                          Synchronizes the access on the list, using
      synchronized (Main.list) {        ◄─── the list instance as a thread monitor
        if (Main.list.size() < 100) {
          int x = r.nextInt();
          Main.list.add(x);
          log.info("Producer " +
              Thread.currentThread().getName() +
              " added value " + x);
        }
      }
    }
  }

}
```

I also gave custom names to each thread. I always recommend this approach. Did you spot the default names the JVM gave our threads in the previous example? Generally, Thread-0, Thread-1, Thread-2, and so on are not names you can easily use to identify a given thread. I prefer giving threads custom names whenever I can to identify them quickly. Moreover, I give them names starting with an underline so it is easier to sort them. First, I defined the constructor in the Consumer and Producer classes (listings 5.4 and 5.5, respectively) and used the super() constructor to name the threads. I then gave them names, as presented in listing 5.6.

Listing 5.6   Setting custom names for the threads

```
public class Main {

  public static List<Integer> list = new ArrayList<>();

  public static void main(String[] args) {
    new Producer("_Producer 1").start();
    new Producer("_Producer 2").start();
    new Consumer("_Consumer 1").start();
    new Consumer("_Consumer 2").start();
  }
}
```

Notice that after starting this app, the console continuously shows logs. The app doesn't stop like it did with example da-ch5-ex1. Let's use VisualVM to observe resource consumption. The CPU utilization widget shows that the app spends less CPU, while the memory usage widget shows that the app uses some of the allocated memory while running. Also, we can observe the activity of the GC. As you will learn later in this chapter, on the right side of the memory graph are valleys resulting from the GC's activity.

The Threads tab shows that the monitor sometimes blocks the threads, allowing only one thread at a time through a synchronized block. The threads don't run continuously, which makes the app consume less CPU, as shown in figure 5.8. Figure 5.9 shows the threads' visualization in the Threads tab.

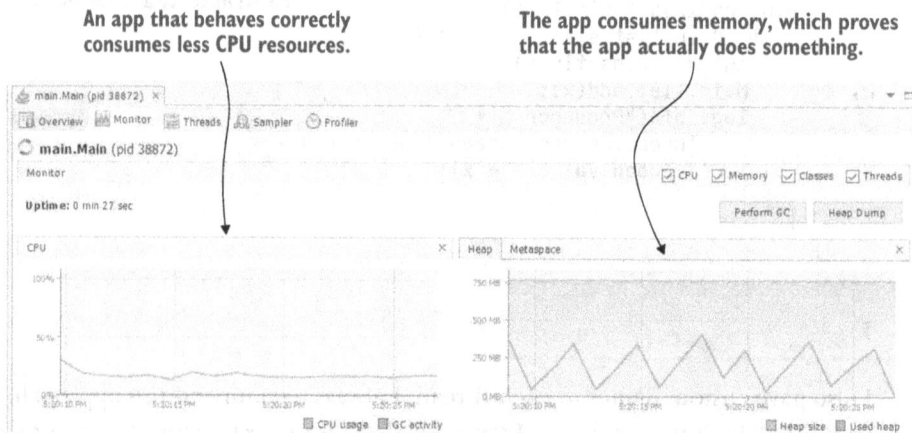

Figure 5.8   After correctly synchronizing the code, the resource consumption widgets look different. The CPU consumption is lower, and the app uses some memory.

The threads are no longer continuously running. The profiler shows when the threads are blocked by a monitor, waiting, or sleeping.

Instructions left out of the synchronized blocks can still cause threads to run concurrently. Observe where the two producer threads appear shaded at the same time on the diagram.

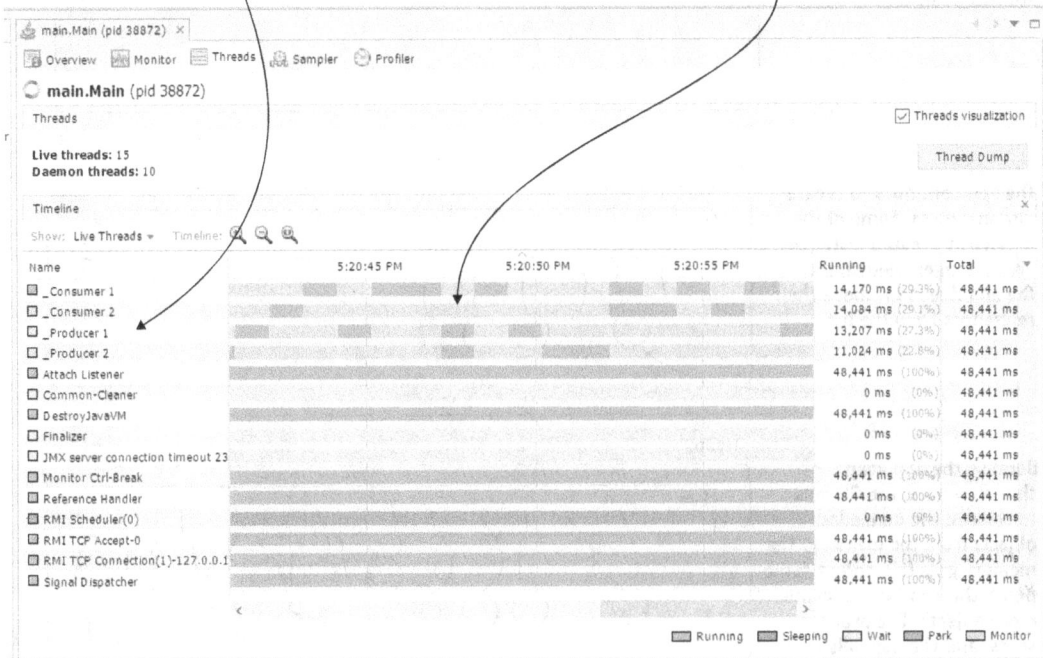

Figure 5.9 The Threads tab helps you visualize the execution of the threads in your app. Since the threads' names start with an underline, you can simply sort them by name to see them grouped. Notice that their execution is interrupted occasionally by the monitor, which allows just one thread at a time through the synchronized blocks of code.

NOTE Even if we added synchronized blocks, some executing code (the `while` condition) still remains outside of these blocks. For this reason, the threads may still appear to run concurrently.

5.2.3 Identifying memory leaks

This section discusses memory leaks and how to spot them before they bring your app to its knees. A memory leak happens when an app holds onto objects it no longer needs—like keeping junk in your closet because you might need it someday (see figure 5.10). Because of these leftover references, the GC—the tool that normally cleans up unused data—can't do its job.

As the app keeps piling on more data, the memory slowly fills up. Eventually, the app runs out of space and throws an `OutOfMemoryError`, basically saying, "I'm full!" before crashing.

1. Suppose you have an app that creates object instances and keeps references to these instances in a list.

Heap

2. The app continues to create new instances. Some of the previously created instances are no longer needed, but the app doesn't remove their references from the list.

Heap

3. Because the app keeps the references, the GC fails to remove the unneeded objects from the memory. The memory gets full, and at some point, the app can't allocate more objects. The process stops, and the app fails with an OutOfMemoryError.

Heap

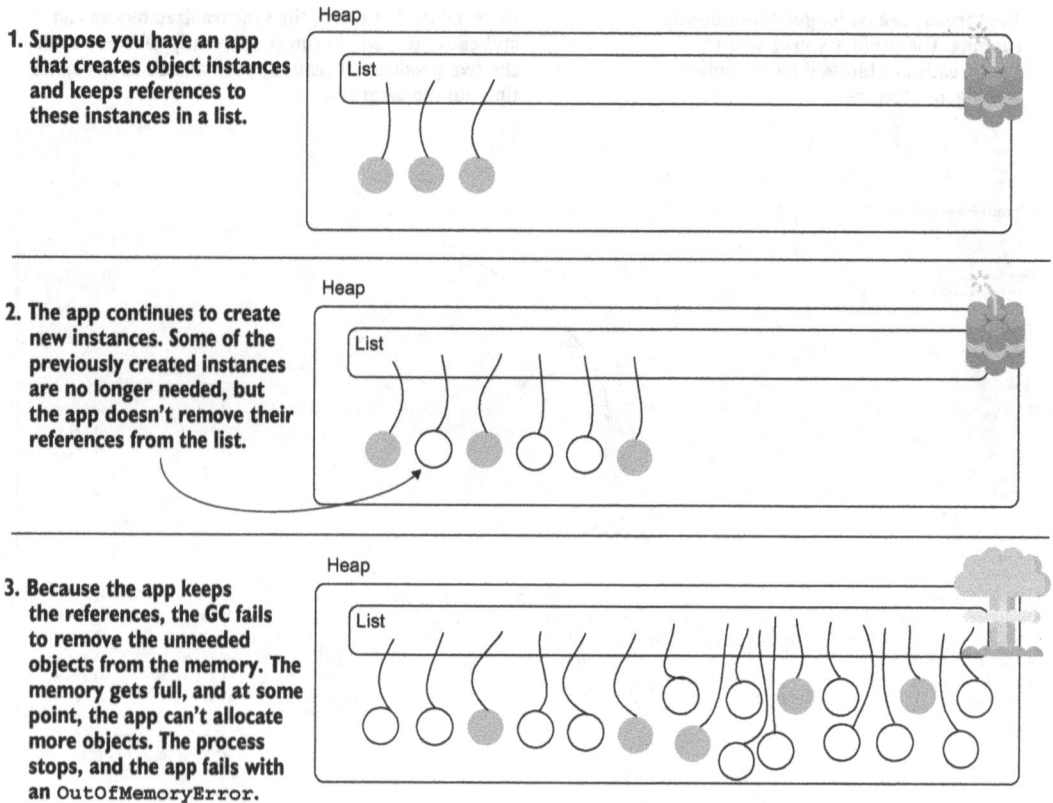

Figure 5.10 An OutOfMemoryError is like a ticking bomb. An app fails to remove references to objects it no longer uses. The GC can't remove these instances from the memory because the app keeps their references. While more objects are created, the memory gets full. At some point, there's no more space in the heap to allocate other objects, and the app fails with an OutOfMemoryError.

To show how this works, we'll use a simple app that intentionally triggers an Out-OfMemoryError. This will help us learn how to spot memory leaks in action using VisualVM before they catch you by surprise.

In the example provided with project da-ch5-ex3, you can find a simple app that stores random instances in a list but never removes their references. The following code provides an example of a simple implementation that produces an OutOfMemoryError.

Listing 5.7 Producing an OutOfMemoryError

```
public class Main {

  public static List<Cat> list = new ArrayList<>();

  public static void main(String[] args) {
    while(true) {
```

```
            list.add(new Cat(new Random().nextInt(10)));
        }
    }
}
```

Continuously adds new instances to a list until the JVM runs out of memory

The class Cat is a simple java object, as presented by the following code snippet:

```
public class Cat {

  private int age;

  public Cat(int age) {
    this.age = age;
  }

  // Omitted getters and setters
}
```

Let's run this app and observe resource usage with VisualVM. We're especially interested in the widget that shows memory usage. When a memory leak affects your app, this widget can confirm that the used memory grows continuously. The GC tries to deallocate unused data from memory, but it removes too few. In the end, the memory gets filled, and the app cannot store the new data, throwing an OutOfMemoryError (figure 5.11).

Note how the used memory grows continuously. The GC attempts to free the memory, but it can't remove most of the instances because the app still keeps their references in memory.

When all the allocated memory is occupied, and the app can't store the new data, the app throws an OutOfMemoryError.

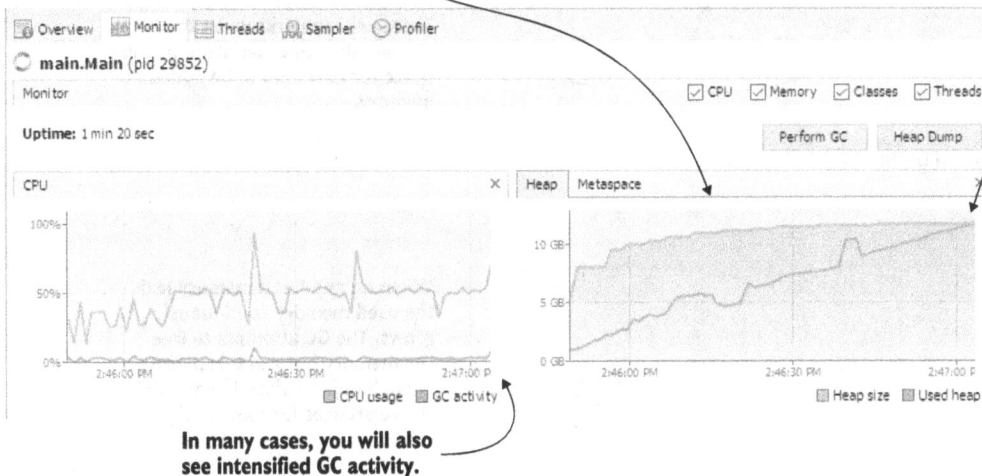

In many cases, you will also see intensified GC activity.

Figure 5.11 When a memory leak affects your app, the used memory grows continuously. GC attempts to free the memory but cannot remove enough data. The used memory increases until the app can't allocate any more new data. At this point, the app throws an OutOfMemoryError and stops. In many cases, a memory leak also causes intensified GC activity, as seen in the CPU resource usage widget.

If you let the app run long enough, you'll eventually see the error stack trace in the app's console:

```
Exception in thread "main" java.lang.OutOfMemoryError: Java heap space
    at java.base/java.util.Arrays.copyOf(Arrays.java:3689)
    at java.base/java.util.ArrayList.grow(ArrayList.java:238)
    at java.base/java.util.ArrayList.grow(ArrayList.java:243)
    at java.base/java.util.ArrayList.add(ArrayList.java:486)
    at java.base/java.util.ArrayList.add(ArrayList.java:499)
    at main.Main.main(Main.java:13)
```

It's important to remember that an `OutOfMemoryError` stack trace doesn't necessarily indicate the place that causes the problem. Since an app has just one heap memory location, a certain thread can cause the problem, whereas another thread may be unlucky enough to be the last one trying to use the memory location and thus gets the error. The only sure way to identify the root cause is using a heap dump, covered in chapter 10.

Figure 5.12 compares normal behavior and the behavior of an app affected by a memory leak, as seen in VisualVM. For the app with a normal execution (not affected

Normal behavior

In an app that behaves normally, you will see this pattern. The memory fills, and at a certain point, the GC cleans the unneeded data, freeing up the memory.

These are moments when the GC cleaned the unneeded data, making space for new data to be added in memory.

Abnormal behavior

When an app has a memory leak, the used memory continuously grows. The GC attempts to free the memory but can't deallocate enough objects since the app holds the references for most of them.

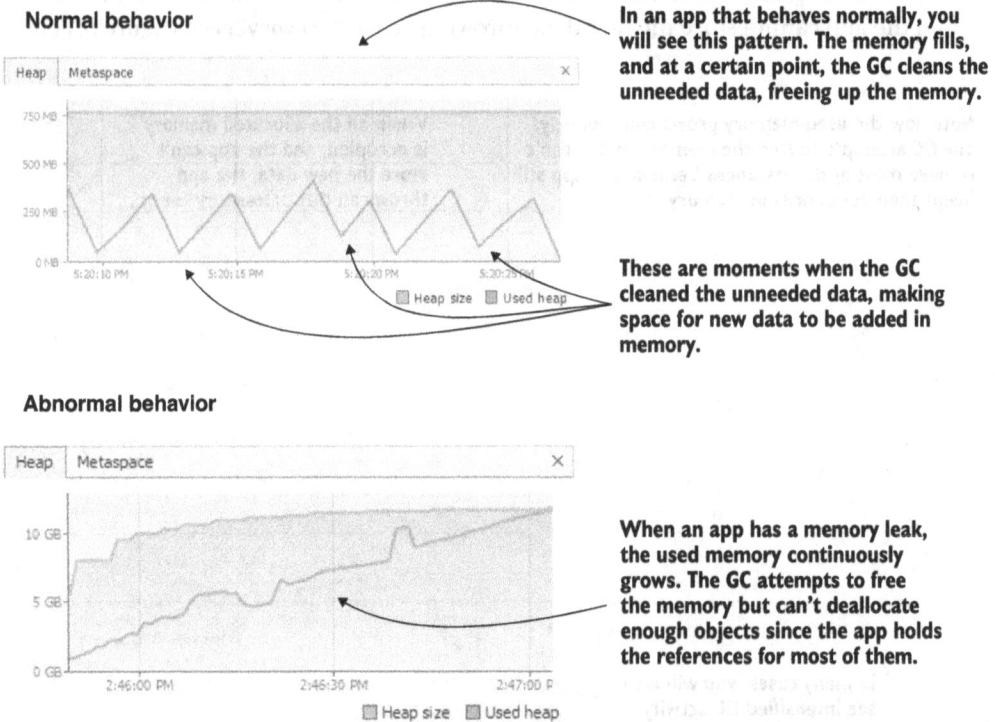

Figure 5.12 A comparison between the memory usage for a healthy app versus an app suffering from a memory leak. The GC frees unneeded data from memory for a healthy app, and the allocated space never fills up. An app with a memory leak prevents the GC from removing enough data. At some point, the memory fills up completely, generating an `OutOfMemoryError`.

by a memory leak), note that the graph has peaks and valleys. The app allocates memory that fills it up (the peaks), and from time to time, the GC removes the data that's no longer needed (the valleys). This ebb and flow is usually a good sign that the capability you are investigating is not affected by a memory leak.

However, if you see that the memory progressively fills and the GC doesn't clean it, your app may have a memory leak. Once you suspect a memory leak, you must investigate further using a heap dump.

You can control the allocated heap size in a Java app. This way, you can enlarge the maximum limit the JVM allocates to your app. However, giving the app more memory is not a solution for a memory leak. However, this approach can be a temporary solution, giving you more time to solve the root cause of the problem. To set a maximum heap size for an app, use the JVM property -Xmx, followed by the amount you want to allocate (e.g., -Xmx1G will allocate a maximum heap size of 1 GB). You can similarly set a minimum initial heap size using the -Xms property (e.g., -Xms500m would allocate a minimum heap size of 500 MB).

Aside from the normal heap space, each app also uses a *metaspace*: the memory location where the JVM stores the class metadata needed for the app's execution. In VisualVM, you can observe the allocation of metaspace in the memory allocation widget. To evaluate the metadata allocation, use the Metaspace tab of the widget, as presented in figure 5.13.

The Metaspace tab of the memory usage widget
shows the size of the metaspace and
how much of it is used.

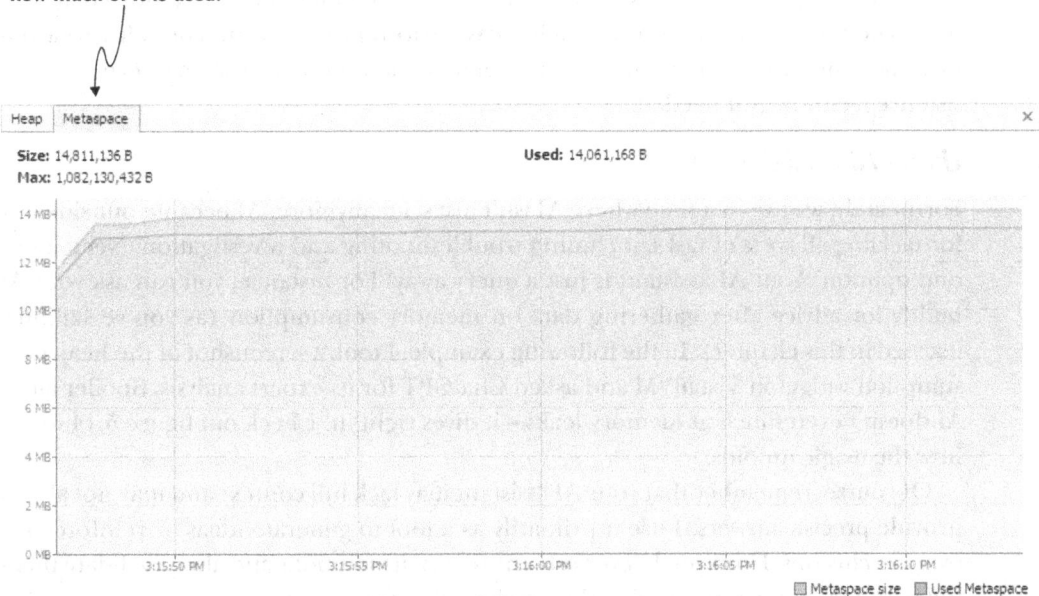

Figure 5.13   The metaspace is a part of the memory used to store class metadata. In some cases, the metaspace can be overflowed. A VisualVM memory allocation widget also shows the usage of the metaspace.

An OutOfMemoryError on the metaspace happens less often, but it's not impossible. I recently dealt with such a case in an app that misused a data persistence framework. Generally, frameworks and libraries using Java reflection are the most likely to generate such problems if misused since they often rely on dynamic proxies and indirect calls.

In my situation, the app was misusing a framework named Hibernate. I would not be surprised if you have already heard about Hibernate since it's one of the most common solutions to manage persistent data in Java apps today. Hibernate is an excellent tool that helps implement the most-used persistence capabilities of an app, while eliminating the need to write unneeded code. Hibernate manages a context of instances and maps the changes to this context to the database. But it's not recommended for a very large context. In other words, don't work with too many records from the database at once!

The app I had trouble with defined a scheduled process, loading many records from a database and processing them in a defined way. It seems that, at some point, the number of records this process was fetching was so large that the load operation itself caused the metaspace to fill; the problem was a misuse of the framework, not a bug. The developers should not have used Hibernate but an alternative, more low-level solution like JDBC.

The problem was critical, and I had to find a short-term solution since a complete refactoring would have taken a long time. Just as for the heap, you can customize the metaspace size. Using the -XX:MaxMetaspaceSize property, you can enlarge the metaspace (e.g., -XX:MaxMetaspaceSize=100M), but remember that this is not a real solution. The long-term solution for such a case is to refactor the functionality to avoid loading so many records at once in the memory and eventually use an alternetive persistence technology if needed.

5.3   *Using AI assistance*

Fortunately, we live in a time where AI isn't just sci-fi anymore. AI became our sidekick for tackling all sorts of tasks, including troubleshooting and investigation. Need a second opinion? Your AI assistant is just a query away! For instance, you can ask your AI buddy for advice after gathering data on memory consumption (as you've skillfully learned in this chapter). In the following example, I took a screenshot of the heap consumption widget in VisualVM and asked ChatGPT for its expert analysis. Spoiler alert: AI doesn't even flinch at memory leaks—it dives right in! Check out figure 5.14 to see how the magic unfolds.

Of course, remember that your AI assistant may lack full context and may not always provide precise answers. I use it primarily as a tool to generate ideas or reinforce my own conclusions. However, I never rely entirely on its solutions and always validate them independently, as emphasized in the previous chapters.

Remember, it's perfectly fine to continue the discussion if needed. You don't have to limit yourself to a simple question-and-answer approach. If the initial response seems

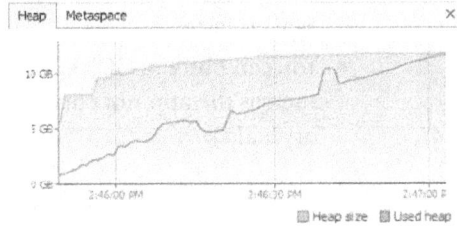

I used a profiler on my app and this is how the memory consumption looks like. Does it look ok for you? Do you think anything is wrong?

This memory chart shows the application's heap memory usage. Here's an analysis based on the image:

1. **Steady Increase in Used Heap:**

   - The `Used heap` (blue area) grows steadily over time and almost matches the maximum `Heap size` (orange area). This indicates that memory usage is increasing, possibly due to objects not being garbage collected.

2. **Garbage Collection Events:**

   - There seems to be a sharp drop in memory usage in one spot (around 2:46:40 PM), indicating a garbage collection (GC) event.

   - However, the memory usage quickly climbs back, which may indicate inefficient memory management or that many objects are being recreated.

Figure 5.14 Consulting ChatGPT for insights on app execution profiling results. The AI assistant offers valuable suggestions for the next steps in your investigation and potential clues about the root cause of the problem (the answer in the image is truncated for brevity).

helpful but not comprehensive enough, feel free to engage further with the AI assistant. Provide additional context or details that could improve the outcome and guide the conversation toward a more complete and precise solution.

Summary

- A profiler is a tool that allows you to observe an app's execution to identify the causes of certain problems that are more difficult to spot otherwise. A profiler shows
  - How an app spends system resources such as the CPU and memory
  - What code executes and the duration of each method execution
  - The execution stack of methods on different threads
  - The executing threads and their status

- The profiler provides excellent visual widgets that let you understand certain aspects faster.
- You can observe GC's execution using the profiler, which helps identify problems such as the app not correctly deallocating unused data from memory (i.e., memory leaks).

Finding hidden problems using profiling techniques

This chapter covers

- Sampling an app's execution to find the currently executing methods
- Observing execution times
- Identifying SQL queries the app executes

In chapter 5, I said a profiler is a powerful tool that can show you a path when all the lights have gone out. But we discussed only a small part of the profiler's capabilities. A profiler offers powerful tools for investigating an app's execution, and learning to use them properly can help you in many scenarios.

In many cases, I have had to evaluate or investigate app executions for codebases I could barely read—old apps with poorly modeled code design, which some companies kept hidden in a wardrobe. In such cases, the profiler was the only efficient way to find what was executing when a specific capability was triggered. Now you can see why I compared a profiler with the light of Eärendil: as Galadriel says, it really was a light in many dark places where all the other lights were out.

In this chapter, we will analyze three investigation techniques through profiling, which I consider extremely valuable:

- Sampling for detecting the part an app's code executes
- Profiling the execution (also called *instrumentation*) to identify wrong behavior and badly performing code that can be optimized
- Profiling the app to identify SQL queries it uses to communicate with a database management system (DBMS)

When used appropriately, these techniques can save you a lot of time finding the causes of various problems. Unfortunately, even though these techniques are powerful, many developers are unfamiliar with them. Some developers know these techniques exist but tend to believe they are challenging to use (in this chapter, I'll show you that the opposite is true). Consequently, they try using other methods to solve problems that could be solved much more efficiently with a profiler (as presented in this chapter).

I created four small projects to show how to use these techniques and the problems that can be investigated. We'll use these projects to apply the profiling techniques we discuss. Section 6.1 discusses sampling—a technique used to identify what code executes at a given time. In section 6.2, you'll learn how a profiler can provide more details about the execution than sampling can offer. Section 6.3 discusses using a profiler to get details about SQL queries an app sends to a DBMS.

6.1   *Sampling to observe executing code*

What is sampling, and how can it benefit you? Sampling is an approach in which a profiling tool is employed to identify the code the app executes. Sampling doesn't provide many details about the execution, but it draws the big picture of what happens, giving you valuable information on what needs to be analyzed further. For this reason, sampling should always be the first step when profiling an app, and as you'll see, sampling may even be enough in many cases. For this section, I prepared project da-ch6-ex1. We'll use a profiling tool to sample this app (VisualVM) to identify problems related to the execution time of a given capability.

The project we'll use to demonstrate sampling is a tiny app that exposes an endpoint, /demo. When someone calls this endpoint using cURL, Postman, or a similar tool, the app further calls an endpoint exposed by httpbin.org.

I like using httpbin.org for many examples and demonstrations. Httpbin.org is an open source web app and tool written in Python that exposes mock endpoints you can use to test different things you're implementing.

Here, we call an endpoint, and httpbin.org responds with a given delay. For this example, we'll use a 5-second delay to simulate a latency scenario in our app, and httpbin.org simulates the root cause of the problem.

The scenario is also illustrated in figure 6.1.

With latency, we understand how an app reacts slower than expected.

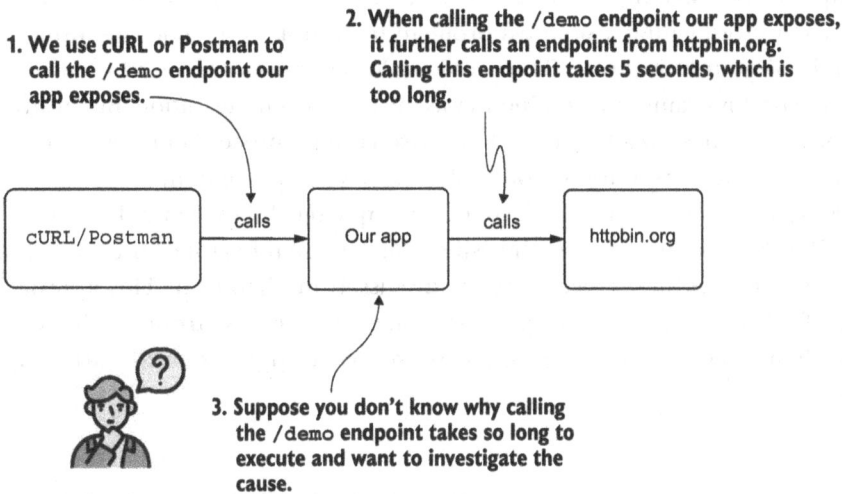

1. **We use cURL or Postman to call the /demo endpoint our app exposes.**

2. **When calling the /demo endpoint our app exposes, it further calls an endpoint from httpbin.org. Calling this endpoint takes 5 seconds, which is too long.**

| cURL/Postman | | calls | | Our app | | calls | | httpbin.org |

3. **Suppose you don't know why calling the /demo endpoint takes so long to execute and want to investigate the cause.**

Figure 6.1   The app we are investigating exposes an endpoint: /demo. When you call this endpoint, you must wait 5 seconds for the app to respond. We need to understand why it takes so long for the endpoint to respond. We know our app calls a mock endpoint from httpbin.org, which causes the delay, but we want to learn how to investigate this scenario with a profiler. This way, you'll know how to use similar techniques for real-world situations.

The profiling approach has two steps:

1 Sampling, to determine what code executes and where you should go into more detail (the approach we discuss in this section)

2 Profiling (also called *instrumentation*), to get more details about the execution of specific pieces of code

Sometimes step 1 (sampling) is enough to understand a problem, and you may not need to profile the app (step 2). As you'll learn in this chapter and chapters 7–9, profiling can provide more details about the execution if needed. But first, you need to know what part of the code to profile, and for that, you use sampling.

How does the problem occur in our example? When calling the /demo endpoint, the execution takes 5 seconds (figure 6.2), which we consider too long. Ideally, we want the

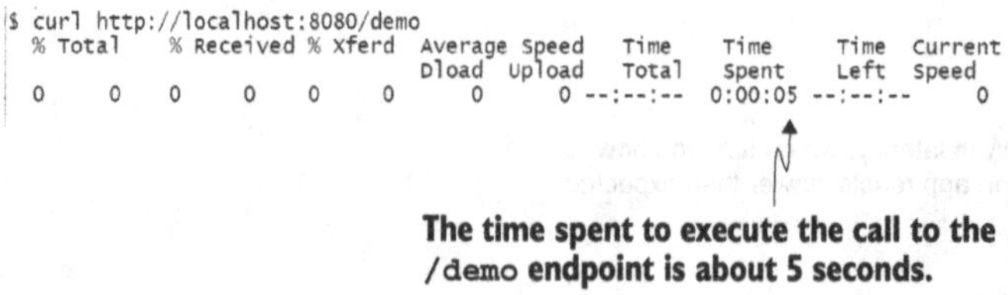

```
$ curl http://localhost:8080/demo
  % Total    % Received % xferd  Average Speed   Time    Time     Time  Current
                                 Dload  Upload   Total   Spent    Left  Speed
  0      0    0      0    0     0      0       0 --:--:-- 0:00:05 --:--:--      0
```

Figure 6.2 **When the endpoint is called (in this figure, using cURL), the app takes about 5 seconds to respond. In our scenario, we use a profiler to investigate this latency problem.**

The time spent to execute the call to the /demo endpoint is about 5 seconds.

execution to take less than 1 second, so we need to understand why calling the /demo endpoint takes so long. What causes the latency? Is it our app or something else?

When investigating a slowness problem in an unknown codebase, using a profiler should be your first choice. The problem doesn't necessarily need to involve an endpoint. For this example, an endpoint was the easiest demonstration. But in any situation involving slowness—calling an endpoint, executing a process, or using a simple method call on a particular event—a profiler should be your first option.

First, start the app we troubleshoot (example da-ch6-ex1) and then VisualVM (the profiling tool we will use for our investigations). Remember to add the VM option -Djava .rmi.server.hostname=localhost, as discussed in chapter 5. This approach allows VisualVM to connect to the process. Select the process from the list on the left, and then select the Sampler tab, as presented in figure 6.3, to start sampling the execution.

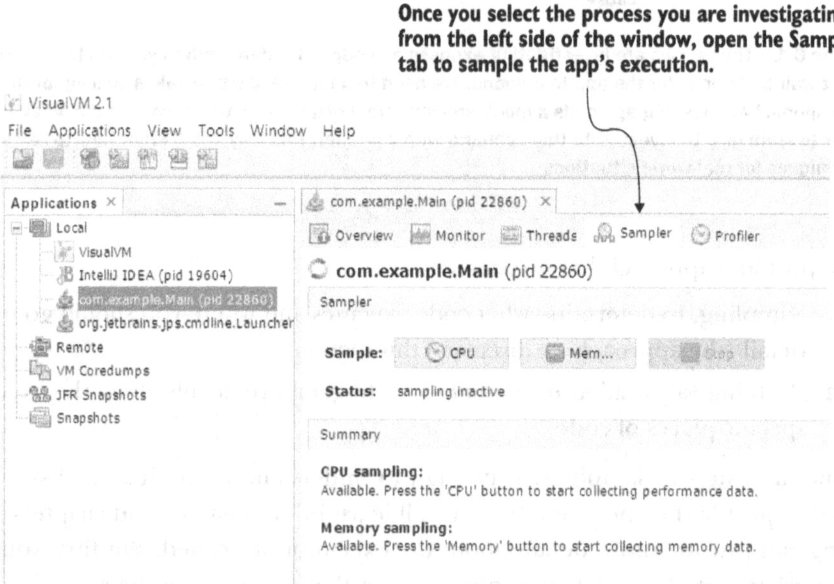

Once you select the process you are investigating from the left side of the window, open the Sampler tab to sample the app's execution.

Figure 6.3 **To start sampling the execution, select the process from the list on the left side, and then select the Sampler tab.**

Sampling the execution has the following three purposes:

- *To find out what code executes*—Sampling shows you what executes behind the scenes and is an excellent way to find the part of the app you need to investigate.

- *To identify CPU consumption*—We'll use this to investigate latency problems and understand which methods share execution time.

- *To identify memory consumption*—In this case, the purpose is to analyze memory-related problems. We'll discuss sampling and profiling memory more in chapter 9.

Select CPU (as shown in figure 6.4) to start sampling performance data. VisualVM displays a list of all the active threads and their stack traces. The profiler then intercepts the process execution and displays all the methods called and the approximate execution time. When you call the /demo endpoint, the profiler shows what happens behind the scenes when the app executes that capability.

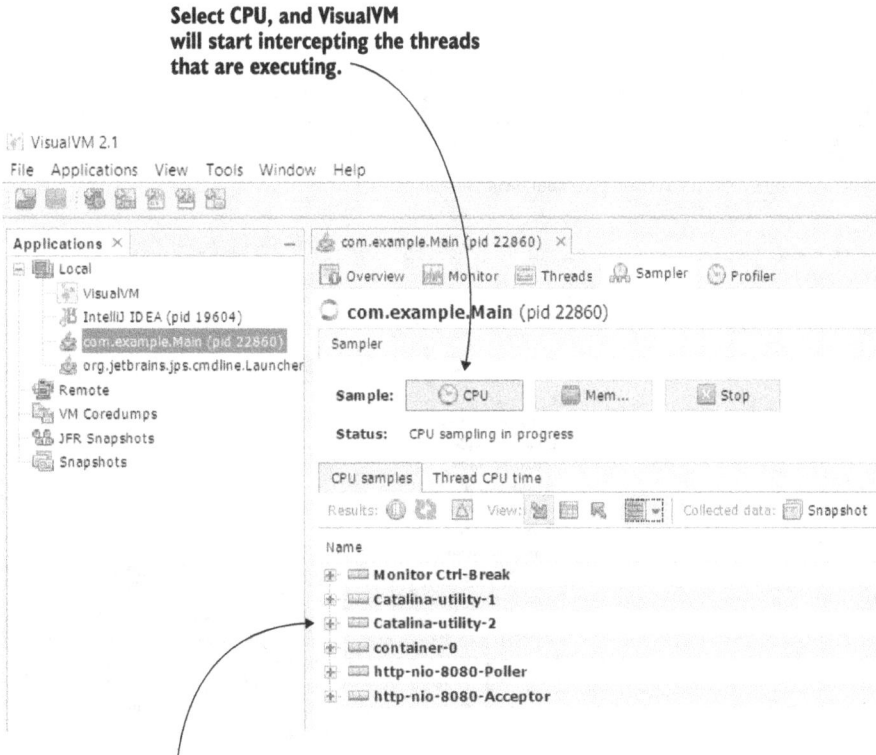

Figure 6.4 The profiler shows all the active threads in a list. You can expand each item to see the execution stack and an approximate execution time. When the app executes, the newly created threads appear in the list, and you can analyze their execution.

We can now call the /demo endpoint and observe what happens. As shown in figure 6.5, some new threads appear in the list. The app started these threads when we called the /demo endpoint. When you open them, you should see precisely what the app does during its execution.

Before we discuss details such as the execution time, I want to highlight how vital this first step is. Many times when I've analyzed code, I used just sampling to figure out where to look for the problem. I may not have even been investigating a performance or latency problem but was simply looking for the point to start debugging. Remember our discussions in chapters 2 and 3: to debug something, you need to know where to add that breakpoint to pause the app's execution. If you have no clue where to add a breakpoint, you can't debug. Sampling can be a way to shed some light on a situation when you can't figure out where to start debugging (especially in cases such as those I mentioned at the beginning of the chapter in which an app lacks clean code design).

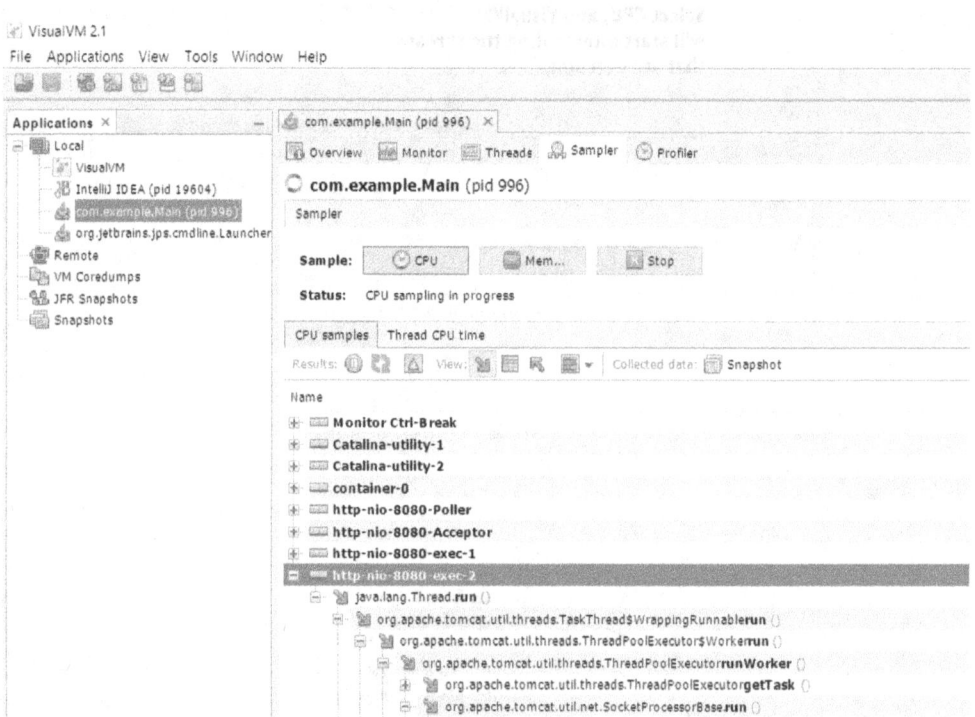

VisualVM reveals the full stack trace the app executed when you called the /demo endpoint. You can use the stack trace to identify which code the app executed and which instructions spent more time executing.

Figure 6.5   The stack trace shows what the app executes. You can see every method and each subsequent method that is called. This view helps you quickly find the code you want to focus on when investigating a certain capability.

Let's look at the execution stack to understand what the profiler shows us. When you want to figure out what code executes, you simply expand the stack trace up to the point where it displays the methods of the app you are interested in. When investigating a latency problem (as in this example), you can expand the stack trace to observe the maximum execution time, as shown in figure 6.6.

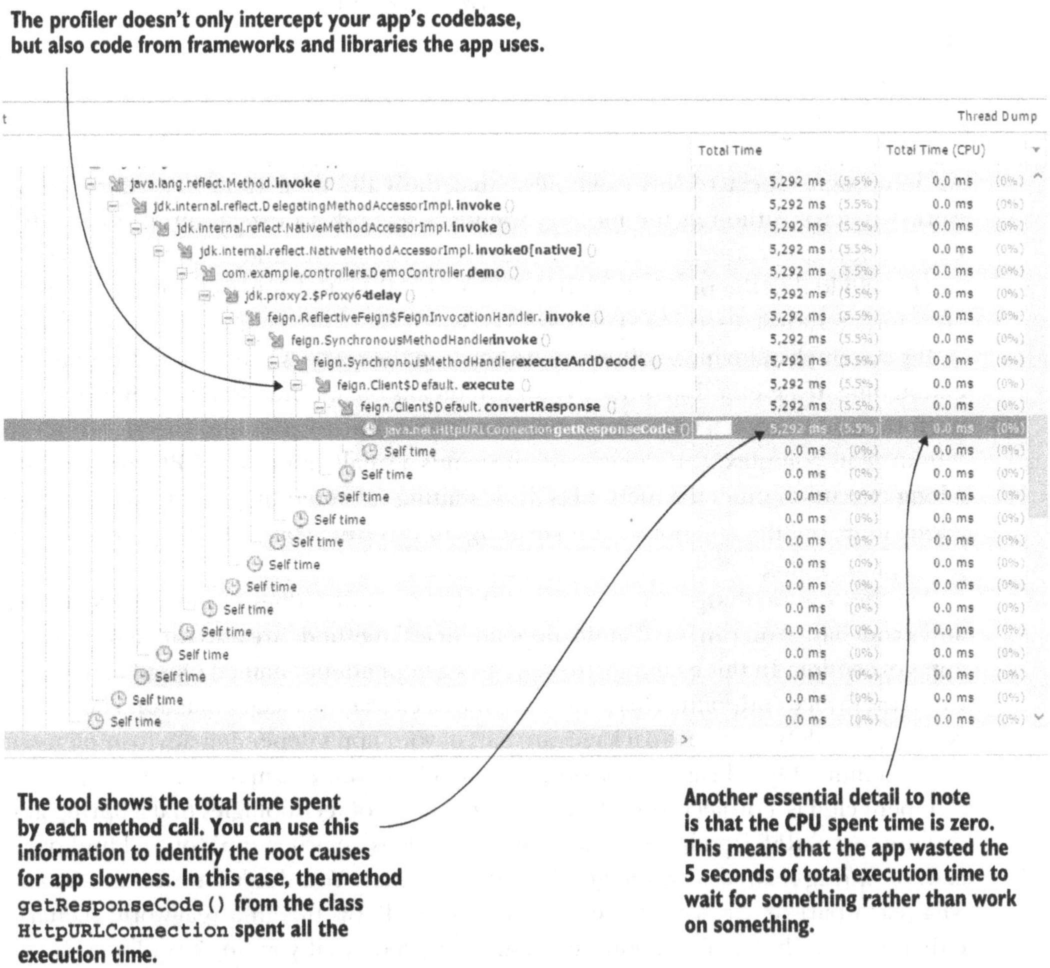

The profiler doesn't only intercept your app's codebase, but also code from frameworks and libraries the app uses.

The tool shows the total time spent by each method call. You can use this information to identify the root causes for app slowness. In this case, the method getResponseCode() from the class HttpURLConnection spent all the execution time.

Another essential detail to note is that the CPU spent time is zero. This means that the app wasted the 5 seconds of total execution time to wait for something rather than work on something.

Figure 6.6   When you expand the execution stack, you find which methods execute and how much time they spend executing. You can also deduce how long they wait and how much they work. The profiler shows both the app's codebase methods and the methods called from specific dependencies (libraries or frameworks) the app uses.

I expanded the execution stack by selecting the small (+) button in the last method. The profiler shows that it took about 5 seconds to understand the execution and find the method that caused the latency. In this particular case, we see that just one method causes the slowness: `getResponseCode()` of the `HttpURLConnection` class.

> **TIP** Remember that it's not always one method that spends all the execution time in real-world scenarios. You'll often find that the time spent is shared among multiple methods that execute. The rule is to first focus on the method that takes the longest time to execute.

An important aspect of this example is that the CPU time (how long the method works) is zero. Although the method spends 5 seconds in execution, it doesn't use CPU resources because it is waiting for the HTTP call to end and to get a response. We can conclude that the problem is not in the app; rather, the app is slow only because it waits for a response to its HTTP request.

It's extremely valuable to differentiate between the total CPU time and the total execution time. If a method spends CPU time, it means the method works. To improve the performance in such a case, you usually have to adjust (if possible) the algorithm to minimize its complexity. If the execution spends a small amount of CPU time but has a long execution time, the method is likely waiting for something: an action may take a long time, but the app doesn't do anything. In this case, you need to figure out what your app is waiting for.

Another essential aspect to observe is that the profiler doesn't just intercept your app's codebase. You can see that the dependencies' methods are also called during the app's execution. In this example, the app uses a dependency named OpenFeign to call the `httpbin.org` endpoint. This is visible in the stack trace packages that don't belong to your app's codebase. These packages are part of your app's dependencies to implement its capabilities. OpenFeign can be one of them, like in this example.

OpenFeign is a project from the Spring ecosystem of technologies that a Spring app can use to call REST endpoints. Since this example is a Spring app, you will find packages of Spring-related technologies in the stack trace. You don't have to understand what each part of the stack trace does. You won't know this in a real-world scenario either. In fact, this book is about understanding code that you don't yet know. If you want to learn Spring, I recommend starting with *Spring Start Here* (Manning, 2021), another book I wrote. You'll also find details about OpenFeign in the same book.

Why is observing dependencies' methods so important? Because, sometimes, it's almost impossible to figure out what executes from a given dependency using other means. Look at the code written in our app to call the `httpbin.org` endpoint (see listing 6.1). You can't see the actual implementation for sending the HTTP request. That's because, as it happens in many Java frameworks today, the dependency uses dynamic proxies to decouple the implementation.

```
@FeignClient(name = "httpBin", url = "${httpBinUrl}")
public interface DemoProxy {

  @PostMapping("/delay/{n}")
  void delay(@PathVariable int n);
}
```

Dynamic proxies give an app a way to choose a method implementation at run time. When an app capability uses dynamic proxies, it might actually call a method declared by an interface without knowing what implementation it will be given to execute at run time (figure 6.7). Using the framework's capabilities is easier, but the disadvantage is that you don't know where to investigate a problem.

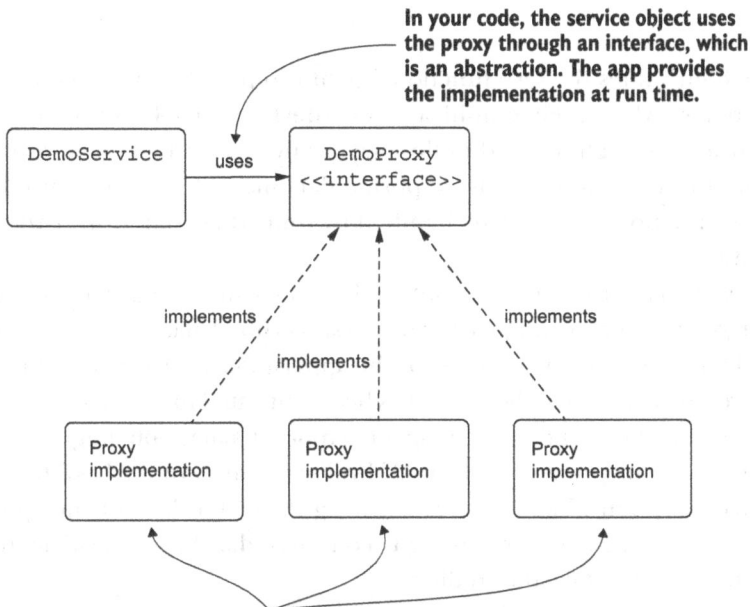

In your code, the service object uses the proxy through an interface, which is an abstraction. The app provides the implementation at run time.

DemoService —uses→ DemoProxy <<interface>>

implements / implements / implements

Proxy implementation   Proxy implementation   Proxy implementation

The frameworks the app uses may provide multiple implementations for the same abstraction. The app decides which implementation to use at run time. Because of this separation, it's more difficult to find which code will execute just by reading the code. You may not even know in which dependency to look to find the dynamic implementations.

Figure 6.7 The framework keeps the implementations for an abstraction separate and provides them dynamically during execution. Because the implementation is decoupled and the app provides it during run time, it's more difficult to find it by reading the code.

We're living in the age of artificial intelligence, where even the dullest tasks can get a clever sidekick. When it comes to sampling and profiling, modern profiling tools often let you export the data into text files—usually in XML or CSV format (because, apparently, those are the universal languages of data). Simply hand that file over to an AI assistant and watch it crunch numbers and spot patterns faster than you can say, "Where did I save that file?" It's like having a superpowered intern, minus the coffee runs.

One of my personal uses for sampling is when learning a new framework or library. Sampling helps me to understand what executes behind the scenes in a new functionality. I applied this approach when learning Hibernate and Spring Security, which have complex functionality, and it helped me quickly understand how to work with the given capabilities.

Figure 6.8 illustrates the save functionality in two popular profiling tools, VisualVM and JProfiler. While their graphical user interfaces (GUIs) differ in appearance, both provide a straightforward option—typically a button—to export profiling data in various formats. Although the exported data may differ in structure between the tools, this variation can easily be handled by your AI assistant for further analysis or processing.

Once you have exported the profiling data, you can share it with your preferred AI assistant to gain valuable insights. Figure 6.9 shows how ChatGPT analyzes the provided data and identifies potential causes for the application's performance problems. Note that the response shown in the figure has been truncated for brevity.

With a few clicks and a sprinkle of exported data, you might turn hours of head-scratching into moments of "Aha!" brilliance. Sure, your AI assistant won't bring you coffee (yet), but when it comes to slicing through call trees and spotting bottlenecks, it's like having a performance guru on speed dial. So go ahead, let the AI do the heavy lifting, and you take the credit.

6.2 *Profiling to learn how many times a method is executed*

Finding what code executes is essential, but sometimes it is not enough. Often, we need more details to precisely understand a given behavior. For example, sampling does not provide the number of method invocations. An app may take only 50 milliseconds to execute, but if it calls the method a thousand times, then it takes 50 seconds to execute when sampling. To demonstrate how to get details about the execution using a profiler and to identify situations where this is useful, we'll again use some projects provided with the book. We'll start with project da-ch6-ex1, which we also used in section 6.1, but this time, we'll discuss profiling (also known as instrumentation) for details about the execution.

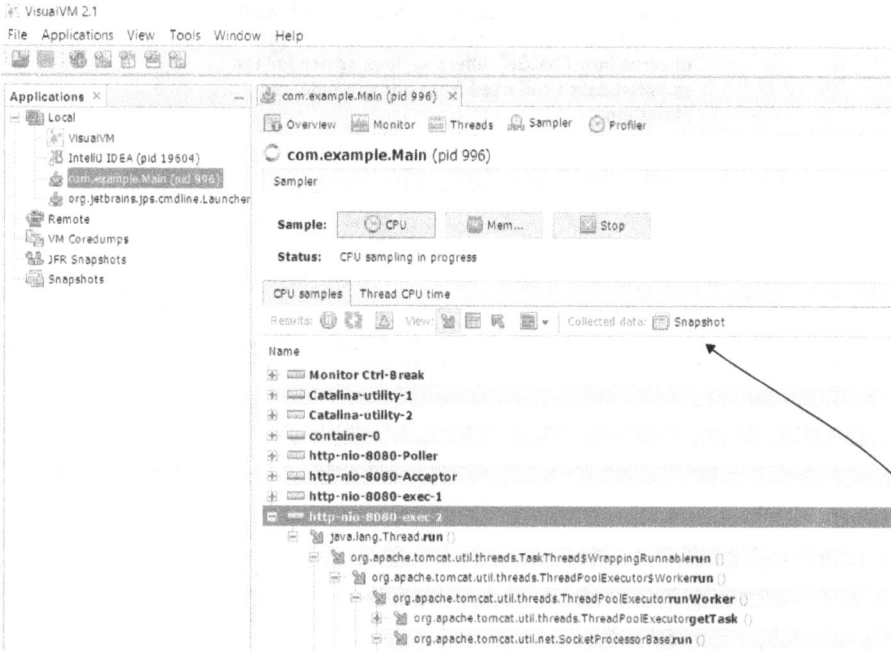

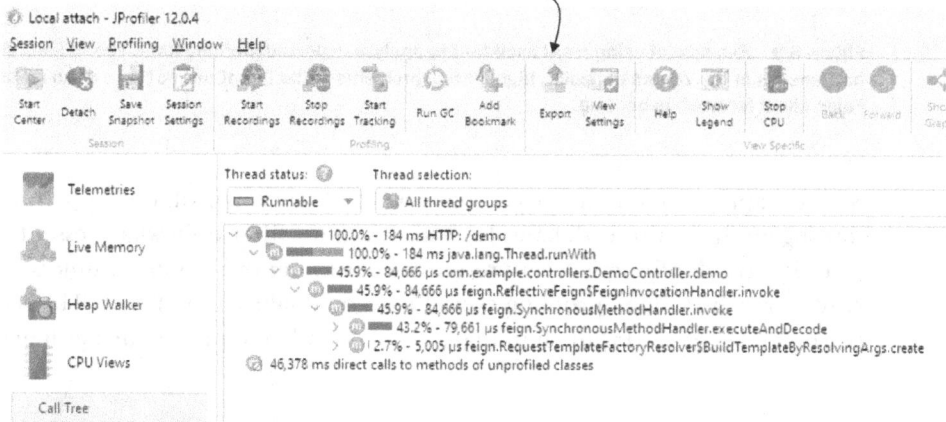

Figure 6.8 Saving sampled data in VisualVM (top) and JProfiler (bottom). VisualVM allows CPU sampling snapshots, while JProfiler provides options to export profiling data, ensuring easy analysis and sharing of performance metrics.

Upload the exported sampled data to your favorite AI assistent and ask for advice. In this case, you observe how ChatGPT offers various advice for the sampled data I collected from our example app execution.

Call_Tree.xml
File

I have a latency problem in my app. It happens when I call the /demo endpoint. Can you give me some advice about what you think the problem is and how I should troubleshoot further?

From the call tree analysis in your XML file, the majority of the latency occurs in the `/demo` endpoint. Here's what stands out:

1. `HTTP: /demo` total time: 184,494 ms

   - Nearly half of this time (45.9%, or 84,666 ms) is spent in the `DemoController.demo` method, which calls a Feign client.

   - The Feign client (`SynchronousMethodHandler.executeAndDecode`) is responsible for the bulk of this latency (43.2%, or 79,661 ms).

2. Self-time in the `runWith` method: 99,828 ms (54%)

   - This could indicate time spent outside of business logic, possibly thread context switching, blocking I/O, or waiting on external dependencies.

Figure 6.9   Example of using an AI assistant to analyze exported profiling data. The AI identifies latency bottlenecks in the /demo endpoint, highlighting problems in the DemoController.demo method and the Feign client for troubleshooting.

Start the app provided with project da-ch6-ex1. When you profile an app, you shouldn't investigate the entire codebase. Instead, you must filter only what's essential to your investigation. Profiling is a very resource-consuming operation, so unless you have a really powerful system, profiling everything would take a ton of time. That's one more reason we always start with sampling—to identify what to profile further if needed.

TIP Never profile the app's entire codebase. You should always first decide, based on sampling, which part of the app you want to profile to get more details.

For this example, we'll ignore the app's codebase (without dependencies) and only take OpenFeign classes from the dependencies. Remember that you can't refer to an app's entire code in a real-world app since that would likely be time- and resource-consumptive. For this small example, it won't be a problem, but for large apps, always restrict the intercepted code as much as possible when profiling.

Figure 6.10 shows how to apply these restrictions. On the right side of the Profiler tab, you can specify which part of the app to intercept. In this example, we use the following:

- `com.example.**`—The code in all the packages and subpackages of `com.example`
- `feign.**`—Code in all the packages and subpackages of `feign`

Profiling helps us to get more information about the execution, but it's also more resource intensive. One of the first supplementary details you see here is the number of executions of a particular method.

Select CPU to start profiling the app.

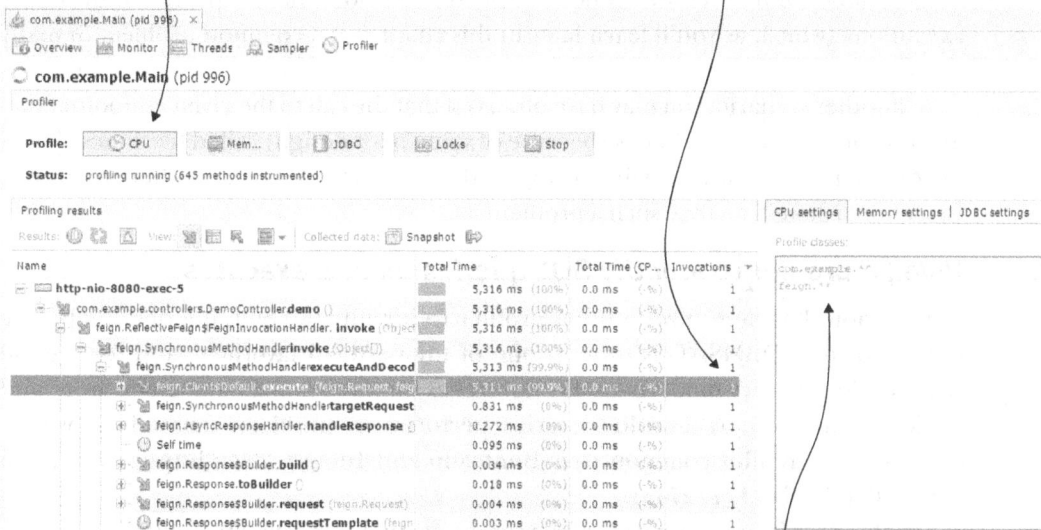

Always profile a small number of packages. Before starting to profile the execution, define the filters to tell the tool which classes need to be intercepted.

Figure 6.10 Profiling a part of the app during execution to get details about the times a given method was invoked. We can see that the method causing the 5 seconds of latency is invoked only once, meaning the number of invocations doesn't cause a problem here.

The syntax you can use to filter the packages and classes you want to profile has just a few simple rules:

- Write each rule on a separate line.
- Use one asterisk (`*`) to refer to a package; for example, we could use `com` `.example.*` if we wanted to profile all classes in the package `com.example`.
- Use two asterisks (`**`) to refer to a package and all its subpackages. In this case, by using `com.example.**`, we mean all classes in the package `com.example`, as well as any of its subpackages.
- Write the full name of a class if you want to profile only that class; for example, we could use `com.example.controllers.DemoController` to profile only this class.

I chose these packages after sampling the execution, as discussed in section 6.1. Because I observed that the method call with the latency problem comes from classes of the `feign` package, I decided to add this package and its subpackages to the list to get more information.

In this particular case, the number of invocations doesn't seem to cause problems: the method executes only once and takes about 5 seconds to finish its execution. A small number of method invocations imply that we don't have repeated unnecessary executions (which, as you'll learn later in this chapter, is a common problem in many apps).

In another scenario, you may have observed that the call to the given endpoint takes just 1 second, but the method is (because of some poor design) called five times. Then, the problem would have been in the app, and we would know how and where to solve it. In section 6.3, we'll analyze such a problem.

6.3   *Using a profiler to identify SQL queries an app executes*

This section illustrates how to use a profiler to identify the SQL queries an application sends to a DBMS. This topic is one of my personal favorites—and for a good reason. Almost every modern application relies on a relational database to store and retrieve data. And in real-world scenarios, performance problems caused by slow SQL queries are incredibly common (see, Bonteanu and Tudose, 2024; https://www.mdpi .com/2076-3417/14/7/2743).

Database performance greatly affects how fast and responsive an application feels to the user. Even if your code is well-written, a single poorly written or slow query can cause your entire app to lag, time out, or even crash under load. This is especially true when your application grows and more users start interacting with it simultaneously.

To make things more complex, many modern apps don't build SQL queries manually. Instead, they use libraries or frameworks—such as JPA, Hibernate, or Spring Data—that automatically generate your queries. This is convenient, but it also means you might not know exactly what SQL is being sent to the database. When performance problems appear, it becomes hard to guess where things are going wrong. That's where a profiler comes in. A good profiler can show you exactly which queries are being executed, how long each one takes, and how often it runs.

We'll use a scenario implemented with project da-ch6-ex2 to learn how often a method executes and intercepts a SQL query the app runs on a relational database. We'll then demonstrate that the executed SQL queries can be retrieved even when the app works with a framework and doesn't handle the queries directly. Finally, we'll discuss this subject further using a couple of examples.

6.3.1 *Using a profiler to retrieve SQL queries not generated by a framework*

This section uses an example to demonstrate using a profiler to obtain the SQL queries an app executes. We'll use a simple app that sends the queries directly to a DBMS directly without using a framework.

Let's start project da-ch6-ex2 and use the Profiler tab, as you learned in section 6.2. Project da-ch6-ex2 is also a small app. It configures an in-memory database with two tables (product and purchase) and populates the tables with a few records.

The app exposes all purchased products when calling the endpoint /products. By "purchased products," I mean products that have at least one purchase record in the purchase table. The purpose is to analyze the app's behavior when calling this endpoint without first analyzing the code. This way, you can see how much we can get just by using the profiler.

In figure 6.11, we use the Profiler tab since you already learned sampling in section 6.1, but remember that in any real-world scenario, you start with sampling. We start the app, and, using cURL or Postman, we call the /products endpoint. The profiler shows us precisely what happens:

1 A method findPurchasedProductNames() that belongs to the PurchaseController class was called.

2 This method delegated the call to the method getProductNamesForPurchases() in class PurchaseService.

3 The method getProductNamesForPurchases() in ProductService calls findAll() in PurchaseRepository.

4 The method getProductNamesForPurchases() in ProductService calls findProduct() in ProductRepository 10 times.

Isn't this amazing? Without even looking at the code, we've already learned so much about what's going on. It's like solving a puzzle without even opening the box! These details are super helpful because now you know exactly where to look in the code and what you're likely to find. The profiler has given you class names, method names, and even how they all work together. Now, let's jump into the code in listing 6.2 and see where all this is happening.

By using the profiler, we can understand that most things happen in the getProductNamesForPurchases() method in the PurchaseService class, so that's most likely the place we need to analyze.

1. The execution starts with the `findPurchasedProductNames()`
method in the `PurchaseController` **class.**

2. The `getProductNamesForPurchases()`
method in `PurchaseService` **is called.**

3. The method in the `PurchaseService` **class**
calls `findAll()` **in** `PurchaseRepository`.

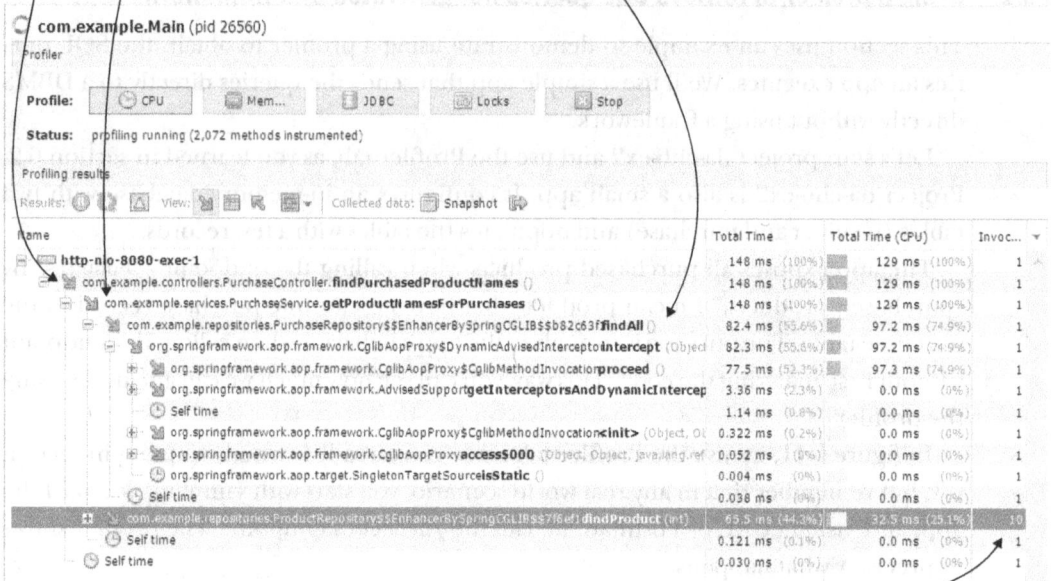

4. After calling `findAll()` **in** `PurchaseRepository`, **the**
method calls `findProduct()` **in** `ProductRepository` **10 times.**

Figure 6.11 When profiling the app, we observe that one of the methods is called 10 times. We now need to ask ourselves whether this is a design problem. Since we now have a big picture of the entire algorithm and we know what code is executed, we can also debug the app if we can't figure out what happens.

Listing 6.2   The algorithm's implementation in the `PurchaseService` **class**

```
@Service
public class PurchaseService {

  private final ProductRepository productRepository;
  private final PurchaseRepository purchaseRepository;

  public PurchaseService(ProductRepository productRepository,
                         PurchaseRepository purchaseRepository) {
    this.productRepository = productRepository;
    this.purchaseRepository = purchaseRepository;
  }

  public Set<String> getProductNamesForPurchases() {
```

```
Set<String> productNames = new HashSet<>();
List<Purchase> purchases = purchaseRepository.findAll();     ◄──────  Gets all the
for (Purchase p : purchases) {                               ◄─────        purchases from
  Product product =                                                        the database
    productRepository.findProduct(p.getProduct());           ◄─────        table
  productNames.add(product.getName());                       ◄─────
}                                                              Iterates through
                                                               each product
                                        Adds the
    return productNames;     ◄──────    product        Gets the details about
  }                         Returns the  into a set     the purchased product
}                           set of products
```

Observe the implemented behavior: the app fetches some data in a list and then iterates over it to get more data from the database. Such an implementation typically indicates a design problem because you can usually reduce the execution of so many queries to one. Obviously, the fewer queries executed, the more efficient the app is.

In this example, it's effortless to retrieve the queries directly from the code. Since the profiler shows us exactly where they are, and the app is tiny, finding the queries isn't a problem. But real-world apps are not small, and in many cases, it's not easy to retrieve the queries directly from the code. But fear no more! You can use the profiler to retrieve all the SQL queries the app sends to a DBMS. You find this demonstrated in figure 6.12. Instead of selecting the CPU button, you select the JDBC button to start profiling for SQL queries.

Click the JDBC button to start profiling for SQL queries the app sends to a DBMS.

When the app sends a SQL query to a DBMS, the profiler intercepts it and shows it in this list. The SQL query appears complete, including the parameters' values.

We can see that this query executed 10 times. Usually, we want to avoid running the same query multiple times to improve the app's performance.

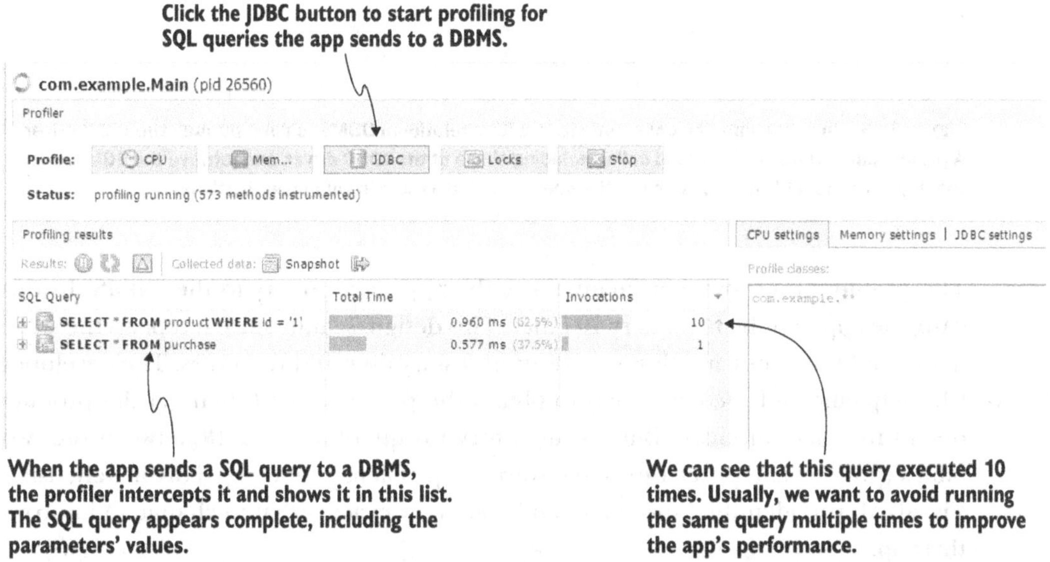

Figure 6.12 The profiler intercepts the SQL queries the app sends to the DBMS through the JDBC driver. This provides you with an easy way to get the queries, run them, observe what part of the codebase runs them, and know how many times a query is executed.

What the tool does behind the scenes is pretty simple: a Java app sends the SQL queries to a DBMS through a JDBC driver. The profiler intercepts the driver and copies the queries before the driver sends them to the DBMS. Figure 6.13 shows this approach. The result is fantastic, as you can simply copy and paste the queries into your database client, where you can run them or investigate their plan.

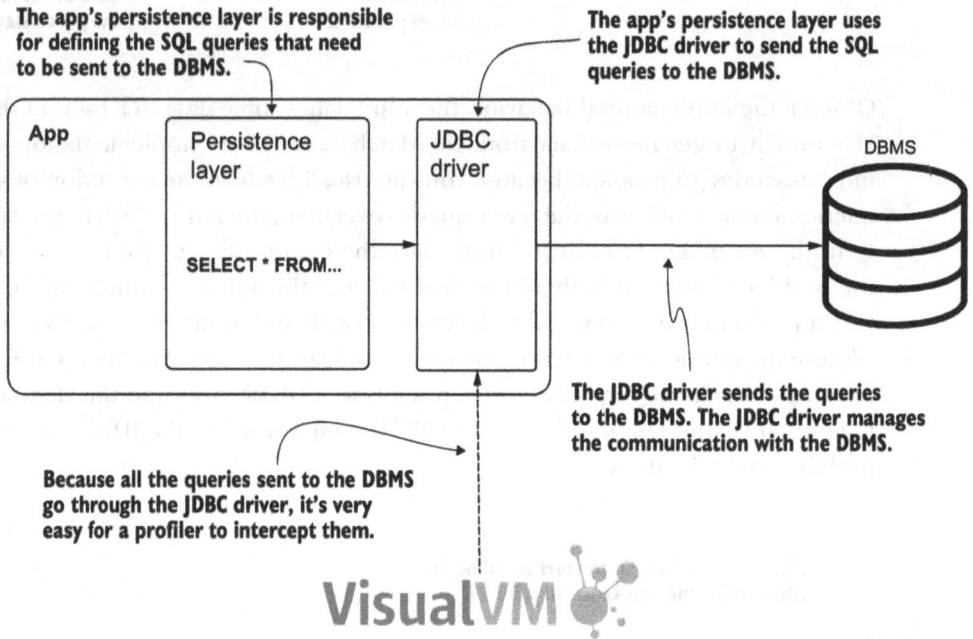

Figure 6.13   In a Java app, the communication with a relational DBMS is done through the JDBC driver. A profiler can intercept all method calls, including those of the JDBC driver, and retrieve the SQL queries the app sends to a DBMS. You can get the queries and use them in your investigations.

The profiler also shows how many times the app sent a query to the DBMS. In this case, the app sent the first query 10 times. This design is faulty since it repeats the same query multiple times and thus spends unnecessary time and resources. The developer who implemented the code tried to obtain the purchases and then get the product details for each purchase. But a straightforward query with a JOIN between the two tables (product and purchase) would solve the problem in one step. Fortunately, using VisualVM, you identified the cause, and you know exactly what to change to improve this app.

Figure 6.14 illustrates how to find the part of the codebase that sent the query. You can expand the execution stack and usually find the first method in the app's codebase.

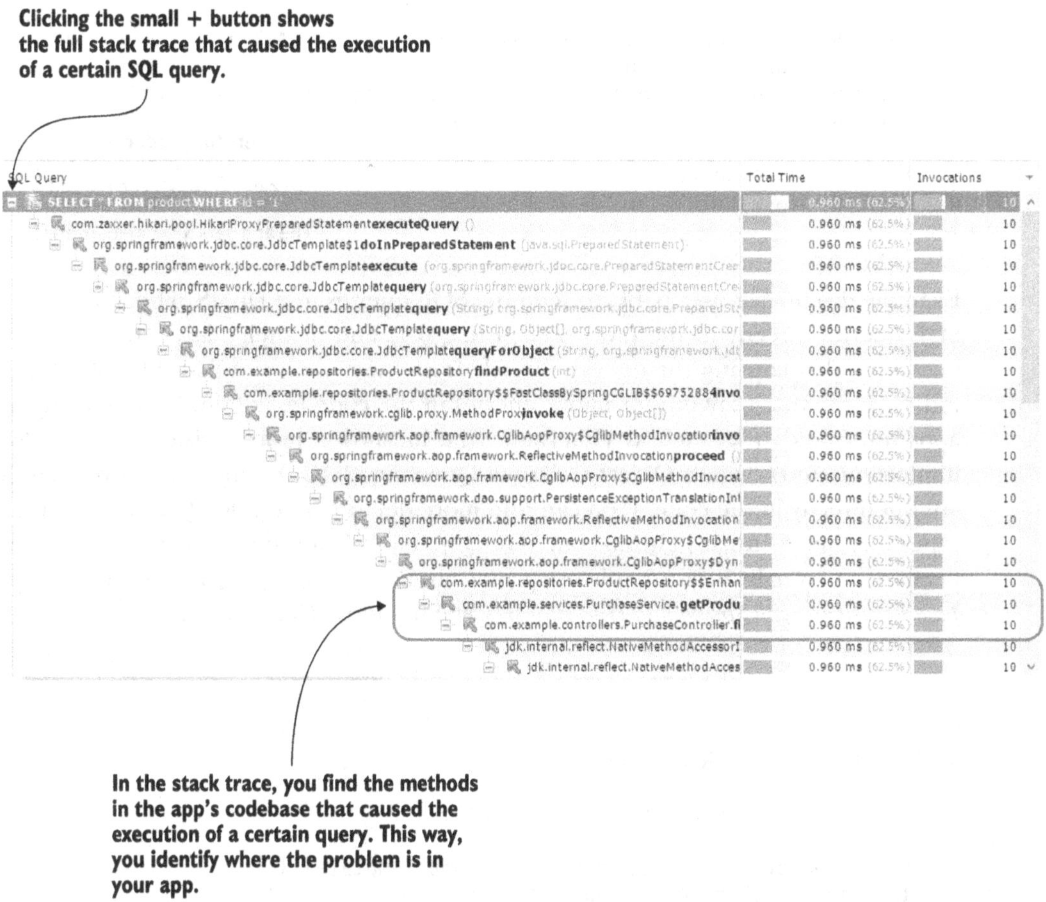

Clicking the small + button shows
the full stack trace that caused the execution
of a certain SQL query.

SQL Query	Total Time	Invocations	
⊟ 🔍 SELECT * FROM product WHERE id = '1'	0.960 ms (62.5%)	10
⊟ 🔍 com.zaxxer.hikari.pool.HikariProxyPreparedStatement**executeQuery** ()	0.960 ms (62.5%)	10
⊟ 🔍 org.springframework.jdbc.core.JdbcTemplate$1**doInPreparedStatement** (java.sql.PreparedStatement)	0.960 ms (62.5%)	10
⊟ 🔍 org.springframework.jdbc.core.JdbcTemplate**execute** (org.springframework.jdbc.core.PreparedStatementCre...	0.960 ms (62.5%)	10
⊟ 🔍 org.springframework.jdbc.core.JdbcTemplate**query** (org.springframework.jdbc.core.PreparedStatementCre...	0.960 ms (62.5%)	10
⊟ 🔍 org.springframework.jdbc.core.JdbcTemplate**query** (String, org.springframework.jdbc.core.PreparedSta...	0.960 ms (62.5%)	10
⊟ 🔍 org.springframework.jdbc.core.JdbcTemplate**query** (String, Object[], org.springframework.jdbc.cor...	0.960 ms (62.5%)	10
⊟ 🔍 org.springframework.jdbc.core.JdbcTemplate**queryForObject** (String, org.springframework.jdb...	0.960 ms (62.5%)	10
⊟ 🔍 com.example.repositories.ProductRepository**findProduct** (int)	0.960 ms (62.5%)	10
⊟ 🔍 com.example.repositories.ProductRepository$$FastClassBySpringCGLIB$$69752884**invo**...	0.960 ms (62.5%)	10
⊟ 🔍 org.springframework.cglib.proxy.MethodProxy**invoke** (Object, Object[])	0.960 ms (62.5%)	10
⊟ 🔍 org.springframework.aop.framework.CglibAopProxy$CglibMethodInvocation**invo**...	0.960 ms (62.5%)	10
⊟ 🔍 org.springframework.aop.framework.ReflectiveMethodInvocation**proceed** ()	0.960 ms (62.5%)	10
⊟ 🔍 org.springframework.aop.framework.CglibAopProxy$CglibMethodInvocat...	0.960 ms (62.5%)	10
⊟ 🔍 org.springframework.dao.support.PersistenceExceptionTranslationInt...	0.960 ms (62.5%)	10
⊟ 🔍 org.springframework.aop.framework.ReflectiveMethodInvocation...	0.960 ms (62.5%)	10
⊟ 🔍 org.springframework.aop.framework.CglibAopProxy$CglibMe...	0.960 ms (62.5%)	10
⊟ 🔍 org.springframework.aop.framework.CglibAopProxy$Dyn...	0.960 ms (62.5%)	10
⊟ 🔍 com.example.repositories.ProductRepository$$Enhan...	0.960 ms (62.5%)	10
⊟ 🔍 com.example.services.PurchaseService.**getProdu**...	0.960 ms (62.5%)	10
⊟ 🔍 com.example.controllers.PurchaseController.**fi**...	0.960 ms (62.5%)	10
⊟ 🔍 jdk.internal.reflect.NativeMethodAccessorl...	0.960 ms (62.5%)	10
⊟ 🔍 jdk.internal.reflect.NativeMethodAcces...	0.960 ms (62.5%)	10

In the stack trace, you find the methods
in the app's codebase that caused the
execution of a certain query. This way,
you identify where the problem is in
your app.

Figure 6.14　For each query, the profiler also provides the execution stack trace. You can use the stack trace to identify the part of your app's codebase that sent the query.

The following listing shows the code whose call we identified using the profiler. Once you identify where the problem comes from, it's time to read the code and find a way to optimize the implementation. In this example, everything could have been merged into one query. It may look like a silly mistake, but trust me, you'll find these cases, even in larger apps implemented by powerful organizations.

Listing 6.3　The algorithm's implementation in the ProductService class

```
@Service
public class PurchaseService {

  // Omitted code

  public Set<String> getProductNamesForPurchases() {
```

```
    Set<String> productNames = new HashSet<>();
    List<Purchase> purchases = purchaseRepository.findAll();
    for (Purchase p : purchases) {
      Product product = productRepository.findProduct(p.getProduct());
      productNames.add(product.getName());
    }
    return productNames;
  }
}
```

Gets the product details

Iterates through each product

The app gets a list of all products.

Example da-ch6-ex2 uses JDBC to send the SQL queries to a DBMS. The app has the SQL queries directly in the Java code (listing 6.4) and in their native shape, so you may think that copying the queries directly from the code is not that difficult. But in today's apps, you'll encounter native queries in the code less often. Nowadays, many apps use frameworks such as Hibernate (the most-used Java Persistence API [JPA] implementation) or Java Object Oriented Querying (JOOQ), and the native queries are not directly in the code. (You can find more details about JOOQ on their GitHub repository here: https://github.com/jOOQ/jOOQ). If you'd like to explore the Java persistence layer in more depth using mainstream technologies, I also recommend *Java Persistence with Spring and Hibernate* by Cătălin Tudose (Manning, 2023).

Listing 6.4   A repository using native SQL queries

```
@Repository
public class ProductRepository {

  private final JdbcTemplate jdbcTemplate;

  public ProductRepository(JdbcTemplate jdbcTemplate) {
    this.jdbcTemplate = jdbcTemplate;
  }

  public Product findProduct(int id) {
    String sql = "SELECT * FROM product WHERE id = ?";
    return jdbcTemplate.queryForObject(sql, new ProductRowMapper(), id);
  }
}
```

A native SQL query the app sends to the DBMS

6.3.2   *Using the profiler to get the SQL queries generated by a framework*

Let's look at something even more extraordinary. To further prove the usefulness of a profiler in investigating SQL queries, let's review project da-ch6-ex3. From an algorithm point of view, this project does the same thing as the previous one: it returns the name of the purchased products. I intentionally kept the same logic to simplify the example and make it comparable.

The next code fragment shows the definition of a Spring Data JPA repository. The repository is a simple interface, and you don't see the SQL queries anywhere. With Spring Data JPA, the app generates the queries behind the scenes based on either the method's names or on a particular way of defining the queries, called Java Persistence Query Language (JPQL), which is based on the app's objects. Either way, there's no simple way to copy and paste the query from the code.

Some frameworks generate the SQL queries behind the scenes based on the code and configurations you write. In these cases, it's more challenging to get the executed queries. But a profiler can help you by extracting them from the JDBC driver before they are sent to the DBMS:

```
public interface ProductRepository
    extends JpaRepository<Product, Integer> {
}
```

The profiler comes to the rescue. Since the tool intercepts the queries before the app sends them to the DBMS, we can still use it to find exactly what queries the app uses. Start app da-ch6-ex3 and use VisualVM to profile the SQL queries the way we did for the previous two projects.

Figure 6.15 shows what the tool displays when profiling the /products endpoint call. The app sent two SQL queries. Notice that the aliases in the query have strange names because the queries are framework generated. Also notice that even if the logic in the service is the same and the app calls the repository method 10 times, the second query is executed only once because Hibernate optimizes the execution where it can. Now you can copy and investigate this query with a SQL development client if needed. In many cases, investigating a slow query requires running it in a SQL client to detect which part of the query causes difficulty for the DBMS.

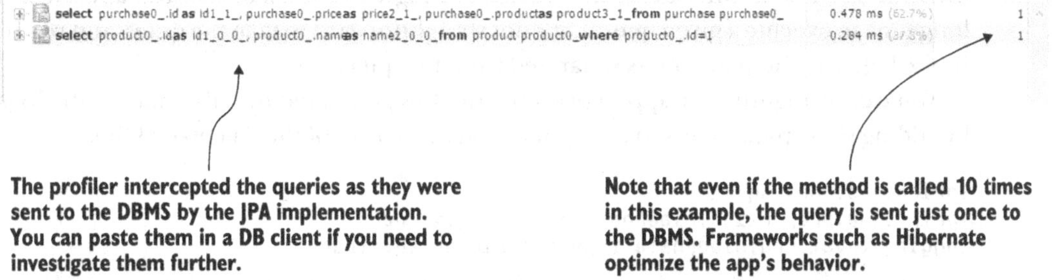

The profiler intercepted the queries as they were sent to the DBMS by the JPA implementation. You can paste them in a DB client if you need to investigate them further.

Note that even if the method is called 10 times in this example, the query is sent just once to the DBMS. Frameworks such as Hibernate optimize the app's behavior.

Figure 6.15 Even when working with a framework, the profiler can still intercept the SQL queries. This makes your investigation a lot easier because you can't copy the query directly from the code like when using JDBC and native queries.

The query is executed only once even though the method is called 10 times. Do persistence frameworks usually do these kinds of tricks? Although they are smart, sometimes, what they do behind the scenes can add complexity. Also, someone who does not properly understand the framework could write code that causes problems. This is another reason to use a profiler to check the queries the framework generates and ensure the app does what you expect.

The problems I mostly encounter with frameworks that require investigation are

- *Slow queries causing latencies*—Easy to spot using a profiler to examine the execution time
- *Multiple unneeded queries generated by the framework (usually caused by what developers call the N + 1 query problem)*—Easy to spot using a profiler to determine the number of executions of a query
- *Long transaction commits generated by poor app design*—Easy to spot using CPU profiling

When a framework needs data from multiple tables, it usually knows to compose one query and get all the data in one call. However, if you don't use the framework correctly, it may take just part of the data with an initial query and then, for each record initially retrieved, run a separate query. So, instead of running just one query, the framework will send an initial query plus *N* others (one for each of the *N* records retrieved by the first); we call this an *N + 1 query problem*, which usually creates significant latency by executing many queries instead of just one.

Most developers are tempted to investigate such problems using logs or a debugger. But in my experience, neither one is the best option for identifying the problem's root cause.

The first problem with using logs for this type of case is that it's challenging to identify which query causes a problem. In real-world scenarios, the app may send dozens of queries—some of these multiple times, and in most cases, they are long and use a large number of parameters. With a profiler, which displays all the queries in a list with their execution time and the number of executions, you can almost instantaneously spot the problem. The second problem is that, even if you identify the potential query causing the undesired behavior (say, while monitoring logs, you observe that the app takes a long time to execute a given query), it's not straightforward to take the query and run it. In the log, you find parameters separated from the query.

You can configure your app to print the queries generated by Hibernate in the logs by adding some parameters to the application properties of the da-ch6-ex3 file:

```
spring.jpa.show-sql=true
spring.jpa.properties.hibernate.format_sql=true
logging.level.org.hibernate.type.descriptor.sql=trace
```

Beware that you'll have to configure the logging differently, depending on the technologies used to implement the app. In the example provided with the book, we use Spring Boot and Hibernate. The next listing shows how the app prints the query in the logs.

Listing 6.5   Logs showing the native queries Hibernate sends

```
Hibernate:
    Select
        product0_.id as id1_0_0_,          ◄────────  The query generated by the app
        product0_.name as name2_0_0_
    from
        product product0_
    where
        product0_.id=?                                          The first parameter's value

2021-10-16 13:57:26.566 TRACE 9512 --- [nio-8080-exec-2]
o.h.type.descriptor.sql.BasicBinder      : binding parameter [1] as
[INTEGER] - [1]
2021-10-16 13:57:26.568 TRACE 9512 --- [nio-8080-exec-2]
o.h.type.descriptor.sql.BasicExtractor   : extracted value ([name2_0_0_] :
[VARCHAR]) - [Chocolate]

                                                            The second parameter's value
```

The logs show us the query and give us both the query's input and output. But you need to bind the parameter values to the query to run it separately. And when multiple queries are logged, looking for what you need can be really frustrating. Logs also don't show which part of the app runs the query, making your investigation even more challenging.

> I recommend always starting with a profiler when investigating latency issues. Your first step should be sampling. When you suspect SQL query-related problems, continue profiling for JDBC. Then, problems will be easy understand, and you can use a debugger or the logs to confirm your speculations as needed.

If you ever find yourself staring at logs with queries you don't fully understand, turning to AI can be a game changer. An AI assistant can help you refactor the query into a more readable format and bind the necessary parameters seamlessly (figure 6.16). Additionally, you can use AI to generate alternative queries with different parameter values, which can be particularly useful for testing or exploring various scenarios.

6.3.3   *Using the profiler to get programmatically generated SQL queries*

To better understand how a profiler works, let's look at another example—this time involving queries created by the application itself, using code. In this example, we investigate a performance problem caused by a query that Hibernate generates behind the scenes.

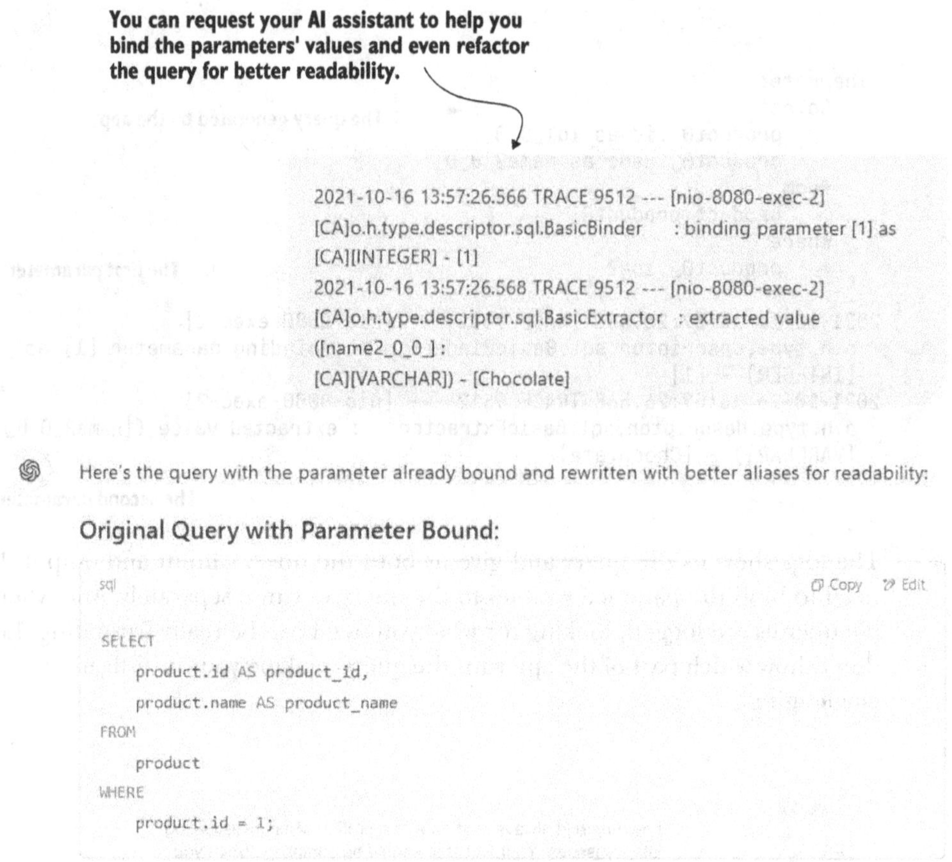

You can request your AI assistant to help you bind the parameters' values and even refactor the query for better readability.

```
2021-10-16 13:57:26.566 TRACE 9512 --- [nio-8080-exec-2]
[CA]o.h.type.descriptor.sql.BasicBinder    : binding parameter [1] as
[CA][INTEGER] - [1]
2021-10-16 13:57:26.568 TRACE 9512 --- [nio-8080-exec-2]
[CA]o.h.type.descriptor.sql.BasicExtractor  : extracted value
([name2_0_0_]:
[CA][VARCHAR]) - [Chocolate]
```

Here's the query with the parameter already bound and rewritten with better aliases for readability:

Original Query with Parameter Bound:

sql   *Copy* *Edit*

```sql
SELECT
    product.id AS product_id,
    product.name AS product_name
FROM
    product
WHERE
    product.id = 1;
```

Figure 6.16   An AI assistant can be a powerful tool for extracting and refactoring data from logs. In this example, I used ChatGPT to transform a partial or complex query into a complete, well-structured, and more readable version, making troubleshooting and analysis much easier.

The app doesn't use plain SQL or JPQL (Java Persistence Query Language) to write its queries directly. Instead, it uses something called criteria queries, which is a more programmatic way to define what data the app wants from the database, using Java code instead of writing the query as a string. The benefit is type safety and flexibility, but it also makes it harder to see what the actual SQL looks like. That's why a profiler is so helpful—it can reveal the real SQL being executed and help you understand where the performance problem is coming from.

As shown in listing 6.6, which presents the `ProductRepository` class reimplemented with a criteria query, this approach is more verbose. It's usually considered more difficult and leaves more room for mistakes. The implementation in project da-ch6-ex4 contains a mistake, which can cause significant performance problems in real-world apps. Let's see if we can find this problem and determine how the profiler can help us understand what's wrong.

Listing 6.6   The repository defined with a criteria query

```java
public class ProductRepository {

  private final EntityManager entityManager;

  public ProductRepository(EntityManager entityManager) {
    this.entityManager = entityManager;
  }

  public Product findById(int id) {
    CriteriaBuilder cb = entityManager.getCriteriaBuilder();
    CriteriaQuery<Product> cq = cb.createQuery(Product.class);

    Root<Product> product = cq.from(Product.class);
    cq.select(product);

    Predicate idPredicate =
      cb.equal(cq.from(Product.class).get("id"), id);
    cq.where(idPredicate);

    TypedQuery<Product> query = entityManager.createQuery(cq);
    return query.getSingleResult();
  }
}
```

Specifies that the query selects products

Creates a new query

Selects the products

Defines the condition that becomes part of the where clause on the next line

Defines the where clause

Runs the query and extracts the result

We use JDBC profiling to intercept the queries the app sends to the DBMS. You can see that it contains a cross join between the product table and itself (figure 6.17). This is a huge problem! With the 10 records in our table, we don't observe anything suspicious here. But in a real-world app, where the table would have more records, this cross join would create huge latencies and eventually even wrong output (duplicated rows). Simply intercepting the query with VisualVM and reading it points to the problem.

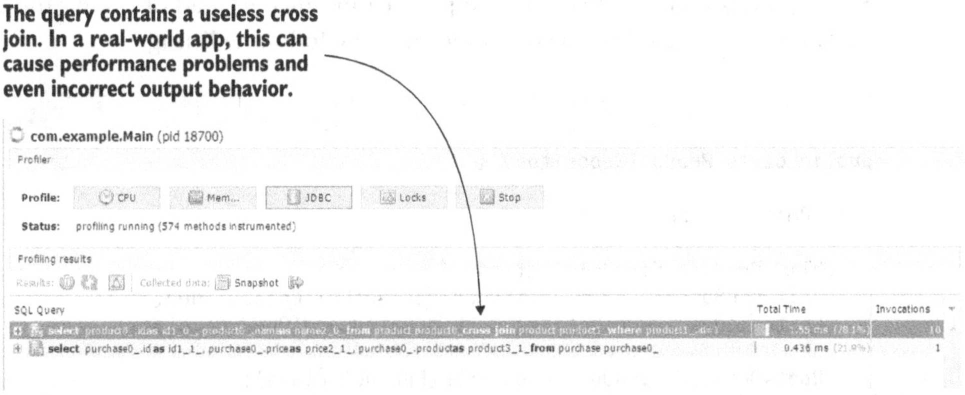

The query contains a useless cross join. In a real-world app, this can cause performance problems and even incorrect output behavior.

Figure 6.17   The profiler can intercept any SQL query sent to the DBMS through the JDBC driver. Here, we spot a problem in the generated query—an unneeded cross join that causes performance problems.

The next question is, "Why did the app generate the query this way?" I like the statement about JPA implementations, such as Hibernate: "The excellent thing is that they make the query generation transparent and minimize work. The bad thing is that they make the query generation transparent, making the app more prone to errors." When working with such frameworks. I generally recommend that developers profile the queries as part of the development process to discover such problems up front. Using a profiler is more for auditing purposes than finding problems, but doing so is a good safety measure.

In the following example, I intentionally introduced this tiny error with a significant effect. I called the from() method twice, instructing Hibernate to make a cross join.

Listing 6.7   The cause of the cross-join problem

```
public class ProductRepository {

  // Omitted code

  public Product findById(int id) {
    CriteriaBuilder cb = entityManager.getCriteriaBuilder();
    CriteriaQuery<Product> cq = cb.createQuery(Product.class);

    Root<Product> product = cq.from(Product.class);     ◄─┐  Calls the CriteriaQuery
    cq.select(product);                                    │  from() method once

    Predicate idPredicate = cb.equal(
      cq.from(Product.class).get("id"), id);     ◄──┐  Calls the CriteriaQuery
    cq.where(idPredicate);                          │  from() method again

    TypedQuery<Product> query = entityManager.createQuery(cq);
    return query.getSingleResult();
  }
}
```

Solving this problem is easy: use the product instance instead of calling the Criteria -Query from() method the second time, as in the following listing.

Listing 6.8   Correcting the cross-join problem

```
public class ProductRepository {

  // Omitted code

  public Product findById(int id) {
    CriteriaBuilder cb = entityManager.getCriteriaBuilder();
    CriteriaQuery<Product> cq = cb.createQuery(Product.class);

    Root<Product> product = cq.from(Product.class);
    cq.select(product);                                    Uses the
                                                           already existing
    Predicate idPredicate = cb.equal(product.get("id"), id);  ◄─┘ Root object
```

```
    cq.where(idPredicate);

    TypedQuery<Product> query = entityManager.createQuery(cq);
    return query.getSingleResult();
  }
}
```

Once you make this small change, the generated SQL query will no longer contain the unneeded cross join (figure 6.18). Still, the app runs the same query multiple times, which is not optimal. The algorithm the app runs should be refactored to get the data, preferably using only one query, same as we did earlier for the example in listing 6.3.

Figure 6.18 By eliminating the supplementary `select()` method call, the cross join disappeared. However, the overall algorithm for this app should be revised, since it still runs the same query multiple times, which is not optimal.

Summary

- A profiler intercepts the app's execution and provides essential details about the code in execution, such as the execution stack trace for each thread, how long it takes for each method to execute, and how many times a certain method was called.
- When investigating latency problems, the first step to using a profiler is *sampling*, which is a way for the profiler to intercept the executing code without getting many details. Sampling is less resource consuming and allows seeing the big picture of execution.

- Sampling provides you with three essential details:
  - *What code executes*—When investigating a problem, you sometimes don't know what part of the code executes, and you can find this aspect by sampling.
  - *Total execution time of every method*—This detail helps identify what part of the code causes potential latency problems.
  - *Total CPU execution time*—This detail helps you identify whether your code spends the execution time working or waiting for something.
- Sometimes, sampling is enough to understand where a problem comes from. But in many cases, you need more details. You can get these details by profiling the execution.
- *Profiling* is a resource-consuming process. With a real-world app, it's almost always impossible to profile the whole codebase. For this reason, when profiling for details, you should filter specific packages and classes on which you want to focus your investigation. You can usually determine what part of the app to focus on by sampling the execution first.
- An essential detail you get by profiling is the number of method invocations. When sampling, you know the total time a method spends executing, but not how often it was called. This aspect is important for identifying a method that is slow or wrongly used.
- You can also use a profiler to get SQL queries the app sends to a DBMS. The profiler intercepts every query, regardless of the technology used to implement the app's persistence layer. This feature is invaluable when investigating slow queries for apps that use frameworks (such as Hibernate) to work with a database.

Investigating locks
in multithreaded
architecture

This chapter covers

- Monitoring an application's threads
- Identifying thread locks and what causes them
- Analyzing threads that are waiting

In this chapter, we dive into the wild world of multithreaded architectures. If you've ever felt like threading is one of the trickiest parts of development, you're not alone. Even the best developers sometimes stare at their code, wondering why their threads behave like unsupervised toddlers. And just when you think you've got it working, making code performant is an entirely new level of pain.

But don't worry! The techniques discussed in this chapter will give you much-needed visibility into the execution of multithreaded apps, helping you pinpoint problems before they become production nightmares.

To get the most out of this chapter, you need a solid grasp of Java's threading basics—things such as thread states and synchronization. If you need a refresher, head over to appendix D. It won't make you a concurrency guru overnight (that would require an entire bookshelf, plus some meditation), but it'll arm you with enough knowledge to tackle the troubleshooting ahead.

7.1 *Monitoring threads for locks*

This section discusses thread locks and how to analyze them to find eventual problems or opportunities to optimize an app's execution. *Thread locks* are caused by different thread synchronization approaches, usually implemented to control the flow of events in a multithreaded architecture. Examples include

- A thread wants to prevent other threads from accessing a resource while it's changing it.
- A thread needs to wait for another thread to finish or reach a certain point in its execution before being able to continue its work.

> **DEFINITION**   A *thread lock* is a mechanism that prevents multiple threads from accessing the same resource simultaneously. It helps avoid conflicts but can also cause problems if threads get stuck waiting for each other.

Thread locks are necessary; they help an app control threads. But implementing thread synchronization leaves a lot of room for mistakes. Wrongly implemented locks may cause app freezes or performance problems. We need to use profiling tools to ensure our implementations are optimal and to make an app more efficient by minimizing the lock time.

In this section, we use a small application (project da-ch7-ex1) that implements a simple multithreaded architecture. We also use a profiler to analyze the locks during the app's execution. We want to find out if the threads are locked and how they behave:

- Which thread locks another
- How many times a thread is locked
- The time at which a thread pauses instead of executing

These details help us understand whether the app execution is optimal and whether there are ways we can improve our app's execution. The app we use for our example implements two threads that run concurrently: the producer and the consumer. The producer generates random values and adds them to a list instance, and the consumer removes values from the same collection used by the producer (figure 7.1).

Let's follow the app implementation in listings 7.1, 7.2, and 7.3 to see what to expect when investigating the execution. In listing 7.1, you find the Main class, which starts the two thread instances. I made the

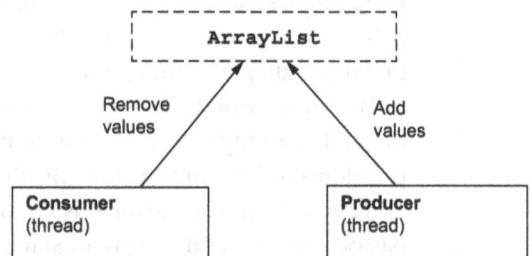

Figure 7.1   The app starts two threads that we refer to as "the producer" and "the consumer." Both threads use a common resource: they change a list instance of type ArrayList. The producer generates random values and adds them to the list, while the consumer concurrently removes the values added by the producer.

app wait 10 seconds before starting the threads to allow us some time to start the profiler and observe the entire threads' timelines. The app names the threads _Producer and _Consumer so we can easily identify them when working with the profiler.

Listing 7.1 App's Main method that starts two threads

```
public class Main {

  private static Logger log = Logger.getLogger(Main.class.getName());

  public static List<Integer> list = new ArrayList<>();

  public static void main(String[] args) {
    try {
      Thread.sleep(10000);               ◄─── Waits 10 seconds, in the beginning, to
                                              let the programmer start the profiling
      new Producer("_Producer").start();  ◄───┐  Starts a producer thread
      new Consumer("_Consumer").start();  ◄───┘
    } catch (InterruptedException e) {       Starts a consumer thread
      log.severe(e.getMessage());
    }
  }
}
```

Listing 7.2 shows the consumer thread's implementation. The thread iterates over a block of code one million times (this number should be enough for the app to run a few seconds and allow us to use the profiler to take some statistics). During every iteration, the thread uses a static list instance declared in the Main class. The consumer thread checks whether the list has values and removes the first value on the list. The whole block of code implementing the logic is synchronized, using the list instance itself as a monitor. The monitor won't allow multiple threads to enter simultaneously in the synchronized blocks it protects.

Listing 7.2 The consumer thread's definition

```
public class Consumer extends Thread {

  private Logger log = Logger.getLogger(Consumer.class.getName());

  public Consumer(String name) {
    super(name);                                   Iterates one million times over the
  }                                                consumer's synchronized block of code

  @Override                                        Synchronizes the block of code
  public void run() {                              using the static list defined in
    for (int i = 0; i < 1_000_000; i++) {  ◄────   the Main class as a monitor

                                                   Tries to consume a value
      synchronized (Main.list) {           ◄────   only if the list is not empty
        if (Main.list.size() > 0) {        ◄────
          int x = Main.list.get(0);          Consumes the first value in
          Main.list.remove(0);               the list and removes that value
```

```
        log.info("Consumer " +
              Thread.currentThread().getName() +        ◄─────┐  Logs the removed value
              " removed value " + x);
      }
    }


  }
  }
}
```

Listing 7.3 presents the producer's thread implementation, which is pretty similar to the consumer's. The producer also iterates one million times over a block of code. For each iteration, the producer generates a random value and adds it to a list statically declared in the Main class. This list is the same one from which the consumer removes the values. The producer adds new values only if the list is shorter than 100.

Listing 7.3 The producer thread's definition

```
public class Producer extends Thread {

  private Logger log = Logger.getLogger(Producer.class.getName());

  public Producer(String name) {                       Iterates one million times over the
    super(name);                                        producer's synchronized block of code
  }

                                                        Synchronizes the block of code
  @Override                                             using the static list defined in
  public void run() {                                   the Main class as a monitor
    Random r = new Random();
    for (int i = 0; i < 1_000_000; i++) {     ◄──────┐  Adds a value only if the list
      synchronized (Main.list) {              ◄────┐    has under 100 elements
        if (Main.list.size() < 100) {         ◄──┐
          int x = r.nextInt();                    Generates a new random
          Main.list.add(x);                       value and adds it to the list
          log.info("Producer " +
                Thread.currentThread().getName() +  ◄──────
                " added value " + x);                        Logs the value
        }                                                    added to the list
      }
    }
  }
}
```

The producer's logic is also synchronized using the list as a monitor. This way, only one of the threads—the producer or the consumer—can change this list at a time. The monitor (the list instance) allows one of the threads to enter its logic, keeping the other thread waiting at the beginning of its block of code until the other thread finishes the execution of the synchronized block (figure 7.2).

Can we find this app's behavior and other execution details using a profiler? Absolutely! Unless you prefer the ancient art of staring at code until the bugs reveal

Producer
(thread)

```
@Override
public void run() {
  Random r = new Random();
  for (int i = 0; i < 1_000_000; i++) {

    synchronized (Main.list) {
      if (Main.list.size() < 100) {
        int x = r.nextInt();
        Main.list.add(x);
        log.info("Producer " +
            Thread.currentThread().getName() +
            " added value " + x);
      }
    }

  }
}
```

Consumer
(thread)

```
@Override
public void run() {
  for (int i = 0; i < 1_000_000; i++) {

    synchronized (Main.list) {
      if (Main.list.size() > 0) {
        int x = Main.list.get(0);
        Main.list.remove(0);
        log.info("Consumer " +
            Thread.currentThread().getName() +
            " removed value " + x);
      }
    }

  }
}
```

While the producer executes the synchronized block (shaded rectangle), the consumer cannot access its synchronized block. The consumer waits for the monitor (list) to allow it to enter its synchronized block.

Figure 7.2 Only one thread at a time can be in the synchronized block. Either the producer executes the logic defined in its run() method or the consumer executes its logic.

themselves out of sheer pity. In a real-world app, things are rarely simple. Threads weave and tangle like holiday lights stuffed in a box, and reading the code alone won't always tell you what's really going on. That's where a profiler comes in.

Remember that the projects we use in this book are simplified and tailored to the purpose of our discussion. Don't take them as best practices and apply them as-is in real-world apps.

Let's use VisualVM to see what this process looks like in the Threads monitoring tab (figure 7.3). Notice that the colors (shading) alternate since most of the code for each thread is synchronized. In most cases, either the producer is running and the consumer waits, or the consumer is running and the producer waits.

These two threads may rarely execute code simultaneously. Since there are instructions outside the synchronized block, the two threads can run simultaneously to execute the code. An example of such code is the for loop, which is defined outside the synchronized block in both cases.

You can see the two threads (consumer and producer) executing on the timeline.

The timelines show alternate colors to indicate when the thread is running and when it's waiting.

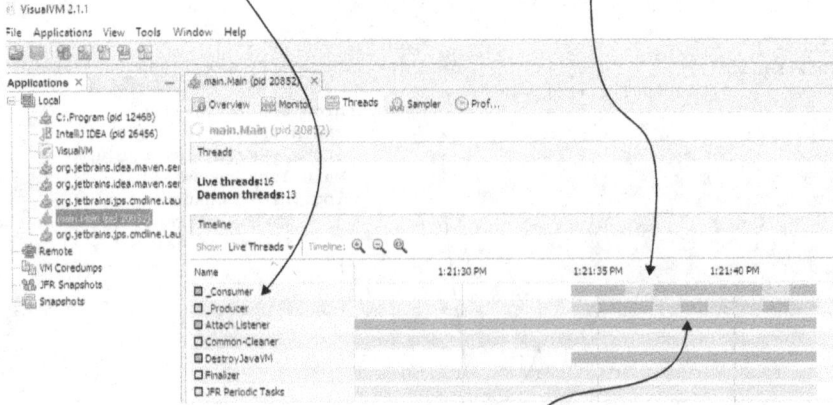

Note that sometimes the threads run concurrently. They can run at the same time when they execute instructions that are outside the synchronized blocks.

Figure 7.3   In most cases, the threads will sequentially lock each other and execute their synchronized blocks of code. The two threads can still concurrently execute the instructions, which are outside the synchronized block.

A thread can be blocked by a synchronized block of code, it can be waiting for another thread to finish its execution (joining), or it can be controlled by a blocking object. In cases where the thread is blocked and it can't continue its execution, we say the thread is *locked*. Figure 7.4 shows the same information presented in JProfiler, which works with the approaches we used.

The executing threads are displayed on a timeline with alternate colors to mark when they are running and when they are blocked.

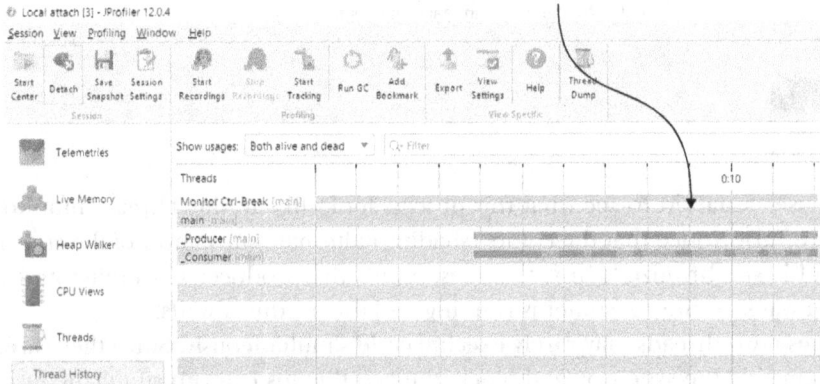

Figure 7.4   You can use other profilers instead of VisualVM. Here, you can see the way thread timelines are displayed in JProfiler.

7.2 Analyzing thread locks

When working with an app architecture that uses thread locks, we want to ensure that the app is optimally implemented. For that, we need a way to identify the locks to find how many times threads are blocked and the length of the lock time. We also need to understand what causes a thread to wait in given scenarios. Can we collect all this information somehow? Yes, a profiler can tell us everything we need to know about the thread's behavior.

We'll continue using the same steps you learned in chapter 6 for profiling investigations:

1 Use sampling to understand what happens during execution at a high level and identify where to go into further detail.

2 Use profiling (instrumentation) to get the details on a specific subject we want to investigate.

Figure 7.5 shows the results of sampling the app's execution. When looking at the execution times, we observe that the total execution time is longer than the total CPU time. In chapter 6, you saw a similar situation, and we figured out that when this happens, it means the app waits for something.

For both threads, the total CPU time is much smaller than the total execution time. This indicates that the method was waiting for something.

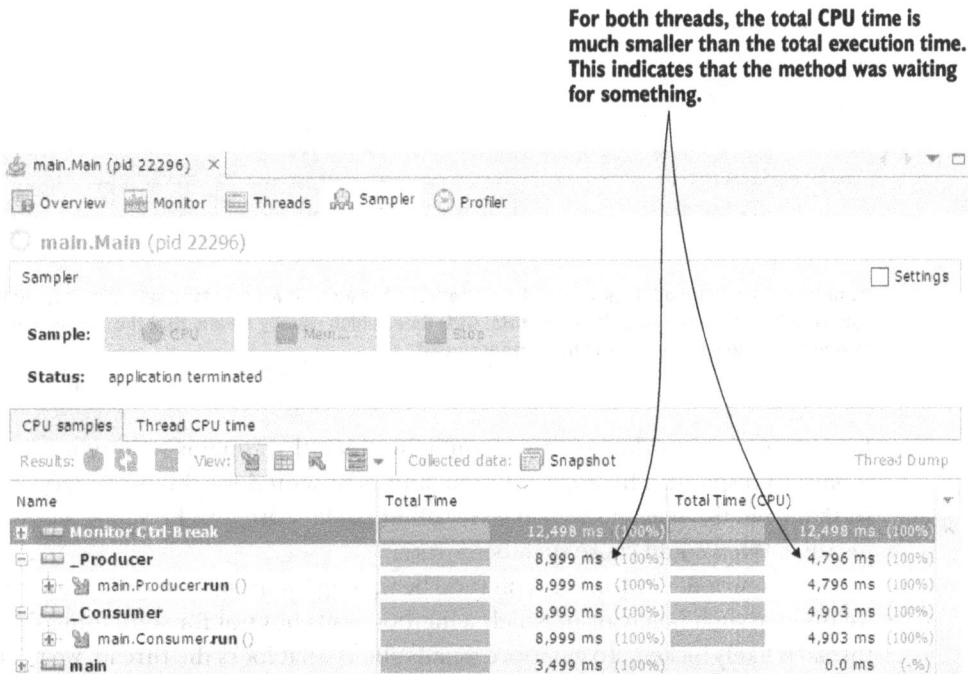

Figure 7.5 When the total CPU time is shorter than the total execution time, it means the app is waiting for something. We want to figure out what the app waits for and if this time can be optimized.

Figure 7.6 shows something interesting: the method waits, but as shown in the sampling data, it doesn't wait for something else. It simply seems to wait on itself. The row marked as "Self time" tells us how much time it took the method to execute. Notice that the method spent only about 700 ms CPU time as self time but a much larger value of 4903 ms as total execution self time.

> Note that the method doesn't wait for something external. Its self-execution time is very long, even though the CPU time is short.

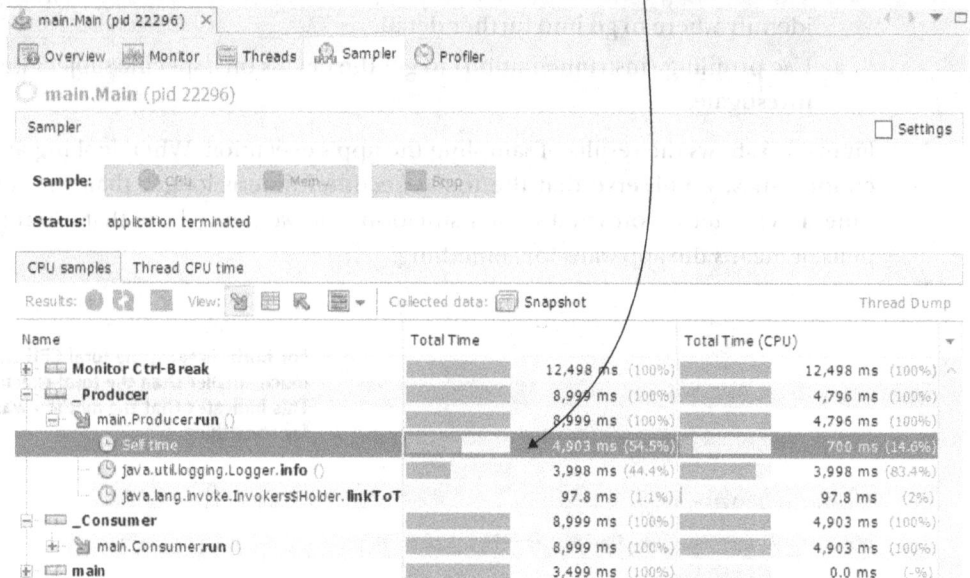

Figure 7.6   The method doesn't wait for something, but instead it waits for itself. We observe that its self-execution time is longer than the total CPU time, which usually means that the thread is locked. The thread could have been blocked by another thread.

In chapter 6, we worked on an example in which the app was waiting for an external service to respond. The app sent a call and then waited for the other service to reply. In that case, the reason the app was waiting made sense, but here, the situation looks peculiar. What could cause such behavior?

You may wonder, "How can a method be waiting for itself? Is it too lazy to run?" When we observe such behavior in which a method waits but not for something external, its thread is likely locked. To get more details about what locks the thread, we need to analyze the method further by profiling the execution.

Sampling didn't answer all our questions. We can see the methods are waiting, but we don't know what they are waiting for. We need to continue with profiling (instrumentation) to get more information. In VisualVM, we use the Profiler tab to start lock monitoring. To start profiling for locks, use the Locks button, as presented in figure 7.7, which shows the profiling result. The button appears disabled in the figure because the process was already stopped at the end of the profiling session.

To start profiling for data about locks, use the Locks button. Once the session ends, the button becomes disabled.

We can see that the threads have been blocked a large number of times. Each thread indicates over 3,600 locks during the execution.

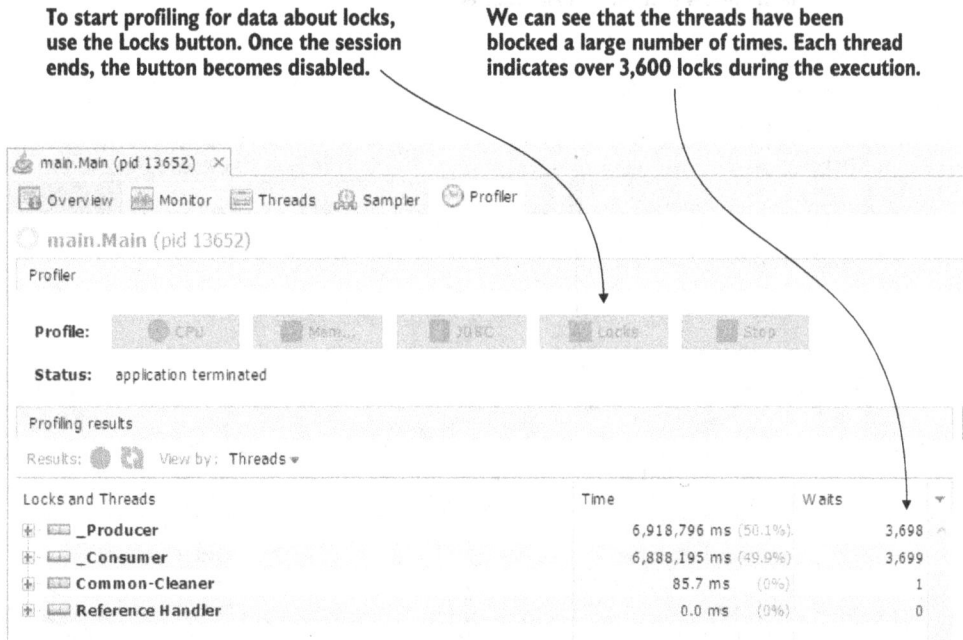

Figure 7.7 To start profiling for locks, use the Locks button in the Profiler tab. At the end of the profiling session, we observe more than 3,600 locks on each of our producer and consumer threads.

For each thread, we can go into detail by selecting the small plus sign (+) to the left of the thread name. Now, you can get details about each monitor object that affected the thread's execution. The profiler shows details about the threads blocked by another thread as well as what blocked the thread.

These details are shown in figure 7.8. We see that the producer thread was blocked by a monitor instance of type ArrayList. The object reference (4476199c in the figure) helps us uniquely identify the object instance to figure out whether the same monitor affected multiple threads. It also allows us to precisely identify the relationship between the threads and the monitor.

What we find in figure 7.8 can be read this way:

- A monitor instance blocked the thread named _Producer with reference 4476199c—an instance of type ArrayList.
- The _Consumer thread blocked the _Producer thread 3,698 times by acquiring the monitor 4476199c.

- The producer thread also held (owned) the monitor with reference 4476199c for 3,699 times, or the thread _Producer blocked the thread _Consumer 3,699 times.

Here, we find the objects (monitors) that caused the thread to be blocked as well as the monitors that the thread acquired.

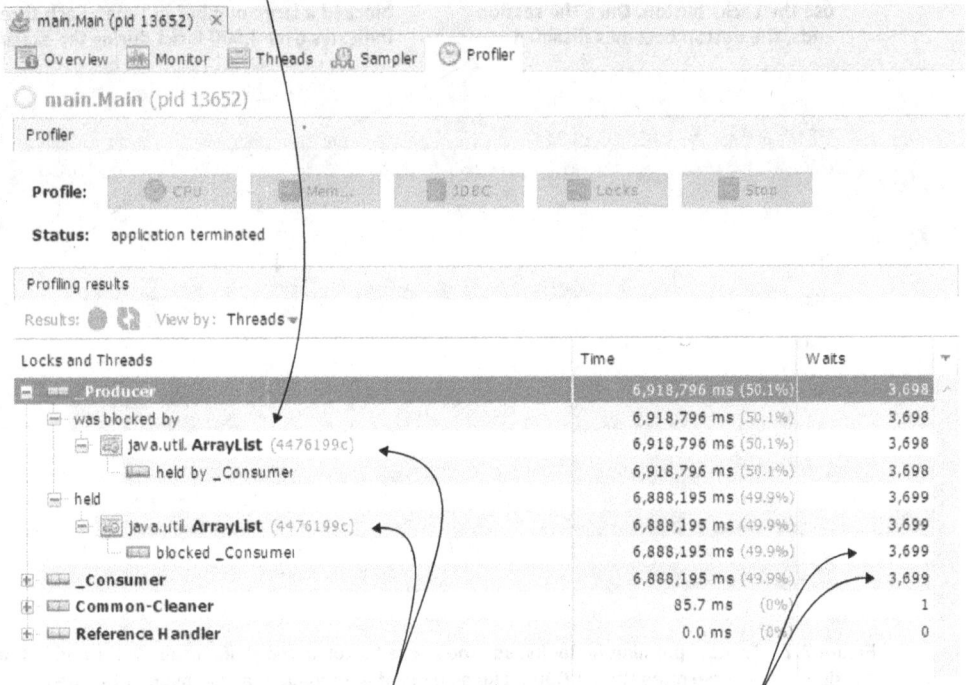

In this case, we see that the same object (an instance of type `ArrayList`) that blocked this thread was also held by it.

Note that the number of locks the producer caused for the consumer is equal to the total number of times the consumer was locked, meaning only the producer locks the consumer.

Figure 7.8   The profiling results give us a good understanding of what creates locks and what is affected by them. We see that there's only one monitor the producer thread works with. Also, the consumer thread blocked the producer thread 3,698 times using the monitor. Using the same monitor instance, the producer blocked the consumer for the same number of times: 3,698.

Figure 7.9 extends the perspective to the consumer thread. You find that all data correlates. Throughout the whole execution, only one monitor instance, an instance of type ArrayList, locks one of the threads or another. The consumer thread ends up being locked 3,699 times, while the producer thread executed a block synchronized by the ArrayList object. The producer thread is blocked 3,698 times, while the consumer thread executed a block synchronized with the ArrayList monitor.

Remember that you won't necessarily get the same numbers when you execute the app on your computer. In fact, it's very likely you won't, even when you repeat the execution on the same computer. Although you may get different values, overall, you can make similar observations.

Both threads (producer and consumer) held and were blocked by the same monitor. This shows that the threads alternately block each other.

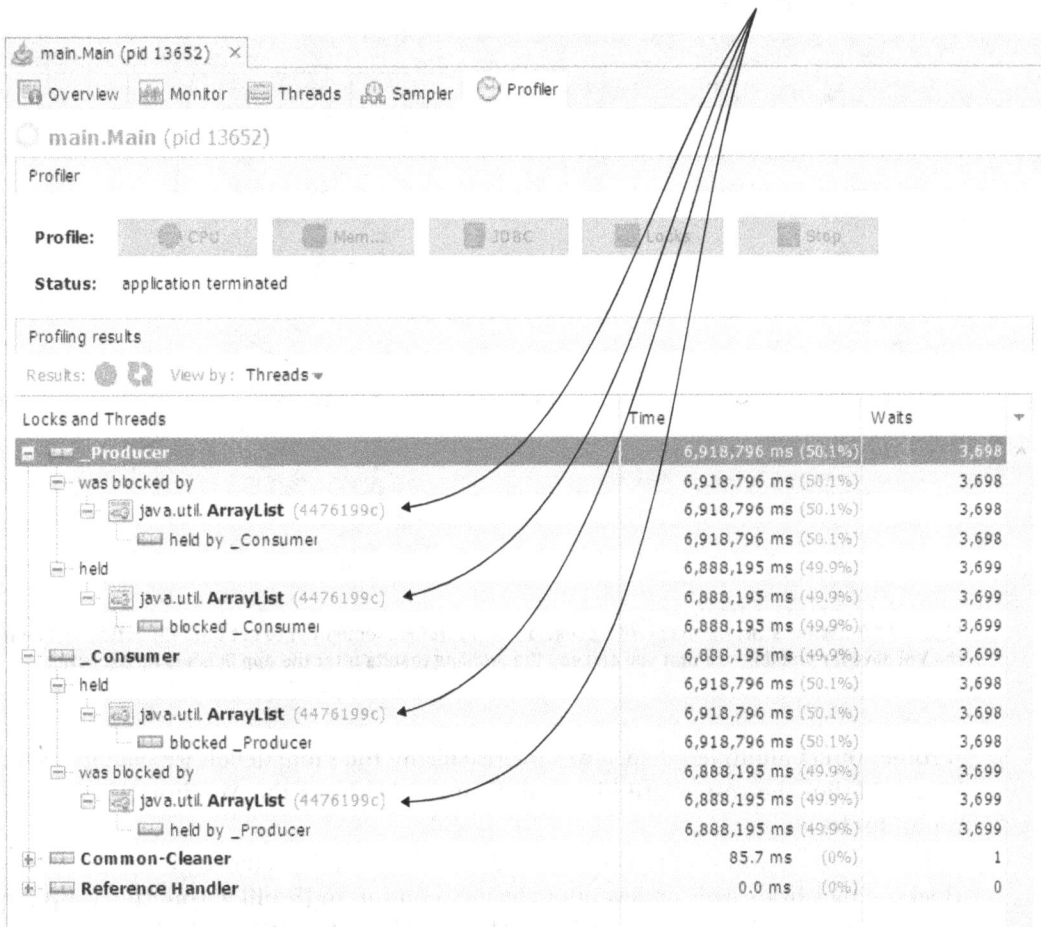

Locks and Threads	Time	Waits
▭ **_Producer**	6,918,796 ms (50.1%)	3,698
▭ was blocked by	6,918,796 ms (50.1%)	3,698
▭ java.util. **ArrayList** (4476199c)	6,918,796 ms (50.1%)	3,698
▭ held by _Consumer	6,918,796 ms (50.1%)	3,698
▭ held	6,888,195 ms (49.9%)	3,699
▭ java.util. **ArrayList** (4476199c)	6,888,195 ms (49.9%)	3,699
▭ blocked _Consumer	6,888,195 ms (49.9%)	3,699
▭ **_Consumer**	6,888,195 ms (49.9%)	3,699
▭ held	6,918,796 ms (50.1%)	3,698
▭ java.util. **ArrayList** (4476199c)	6,918,796 ms (50.1%)	3,698
▭ blocked _Producer	6,918,796 ms (50.1%)	3,698
▭ was blocked by	6,888,195 ms (49.9%)	3,699
▭ java.util. **ArrayList** (4476199c)	6,888,195 ms (49.9%)	3,699
▭ held by _Producer	6,888,195 ms (49.9%)	3,699
⊞ **Common-Cleaner**	85.7 ms (0%)	1
⊞ **Reference Handler**	0.0 ms (0%)	0

Figure 7.9   Both threads use the same monitor to block each other. While one thread executes the synchronized block with an `ArrayList` instance monitor, the other waits. This way, one thread is locked for 3,698 times and the other for 3,698.

For this demonstration, I used VisualVM because it's free and I'm comfortable with it. However, you can also apply this approach to other tools, such as JProfiler.

After attaching JProfiler to a process (as discussed in chapter 6), make sure you set the JVM exit action to Keep the VM Alive for Profiling, as presented in figure 7.10.

When you attach JProfiler to a process, configure the JVM exit action to keep the VM alive so that you can still see the statistics after the profiled app ends its execution.

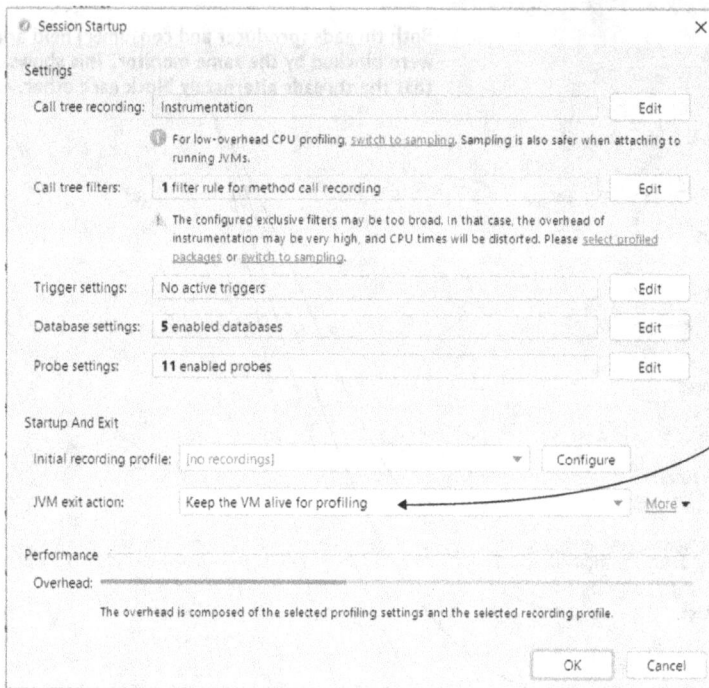

Figure 7.10   When starting the profiling session with JProfiler, remember to set the JVM action to "Keep the VM alive for profiling" so that you can see the profiling results after the app finishes its execution.

JProfiler offers multiple perspectives for visualizing the same details we obtained with VisualVM, but the results are identical. Figure 7.11 shows the Monitor History view report for locks.

In most cases, you don't need such a detailed report. I prefer to group the events (locks) either by threads or, less often, by the monitor. In JProfiler, you can group the events as presented in figure 7.12. From Monitor Usage Statistics in the left menu, you can choose to group the events either by threads involved or the monitors that caused the locks. JProfiler even has a more exotic option in which you can group the locks by the monitor objects' classes.

To access the lock history in JProfiler, select Monitor History under Monitors & Locks in the left menu.

JProfiler shows a complete history of the lock events: the lock duration, the monitor used, the thread that acquired the lock (owning thread), the thread that was blocked (waiting thread), and the exact time of the event.

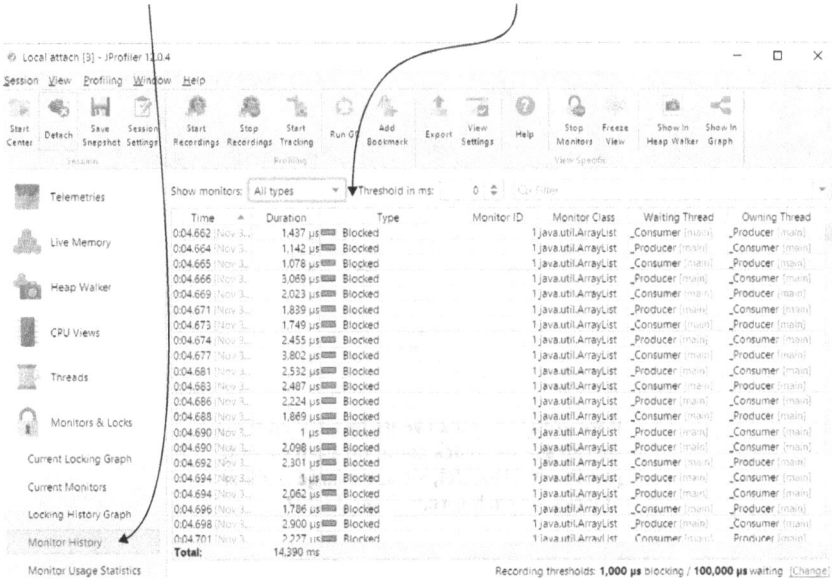

Figure 7.11 JProfiler shows a detailed history of all the locks the app's threads encountered. The tool displays the exact time of the event, the event duration, the monitor that caused the lock, and the threads involved.

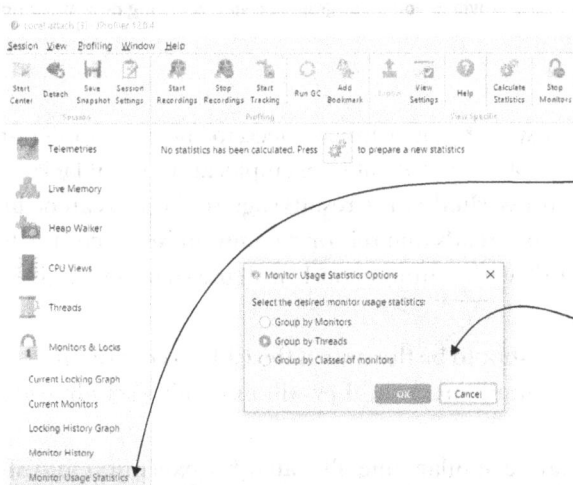

In JProfiler, you can use the Monitor Usage Statistics section to get information about locks grouped by affected threads or by the monitor that caused the lock.

To get statistics of all the intercepted lock events grouped by affected threads, select Group by Threads and then click OK.

Figure 7.12 You can group the lock events by threads involved or by monitors using the Monitor Usage Statistics section. You can use the aggregated view to understand which threads are more affected and what affects them or which monitor causes the threads to stop more often.

If you group the lock events by involved threads, you get a statistic similar to the one provided by VisualVM. Each thread is locked over 3,600 times during the app's execution (figure 7.13).

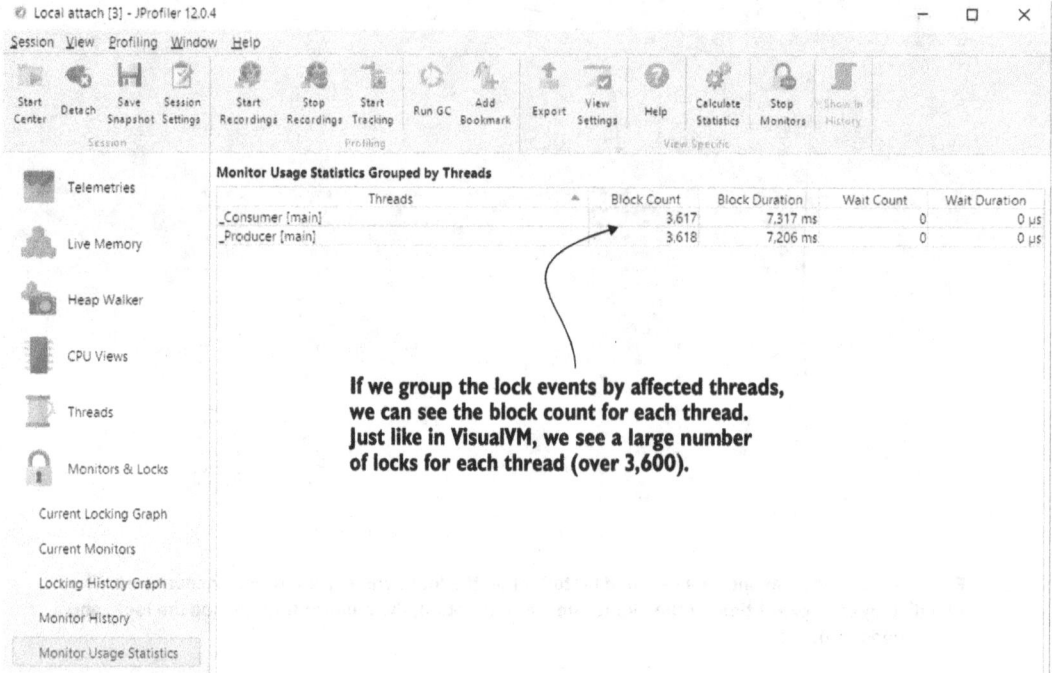

Figure 7.13   Grouping the lock events by threads provides you an aggregated view showing how many times each of the threads locked during its execution.

Is the execution optimal? To answer this question, we need to know the app's purpose. In our case, the app serves as a simple, demonstrative example, and since it lacks a real purpose, it's challenging to fully assess whether the results suggest the app can be improved.

But because the app uses two threads that rely on a common resource (the list), if we consider the fact that they can't work simultaneously with the shared resource, then we expect the following:

- The total execution time should be the sum of the CPU execution times (because the threads can't work simultaneously, they will mutually exclude each other), approximately.
- The threads should have a similar time allocated for execution and should be locked approximately the same number of times. If one of the threads is preferred, the other can end up in *starvation*—the situation in which a thread is blocked in an unfair way and doesn't get to execute.

If you look again at the thread analysis, you can see that the two threads are fairly treated. They indeed get locked a similar number of times, and they mutually exclude each other but have a similar active (CPU time) execution. This is optimal, and there's not much we can do to enhance it. But remember that it depends on what the app does and our expectations about how should it execute.

Here's an example of a different scenario in which the app would not necessarily be considered optimal. Suppose that you had an app that was processing values. Say that the producer needed more time to add each value to the list than the consumer needed to process the value afterward. In a real-world app, something like this can happen: the threads don't need to have equivalent difficult "work" to do.

In such a case, you can enhance the app:

- Minimize the number of locks for the consumer and make it wait to allow the producer work more.
- Define more producer threads or make the consumer thread read and process the values in batches (multiple at a time).

Everything depends on what the app does, but understanding what you can do to make it better starts with analyzing the execution. Because you never have one approach you can apply to all apps, I always recommend developers use a profiler and analyze the changes in app execution when they implement a multithreaded app.

Remember that in chapter 6, we also discussed about exporting the results of your profiling to ask help from your favorite AI assistant. You can do the same here to get some ideas of what's going on, especially if you find yourself investigating large numbers of details. This app we use in the current chapter is just a small example and may not seem complex to understand. I designed it this way to ensure we have a smooth discussion over the topics you learn about in this chapter. But real-world apps are more like a jungle. Thus, having some AI-powered tool helping with deciphering what's going on might save you time.

Remember back in chapter 6 when we talked about exporting your profiling results to get a second opinion from your favorite AI assistant? Well, guess what? You can do the same here! If you ever find yourself drowning in a sea of cryptic logs and spaghetti-like stack traces, handing some of that mess over to an AI might just save your sanity.

That's where AI-powered tools can come in handy. They act like a digital machete, helping you cut through chaos and make sense of what's happening. So, don't hesitate to get some machine-assisted wisdom. It might just save you from hours of debugging despair!

7.3 Analyzing waiting threads

In this section, we analyze threads that are waiting to be notified. Waiting threads are different than locked threads. A monitor locks a thread for the execution of a synchronized block of code. In this case, we don't expect the monitor to execute a specific action to tell the blocked thread to continue its execution. However, a monitor can cause the thread to wait for an indefinite amount of time and later decide when to allow the thread to continue its execution. Once a monitor makes a thread wait, the thread will return to execution only after being notified by the same monitor. The ability to make a thread wait until being notified provides great flexibility in controlling threads, but it can also cause problems when not used correctly.

To visualize the difference between locked and waiting threads, take a look at figure 7.14. Imagine the synchronized block is a restricted area managed by a police officer. The threads are cars. The police officer allows just one car to run at a time in the restricted area (the synchronized block). So, we say the cars that are unable to move are *locked*. The police officer can also manage the cars running in the restricted area. The police officer can order a car running inside this area to wait until they are explicitly ordered to continue; we say they are *waiting*.

These threads are in a blocked state. They cannot continue execution while another thread is running inside the synchronized block. We say they are locked.

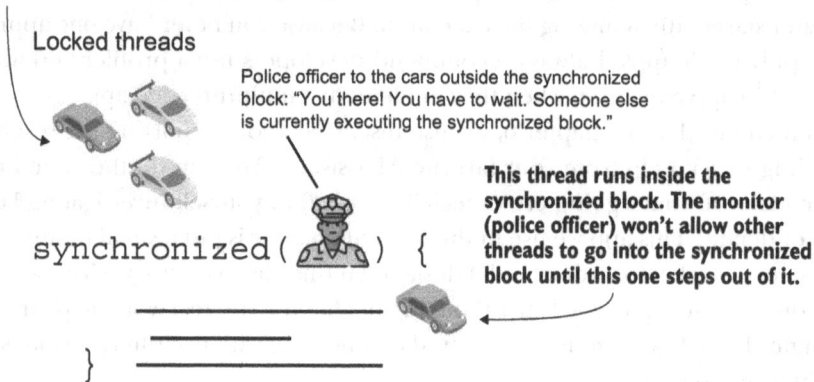

Locked threads

Police officer to the cars outside the synchronized block: "You there! You have to wait. Someone else is currently executing the synchronized block."

This thread runs inside the synchronized block. The monitor (police officer) won't allow other threads to go into the synchronized block until this one steps out of it.

```
synchronized(      ) {

}
```

Waiting threads

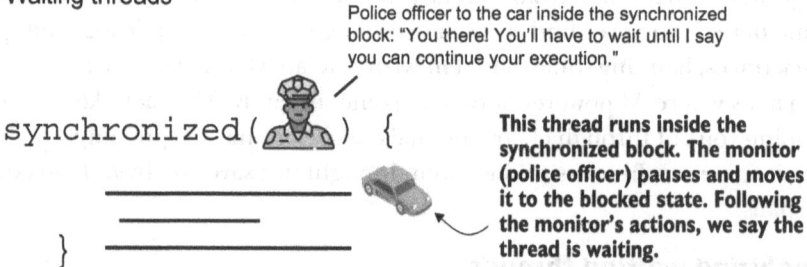

Police officer to the car inside the synchronized block: "You there! You'll have to wait until I say you can continue your execution."

This thread runs inside the synchronized block. The monitor (police officer) pauses and moves it to the blocked state. Following the monitor's actions, we say the thread is waiting.

```
synchronized(      ) {

}
```

Figure 7.14 Locked versus waiting threads. A locked thread is blocked at the entrance of a synchronized block. The monitor won't allow a thread to enter a synchronized block while another thread actively runs inside the block. A waiting thread is a thread that the monitor has explicitly set to the blocked state. The monitor can make any thread inside the synchronized block it manages wait. The waiting thread can continue its execution only after the monitor explicitly tells it that it can proceed.

We'll use the same application we analyzed earlier in this chapter and consider the following scenario: one of the developers working on the app thought about improving our producer–consumer architecture. Now, the consumer thread can't do anything when the list is empty, so it just iterates multiple times over a false condition until the JVM makes it wait to allow a producer thread to run and add values to the list. The same thing happens when the producer adds 100 values to the list. The producer thread runs over a false condition until the JVM allows a consumer to remove some of the values.

Can we do something to make the consumer wait when it has no value to consume and make it run only when we know the list contains at least one value (figure 7.15)? Similarly, can we make the producer wait when there are already too many values in the list and allow it to run only when it makes sense to add other values? Would this approach make our app more efficient?

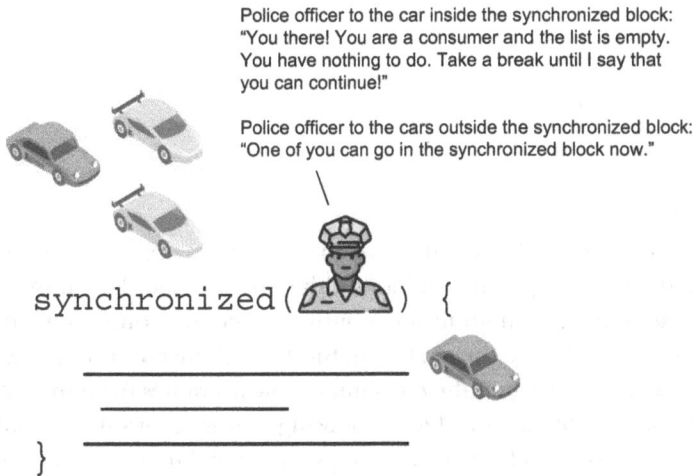

Police officer to the car inside the synchronized block: "You there! You are a consumer and the list is empty. You have nothing to do. Take a break until I say that you can continue!"

Police officer to the cars outside the synchronized block: "One of you can go in the synchronized block now."

```
synchronized(      ) {
    _____
    _____
    _____
}
```

After a producer adds a value to the list . . .

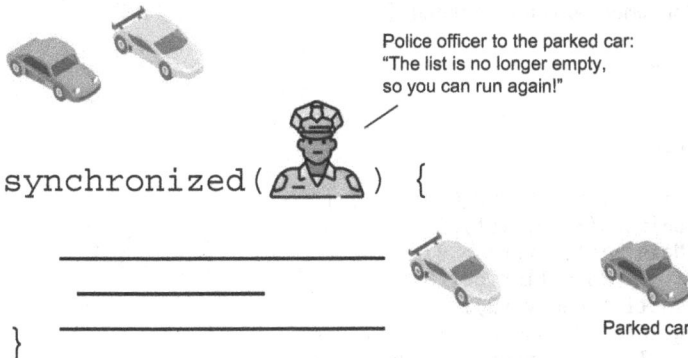

Police officer to the parked car: "The list is no longer empty, so you can run again!"

```
synchronized(      ) {
    _____
    _____
    _____
}
```

Parked car

Figure 7.15 Some of the cars are consumer threads, and others are producer threads. The police officer orders a consumer to wait if the list doesn't have values that can be consumed, allowing producers to work and add values. Once the list contains at least a value that can be consumed, the officer orders the waiting consumer to continue its execution.

We'll modify the application to implement this new behavior, but—spoiler alert—it won't make things any more efficient. In fact, quite the opposite! The execution will be less optimal.

At first glance, making threads wait when they can't access the shared resource (the list) might seem like a smart move. After all, if they can't do their job, shouldn't they just sit tight and wait their turn? But as you'll see, this well-intentioned change ends up doing more harm than good, dragging performance down instead of speeding things up.

This is a perfect example of why, in multithreaded programming, what seems like a good idea in theory can turn into a performance nightmare in practice. The take-away? Always experiment, measure, and analyze before declaring your optimization a success—because sometimes, the only thing you're optimizing is your frustration!

I always recommend using a profiler during development to prove that the app executes optimally.

Listing 7.4 shows the new implementation of the consumer thread. The consumer thread waits when the list is empty since it has nothing to consume. The monitor makes the consumer thread wait and will notify it to continue executing only after a producer adds something to the list. We use the `wait()` method to tell the consumer to wait if the list is empty. At the same time, when the consumer removes values from the list, it notifies the waiting threads so that if a producer is waiting, it now knows it can continue its execution because the list is no longer full. We use the `notifyAll()` method to notify the waiting threads. You can find this implementation in project da-ch7-ex2.

Listing 7.4   Making the consumer thread wait when the list is empty

```java
public class Consumer extends Thread {

  // Omitted code

  @Override
  public void run() {
    try {
      for (int i = 0; i < 1_000_000; i++) {
        synchronized (Main.list) {
          if (Main.list.size() > 0) {
            int x = Main.list.get(0);
            Main.list.remove(0);
            log.info("Consumer " +
                Thread.currentThread().getName() +
```

```
                           " removed value " + x);
              Main.list.notifyAll();
            } else {
              Main.list.wait();
            }
          }
        }
      } catch (InterruptedException e) {
        log.severe(e.getMessage());
      }
    }
  }
}
```

After consuming an element from the list, the consumer notifies the waiting threads a change has been made in the list contents.

When the list is empty, the consumer waits until it gets notified something has been added to the list.

The following listing shows the implementation of the producer thread. Similar to the consumer thread, the producer thread waits if there are too many values in the list. A consumer will eventually notify the producer and allow it to run again when it consumes a value from the list.

Listing 7.5 Making the producer thread wait if the list is already full

```
public class Producer extends Thread {

  // Omitted code

  @Override
  public void run() {
    try {
      Random r = new Random();
      for (int i = 0; i < 1_000_000; i++) {
        synchronized (Main.list) {
          if (Main.list.size() < 100) {
            int x = r.nextInt();
            Main.list.add(x);
            log.info("Producer " +
                Thread.currentThread().getName() +
                " added value " + x);
            Main.list.notifyAll();
          } else {
            Main.list.wait();
          }
        }
      }
    } catch (InterruptedException e) {
      log.severe(e.getMessage());
    }
  }
}
```

After adding an element to the list, the producer notifies the waiting threads a change has been made in the list contents.

When the list has 100 elements, the producer waits until it gets notified something has been removed from the list.

As you know, we start our investigations by sampling the execution. We already see something suspicious: the execution seems to take much longer (figure 7.16). If you go back to the observations we made in section 7.1, you'll see that the whole execution was only about 9 seconds long. Now, the execution takes about 50 seconds—a huge difference.

The execution takes longer, and there is a big difference between the total time and the total CPU time, indicating that the app still does a lot of waiting.

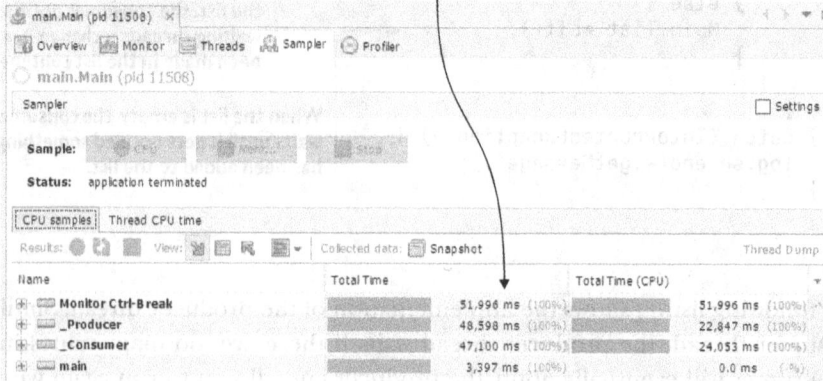

Figure 7.16   By sampling the execution, we see that the execution time is slower than before we made threads wait.

Sample details (figure 7.17) show us that the wait() method we added caused most of the thread waiting time. The thread is not locked for long since the self-execution time is very close to the CPU execution time. Still, our purpose is to make our app more efficient overall, but it seems we only shifted the waiting from one side to the other and made the app slower in the process.

The execution details indicate that most of the waiting time is caused by the wait() method the monitor invokes.

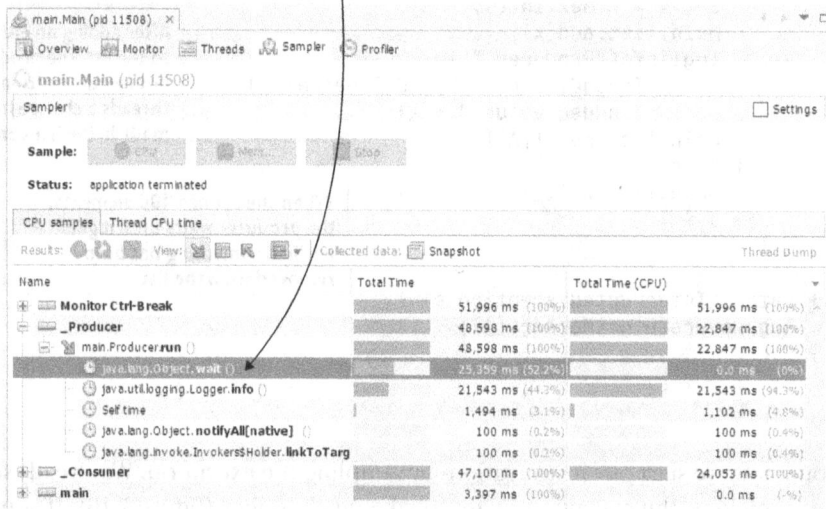

Figure 7.17   By analyzing the details, we can see that the self-execution time is not that long, but the thread is blocked and thus waits for a longer time.

We continue by profiling for more detail (figure 7.18). Indeed, the profiling results show fewer locks, but that doesn't help much since the execution is much slower.

Note that the number of locks decreased. Even so, the total execution time increased.

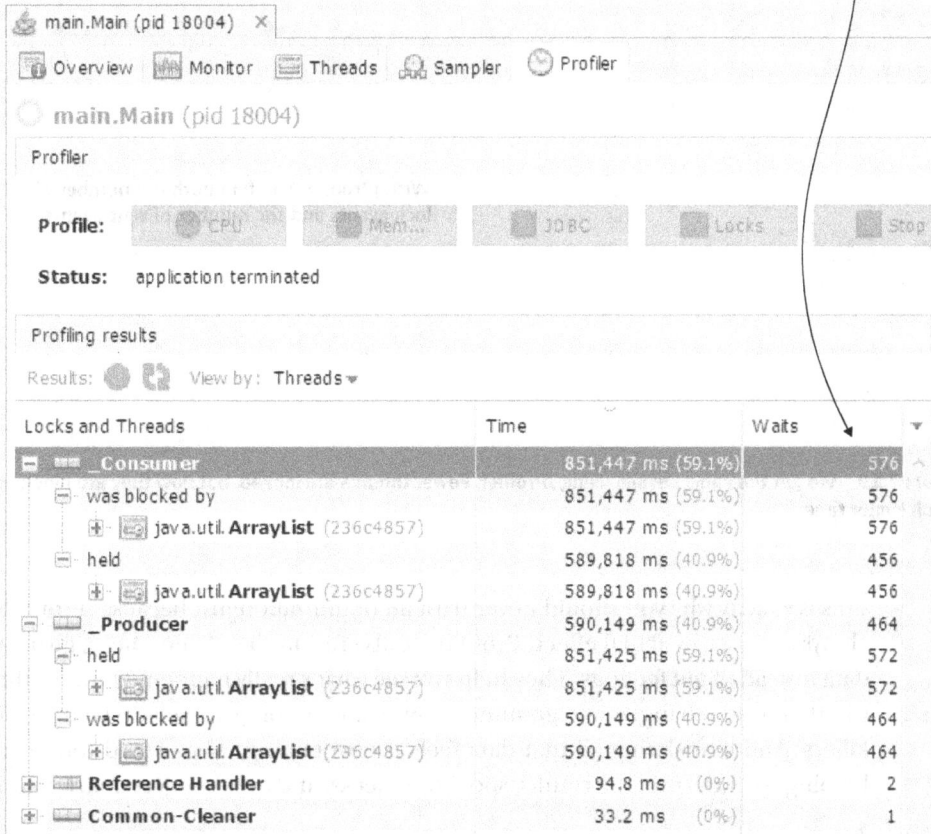

Locks and Threads	Time	Waits
⊟ ▦▦ _Consumer	851,447 ms (59.1%)	576
⊟ was blocked by	851,447 ms (59.1%)	576
⊞ 🗂 java.util. **ArrayList** (236c4857)	851,447 ms (59.1%)	576
⊟ held	589,818 ms (40.9%)	456
⊞ 🗂 java.util. **ArrayList** (236c4857)	589,818 ms (40.9%)	456
⊟ ▭▭▭ _Producer	590,149 ms (40.9%)	464
⊟ held	851,425 ms (59.1%)	572
⊞ 🗂 java.util. **ArrayList** (236c4857)	851,425 ms (59.1%)	572
⊟ was blocked by	590,149 ms (40.9%)	464
⊞ 🗂 java.util. **ArrayList** (236c4857)	590,149 ms (40.9%)	464
⊞ ▭▭▭ Reference Handler	94.8 ms (0%)	2
⊞ ▭▭ Common-Cleaner	33.2 ms (0%)	1

Figure 7.18 The lock pattern is similar to our previous results, but the threads are locked less frequently.

Figure 7.19 shows the same investigation details obtained using JProfiler. In JProfiler, once we group the lock events by threads, we get both the number of locks and the waiting time. In the previous exercise, the waiting time was zero, but we had many more locks. Now we have fewer locks but a longer waiting time. This tells us that the JVM changes more slowly between threads when using a wait/notify approach than when allowing the threads to get naturally locked and unlocked by the monitor of a synchronized block.

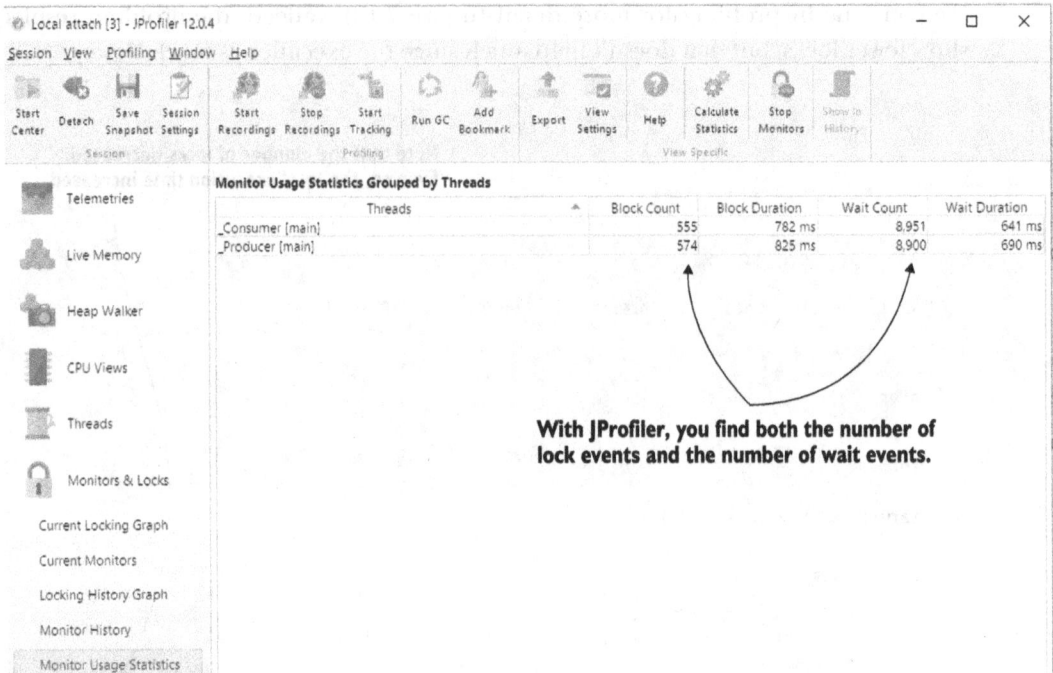

Figure 7.19   We get the same details using JProfiler. Fewer threads are locked, but now they are blocked for a much longer time.

This is exactly why you should never trust an optimization just because it sounds good—always measure its actual effect! Profiling tools are your best friend here, giving you hard data instead of gut feelings. They help you see what's really happening under the hood—whether your changes are genuine improvements or just well-dressed performance killers. And if analyzing all that data feels overwhelming, AI-powered tools can step in, helping you interpret the results, spot bottlenecks, and even suggest smarter approaches.

Summary

- A thread can be locked and forced to wait by a synchronized block of code. Locks appear when threads are synchronized to avoid changing shared resources simultaneously.

- Locks are needed to avoid race conditions, but sometimes apps use faulty thread synchronization approaches, which can lead to undesired results such as performance problems or even app freezes (in the case of deadlocks).

- Locks caused by synchronized code blocks slow down the app's execution because they force threads to wait instead of letting them work. Locks may be needed in certain implementations, but it's better to find ways to minimize the time an app's threads are locked.

- We can use a profiler to identify when locks slow down an app, how many locks the app encounters during execution, and how much they slow down performance.

- When using a profiler, always sample the execution first to figure out if the app's execution is affected by locks. You'll usually identify locks when sampling by observing that a method is waiting on itself.

- If you find by sampling that locks may be affecting the app's execution, you can continue investigating using lock profiling (instrumentation), which will show the threads affected, the number of locks, the monitors involved, and the relationship between locked threads and threads that cause the locks. These details help you decide if the app's execution is optimal or if there are any ways to enhance it.

- Each app has a different purpose, so there's no unique formula for understanding thread locks. In general, we want to minimize the time threads are locked or waiting and make sure threads are not unfairly excluded from execution (starving threads).

Investigating deadlocks with thread dumps

8

Picture this: You're at your favorite coffee shop, about to enjoy a well-earned break. You order a cappuccino, and just as you're about to pay, the cashier's system freezes. The barista taps the screen, then tries again. Nothing happens. Meanwhile, the queue behind you is growing.

Behind the counter, two cash registers are blinking with error messages. It turns out, register A is waiting for register B to confirm a payment, while register B is waiting for register A to process it first. Neither register can proceed, and the entire coffee shop grinds to a halt. Baristas glance at each other helplessly. Customers sigh. Someone dramatically proclaims, "I just wanted coffee!"

Congratulations, you've just witnessed a deadlock—only instead of two software threads, it's two cash registers locked in an eternal standoff. And a reboot or some clever debugging to break the cycle is the only way to fix it.

Now, imagine a similar situation happening inside a Java application. Multiple threads get stuck waiting for each other, and your app stops responding. How do you figure out what went wrong? That's where thread dumps come in.

A thread dump captures the state of all threads in a JVM at a particular moment. It helps us diagnose deadlocks, high CPU usage, slow performance, and other threading problems by showing which threads are running, waiting, or being stuck. Unlike profiling techniques discussed in chapters 5 through 7, which rely on sampling over time, a thread dump provides a snapshot of execution at a single point—crucial when an application is completely frozen.

This chapter explores how to generate and analyze thread dumps to identify problems such as deadlocks and performance bottlenecks. By the end of it, you'll learn you how to use the tools to diagnose and resolve thread-related problems before they bring down your metaphorical coffee shop. And since thread dumps can be sometimes large and cryptical, I'll show you how to make things easier using some AI assistance.

8.1 Getting a thread dump

This section analyzes ways to obtain a thread dump. We'll use a small application that intentionally creates deadlocks. You can find this app in project da-ch8-ex1. We'll run this app and wait for it to freeze (this should happen in a few seconds), and then we'll discuss multiple ways to get thread dumps. Once you learn how to obtain thread dumps, we discuss how to read them (section 8.2).

Let's examine how the app we'll use is implemented and why its execution causes deadlocks. The app uses two threads to change two shared resources (two list instances). A thread named the "_Producer" adds values to one list or another during execution. Another thread called the "_Consumer" removes values from these lists. If you read chapter 6, you may recall we worked on a similar app. But since the app's logic is irrelevant to our example, I've omitted it from the listings and kept only the part important to our demonstration—the synchronized blocks.

The example is simplified to allow you to focus on the investigation techniques. In a real-world app, things usually get more complicated. Also, wrongly used synchronized blocks are not the only way to get into deadlocks. Faulty use of blocking objects such as semaphores, latches, or barriers can also cause such problems. But the steps used to investigate the problems are the same.

In listings 8.1 and 8.2, notice that the two threads use nested synchronized blocks with two different monitors: `listA` and `listB`. The problem is that one of the threads uses monitor `listA` for the outer synchronized block, while `listB` is used for the inner. The other thread uses them in reverse order. Such code design leaves room for deadlocks.

> **Listing 8.1 Using nested synchronized blocks for the "_Consumer" thread**

```
public class Consumer extends Thread {

    // Omitted code
```

```
    @Override
    public void run() {
      while (true) {
        synchronized (Main.listA) {          ◄──┐ The outer synchronized block
                                                  uses the listA monitor.

          synchronized (Main.listB) {        ◄──┐ The inner synchronized block
            work();                               uses the listB monitor.
          }
        }
      }
    }

    // Omitted code
}
```

In listing 8.1, the "_Consumer" thread uses listA as the monitor for the outer synchronized block. In listing 8.2, the "_Producer" thread uses the same monitor for the inner block, while the listB monitor is also swapped between the two threads.

Listing 8.2   Using nested synchronized blocks for the "_Producer" thread

```
public class Producer extends Thread {

  // Omitted code

  @Override
  public void run() {
    Random r = new Random();
    while (true) {
      synchronized (Main.listB) {          ◄──┐ The listB monitor is used by
                                                the outer synchronized block.

        synchronized (Main.listA) {        ◄──┐ The listA monitor is used by
          work(r);                              the inner synchronized block.
        }
      }
    }
  }

  // Omitted code
}
```

Figure 8.1 shows how the two threads can run into a deadlock.

8.1.1   Getting a thread dump using a profiler

What do we do when we have a frozen app and want to identify the problem's root cause? Using a profiler to analyze the locks is unlikely to be effective in a scenario where the app, or part of it, is frozen. Instead of analyzing the locks during execution as we did in chapter 6, we'll take a snapshot just of the app's thread states. We'll review this snapshot (i.e., thread dump) and identify which threads are interacting with each other, causing the app to freeze.

1. Suppose that, while running, two threads enter the outer synchronized block but don't go into the inner synchronized block. The arrows indicate where each thread is during the execution.

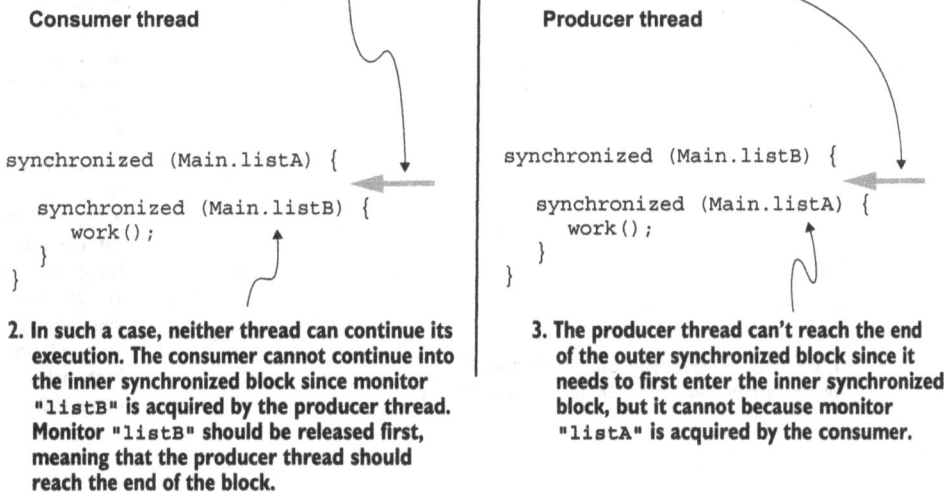

Consumer thread

```
synchronized (Main.listA) {

  synchronized (Main.listB) {
    work();
  }
}
```

Producer thread

```
synchronized (Main.listB) {

  synchronized (Main.listA) {
    work();
  }
}
```

2. In such a case, neither thread can continue its execution. The consumer cannot continue into the inner synchronized block since monitor "listB" is acquired by the producer thread. Monitor "listB" should be released first, meaning that the producer thread should reach the end of the block.

3. The producer thread can't reach the end of the outer synchronized block since it needs to first enter the inner synchronized block, but it cannot because monitor "listA" is acquired by the consumer.

Figure 8.1   If both threads enter the outer synchronized block, but not the inner one, they remain stuck and wait for each other. We say that they went into a deadlock.

You can obtain a thread dump either by using a profiling tool (e.g., VisualVM, JProfiler) or by directly calling a tool provided by the JDK using the command line. In this section, we'll discuss how to obtain a thread dump using a profiler, and in section 8.1.2, you'll learn how to get the same information using the command line.

We'll start our application (project da-ch8-ex1) and wait a few seconds for it to enter a deadlock. You'll know the app gets into a deadlock when it no longer writes messages in the console (it gets stuck).

Getting a thread dump using a profiler is a simple approach. It's no more than the click of a button. Let's use VisualVM to get a thread dump. Figure 8.2 shows the Visual VM interface. You can see that VisualVM is smart and that it figured out that some of the threads of our process ran into a deadlock. This is indicated in the Threads tab.

After the thread dump is collected, the interface looks like figure 8.3. The thread dump is represented as plain text, describing the app threads and providing details about them (their state in the life cycle, who blocks them, etc.).

8.1.2   Generating a thread dump from the command line

A thread dump can also be obtained using the command line. This approach is particularly useful when you need to get a thread dump from a remote environment. Most of the time, you won't be able to remote profile an app installed in an environment (and remember, remote profiling and remote debugging aren't recommended in a production environment, as discussed in chapter 6). Since in most cases you can only access a

VisualVM indicates a deadlock.

To get a thread dump, click the Thread Dump button.

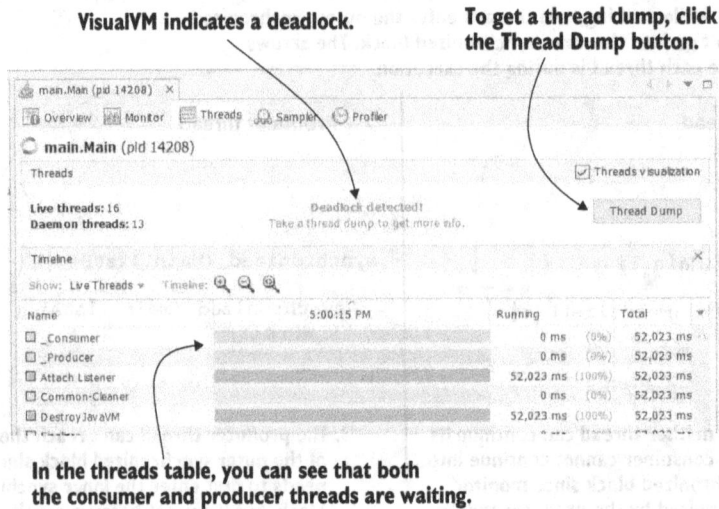

Figure 8.2 When some of the app's threads get into a deadlock, VisualVM indicates the situation with a message in the Threads tab. Notice that both the _"_Consumer" and _"_Producer" threads are locked on the graphic timeline. To get a thread dump, you simply select the Thread Dump button in the window's upper-right corner.

In the threads table, you can see that both the consumer and producer threads are waiting.

The thread dump shows information about each active thread. You find the producer and consumer threads in the generated thread dump.

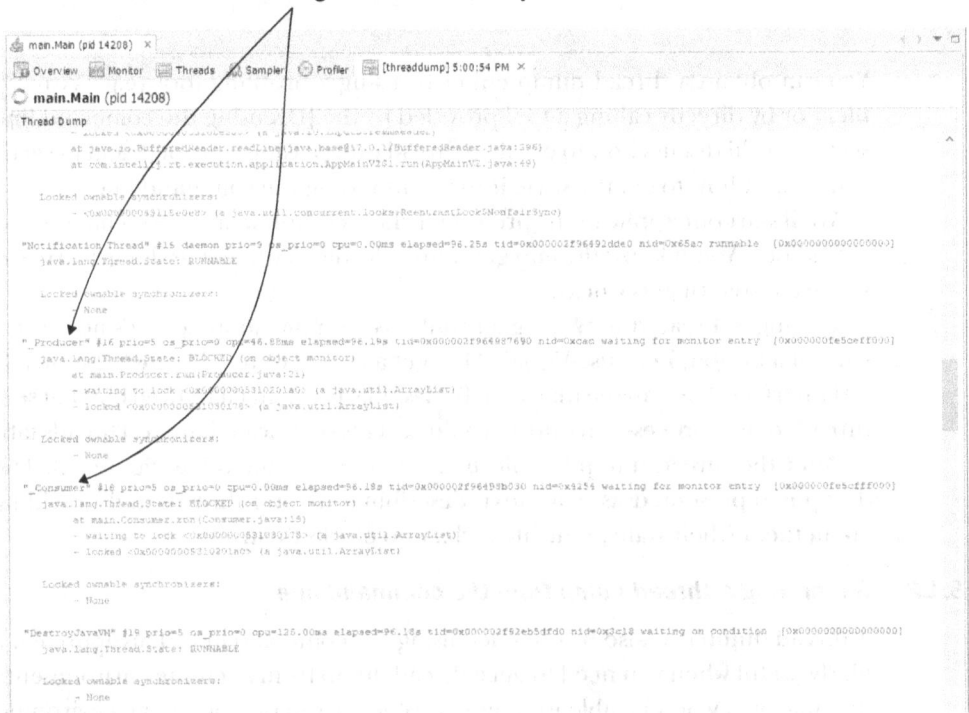

Figure 8.3 A thread dump in plain text that describes an app's threads. In the thread dump we collected, we can find the two deadlocked threads "_Consumer" and "_Producer".

At first, you might not understand the thread dump text in figure 8.3. Later in this chapter, you'll learn how to read it.

remote environment using the command line, you need to know how to get a thread dump this way, too.

Fortunately, getting a thread dump using the command line is quite easy (figure 8.4):

1 Find the process ID for which you want a thread dump.
2 Get the thread dump as text data (raw data) and save it in a file.
3 Load the saved thread dump to make it easier to read in a profiler tool.

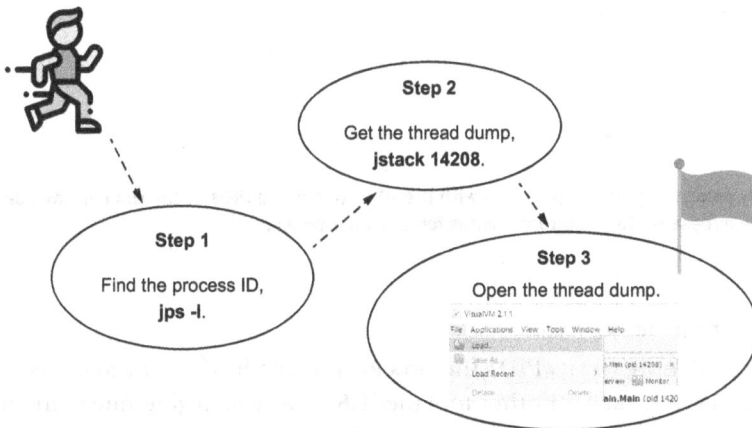

Step 2

Get the thread dump, **jstack 14208.**

Step 1

Find the process ID, **jps -l.**

Step 3

Open the thread dump.

Figure 8.4 Follow these simple steps to get a thread dump using the command line. First, find the process ID for which you want the thread dump. Second, use a JDK tool to get the thread dump. Finally, open the thread dump in a profiling tool to read it.

STEP 1: FIND THE PROCESS ID FOR THE PROCESS UNDER INVESTIGATION

Thus far, we have identified the process we want to profile using its name (represented as the main class's name). But when getting a thread dump using the command line, you need to identify the process using its ID. How do you get a process ID (PID) for a running Java app? The simplest way is using the jps tool provided with the JDK.

The next snippet shows the command you need to run. We use the -l (lowercase "L") option to get the main class names associated with the PIDs. This way, we can identify the processes the same way we did in chapters 5–7 where we learned to profile an app's execution:

```
jps -l
```

Figure 8.5 shows the result of running the command. The numeric values in the output's first column are the PIDs. The second column associates the main class name with each PID. This way, we get the PID that we'll use in step 2 to obtain the thread dump.

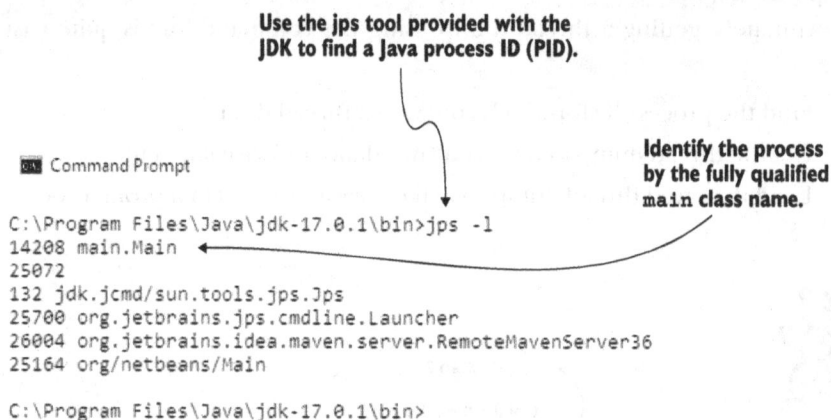

Use the jps tool provided with the
JDK to find a Java process ID (PID).

Identify the process
by the fully qualified
main class name.

```
Command Prompt

C:\Program Files\Java\jdk-17.0.1\bin>jps -l
14208 main.Main
25072
132 jdk.jcmd/sun.tools.jps.Jps
25700 org.jetbrains.jps.cmdline.Launcher
26004 org.jetbrains.idea.maven.server.RemoteMavenServer36
25164 org/netbeans/Main

C:\Program Files\Java\jdk-17.0.1\bin>
```

Figure 8.5   By using the `jps` tool provided with the JDK, we get the PIDs of the running Java processes. These PIDs are necessary to get thread dumps for a given process.

STEP 2: COLLECT THE THREAD DUMP

Once you can identify (by its PID) the process for which you want to collect a thread dump, you can use jstack, another tool the JDK provides, to generate a thread dump. When using jstack, you only need to provide the process ID as a parameter (instead of <<PID>>, you need to use the PID value you collected in step 1):

```
jstack <<PID>>
```

An example of such a command execution is

```
jstack 14208
```

Figure 8.6 shows you the result of running the jstack command followed by a PID. The thread dump is provided as plain text you can save in a file to move or load into a tool for investigation.

Use the jstack tool provided with the JDK to get a thread dump.
The only mandatory parameter is the process ID (PID) for the
process you want to generate the thread dump.

```
Command Prompt                                                                    —  □  ×

C:\Program Files\Java\jdk-17.0.1\bin>jstack 14208
2021-12-01 17:10:51
Full thread dump OpenJDK 64-Bit Server VM (17.0.1+12-39 mixed mode, sharing):

Threads class SMR info:
_java_thread_list=0x000002f96843b110, length=25, elements={
0x000002f9646faaf0, 0x000002f9646fc110, 0x000002f96470ec20, 0x000002f9647107e0,
0x000002f964713a40, 0x000002f964718090, 0x000002f964719cb0, 0x000002f96471a750,
0x000002f96472e0b0, 0x000002f9647c08b0, 0x000002f964921580, 0x000002f96492dde0,
0x000002f964987690, 0x000002f96498b030, 0x000002f92eb5dfd0, 0x000002f965cb8cee,
0x000002f966f07490, 0x000002f967087840, 0x000002f9666ba6a0, 0x000002f96747e060,
0x000002f96747f870, 0x000002f96747fd40, 0x000002f964a76010, 0x000002f964a746c0,
0x000002f967480210
}

"Reference Handler" #2 daemon prio=10 os_prio=2 cpu=0.00ms elapsed=692.87s tid=0x000002f9646faaf0 nid=0x6888 waiting on
condition  [0x000000fe5c1ff000]
   java.lang.Thread.State: RUNNABLE
        at java.lang.ref.Reference.waitForReferencePendingList(java.base@17.0.1/Native Method)
        at java.lang.ref.Reference.processPendingReferences(java.base@17.0.1/Reference.java:253)
        at java.lang.ref.Reference$ReferenceHandler.run(java.base@17.0.1/Reference.java:215)

"Finalizer" #3 daemon prio=8 os_prio=1 cpu=0.00ms elapsed=692.87s tid=0x000002f9646fc110 nid=0x5fa8 in Object.wait()  [0
x000000fe5c2ff000]
   java.lang.Thread.State: WAITING (on object monitor)
        at java.lang.Object.wait(java.base@17.0.1/Native Method)
        - waiting on <0x0000000531818640> (a java.lang.ref.ReferenceQueue$Lock)
        at java.lang.ref.ReferenceQueue.remove(java.base@17.0.1/ReferenceQueue.java:155)
        - locked <0x0000000531818640> (a java.lang.ref.ReferenceQueue$Lock)
```

Figure 8.6 The `jstack` command followed by a PID will generate a thread dump for the given process. The thread
dump is shown as plain text (also called a raw thread dump). You can collect the text in a file to import it and
investigate it later.

STEP 3: IMPORT THE COLLECTED THREAD DUMP INTO A PROFILER TO MAKE IT EASIER TO READ

Usually, you save the output of the `jstack` command, the thread dump, into a file. Storing the thread dump in a file allows you to move, store, or import it into tools that help you investigate its details.

Figure 8.7 shows how you can place the output of the `jstack` command in a file in the command line. Once you have the file, you can load it in VisualVM using the File > Load menu.

8.2   *Reading thread dumps*

Imagine you've just received a thick stack of printed medical records—pages upon pages of test results, doctor's notes, and mysterious abbreviations. You could call a specialist to decode them for you, but what if they're unavailable? You'd better brush up on your medical jargon.

Thread dumps are similar. When your application freezes, crashes, or behaves oddly, you collect a thread dump—but then what? It's a dense wall of text, filled with stack traces, thread states, and synchronization details. Fortunately, you don't have to decode everything manually. Tools such as `fastThread` (https://fastthread.io/) can visualize the data for you, much like a medical professional summarizing your test results.

**A good approach is to put the contents jstack outputs into
a file so that you can save it, send it, and investigate it.**

```
Command Prompt

C:\Program Files\Java\jdk-17.0.1\bin>jstack 14208 > C:\MANNINGS\stack_trace.tdump

C:\Program Files\Java\jdk-17.0.1\bin>
```

**You can open a saved thread dump in any profiler
to easily read it. For example, in VisualVM, you
can open it using File > Load.**

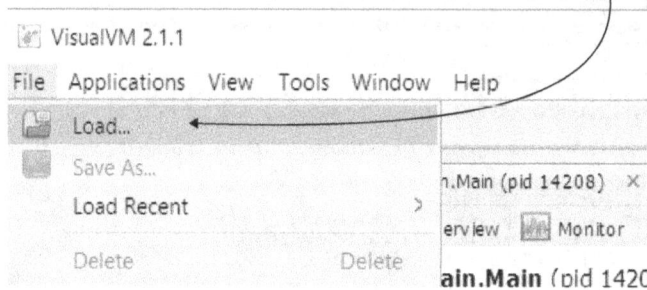

```
VisualVM 2.1.1

File  Applications  View  Tools  Window  Help

    Load...  ◄

    Save As...                          n.Main (pid 14208)  ✕

    Load Recent                  >
                                        erview    Monitor
    Delete              Delete
                                        ain.Main (pid 1420
```

**Figure 8.7 Once you save the thread dump into a file, you can open it in various tools to investigate it.
For example, to open it in VisualVM, you select File > Load.**

And, of course, there's AI. AI-powered assistants can now parse thread dumps, highlight problematic threads, and even suggest possible causes of deadlocks or performance problems. But while AI is a great helper, it's not perfect—sometimes, it misinterprets the data, or the best tools aren't available in your environment. That's why knowing how to read a plain-text thread dump manually is still an essential skill.

This section covers both approaches:

- *Section 8.2.1*—Reading raw thread dumps as generated by `jstack` (see section 8.1.2)
- *Section 8.2.2*—Using `fastThread` to visualize and analyze thread dumps more easily.

While we all love good visualizations, there are times when you won't have access to advanced tools. In those cases, your ability to manually dissect a thread dump can mean the difference between resolving a problem faster or staring at a frozen app in despair. Let's dive in!

8.2.1 Reading plain-text thread dumps

When you collect a thread dump, you get a description of the threads in plain-text format (i.e., raw data). Although we have tools you can use to easily visualize the data (see section 8.2.2), I've always considered it important for a developer to understand the raw representation as well. You may encounter a situation where you can't remove the raw thread dump from the environment you generated it in. Say you connect to a container remotely and can only use the command line to dig into the logs and investigate what happens with the running app. You suspect a thread-related problem, so you want to generate a thread dump. If you can read the thread dump as text, you need nothing more than the console itself.

Let's look at listing 8.3, which shows one of the threads in the thread dump. It is nothing more than similarly displayed details for each thread active in the app when the dump was taken. Here are the details you get for a thread:

- *Thread name*—The name assigned to the thread, which helps you identify it in logs and debugging tools
- *Thread ID*—A unique identifier assigned to the thread by the Java Virtual Machine (JVM)
- *Native thread ID*—The identifier assigned to the thread by the operating system, useful for low-level debugging
- *Priority of the thread at the operating system level*—The priority level set for the thread, which influences how the OS schedules its execution
- *Total and CPU time the thread consumed*—The total execution time of the thread and the amount of CPU time it has used
- *State description*—A detailed explanation of the thread's current execution status
- *State name*—The standardized state of the thread, such as runnable, waiting, or blocked
- *Stack trace*—A snapshot of the method calls that the thread is currently executing
- *Who's blocking the thread*—Information about any other thread preventing this particular thread from proceeding
- *What locks the thread acquires*—A list of synchronization locks the thread currently holds, which can help diagnose deadlocks or contention problems

Listing 8.3   The anatomy of a thread's details in a thread dump

Thread stack trace

Thread state

Thread ID and state description

Thread name and details about resource
consumption and execution time

```
"_Producer" #16 prio=5 os_prio=0 cpu=46.88ms elapsed=763.96s
  tid=0x000002f964987690 nid=0xcac waiting for monitor entry
  [0x000000fe5ceff000]
    java.lang.Thread.State: BLOCKED (on object monitor)
      at main.Producer.run(Unknown Source)
```

```
- waiting to lock <0x000000052e0313f8> (a java.util.ArrayList)
- locked <0x000000052e049d38> (a java.util.ArrayList)
```

**Lock ID of the lock produced
by the current thread**

**Lock ID that blocks the current thread
and type of the monitor object**

The first thing displayed is the *thread name*—in our case, "_Producer". The thread name is essential as it's one of the ways you identify the thread in the thread dump later if you need it. The JVM also associates the thread with a *thread ID* (in listing 8.3, tid=0x000002f964987690). Since the developer gives the name, there's a small chance some threads will be named the same. If this unlucky situation happens, you can still identify a thread in the dump by its ID (which is always unique).

In a JVM app, a thread is a wrapper over a system thread, meaning you can always identify the operating system (OS) thread running behind the scenes. If you ever need to do that, look for the *native thread ID* (nid=0xcac in listing 8.3).

Once you have identified a thread, you identify the details you are interested in. The first three pieces of information you get in a thread dump are the *thread's priority*, the *CPU execution time*, and the *total execution time*. Every OS associates a priority to each of its running threads. I don't often use this value in a thread dump. But if you see that a thread isn't as active as you think it should be, and you see that the OS designates it as a lower priority, then this may be the cause. In this situation, the total execution time would also be much higher than the CPU execution time. Remember from chapter 6 that the total execution time is how long the thread was alive, while the CPU execution time is how long it worked.

State description is a valuable detail. It tells you in plain English what happens to the thread. In our case, the thread is "waiting for monitor entry," meaning it is blocked at the entrance to a synchronized block. The thread could have been "timed waiting on a monitor," which would mean it's sleeping for a defined time or is running. A *state name* (running, waiting, blocked, etc.) is associated with the state description. Appendix D offers a good refresher on thread life cycle and thread states in case you need it.

The thread dump provides a *stack trace* for every thread, which shows exactly what part of the code the thread was executing when the dump was taken. The stack trace is valuable since it shows you exactly what the thread was working on. You can use the stack trace to find a specific piece of code you want to further debug, or in the case of a slow thread, determine exactly what delays or blocks that thread.

Finally, for threads that acquire locks or are locked, we can find *which locks they acquire* and *which locks they are waiting for*. You'll use these details every time you investigate a deadlock. They can also give you optimization hints. For example, if you see that a thread acquires many locks, you may wonder why and how you can change its behavior so that it doesn't block so many other executions.

It is important to remember that thread dumps give you almost as many details as normal lock profiling (discussed in chapter 7). Lock profiling offers one key advantage over a thread dump: it shows execution dynamics. It's like the difference between a security camera feed and a single frame from that feed—profiling gives you the full movie, showing how events unfold, while a thread dump is just a single snapshot in time.

Of course, sometimes, all you need is that one snapshot. If you're trying to catch a raccoon sneaking into your kitchen at night, a full recording would be nice—but if your security cam grabs a picture of the little bandit mid-cookie theft, you already have your culprit. Likewise, while profiling can give you a dynamic view of execution, a well-timed thread dump can still be enough to catch a problem in the act. And as a bonus, it's much easier to obtain than full profiling data.

Sometimes it is enough to use a thread dump instead of a profiler.

If you only need to know what is executed by code at a given time, a thread dump is sufficient. You have learned to use sampling for this purpose, but it's good to know a thread dump can do this, too. Say you don't have access to remotely profile an app, but you must find out what code executes behind the scenes. You can get a thread dump.

Let's now focus on how you can find the relationship between threads with a thread dump. What methods can we use to analyze how threads interact with one another? We are particularly interested in threads locking each other. In listing 8.4, I added the details from the thread dump for the two threads we know are deadlocked. But the question is, "How would we find they are in a deadlock if we didn't know this detail up front?"

If you suspect a deadlock, you should focus your investigation on the locks the threads cause (figure 8.8):

1 Filter out all threads that are not blocked so you can focus on the threads that can cause the deadlock.

2 Start with the first candidate thread (a thread you didn't filter in step 1), and search for the lock ID that causes it to be blocked.

3 Find the thread causing that lock, and check what blocks that thread. If, at some point, you return to the thread you started with, all the threads you parsed are in a deadlock.

STEP 1: FILTER OUT THREADS THAT ARE NOT LOCKED

First, filter out all the threads that are not locked so that you can focus only on the threads that are potential candidates for the situation you are investigating—the

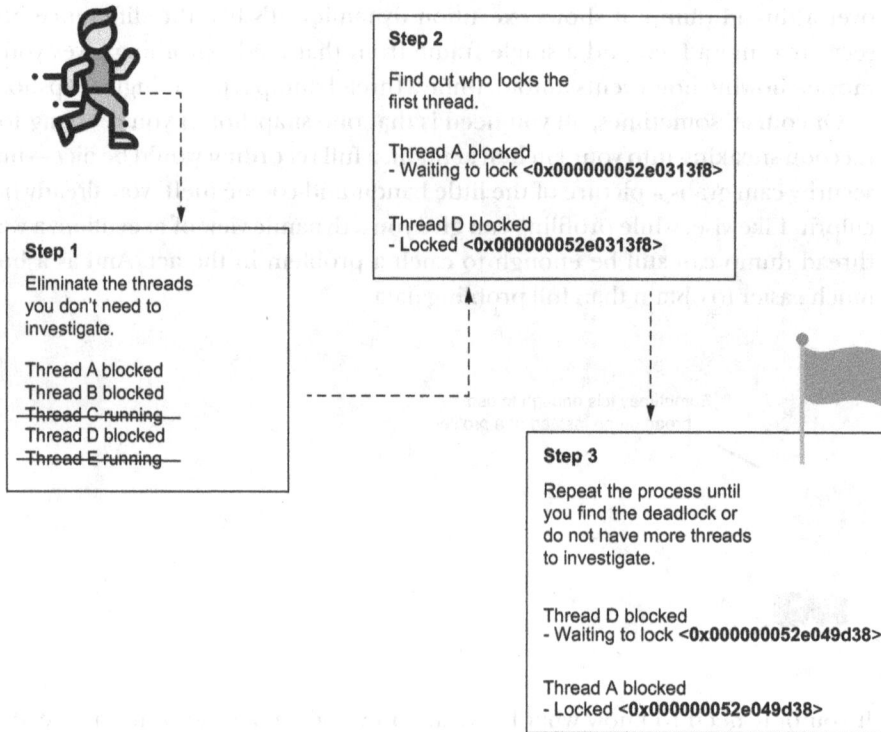

Step 1

Eliminate the threads you don't need to investigate.

Thread A blocked
Thread B blocked
~~Thread C running~~
Thread D blocked
~~Thread E running~~

Step 2

Find out who locks the first thread.

Thread A blocked
- Waiting to lock <0x000000052e0313f8>

Thread D blocked
- Locked <0x000000052e0313f8>

Step 3

Repeat the process until you find the deadlock or do not have more threads to investigate.

Thread D blocked
- Waiting to lock <0x000000052e049d38>

Thread A blocked
- Locked <0x000000052e049d38>

Figure 8.8 To find a deadlock with a thread dump, follow these three easy steps. First, remove all threads that are not blocked. Then, start with one of the blocked threads and find what is blocking it using the lock ID. Continue this process for each thread. If you return to a thread you already investigated, it means you found a deadlock.

deadlock. A thread dump can describe dozens of threads. You want to eliminate the noise and focus only on the blocked threads.

STEP 2: TAKE THE FIRST CANDIDATE THREAD AND FIND WHAT BLOCKS IT

After eliminating the unnecessary thread details, start with the first candidate thread and search by the lock ID that causes a thread to wait. The lock ID is the one between angle brackets (in listing 8.4, "_Producer" waits for a lock with ID 0x000000052e0313f8).

STEP 3: FIND WHAT BLOCKS THE NEXT THREAD

Repeat the process. If at some point you get to a thread that was already investigated, you've found a deadlock (see the following listing).

Listing 8.4   Finding threads that lock each other

```
"_Producer" #16 prio=5 os_prio=0 cpu=46.88ms
 elapsed=763.96s tid=0x000002f964987690
 nid=0xcac waiting for monitor entry [0x000000fe5ceff000]
   java.lang.Thread.State: BLOCKED (on object monitor)
```

```
    at main.Producer.run(Unknown Source)
    - waiting to lock <0x000000052e0313f8>
(a java.util.ArrayList)
    - locked <0x000000052e049d38>
(a java.util.ArrayList)
```

The "_Producer" thread waits for a lock initiated by the "_Consumer" thread.

The "_Consumer" thread waits for a lock initiated by the "_Producer" thread.

```
"_Consumer" #18 prio=5 os_prio=0 cpu=0.00ms
 elapsed=763.96s tid=0x000002f96498b030
 nid=0x4254 waiting for monitor entry  [0x000000fe5cfff000]
   java.lang.Thread.State: BLOCKED (on object monitor)
    at main.Consumer.run(Unknown Source)
    - waiting to lock <0x000000052e049d38> (a java.util.ArrayList)  ◀
    - locked <0x000000052e0313f8> (a java.util.ArrayList)  ◀
```

Our example demonstrates a simple deadlock that assumes two threads lock each other. Following the three-step process discussed earlier, you'll see that the "_Producer" thread blocks the "_Consumer" thread, and vice versa. A complex deadlock happens when more than two threads are involved. For example, thread A blocks thread B, thread B blocks thread C, and thread C blocks thread A. You can discover a long chain of threads that lock each other. The longer the chain of threads in the deadlock, the more difficult the deadlock is to find, understand, and solve. Figure 8.9 shows the difference between a complex deadlock and a simple one.

Simple deadlock

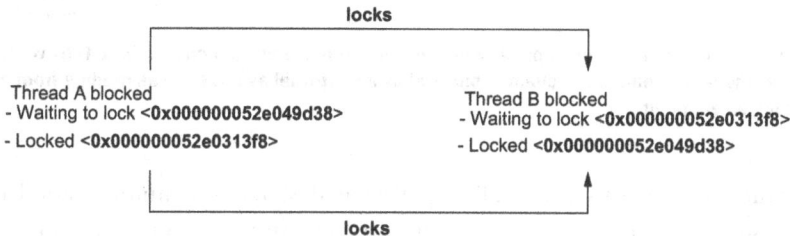

locks

Thread A blocked
- Waiting to lock <0x000000052e049d38>
- Locked <0x000000052e0313f8>

Thread B blocked
- Waiting to lock <0x000000052e0313f8>
- Locked <0x000000052e049d38>

locks

Complex deadlock (more than two threads)

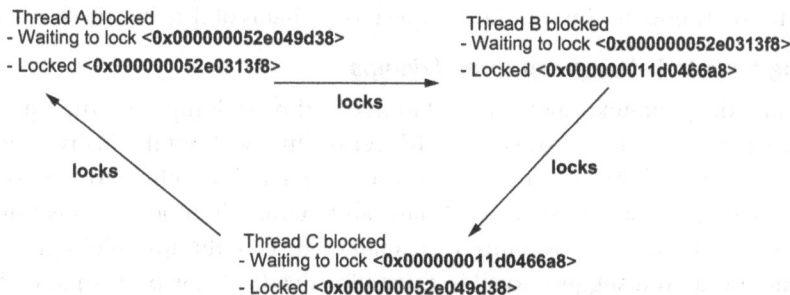

Thread A blocked
- Waiting to lock <0x000000052e049d38>
- Locked <0x000000052e0313f8>

Thread B blocked
- Waiting to lock <0x000000052e0313f8>
- Locked <0x000000011d0466a8>

locks

locks

locks

Thread C blocked
- Waiting to lock <0x000000011d0466a8>
- Locked <0x000000052e049d38>

Figure 8.9 When only two threads block each other, it's called a simple deadlock, but a deadlock can be caused by multiple threads that block each other. More threads means more complexity. Thus, when more than two threads are involved, it's called a complex deadlock.

Sometimes a complex deadlock can be confused with cascading blocked threads (figure 8.10). *Cascading blocked threads* (also known as *cascading locks*) are a different problem you can spot using a thread dump. To find cascading threads, follow the same steps as when investigating a deadlock. But instead of finding that one of the threads is blocked by another in the chain (as in the case of a deadlock), in a cascade of locks, you'll see that one of the threads is waiting for an external event, causing all others to also wait.

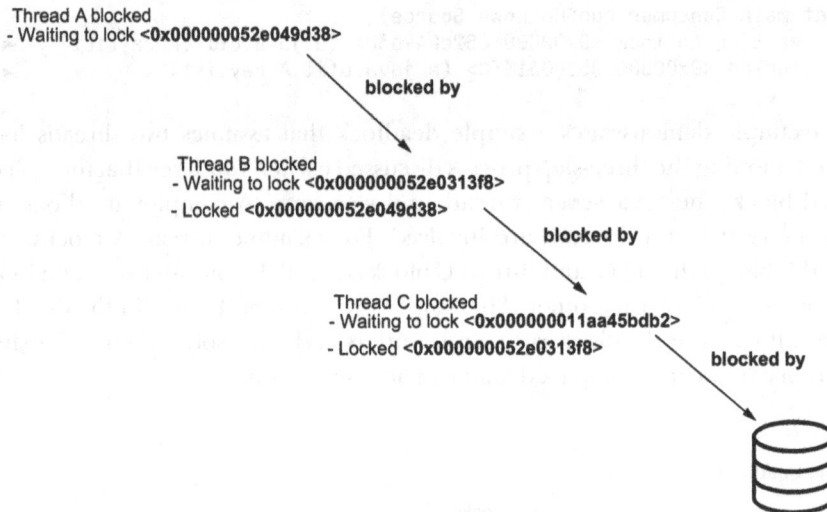

Thread A blocked
- Waiting to lock <0x000000052e049d38>

blocked by

Thread B blocked
- Waiting to lock <0x000000052e0313f8>
- Locked <0x000000052e049d38>

blocked by

Thread C blocked
- Waiting to lock <0x000000011aa45bdb2>
- Locked <0x000000052e0313f8>

blocked by

Figure 8.10   Cascading locks appear when multiple threads enter a chain where they wait for one another. The last thread in the chain is blocked by an external event, such as reading from a data source or calling an endpoint.

Cascading blocked threads usually signal a bad design in the multithreaded architecture. When we design an app with multiple threads, we implement threading to allow the app to process things concurrently. Having threads waiting for one another defeats the purpose of a multithreaded architecture. Although sometimes you need to make threads wait for one another, you shouldn't expect long chains of threads with cascading locks.

8.2.2   *Using tools to better grasp thread dumps*

Reading the plain-text raw representation of a thread dump is useful, but let's be honest, it can feel like trying to assemble IKEA furniture without the instructions. Sure, the information is all there, but making sense of it? That's another story. Most developers prefer a simpler way to visualize the data, and thankfully, modern tools can help.

Today, AI-powered assistants can analyze thread dumps, highlight problematic threads, and even suggest possible causes for deadlocks or performance bottlenecks. You can even upload a thread dump text file to AI assistants such as ChatGPT, Bard, or Gemini (or whichever similar AI assistant is your favorite) and get insights into which threads are stuck, which locks might be causing problems, and possible next steps. We did that with sampling and profiling data in chapter 6. While AI doesn't always get it right, it can provide valuable clues and save time when diagnosing complex problems.

Another good piece of advice is to use a dedicated GPT for analyzing thread dumps. For example, if you're using ChatGPT, you can search for a GPT specialized in investigating thread dumps through the Explore GPTs section. AI assistants tailored to specific tasks like this one often yield better results and enhance your investigation.

Whenever possible, I extract the thread dump from the environment where I collect it and analyze it externally. My go-to tool for this is fastThread (fastthread.io), which provides a clear visualization of the dump, saving me from manually sifting through raw data like someone trying to figure out a correct placement of the 47 identical screws in an Ikea construction. Of course, AI and visualization tools are great, but it's always good to understand the raw format in case you need to dig deeper or when tools aren't available.

fastThread is a web tool designed to assists users read thread dumps. It offers both free and paid plans, but the free plan has always been enough for my needs. Simply upload a file containing the thread dump raw data and wait for the tool to extract the details you need and put them in a shape that is easier to grasp. Figure 8.11 shows the starting page, where you choose the file containing the thread dump raw data from your system and upload it for analysis.

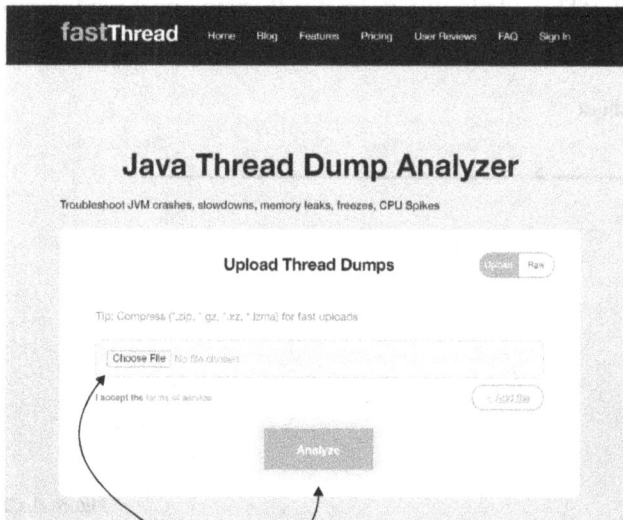

To analyze a thread dump, upload the file with the raw data and then click Analyze.

Figure 8.11 To analyze a thread dump, upload a file containing the thread dump raw data to fastThread.io and wait for the tool to present the details in a easy-to-understand shape.

The fastThread analysis shows various details from the thread dump, including dead-lock detection, dependency graphs, stack traces, resource consumption, and even a flame graph (figure 8.12).

After analyzing the thread dump, the tool presents multiple
visualization widgets, such as identifying deadlocks, CPU consumption
per thread, and even a flame graph representation of the process.

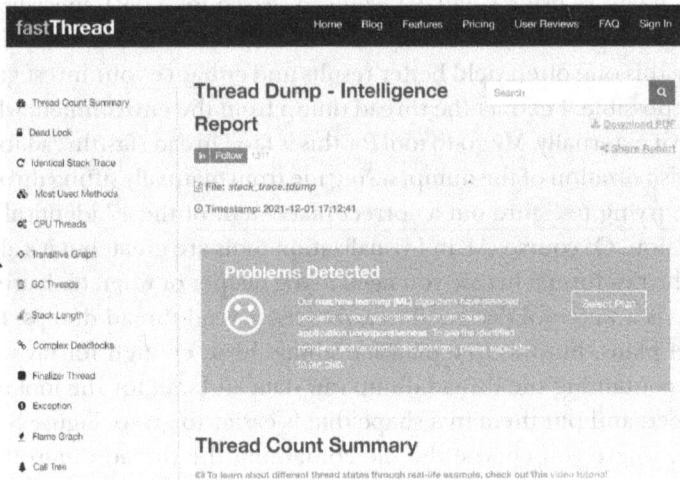

Figure 8.12
**fastThread provides
various details in
an easy-to-read
format. These
details include
deadlock detection,
dependency
graphs, resource
consumption, and a
flame graph.**

Figure 8.13 shows how fastThread identified the deadlock in our thread dump.

The tool identifies the deadlock
and the threads causing it.

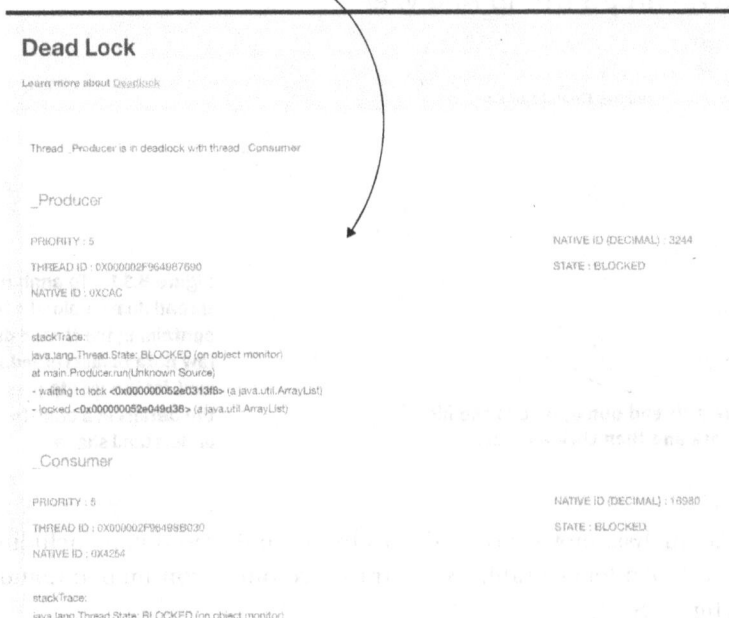

**Figure 8.13   After
analyzing the
thread dump raw
data, fastThread
identifies and
provides details
about the deadlock
caused by the
"_Consumer"
and "_Producer"
threads.**

After all, when it comes to investigating thread dumps, having an AI sidekick is like having Dr. Watson for your Java mysteries, with you playing the role of Sherlock. And remember, while the AI might not demand tea and biscuits, it'll still serve you threads of truth—without the deduction pipe!

Summary

- When two or more threads get blocked while waiting for each other, they are in a deadlock. When an app gets into a deadlock, it usually freezes and can't continue its execution.

- You can identify the root cause of a deadlock using thread dumps, which show the status of all threads of an app at the time the thread dump was generated. This information helps you identify the thread waiting for another.

- A thread dump also shows details such as resource consumption and stack traces for each thread. If these details are sufficient, you can use a thread dump instead of instrumentation for your investigation. Imagine the difference between a thread dump and profiling as the difference between a picture and a movie. With a thread dump, you only have a still image, so you miss the execution dynamics, but you can still get a lot of relevant and helpful details.

- The thread dump provides information about the threads that were executing in the app when the dump was taken. The thread dump shows essential details about the threads in a plain-text format, including resource consumption, thread state in its life cycle, if the thread is waiting for something, and which locks it's causing or being affected by.

- You can generate a thread dump using either a profiler or the command line. Using a profiling tool to get the thread dump is the easiest approach, but when you can't connect a profiler to the running process (e.g., due to network constraints), you can use the command line to get the dump. The thread dump will allow you to investigate the running threads and the relationships between them.

- The plain-text thread dump (also known as a raw thread dump) can be challenging to read. Tools such as fastThread.io help you to visualize the details.

Part 3

Diagnosing
memory-related problems

In the previous part, we looked at problems tied to CPU and execution flow. But another major source of trouble lies in how an application uses memory. Memory problems can creep in slowly. They cause the app to slow down, pause unpredictably, or even crash. And they can appear suddenly in high-load scenarios.

This part is all about spotting these memory-related problems. We'll start by profiling the heap to see which parts of the code are allocating objects and in what quantities. Then we'll move on to heap dumps, which are snapshots of everything in memory. We'll use them to find leaks, unexpected object retention, or bloated data structures. Finally, we'll look at garbage collection logs to understand how the JVM is reclaiming memory and how tuning or fixing code can help reduce GC pauses and improve stability.

By the end of this part, you'll know how to measure memory usage, uncover leaks, and interpret JVM behavior so you can keep your application running smoothly.

Profiling memory-related problems

This chapter covers

- Sampling an execution to find memory allocation problems
- Profiling code to identify the root causes of memory allocation problems

Every app needs memory to function—it's like a workspace where it lays out all the tools, papers, and half-empty coffee cups while processing data. But here's the problem: that workspace isn't infinite. Every app running on a system competes for a share of the same limited memory. And if an app overuses it, it can consume too much, slow itself down, or even crash entirely when it runs out of resources.

Imagine trying to work at a tiny desk cluttered with files, snacks, and a cat that refuses to move. That's what happens when an app mismanages memory—it chokes on its own inefficiency. If memory allocation isn't optimized, the app slows down, struggles to perform, and eventually collapses under the weight of its own excess. Worst case? It crashes entirely, throwing a dramatic error message as its final words.

Efficient memory management isn't just about survival but about performance. An app that uses memory wisely runs smoothly, avoiding unnecessary slowdowns and embarrassing system meltdowns. So, unless you want your app to be that colleague who takes up all the meeting time and then forgets their point, it's time to manage memory like a pro.

If the app doesn't allocate the data it processes in an optimized way, it may force the GC to run more often, so the app will become more CPU-consumptive.

An app should be a responsible citizen when it comes to managing its resources. After all, nobody likes a program that consumes all the CPU and memory, leaving the rest of the system struggling to keep up. When we talk about an app's resources, we mainly refer to two key players: CPU (processing power) and memory. In chapters 5–8, we rolled up our sleeves and tackled CPU consumption problems. Now it's time to dive into the other half of the equation—how an app handles memory allocation.

We kick things off in section 9.1 by exploring memory execution sampling. We then continue with discussing memory profiling in section 9.2. These will help you spot whether your app has memory problems and, more importantly, track down the culprit. Is it an innocent-looking object overstaying its welcome? A memory leak lurking in the shadows? You'll soon find out.

Before we dive in, though, it's important to have a solid grasp of how a Java app allocates and uses memory. If your memory (pun intended) needs a refresher, Appendix E has your back with all the essential details.

9.1   *Sampling to identify memory allocation problems*

In this section, we use a small application that simulates a faulty implemented capability that uses too much of the allocated memory. We use this app to discuss investigation techniques you can use to identify problems with memory allocation or places in code that can be optimized to use the system's memory more efficiently.

Suppose you implement a real-world application and notice that a particular feature runs slowly. You use the techniques discussed in chapter 5 to analyze resource consumption and find that although the app doesn't work very often (consume CPU resources), it uses a large amount of memory. When an app uses too much memory, the JVM can trigger the garbage collector (GC), which will further consume CPU resources (chapter 6). Remember that the GC is the mechanism that automatically deallocates unneeded data from memory (see appendix E for a refresher).

Look at figure 9.1. When discussing how to analyze resource consumption in chapter 5, we used the Monitor tab in VisualVM to observe what resources the app consumes. You can use the memory widget in this tab to find when the app uses an extensive amount of memory.

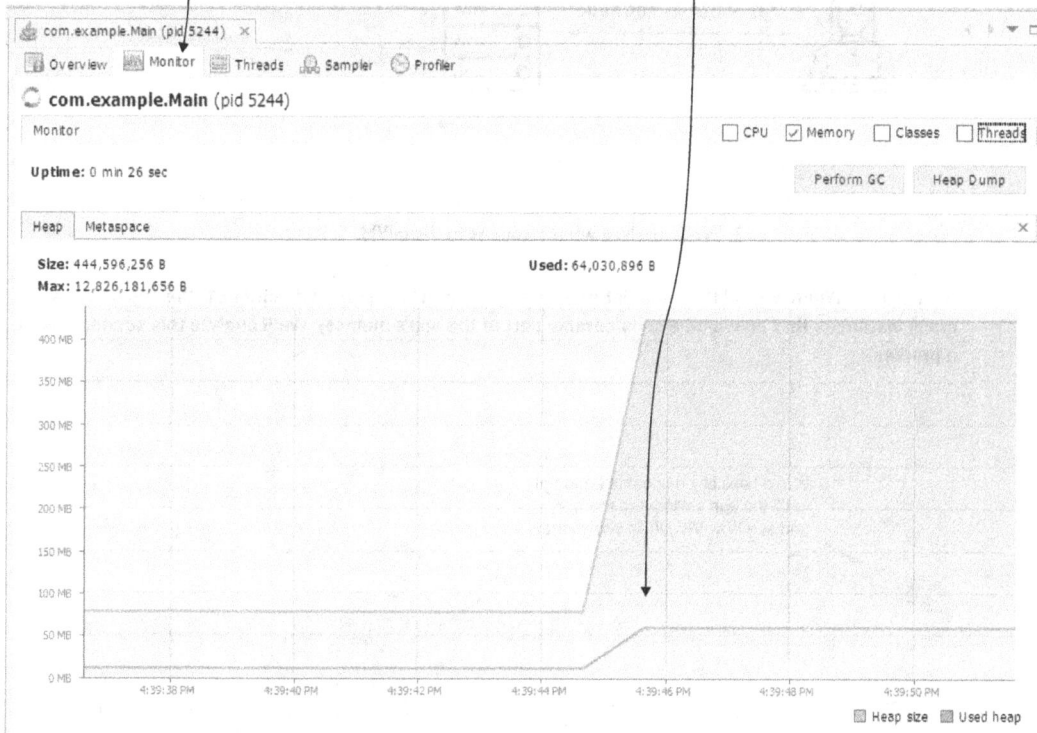

Figure 9.1 The memory widget in the Monitor tab in VisualVM helps to identify whether the app spends more memory than usual at any given time. Often, widgets in the Monitor tab, such as CPU and memory consumption, give us clues on how to continue our investigation. When we see that the app consumes an abnormal amount of memory, we may decide to continue with memory profiling the execution.

The application we use in this chapter is in project da-ch9-ex1. This small web application exposes an endpoint. When calling this endpoint, we provide a number, and the endpoint creates that many object instances. We request the creation of one million objects (a sufficiently large number for our experiment) and then examine what a profiler reports about the execution of this request. This endpoint execution simulates what happens in a real-world situation when a given app capability consumes a significant portion of the app's memory resources (figure 9.2).

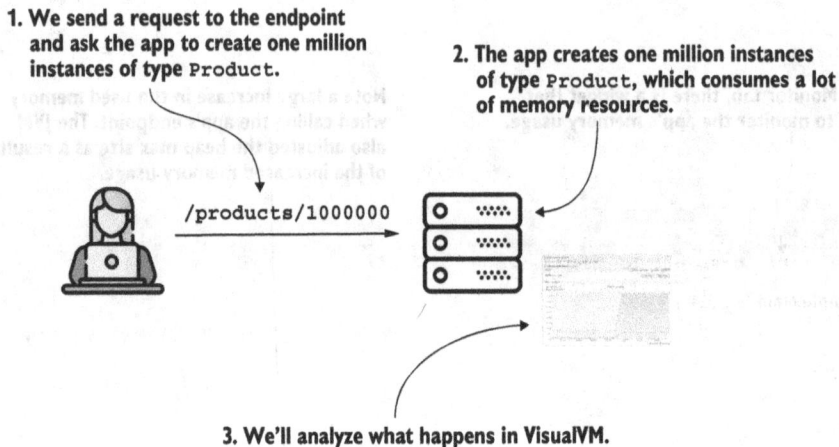

1. We send a request to the endpoint and ask the app to create one million instances of type Product.

`/products/1000000`

2. The app creates one million instances of type Product, which consumes a lot of memory resources.

3. We'll analyze what happens in VisualVM.

Figure 9.2   When we call the endpoint exposed by the provided project da-ch9-ex1, the app creates many instances that consume a considerable part of the app's memory. We'll analyze this scenario using a profiler.

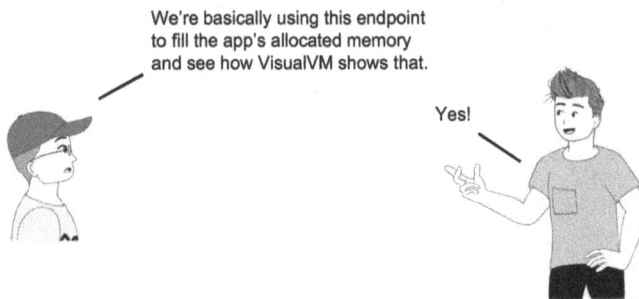

We're basically using this endpoint to fill the app's allocated memory and see how VisualVM shows that.

Yes!

To start the project, follow these steps:

1 Start project da-ch9-ex1.

2 Start VisualVM.

3 Select a process for project da-ch9-ex1 in VisualVM.

4 Go to the Monitor tab in VisualVM.

5 Call the /products/1000000 endpoint.

6 Observe the memory widget in the Memory tab in VisualVM.

In the Monitor tab in the memory widget, you can see that the app uses a lot of memory resources. The widget looks similar to figure 9.1. What should we do when we suspect some app capability doesn't optimally use the memory resources? The investigation process follows two major steps:

1. Use memory sampling to get details about the object instances the app stores.
2. Use memory profiling (instrumentation) to get additional details about a specific part of the code in execution.

Let's follow the same approach you learned in chapters 5–8 for CPU resource consumption: get a high-level view of what happens using sampling. To sample an app execution for memory usage, select the Sampler tab in VisualVM. Then select the Memory button to start a memory usage sampling session. Call the endpoint and wait for the execution to end. The VisualVM screen will display the objects the app allocates.

We are looking for what occupies most of the memory. In most cases, that will be one of these two situations:

- Many object instances of certain types are created and fill up the memory (this is what happens in our scenario).
- There are not many instances of a certain type, but each instance is very large.

Many instances filling up the allocated memory makes sense, but how could a small number of instances do this? Imagine this scenario: your app processes large video files. The app loads maybe two or three files at a time, but since they are large, they fill the allocated memory. A developer can analyze whether the capability can be optimized. Maybe the app doesn't need the full files loaded in memory but just fragments of them at a time. In such a case, you'll also notice the specific patterns of insufficient memory in the GC logs, which we'll discuss in chapter 11.

When we start our investigation, we don't know which scenario we'll fall into. I usually sort, in descending order, by the amount of memory occupied and then by the number of instances. Notice in figure 9.3 that VisualVM shows you the memory spent and the number of instances for each sampled type. You need to sort, in descending order, by the second and the third columns in the table.

Figure 9.3 clearly shows that I sorted the table in descending order by Live Bytes (space occupied). We can then look for the first type in our app's codebase that appears in the table. Don't look for primitives, strings, arrays of primitives, or arrays of strings. These are usually at the top since they are created as a side effect. However, in most cases, they don't provide any clues about the problem.

Figure 9.3 clearly shows that type Product is causing trouble. It occupies a large part of the allocated memory, and in the Live Objects column, we see that the app created one million instances of this type.

If you need the total number of instances of the type created throughout execution, you must use profiling (instrumentation) techniques. We'll do this later in this chapter.

2. Find the first object type that belongs to your codebase or a library that your app uses. Don't look for types coming from the JDK.

1. Sort in descending order by allocated memory.

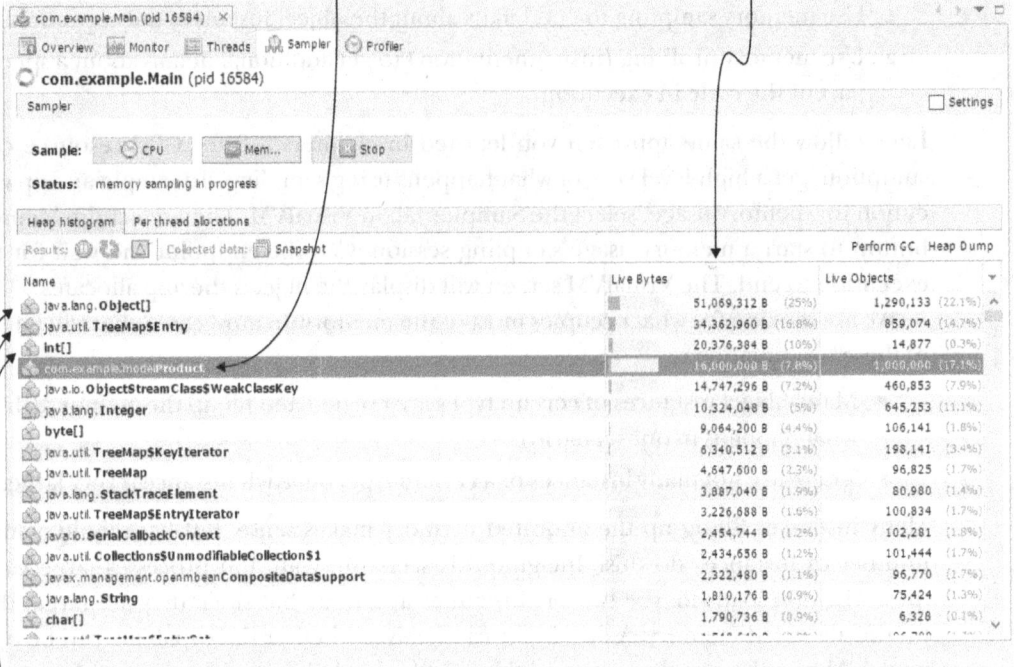

com.example.Main (pid 16584) ×

Overview   Monitor   Threads   Sampler   Profiler

○ **com.example.Main** (pid 16584)

Sampler   ☐ Settings

Sample: ○ CPU   Mem...   ■ Stop

Status: memory sampling in progress

Heap histogram | Per thread allocations

Results: Collected data: Snapshot   Perform GC   Heap Dump

Name	Live Bytes	Live Objects
java.lang.Object[]	51,069,312 B (25%)	1,290,133 (22.1%)
java.util.TreeMap$Entry	34,362,960 B (16.8%)	859,074 (14.7%)
int[]	20,376,384 B (10%)	14,877 (0.3%)
com.example.model.Product	16,000,000 B (7.8%)	1,000,000 (17.1%)
java.io.ObjectStreamClass$WeakClassKey	14,747,296 B (7.2%)	460,853 (7.9%)
java.lang.Integer	10,324,048 B (5%)	645,253 (11.1%)
byte[]	9,064,200 B (4.4%)	106,141 (1.8%)
java.util.TreeMap$KeyIterator	6,340,512 B (3.1%)	198,141 (3.4%)
java.util.TreeMap	4,647,600 B (2.3%)	96,825 (1.7%)
java.lang.StackTraceElement	3,887,040 B (1.9%)	80,980 (1.4%)
java.util.TreeMap$EntryIterator	3,226,688 B (1.6%)	100,834 (1.7%)
java.io.SerialCallbackContext	2,454,744 B (1.2%)	102,281 (1.8%)
java.util.Collections$UnmodifiableCollection$1	2,434,656 B (1.2%)	101,444 (1.7%)
javax.management.openmbean.CompositeDataSupport	2,322,480 B (1.1%)	96,770 (1.7%)
java.lang.String	1,810,176 B (0.9%)	75,424 (1.3%)
char[]	1,790,736 B (0.9%)	6,328 (0.1%)

3. Ignore primitives, arrays of primitives, or JDK objects.

Figure 9.3   We sort the sampled results in descending order by memory occupied. This way, we can see which objects consume most of the memory. We don't usually look for primitives, strings, and arrays of strings or JDK objects in general. We are mostly interested in finding the object directly related to our codebase, that is causing the problem. In this case, the Product type (which is part of our codebase) occupies a large part of the memory.

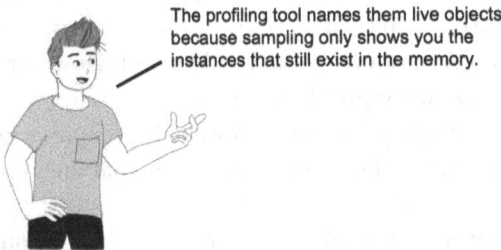

The profiling tool names them live objects because sampling only shows you the instances that still exist in the memory.

This app is just an example, but in a real-world app, simply sorting by the occupied space may not be enough. We need to figure out whether the problem is a large number of instances or whether each instance takes a lot of space. I know what you're thinking: Isn't it clear in this case? Yes, but it may not be in a real-world app, so I always recommend that developers also sort in descending order by the number of instances to make sure. Figure 9.4 shows the sampled data sorted in descending order by the number of instances the app created for each type. Again, type Product is at the top.

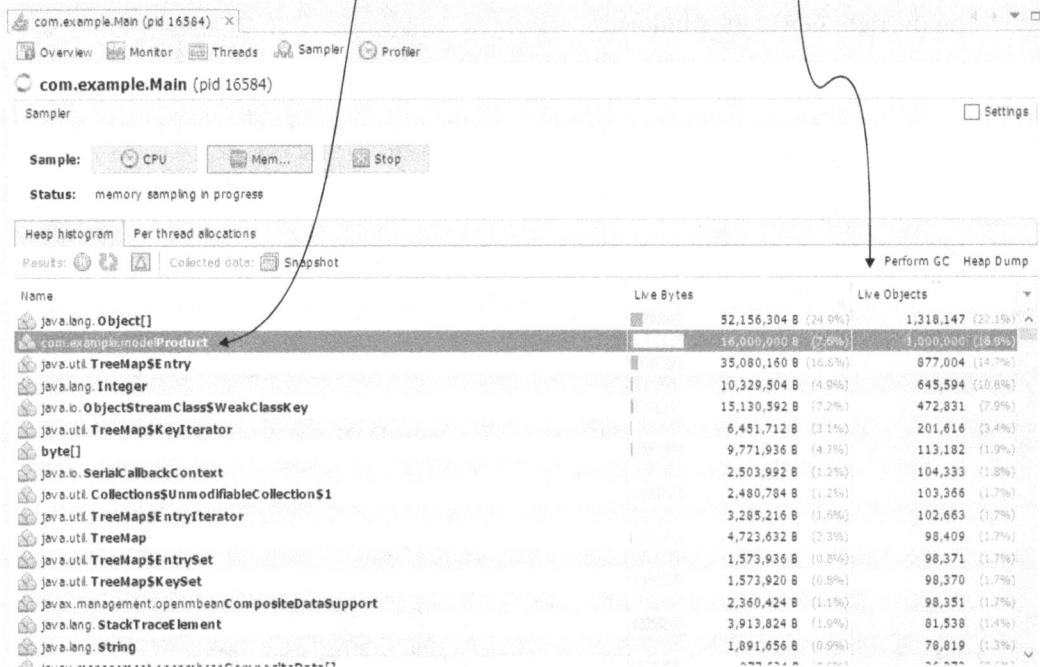

Figure 9.4 We can sort the sampled results by the number of instances (live objects). This gives us clues on whether some capability creates many objects that are negatively affecting the memory allocation.

9.2 Profiling to find the culprit

Sometimes, sampling is all you need to spot what's going wrong. It's fast, lightweight, and often provides a clear indication of the problem. But what if it doesn't? What if you still don't know which part of your app is creating all those objects? You look at the results and think, "Okay… but who's actually doing this?"

That's when it's time to switch gears and try profiling (also called instrumentation). While sampling, watches the program from a distance and takes notes occasionally, profiling gets up close and watches everything. It tells you exactly which part of your code is creating those objects, and how often.

However, profiling isn't free; it can slow things down and provide too much data. That's why we always follow one simple rule: don't profile until you know what to profile. If you start profiling everything, you'll waste time and possibly make things worse. We always begin by sampling to narrow things down. Once you have an idea where the problem might be, then you can zoom in with profiling.

Since we know the problem is with the Product type, we will profile for it. Like you did in chapters 5–8, you must specify which part of the app you want to profile using an expression. In figure 9.5, I profile only for the Product type. I do this by using the fully qualified name (package and class name) of the class in the Memory settings textbox on the right side of the window.

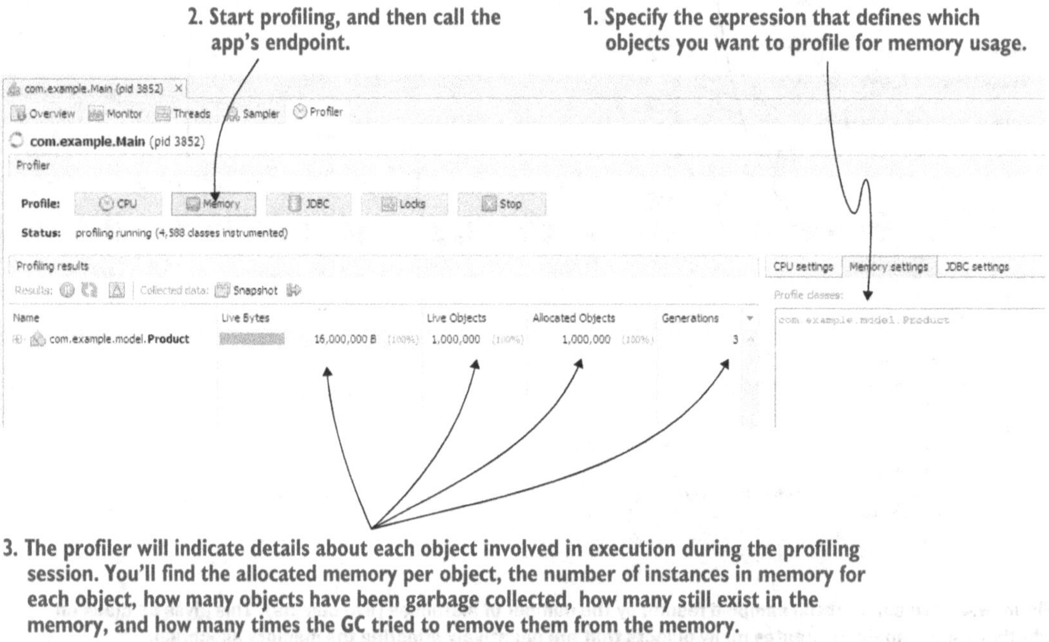

2. Start profiling, and then call the
   app's endpoint.

1. Specify the expression that defines which
   objects you want to profile for memory usage.

3. The profiler will indicate details about each object involved in execution during the profiling session. You'll find the allocated memory per object, the number of instances in memory for each object, how many objects have been garbage collected, how many still exist in the memory, and how many times the GC tried to remove them from the memory.

Figure 9.5   To profile for memory allocation, first specify which packages or classes you want to profile, and then start the profiling by pressing the Memory button. The profiler will give you relevant details about the profile types, including used memory, number of instances, the total number of allocated objects, and the number of GC generations.

Just as in the case of CPU profiling (chapter 6), you can profile multiple types at once or even specify entire packages. Some of the most commonly used expressions are

- *Strict-type, fully qualified name (e.g.,* `com.example.model.Product`*)*—Only searches for that specific type
- *Types in a given package (e.g.,* `com.example.model.*`*)*—Only searches for types declared in the package `com.example.model` but not in its subpackages
- *Types in a given package and its subpackages (e.g.,* `com.example.**`*)*—Searches in the given package and all its subpackages

Always remember to restrict the types you profile as much as possible. If you know product causes the problem, then it makes sense to profile only this type.

In addition to the live objects (instances that still exist in memory for that type), you will also receive the total number of instances of that type that the app has created. Moreover, you will see how often those instances survived the GC (what we call *generations*). As you'll find out in chapter 11, you can mix this with investigating GC logs to get extra details about the GC activity.

All these details are valuable, but finding what part of the code creates the objects is often even more useful. As shown in figure 9.6, for each profiled type, the tool displays where the instances were created. Click the plus sign (+) on the left side of the line in the table, which will quickly lead you the root cause of the problem.

At this point, you should have a solid understanding of how to sample and profile memory usage, identifying the trouble spots in your app's allocation patterns. But profiling only works when the app is actually running—and cooperative.

What if your app decides to throw a tantrum and crash before you can even fire up the profiler? Or worse, what if the problem only happens in production, where you can't just attach a profiler like it's your personal playground?

That's where heap dumps come in. Instead of watching memory in real time, you take a snapshot of the entire memory state, capturing everything your app was holding onto at the moment of its demise. Think of it as a freeze-frame of the crime scene—except that instead of footprints and fingerprints, you're analyzing objects and references.

So, if profiling leaves you empty-handed, don't worry. In chapter 10, we'll dive into heap dumps and how they can help you catch memory leaks red-handed. Let's go play detective!

For each profiled object type, the profiler indicates the part of code that created it during execution. This way, you can find the potential problem.

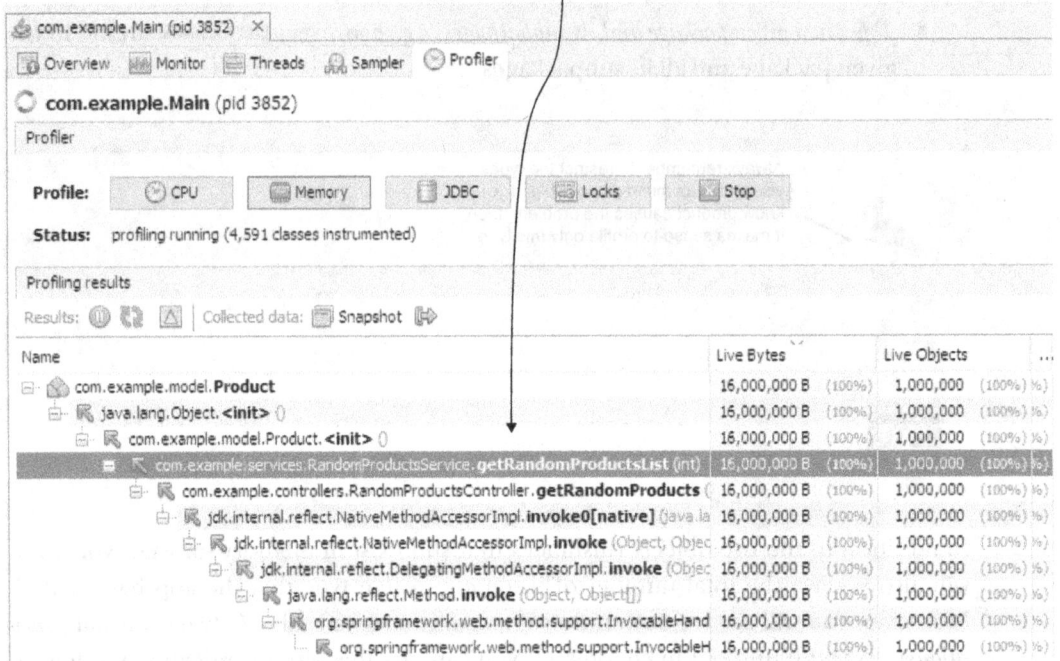

Figure 9.6 The profiler shows the stack trace of the code that created the instances of each of the profiled types. This way, you can easily identify what part of the app created the problematic instances.

Summary

- An application that doesn't manage memory efficiently can suffer from serious performance problems. Optimizing how data is allocated and released ensures stability and responsiveness.

- A profiling tool allows you to monitor memory usage in real time. This helps identify inefficient allocations and areas that need optimization.

- If object instances continue to accumulate without being dereferenced, the GC will be unable to free memory. Eventually, the heap fills up, leading to an OutOf-MemoryError and application failure.

- Understanding and managing heap memory efficiently prevents performance degradation. With the right tools and techniques, you can keep your application running smoothly and avoid critical memory problems.

Investigating memory
problems with heap dumps

10

This chapter covers

- Obtaining heap dumps for an app execution
- Using heap dumps to investigate memory allocation problems
- Using OQL to query object instances in heap dumps
- Using AI to simplify heap dump investigation

When you're testing the app, you can profile it to spot any memory-hungry capabilities that need optimization. But what if the app doesn't give you that luxury? What if it crashes spectacularly before you can even lift a profiler?

In many cases, crashes are the tragic result of memory allocation problems, with the usual suspect being memory leaks. These leaks happen when an app clings to objects in memory like a hoarder refusing to throw anything away—even when it has no use for them anymore. Over time, the memory fills up, and eventually, the JVM throws in the towel, leaving you with the dreaded `OutOfMemoryError`.

Think of it like a messy office. If you keep piling up papers, coffee cups, and half-eaten snacks without ever cleaning up, at some point, you'll run out of space to work.

In the digital world, instead of an exasperated coworker staging an intervention, your app simply crashes and burns.

So when profiling isn't an option and the app has already thrown its memory tantrum, what can you do? You freeze the moment—by grabbing a heap dump. If the app is not running, you can't attach a profiler to investigate the execution. But, even so, you have other alternatives to investigate the problem. You can use a *heap dump*, which is a snapshot of the heap memory's state at the time the app crashed. Although you can collect a heap dump anytime, it is most useful when you can't profile the app for some reason—maybe because the app crashed or you simply don't have access to profile the process, and you want to determine whether it suffers from any memory allocation problems.

> **DEFINITION** A heap dump is a snapshot of an application's memory at a specific moment, showing all the objects stored in the heap and their relationships.

In section 10.1, we'll discuss three possible ways to obtain a heap dump, and in section 10.2, I'll show you how to use the heap dump to identify memory allocation problems and their root causes. In section 10.3, we'll discuss a more advanced way of reading a heap dump using a query language called Object Query Language (OQL). OQL is similar to SQL, but instead of querying a database, you use OQL to query the data in a heap dump.

10.1 Obtaining a heap dump

Before being able to use a heap dump, you obviously need to know how to get one. This section discusses three ways to generate a heap dump:

- Configuring the application to generate one automatically in a specified location when the app crashes due to a memory problem
- Using a profiling tool (such as VisualVM)
- Using a command-line tool (such as `jcmd` or `jmap`)

You can even get a heap dump programmatically. Some frameworks have capabilities that can generate a heap dump, allowing developers to integrate app-monitoring tools.

10.1.1 Configuring an app to generate a heap dump when it encounters a memory problem

Developers often use a heap dump to investigate an app crash when they suspect faulty memory allocation is causing a problem. For this reason, apps are most often configured to generate a heap dump of what the memory looked like when the app crashed. You should always configure an app to generate a heap dump when it stops due to a memory allocation problem. Fortunately, the configuration is easy. You just need to add a couple of JVM arguments when the app starts:

```
-XX:+HeapDumpOnOutOfMemoryError
-XX:HeapDumpPath=heapdump.bin
```

The first argument, `-XX:+HeapDumpOnOutOfMemoryError`, tells the app to generate a heap dump when it encounters an `OutOfMemoryError` (the heap gets full). The second argument, `-XX:HeapDumpPath=heapdump.bin`, specifies the path in the filesystem where the dump will be stored. In this case, the file containing the heap dump will be named `heapdump.bin` and located near the executable app, from the root of the `classpath` (because we used a relative path). Make sure the process has write privileges on this path to be able to store the file in the given location.

> **NOTE** Remember to configure the app to generate the heap dump in a non-volatile location. If you're running your app in a Docker container, avoid placing the heap dump on the `classpath`, as it will be automatically destroyed when the container restarts. Instead, ensure that the app saves the heap dump in a persistent volume to retain it for analysis. Also, ensure that there's enough space in the location on the disk to store the heap dump, as it might be large.

The following snippet shows the full command for running an app:

```
java -jar -XX:+HeapDumpOnOutOfMemoryError
  -XX:HeapDumpPath=heapdump.bin app.jar
```

We'll use a demo app named da-ch10-ex1 to demonstrate this approach. You can find this app in the projects provided with the book. The app in the following listing continuously adds instances of type `Product` to a list until the memory fills.

Listing 10.1 Generating a large number of instances that can't be deallocated

```
public class Main {

  private static List<Product> products = new ArrayList<>();

  public static void main(String[] args) {
    Random r = new Random();
    while (true) {                              ◄─── The loop iterates forever.
      Product p = new Product();
      p.setName("Product " + r.nextInt());      ◄─── Adds instances to the list
      products.add(p);                               until the memory gets full
    }
  }
}
```

The next code snippet shows what the simple `Product` type looks like:

```
public class Product {

  private String name;

  // Omitted getters and setters

}
```

Perhaps you're wondering why there's a random name for the product instances. We'll need that later when we discuss reading a heap dump in section 10.2. For the moment, we're only interested in generating a heap dump to determine why this app is filling its heap memory in seconds.

You can use the IDE to run the app and set the arguments. Figure 10.1 illustrates how to set JVM arguments in IntelliJ. I also added the -Xmx argument to limit the app's heap memory to 100 MB. That will make the heap dump file smaller and our example easier.

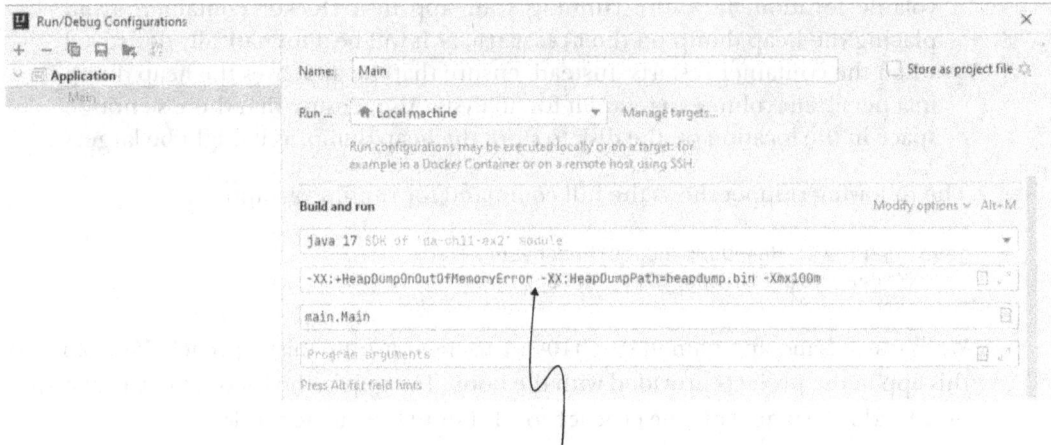

**Set the JVM arguments in the
Run/Debug Configuration window.**

Figure 10.1   You can configure the JVM arguments from your IDE. Add the values in the Run/Debug Configurations before starting the application.

When you run the application, wait a moment, and the app will crash. With only 100 MB of heap space, the memory shouldn't take more than a few seconds to get full. The project folder contains a file named heapdump.bin, which includes all the details about the data in the heap the moment the app stopped. You can open this file with VisualVM to analyze it, as presented in figure 10.2.

10.1.2   *Obtaining a heap dump using a profiler*

Sometimes, you need to get a heap dump for a running process on your local machine. In this case, the easiest solution is to use VisualVM (or a similar profiling tool) to generate the dump. Getting a heap dump with VisualVM is as easy as clicking a button. Just use the Heap Dump button in the Monitor tab, as shown in figure 10.3.

10.1.3   *Obtaining a heap dump with the command line*

If you need to get a heap dump for a running process, but your app is deployed in an environment where you don't have access to connect a profiler to it, don't panic; you

Use the Load button to find the file where it was generated. Then open the file.

Once you open the file, VisualVM displays it as a tab.

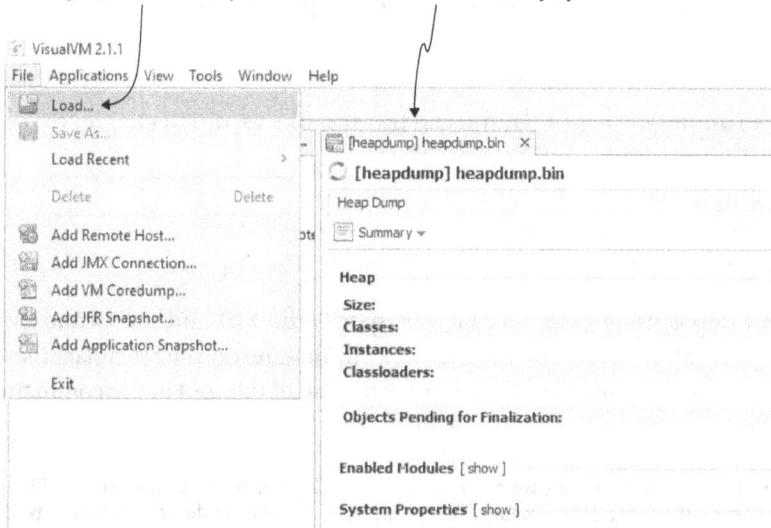

VisualVM 2.1.1

File Applications View Tools Window Help

Load...

Save As...

Load Recent

Delete   Delete

Add Remote Host...

Add JMX Connection...

Add VM Coredump...

Add JFR Snapshot...

Add Application Snapshot...

Exit

[heapdump] heapdump.bin ×

[heapdump] heapdump.bin

Heap Dump

Summary ▾

Heap

Size:

Classes:

Instances:

Classloaders:

Objects Pending for Finalization:

Enabled Modules [show]

System Properties [show]

Figure 10.2 You can use VisualVM to open the heap dump file for analysis. Use the Load button in the menu to find the file. Open the file, and VisualVM will display the heap dump as a tab.

still have options. You can use `jmap`, a command-line tool provided with the JDK, to generate the heap dump.

Click the Heap Dump button in the Monitor tab to get a heap dump. VisualVM opens the dump as a tab, and you'll be able to investigate it or save it anywhere you want.

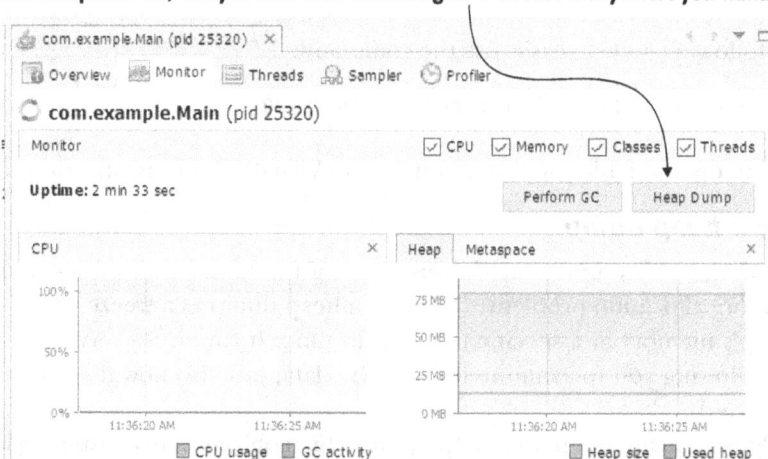

com.example.Main (pid 25320) ×

Overview Monitor Threads Sampler Profiler

com.example.Main (pid 25320)

Monitor   ☑ CPU ☑ Memory ☑ Classes ☑ Threads

Uptime: 2 min 33 sec   Perform GC   Heap Dump

CPU   ×   Heap   Metaspace   ×

100%   75 MB

50%   50 MB

                                      25 MB

0%   0 MB

11:36:20 AM   11:36:25 AM   11:36:20 AM   11:36:25 AM

■ CPU usage ■ GC activity   ■ Heap size ■ Used heap

Figure 10.3 Click the Heap Dump button in VisualVM's Monitor tab to get a heap dump for the selected process. VisualVM opens the dump as a tab, and you can further investigate it or save it anywhere you want.

There are two steps for collecting a heap dump with jmap:

1 Find the process ID (PID) of the running app for which you want to get the heap dump.

2 Use jmap to save the dump to a file.

To find the running-process PID, you can use jps, like we did in chapter 8:

```
jps -l
25320 main.Main
132 jdk.jcmd/sun.tools.jps.Jps
25700 org.jetbrains.jps.cmdline.Launcher
```

The second step is using jmap. To call jmap, specify the PID and the location where the heap dump file will be saved. You must also specify that the output is a binary file using the -dump:format=b parameter. Figure 10.4 shows the use of this tool in the command line.

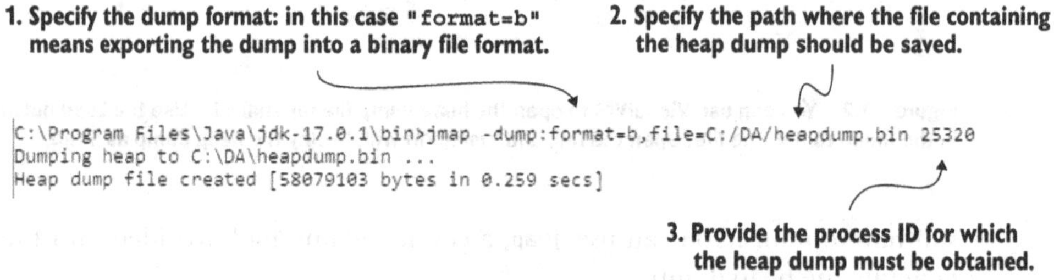

1. Specify the dump format: in this case "`format=b`" means exporting the dump into a binary file format.   **2. Specify the path where the file containing the heap dump should be saved.**

```
C:\Program Files\Java\jdk-17.0.1\bin>jmap -dump:format=b,file=C:/DA/heapdump.bin 25320
Dumping heap to C:\DA\heapdump.bin ...
Heap dump file created [58079103 bytes in 0.259 secs]
```

3. Provide the process ID for which the heap dump must be obtained.

Figure 10.4   Using jmap in the command line to get a heap dump. You need to specify the path where the file containing the dump will be saved and the process ID for which you generate the dump. The tool saves the heap dump as a binary file in the requested location.

Copy the following code to easily use the command:

```
jmap -dump:format=b,file=C:/DA/heapdump.bin 25320
```

Now you can open the file you saved with jmap in VisualVM for investigation.

10.2 *Reading a heap dump*

In this section, we dive into heap dumps—one of the most powerful tools for uncovering memory allocation problems. Think of a heap dump as a freeze-frame snapshot of your app's memory at a specific moment in time. It captures everything stored in the heap, allowing you to examine not just the data, but also how it's structured and interconnected.

By analyzing a heap dump, you can pinpoint which objects were consuming large portions of memory and, more importantly, why they weren't deallocated. Is it a classic memory leak? A rogue collection growing out of control? A forgotten cache hoarding data like a dragon? The answers are all in the heap dump—you just need to know how to look.

Remember that in the "picture" (heap dump), you can see everything. If unencrypted passwords or any kind of private data is in memory, someone with the heap dump will be able to get these details.

Unlike a thread dump, you cannot analyze a heap dump as plain text. Instead, you must use VisualVM (or any profiling tool in general). In this section, we'll use VisualVM to analyze the heap dump we generated for project da-ch10-ex1 in section 10.1. You'll learn how to use this approach to find the root cause of an OutOfMemoryError.

When you open a heap dump in VisualVM, the profiling tool displays a summary view of the heap dump (figure 10.5), which provides quick details on the heap dump

For a real-world app, the heap dump is usually much larger than the one in our example.

The summary shows quick details about the dump and the environment where the app was running.

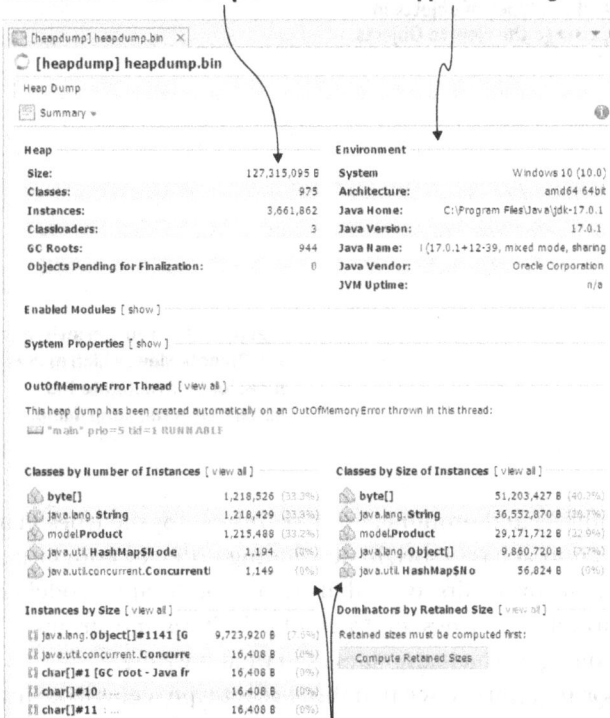

The summary presents a quick view of the types that occupy the most memory or that created a large number of instances.

Figure 10.5 In the initial screen after opening a heap dump, VisualVM provides a summary of the heap dump, which includes information about the dump itself and the system where the app was running. The view also shows the types that occupy the largest amount of memory.

file (e.g., the file size, total number of classes, total number of instances in the dump). You can use this information to ensure you have the correct dump, in case you weren't the one who extracted it.

There have been times I've had to investigate heap dumps from a support team that had access to the environments where the app was running. However, I couldn't access those environments myself, so I had to rely on someone else to get the data for me. More than once, I was surprised that I had been given the wrong heap dump. I was able to identify the error by examining the size of the dump and comparing it to the maximum value configured for the process, or by reviewing the operating system or Java version.

My advice is to first quickly review the summary page and ensure you have the correct file. On the summary page, you'll also find types that occupy a large amount of space. I usually don't rely on this summary and instead go directly to the Objects view, where I start my investigation. In most cases, the summary isn't enough for me to draw a conclusion.

To switch to the objects view, select Objects from the drop-down menu in the upper-left corner of the heap dump tab (figure 10.6). This step will allow you to investigate the object instances in the heap dump.

To get a view of all the types of objects in the heap dump, change the view to Objects.

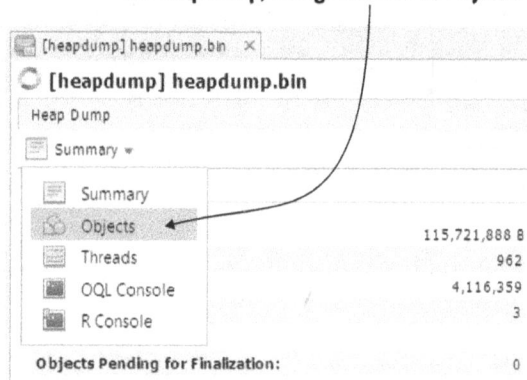

Figure 10.6 You can switch to the Objects view, which makes it easier to investigate the instances in the heap dump.

Just as with memory sampling and profiling, we're searching for the types that use the most memory. The best approach is to sort, in descending order, by both instances and occupied memory, and look for the first types that are part of the app's codebase. Don't look for types such as primitives, strings, or arrays of primitives and strings. There are usually a lot, and they won't give you many clues as to what is wrong.

In figure 10.7, after sorting, you can see that the Product type seems to be involved in the problem. The Product type is the first type that is part of the app's codebase, and it uses a large part of the memory. We need to figure out why so many instances have been created and why the GC can't remove them from the memory.

Look for the object type in your app's codebase that occupies the most memory.

Name	Count		Size		Retained	
⊞ byte[]	1,218,526	(33.3%)	51,203,427 B	(40.2%)	51,199,918 B	(40.2%)
⊞ java.lang.String	1,218,429	(33.3%)	36,552,870 B	(28.7%)	87,705,789 B	(68.9%)
⊞ model.Product	1,215,488	(33.2%)	29,171,712 B	(22.9%)	116,665,403 B	(91.6%)
⊞ java.util.HashMap$Node	1,194	(0%)	52,536 B	(0%)	104,234 B	(0.1%)
⊞ java.util.concurrent.ConcurrentHashMap$	1,149	(0%)	50,556 B	(0%)	68,717 B	(0.1%)
⊞ java.lang.Object[]	1,141	(0%)	9,860,720 B	(7.7%)	126,583,190 B	(99.4%)
⊞ java.lang.module.ModuleDescriptor$Expo	370	(0%)	14,800 B	(0%)	18,824 B	(0%)
⊞ java.util.HashMap	328	(0%)	20,992 B	(0%)	137,786 B	(0.1%)
⊞ java.util.HashMap$Node[]	325	(0%)	56,824 B	(0%)	129,794 B	(0.1%)
⊞ java.util.HashSet	264	(0%)	6,336 B	(0%)	89,204 B	(0.1%)
⊞ java.lang.Integer	262	(0%)	5,240 B	(0%)	5,240 B	(0%)

Figure 10.7 Use sorting on columns to identify which type created a large number of instances or takes up a lot of space. Always look for the first object in your app codebase. In this case, both in number of instances and size, the Product type is the first in the list.

You can select the small plus sign (+) on the left side of the row to get details about all the instances for that type. We already know there are more than one million Product instances, but we still need to find

- What part of the code creates those instances
- Why the GC can't remove them in time to avoid the app's failure

You can find what each instance refers to (through fields) and what refers to that instance. Since we know the GC cannot remove an instance from the memory unless it has no referrers, we look for what refers the instance to see whether it is still needed in the processing context or if the app forgot to remove its reference.

This behavior can hint at a memory problem—letting you know that something is off—but they won't pinpoint exactly where the problem lies. That's where memory profiling and heap dumps come into play.

Profiling works well when the app is running. But if the app crashes or profiling isn't feasible, a heap dump becomes your best friend.

Figure 10.8 shows the expanded view for the details of one of the Product instances. We can see that the instance refers to a String (the product name), and its reference is kept in an Object array, which is part of an ArrayList instance. Moreover, the ArrayList instance seems to keep a large number of references (over one million). This is usually not a good sign, as either the app implements an unoptimized capability or we found a memory leak.

**The object referencing this `Product` instance is an
`ArrayList` that holds 1,215,487 other references.**

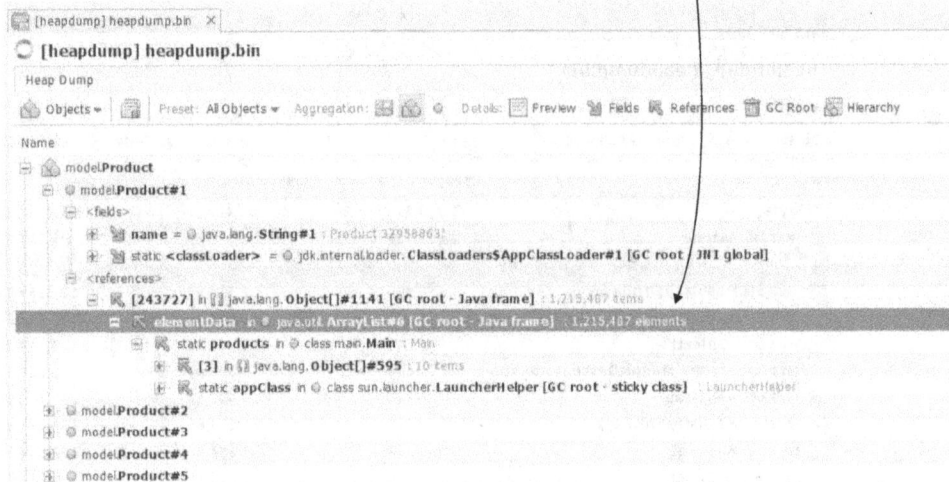

Figure 10.8   References to an instance. By using the heap dump, you can find, for each instance, what other instances were being referenced at the time the dump was generated. The profiling tool also tells you where a given reference is stored in the code. In this case, `ArrayList`, which holds over one million references, is a static variable in the `Main` class.

To find which is the case, we need to investigate the code using the debugging and logging techniques discussed in chapters 2–4. Fortunately, the profiler indicates exactly where to locate the list in the code. In our case, the list is declared as a static variable in the `Main` class.

Using VisualVM, we can easily understand the relationships between objects. By combining this technique with other investigation techniques you've learned throughout the book, you have all the tools you need to address these kinds of problems. Complex problems (and apps) may still require significant effort, but using this approach will save you a lot of time.

You might now be wondering about AI assistants—can we use them to investigate heap dumps? The answer is yes, but analyzing heap dumps with AI is significantly more challenging than working with thread dumps or profiling data. This is primarily due to the sheer size of heap dumps in real-world scenarios

Take, for example, the heap dump we analyzed in this scenario—it is just over 100 MB. As an experiment, you could try feeding it to an AI assistant such as Gemini or ChatGPT. However, you'll notice that processing it takes a considerable amount of time and may not yield immediate insights. Now, imagine handling a real-world heap dump of 4 GB or larger—such a task would be impractical for most AI assistants.

For this reason, I take a different approach when using AI for heap dump analysis. First, I investigate the data using a dedicated profiling tool such as VisualVM. Next, I extract relevant portions of the data and, if needed, consult an AI assistant to generate ideas or help me overcome roadblocks. However, I never rely on AI to analyze an entire heap dump file directly.

First, I follow the steps we have already discussed in this section. I begin by sorting instances based on their size and count. This is, in fact, the most crucial part of preparing investigation data—there's generally no need to examine types with only a small number of instances.

Second, if the heap dump file is particularly large and complex, I use OQL queries to explore the data as if it were a relational database. OQL enables precise filtering, allowing us to focus on only the most relevant objects. Section 10.3 discusses OQL queries in detail—this powerful yet often overlooked tool can significantly enhance your ability to isolate essential data when investigating memory problems in heap dumps.

10.3 *Using the OQL console to query a heap dump*

Alright, you've wrestled with heap dumps the old-fashioned way—sorting instances, eyeballing sizes, and maybe even muttering a few choice words when things didn't add up. But now, it's time to work smarter, not harder.

In this section, we're stepping up our game by using a query language similar to SQL to extract details from a heap dump with precision. The basic techniques from section 10.2 work fine for identifying memory problems, but they fall short when you need to compare multiple heap dumps—say, from different versions of your app.

Sure, you could open each heap dump manually, flip between them, and try to spot differences with sheer determination. But let's be real—that's like comparing two novels by reading them side by side. Instead, I'll show you how to write queries that do the heavy lifting for you.

This is where OQL shines. It lets you sift through heap dumps like a pro, extracting exactly what you need without endless scrolling. Figure 10.9 shows how to switch to the OQL console and unleash its power.

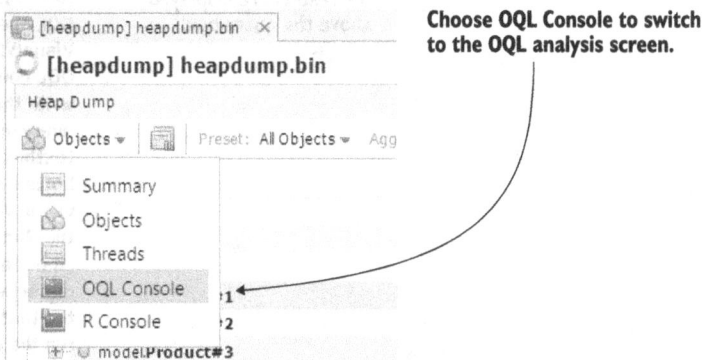

Figure 10.9 To switch to the OQL view in VisualVM, choose OQL Console from the drop-down menu in the upper-left corner of the heap dump tab.

We'll discuss a few useful examples, but remember that OQL syntax is more complex than the examples we'll be able to cover in this section. (You can find more information on its functions at http://mng.bz/Pod2.)

Let's start with a simple example: selecting all the instances of a given type. Suppose we want to retrieve all instances of type Product from the heap dump. To use a SQL query to get all the product records from a table in a relational database, we would write something like

```
select * from product
```

To query all the Product instances in a heap dump using OQL, you need to write this:

```
select p from model.Product p
```

> **NOTE** For OQL, keywords such as "select," "from," or "where" are always written in lowercase. The types are always given with their fully qualified name (package + class name).

Figure 10.10 shows the result of executing the simple query that retrieves all the Product instances from the heap dump.

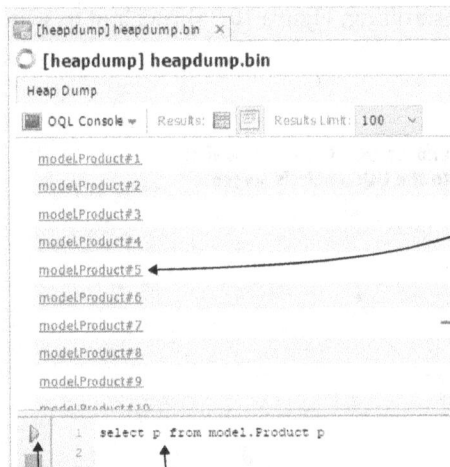

3. After running an OQL query, the results are displayed above the query box.

1. Write the OQL query in the text box.
2. Click the Run button.

Figure 10.10 Running an OQL query with VisualVM. In the OQL console, write the OQL query in the textbox on the bottom of the window and click the Run button (the green arrow on the left of the text box) to run the query. The results will appear above the text box.

NOTE When learning OQL, use small heap dumps. Real-world heap dumps are usually large (4 GB or larger). The OQL queries will be slow. If you are studying only, generate and use small-sized heap dumps like we do in this chapter.

You can select any of the queried instances to get its details. You can find what keeps a reference to that instance, what that instance refers to, and its values (figure 10.11).

Selecting any of the rows in the result (which represents an object instance) gives you details about that instance.

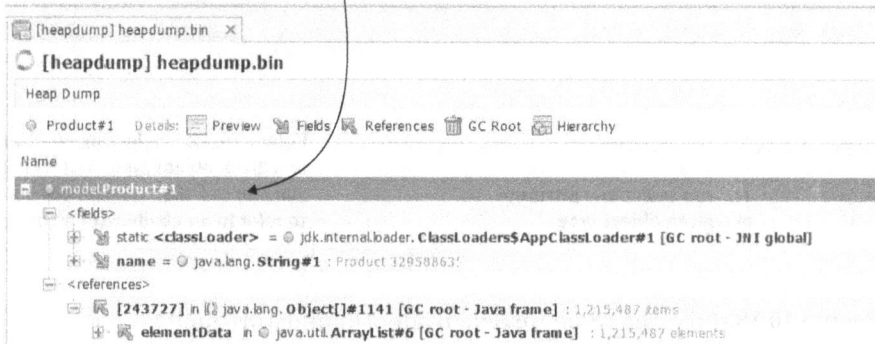

Figure 10.11 You can access the details about a queried instance (referees and referrers) by clicking it.

You can also select values or references referred from certain instances. For example, if we want to get all the product names instead of the product instances, we can write the following query (figure 10.12):

```
select p.name from model.Product p
```

With OQL, you can extract multiple values at the same time. To do so, you need to format them as JSON, as shown in the next listing.

Listing 10.2 Using a JSON projection

```
select
{
    name: p.name,
```

Curly braces surround the JSON object representation.

The attribute name takes the value of the product name.

```
        name_length: p.name.value.length
}

from model.Product p
```

◄——— The attribute name_length takes the value of the number of characters in the product name.

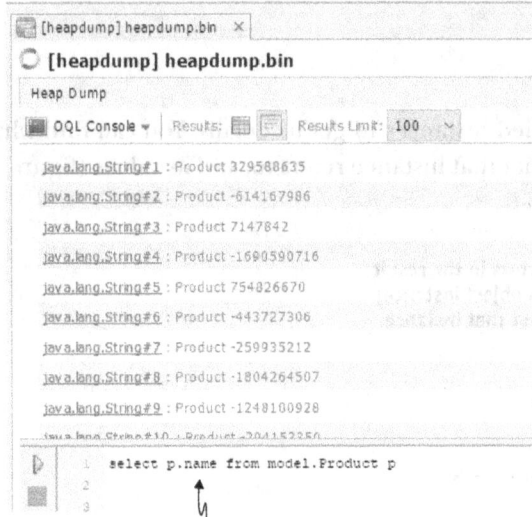

You can select any attribute of a given object type.

Figure 10.12 Selecting an attribute of a given object type. Just as in Java, you can use the standard dot operator to refer to an attribute of an instance.

Figure 10.13 shows the result we obtain after running this query.

To see the results clearly, use the formatter display.

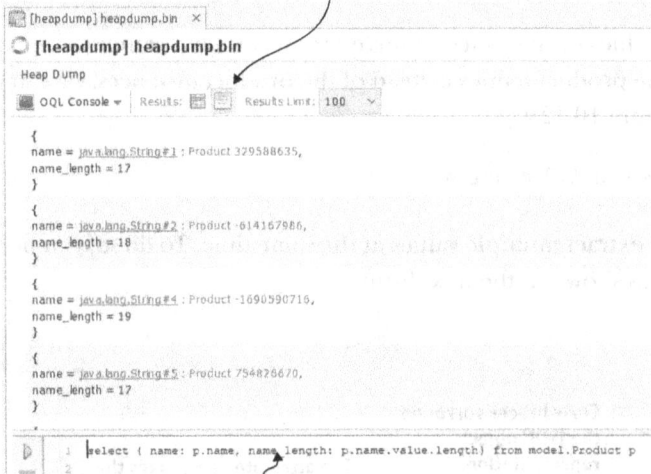

To select multiple values, use JSON formatting.

Figure 10.13 Selecting multiple values. You can use JSON formatting to obtain multiple values with one query.

You can change this query to, for example, add conditions on one or more of the selected values. Say you want to select only the instances that have a name longer than 15 characters. You could write a query as presented in the next snippet:

```
select { name: p.name, name_length: p.name.value.length}
from model.Product p
where p.name.value.length > 15
```

Let's move on to something slightly more advanced. A query I often use when investigating memory problems utilizes the `referrers()` method to retrieve the objects that refer to instances of a specific type. By using built-in OQL functions such as this one, you can do plenty of helpful things:

- *Find or query instance referees*—Can tell you if the app has memory leaks
- *Find or query instance referrals*—Can tell you if specific instances are the cause of memory leaks
- *Find duplicates in instances*—Can tell you if specific capabilities can be optimized to use less memory
- *Find subclasses and superclasses of certain instances*—Gives you insight into an app's class design without needing to see the source code
- *Identify long life paths*—Can help you to identify memory leaks

To get all the unique referrers for instances of type `Product`, you can use the following query:

```
select unique(referrers(p)) from model.Product p
```

Figure 10.14 shows the result for running this query. In this case, we can see that all the product instances are referred to by one object—a list. Usually, when a large number of instances have a small number of referrals, it's a sign of a memory leak. In our case, a list keeps references to all the `Product` instances, preventing the GC from removing them from memory.

If the result is not unique, you can count the referrals by instance using the next query to find the instances that are potentially involved in a memory leak:

```
select { product: p.name, count: count(referrers(p))} from model.Product p
```

The OQL queries provide a lot of opportunities, and once you write a query, you can run it as many times as you need and on different heap dumps.

Now, don't get too lazy—but do remember that AI assistants can help you craft and refine queries such as these. Some OQL queries can get pretty complex, and let's be honest, there's no need to become an expert in every little detail of the language. After all, it's not something you use every day.

So, work smarter! When investigating heap dumps, don't hesitate to offload some of the grunt work to an AI assistant. Whether it's generating queries, tweaking filters, or

By running the query, you can see that
all the products have a unique referrer.

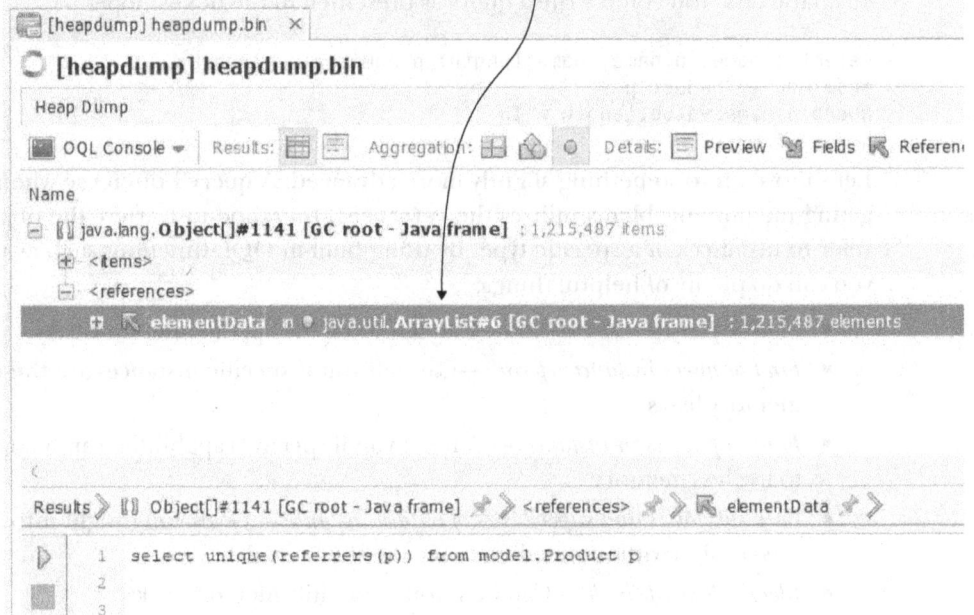

Figure 10.14   Selecting all the unique referrers for instances of a type shows you if there's one object that prevents the GC from removing the instances from memory. This can be a quick way to identify a memory leak.

explaining results, a little help can go a long way in simplifying your analysis. Just don't let the AI take all the credit!

And with that, you're now equipped to navigate heap dumps like a pro—one query at a time.

Summary

- A heap dump captures the entire memory state at a given moment. Analyzing it helps diagnose memory leaks, excessive object retention, and inefficient data structures.

- The JVM can be configured to generate a heap dump automatically when an OutOfMemoryError occurs. This makes post-crash investigations much easier.

- Heap dumps can be manually created using profiling tools such as VisualVM or command-line utilities such as jmap. These tools help capture and inspect memory usage at any time.

- Loading a heap dump into VisualVM facilitates exploring object instances, references, and relationships. This helps pinpoint performance bottlenecks and memory leaks.

- OQL (Object Query Language) lets you filter and analyze heap dump data efficiently. Instead of manually browsing through thousands of objects, you can retrieve specific information using queries.
- AI assistants such as ChatGPT or Gemini can help analyze heap dumps by generating OQL queries, summarizing data, and suggesting optimizations. While AI won't replace manual analysis, it can significantly speed up the process.

Analyzing potential JVM problems with GC logs

This chapter covers

- Enabling and accessing GC logs
- Understanding the structure and content of GC logs
- Using GC logs to identify root causes
- Analyzing large volume GC logs with AI assistance

Let's embark on a journey into the often misunderstood yet indispensable world of garbage collection (GC) logs. If you've ever stared at a stream of cryptic JVM output and thought, "This looks like *The Matrix*, but with less Keanu and more confusion," you're not alone. Fear not, for by the end of this chapter, GC logs will transform from chaotic hieroglyphics into an invaluable troubleshooting ally. But before we dive in, let me set the stage with a little story—a cautionary tale of what happens when GC logs are ignored.

Alex is a senior developer at an e-commerce startup, known for their love of coffee, code, and, unfortunately, cutting corners. One fateful Friday afternoon, Alex deployed a major update to the production environment—an update heralded as the solution to all scalability woes. But as the weekend wore on, the reality was anything but celebratory.

By Sunday morning, the site was slower than a dial-up modem from the 1990s. The server logs painted a picture of doom: memory spikes, sluggish response times, and CPU usage hovering at 99%. The worst part? The system was spawning threads faster than it could clean them up, leading to what Alex dubbed "zombie threads."

Desperate and sleep-deprived, Alex dove into the JVM's GC logs, a treasure trove of information they had always ignored in favor of more user-friendly tools. With the clock ticking and their caffeine stash running low, Alex turned to an AI assistant for help deciphering the logs.

Within minutes, the culprit was uncovered—an overly aggressive full GC cycle triggered by an improperly tuned heap size. The logs revealed excessive stop-the-world events, freezing the application at the worst possible times. A few adjustments to the JVM options, and voilà—the zombie threads were finally put to rest.

Why do GC logs matter? GC logs are like your JVM's memory diary. They document every GC event, from minor collections to full-scale memory cleanups. In this chapter, we'll start with the basics: enabling GC logs and understanding their structure. From there, we'll identify and solve common JVM performance problems, such as excessive GC pauses or memory leaks. And yes, I'll show you how to use AI assistants to make sense of the data faster than you can say "OutOfMemoryError."

Let's dive into the world of GC logs. Who knows? By the end of this chapter, you might just find yourself enjoying the process—or at least appreciating it a little more. After all, as Alex learned the hard way, sometimes the answers you seek are hidden in plain sight, waiting to be decoded.

We begin by learning how to enable GC logging in section 11.1, followed by configuring these logs to be stored in files in section 11.2. Next, in section 11.3, we explore techniques for optimizing log storage, including log rotation and selective logging levels, to enhance the troubleshooting experience. Finally, in section 11.4, we examine the most common real-world GC log patterns and analyze how to troubleshoot them effectively.

11.1 Enabling GC logs

This section covers key options and configurations for enabling GC logging for Java apps. Whether you're troubleshooting excessive GC pauses, high CPU usage, or memory leaks, enabling GC logs is the first step toward a deeper understanding of how the JVM manages memory.

Garbage collection plays a crucial role in Java application performance, but understanding its behavior can be challenging without proper visibility. GC logs provide valuable insights into memory allocation, collection pauses, and overall heap management, helping developers diagnose performance bottlenecks and fine-tune the JVM for optimal efficiency.

> **DEFINITION** *Garbage collection* is the process by which Java automatically finds and removes objects from memory that are no longer used by the application, freeing up space so the app can keep running efficiently.

Before we dive into GC analysis, let's first see how to enable GC logging. By default, GC logging is turned off when an application runs. This is because GC logs can be quite large, which may slow down the application and fill up the log files with extra data.

Since these logs can make it harder to find important information, it's best to enable them only when needed—such as when troubleshooting problems such as slow performance, high CPU usage, or memory problems. When used correctly, GC logs can help you understand how the JVM handles memory and find the root cause of performance problems.

First, I'll display the GC logs in the terminal so you can familiarize yourself with their appearance. Then, I'll show you how to save them to files, which is useful for long-term analysis or using AI tools to help with troubleshooting. AI can quickly scan through large GC logs and point out patterns or problems you might miss. It will save you time and make your investigation easier.

The following code snippet shows the VM attribute you must use to activate the GC logging:

```
-Xlog:gc*
```

If you're running the application in an IDE, you need to add the `-Xlog:gc*` VM option to your run configuration. This enables GC logging during execution. Figure 11.1 illustrates how I configured this option in IntelliJ IDEA in example da-ch11-ex1.

The example da-ch11-ex1 follows a producer-consumer multithreaded architecture, similar to the one we analyzed in chapter 5. To keep the focus on GC logs, I have removed all other application logs. This way, once we start the app, we can clearly observe the GC-related output without distractions.

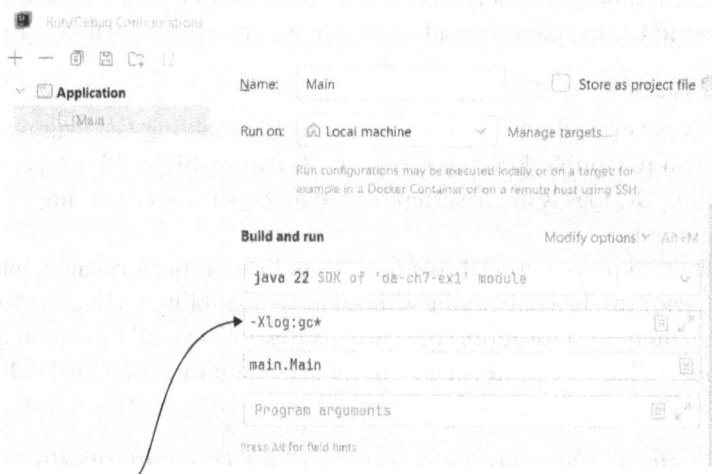

Add the necessary property to enable GC logging.

Figure 11.1 Enabling the GC logs in IntelliJ IDEA running configuration to display the GC logs in the execution console

If you run the application in a console—typically in a real-world environment where your app is started in a Docker container—you need to add the VM parameter to the execution command:

```
java -Xlog:gc* -jar app.jar
```

Listing 11.1 shows an example of GC logs that appear in the console when you run the application with the appropriate VM parameter. These first logs are also called initialization logs since they uncover the essential parameters related to the GC initialization.

We'll break down the most important lines together. As you get more familiar with them, what once seemed like an unreadable mess will start making sense. Over time, these logs will go from being an ominous wall of text to a helpful guide in your troubleshooting journey.

Next, we'll walk through the upcoming listings to give you a sneak peek at what GC logs look like—so they won't feel like an alien language anymore. We'll also discuss how to use these logs for troubleshooting and, most importantly, which ones deserve your attention first (Spoiler: Not all logs are created equal!). For a deeper dive into practical troubleshooting, stay tuned for section 11.2, where we'll turn GC logs from cryptic riddles into useful clues.

Listing 11.1 Initialization GC logs appearing in the app terminal

```
[0.059s][info][gc,init] CardTable entry size: 512          Which garbage collector is used
[0.059s][info][gc     ] Using G1                            Which JVM version is used
[0.065s][info][gc,init] Version: 22.0.1+8 (release)
[0.065s][info][gc,init] CPUs: 8 total, 8 available          Information about the
[0.065s][info][gc,init] Memory: 48899M                      system where the JVM runs
[0.065s][info][gc,init] Large Page Support: Disabled
[0.065s][info][gc,init] NUMA Support: Disabled
[0.065s][info][gc,init] Compressed Oops: Enabled (Zero based)
[0.065s][info][gc,init] Heap Region Size: 8M
[0.065s][info][gc,init] Heap Min Capacity: 8M               Information about
[0.065s][info][gc,init] Heap Initial Capacity: 768M         heap allocation for
[0.065s][info][gc,init] Heap Max Capacity: 12232M           the current execution
[0.065s][info][gc,init] Pre-touch: Disabled
[0.065s][info][gc,init] Parallel Workers: 8                 Information about GC
[0.065s][info][gc,init] Concurrent Workers: 2               parallelism configuration
[0.065s][info][gc,init] Concurrent Refinement Workers: 8
[0.065s][info][gc,init] Periodic GC: Disabled
```

The details in listing 11.1 provide a crucial first glance before I investigate a problem further. This initial overview helps me understand the basic configuration of the current application's execution.

Key aspects, such as the JVM version and the type of GC, are fundamental. They set expectations for how memory is managed. Different JVM versions may introduce improvements in memory allocation and storage, while different GC types handle object evacuation in distinct ways. Understanding these nuances allows you to anticipate potential events that might lead to higher latencies or unexpected behavior during execution.

System details matter because they tell you how many resources are available for the application. If the system lacks CPU or memory, the app might slow down, experience longer pauses, or even behave unpredictably. For example, running the same process on a single-core machine versus a multicore setup can yield different results.

Sometimes, weird bugs only show up when the system has fewer resources. I once spent way too many hours chasing down a mysterious problem in a multithreaded application. The problem? It happened randomly—sometimes everything worked fine, sometimes it didn't. After a lot of head-scratching, we finally realized that the bug showed up more often when the app ran in a virtual environment with limited CPU power. It turns out, our multithreading logic was not as smart as we thought, and the lower processing power made the flaw much more obvious.

Heap information is also crucial when investigating performance or memory-related problems. Suppose I notice that the heap has been allocated only a small amount of memory. In that case, it's one of the first things I suspect when troubleshooting GC performance or general memory problems.

No matter how efficient our algorithms are, they still need enough memory to run smoothly. Sometimes, tweaking memory configurations can reveal unexpected behaviors, uncover hidden flaws, or even expose inefficient memory management patterns. Adjusting heap settings isn't just about improving performance—it's also a great way to test how resilient an application is under different conditions. After all, if your app starts acting strangely just because it got a little less memory, maybe it was never that stable to begin with!

How is the heap organized

Before diving deeper into the structure of GC event log messages and how to analyze them, let's first refresh our understanding of how memory works. It can also be beneficial to review appendix E. In addition to what appendix E covers, let's explore the structure of the heap in greater depth and use some analogies to help you understand the complexities more easily.

Imagine the JVM process heap as a closet where you store clothes. But instead of just throwing everything in randomly (I know not everyone does that, but I'm usually guilty of that), you have a system to keep things organized. The heap has different sections based on how long the clothes (or data) are expected to stay:

1 *Eden (new clothes section)*—Think of Eden as the place where you put brand-new clothes you just bought. These are fresh items, and you're not sure yet if you'll keep them forever or get rid of them after a short time. New objects in a Java program start here.

2 *Survivor (still in use section)*—Some clothes from Eden are worn often, so you move them to a special section called Survivor. If something is still useful after

a few wears (or in Java's case, after surviving a few GC cycles), it gets moved here. There are two small areas in Survivor, and clothes (or data) get shuffled between them before moving to a more permanent place.

3 *Old generation (the classics)*—Some clothes become favorites: you wear them all the time, and they stay in your closet for years. This is the Old Generation in Java memory. Objects that survive long enough in Survivor move here because they're needed for the long run.

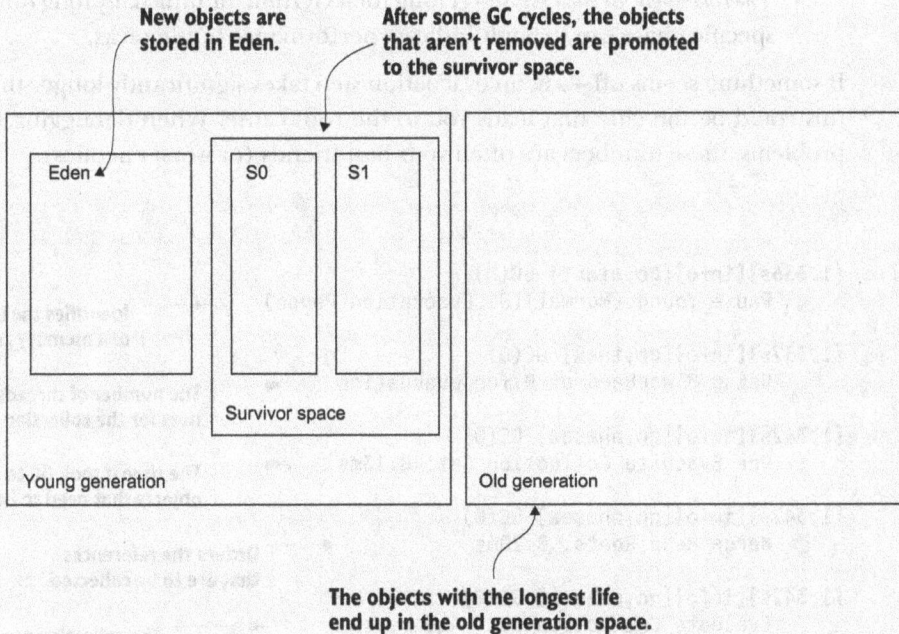

New objects are stored in Eden.

After some GC cycles, the objects that aren't removed are promoted to the survivor space.

Eden	S0	S1	
	Survivor space		Old generation
Young generation			

The objects with the longest life end up in the old generation space.

A visual representation of heap memory management illustrates how the heap is structured and how objects are organized based on their life cycle. The heap is divided into multiple regions, where objects are stored according to their age, which is determined by the number of GC cycles they have survived. As objects persist through successive GC cycles, they may be promoted from one region to another, optimizing memory usage and performance.

When the closet gets too full, you need to clean it out. This is what GC does—it removes clothes (data) you don't use anymore. Eden gets cleaned frequently because a lot of new stuff comes in and out. Survivor gets tidied up less often. The Old Generation is cleaned rarely because it holds important items.

Understanding the heap structure is crucial when analyzing GC logs because it helps identify patterns in GC events that may indicate potential problems in your application. By recognizing these patterns, you can diagnose performance problems, memory inefficiencies, and possible malfunctions more effectively.

Listing 11.2 shows an example of a GC event. These events are critical when trouble-shooting performance problems, especially if you suspect that GC is contributing to—or even causing—the problem.

One key detail to note is that each major phase of the collection process is measured separately. The two most important things to focus on are

- *The type of GC event*—This helps you understand whether it's a minor, full, mixed, or emergency collection. As you'll learn further in this chapter, these types represent events that serve distinct purposes in cleaning the memory.

- *The time spent in each phase*—A long total GC time or unusually long duration for a specific phase can strongly indicate performance bottlenecks.

If something seems off—say, an evacuation step takes significantly longer than usual—this could be the clue that leads you to the root cause. When debugging GC-related problems, these numbers are often your best friends (or worst enemies).

Listing 11.2   Logs related to events of a GC event of memory collecting

```
[1.336s][info][gc,start] GC(0)
     Pause Young (Normal)(G1 Evacuation Pause)          Identifies the initiation
                                                        of a memory collection

[1.337s][info][gc,task] GC(0)
     Using 8 workers of 8 for evacuation                The number of threads the GC
                                                        uses for the collection operation

[1.342s][info][gc,phases] GC(0)
     Pre Evacuate Collection Set: 0.13ms                The time it took GC to identify the
                                                        objects that need to be deallocated

[1.342s][info][gc,phases] GC(0)
     Merge Heap Roots: 0.20ms                    Orders the references
                                                 that are to be collected

[1.342s][info][gc,phases] GC(0)
     Evacuate Collection Set: 4.04ms                    The collecting operation
                                                        that implies moving some
                                                        references to the next
[1.342s][info][gc,phases] GC(0)                         hierarchic memory zone
     Post Evacuate Collection Set: 0.73ms               and removing others
[1.342s][info][gc,phases] GC(0) Other: 0.71ms

                                                 The final cleanup
                                                 phase after evacuation
```

For instance, in listing 11.2, there are no signs of concern. The event type is labeled as Normal, indicating that this is a routine collection event—not one triggered by memory pressure or any other urgent condition.

Moreover, all the execution times for each phase are measured in milliseconds, which are brief enough to rule out any significant problems with memory deallocation. The quick execution suggests that the garbage collector works efficiently, without causing noticeable delays or disruptions in application performance.

Listing 11.3 shows a summary of the changes made during the collection event. These logs provide insights into how many objects were promoted from one region to another and how many humongous objects (extra-large objects that occupy more than half of a memory region) were removed. This breakdown helps assess how memory is being managed and whether object movement patterns align with expected GC behavior.

Listing 11.3 Logs that show the changes after a collection

No survivor regions were used before the collection event.
After the collection event, one survivor region is used. In
total there is only one survivor region available.

Before the collection event, the app was using four
Eden regions that were all cleared during the collection
event. The app has five available Eden regions.

```
[1.342s][info][gc,heap] GC(0) Eden regions: 4->0(5)
[1.342s][info][gc,heap] GC(0) Survivor regions: 0->1(1)
[1.342s][info][gc,heap] GC(0) Old regions: 0->0
[1.342s][info][gc,heap] GC(0) Humongous regions: 0->0
```

There were no large
objects collected.

No objects were
promoted to the
old generation.

From the logs in listings 11.1, 11.2, and 11.3, we can draw the following conclusions as a summary:

- G1 GC is used, with an 8 MB heap region size and a max heap of approximately 12 GB.
- GC was triggered at 1.336s, doing a Young Generation collection.
- All Eden space was cleared, and one Survivor region was used.
- GC pause lasted only a few milliseconds, showing a well-tuned GC.

11.2 Storing GC logs in files

Logging GC activity directly in the terminal is useful for learning and quick debugging, but it's far from ideal in real-world scenarios. These logs often get mixed with other applications in a live console, making them hard to follow. Additionally, GC logs can be quite large, further cluttering the console and making real-time analysis difficult.

GC logs should be stored in separate files for practical troubleshooting. This allows easier collection, filtering, and analysis, especially when dealing with large volumes of data. For this reason, let's now explore how to store GC logs in files, ensuring they remain organized and accessible for deeper investigation.

The following code snippet shows the VM parameter you need to use to redirect the GC logs in a specific file. Make sure that the JVM process has write permissions to the directory where the GC log file should be created:

```
-Xlog:gc*:file=<file_path>:time,uptime,level,tags
```

In the snippet you've just read, the options `time`, `uptime`, `level`, and `tags` are data you want to be added to the log messages format. Usually, these four are the most useful and frequently used, representing

- `time`—Adds a timestamp to each log entry.
- `uptime`—Logs the JVM uptime in seconds/milliseconds when the GC event occurred.
- `level`—Includes the log level (e.g., info, debug, trace). See chapter 4 where we talked more about logging levels.
- `tags`—Shows tags (categories) associated with each log message.

You can add this VM option to the Java command when running the application from a terminal or configure it in your IDE's runtime settings. The following snippet shows an example of using the VM attribute in the command line, while figure 11.2 shows how to configure it in the running configuration of IntelliJ IDEA:

```
java -Xlog:gc*:file=gc.log:time,uptime,level,tags -jar yourApp.jar
```

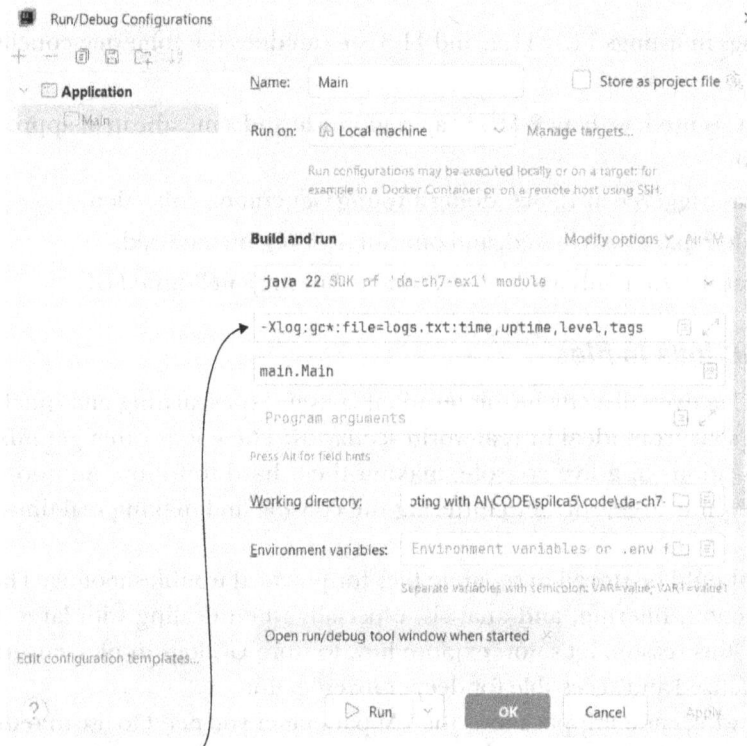

Add the VM property to store
the GC logs in a given file.

Figure 11.2   Adding a VM property to store GC logs for the application's execution in a specified file

After running the application for some time, a file will appear in the specified location. This file contains GC logs formatted according to the specified option (figure 11.3).

The GC logs were stored at the requested location.

The message is formatted according to the options you provided: time, uptime, level, and tags.

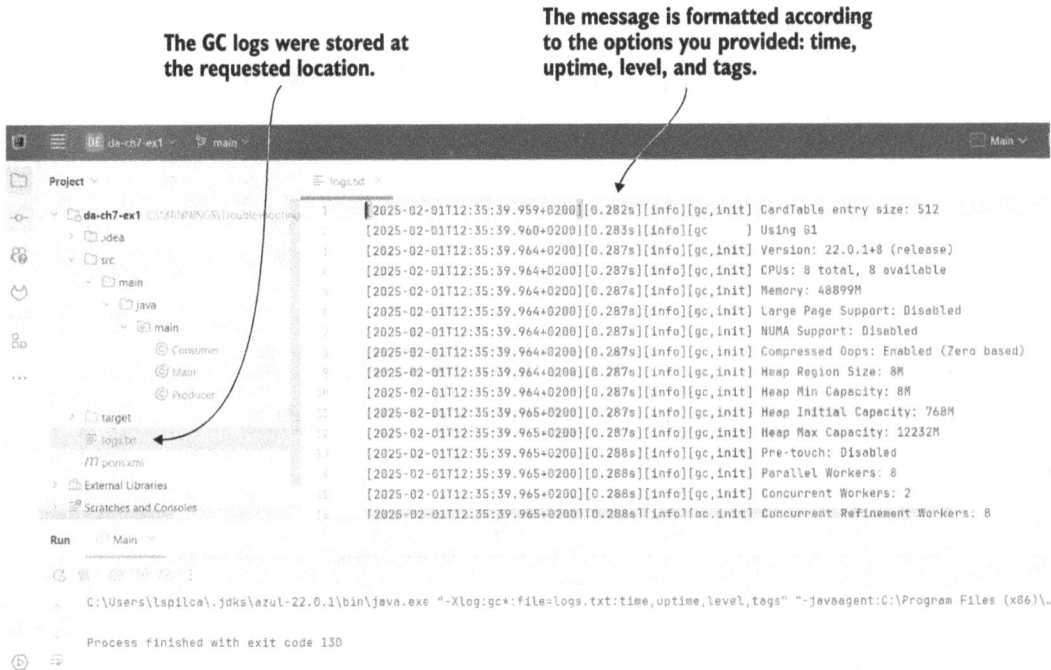

Figure 11.3 Properly formatted GC logs are stored in the specified file, as defined by the VM parameter.

Storing GC logs in a file not only makes it easier to retain and share them but also allows you to employ specialized tools for in-depth analysis. In figure 11.4, you can see how I uploaded the file to GCeasy.io, a well-known tool for investigating GC logs. Additionally, the figure demonstrates how AI assistants, such as ChatGPT or Gemini, can help analyze the contents of the GC log file, providing valuable insights and suggesting effective troubleshooting strategies.

To end this section, let me tell you a short story. Once upon a time, in a chaotic tech company (aren't they all the same?), a junior developer named Jake was given a simple task: enable and store GC logs in a file. It was supposed to be easy—just a couple of JVM flags and voilà, problem solved. Jake confidently added the configuration and deployed the app, going home early and dreaming of a promotion.

The following day, the senior dev, Maria, stormed over.

Maria: "Where are the GC logs?"

Jake: "They should be in /var/logs/gc.log."

Maria: "They are not."

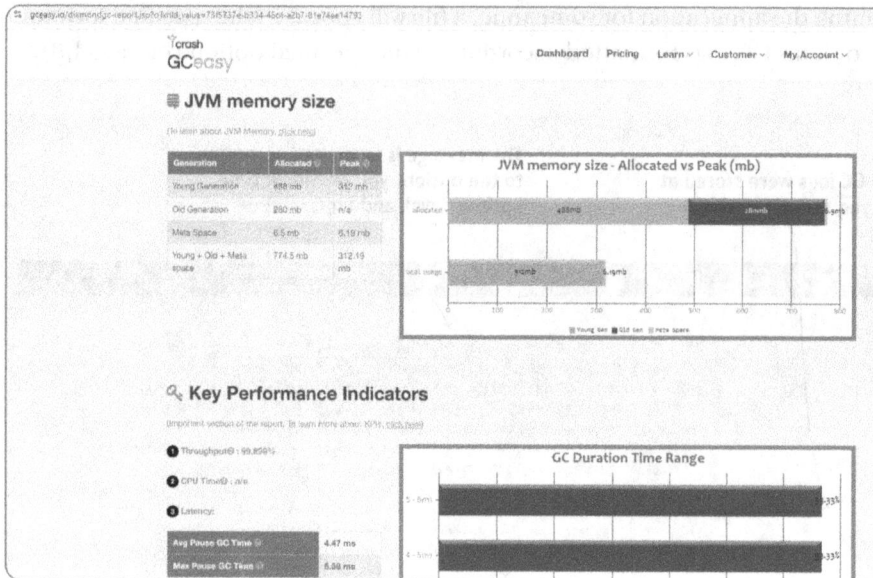

Figure 11.4   Using tools such as GCeasy or AI chat assistants to help you troubleshoot the GC logs.

Jake opened the directory and, sure enough, the file was missing. In a frenzy, he tried rerunning the app. The log file appeared! Victory! But moments later, it vanished into the digital abyss. Determined to solve the mystery, Jake turned to Stack Overflow (as all great engineers do, or was it ChatGPT today?) and discovered that the log file was getting overwritten on every restart.

Embarrassed but undeterred, Jake updated the JVM options to add a timestamp at the end of the filename. This time, the logs stayed put, each with a timestamp. Crisis averted.

Maria: "Good. Now, where are the old logs?"

Jake turned pale. He hadn't enabled log rotation (we'll discuss log rotation next, in section 11.3). Somewhere, deep in the server, an ancient GC log from five years ago still lurked, consuming disk space like an ever-hungry garbage collector that refused to be collected.

Moral of the story? Always configure log rotation. Or else, your past mistakes will haunt you—literally. For this reason, we continue talking about particular configurations that you'll find useful in real-world situations.

11.3 *Particular configurations for storing GC logs*

Simply writing all logs into a single file is not always practical. GC can generate a significant amount of logs, and ending up with a multi-gigabyte file can make storage, transfer, and analysis cumbersome. In this section, we discuss several configurations to improve the troubleshooting experience with GC logs, including file rotation and selecting the appropriate logging level for the messages you want to retain.

Let's begin with file rotation. You can configure the GC to split logs into multiple files, preventing a single log file from growing indefinitely. This approach improves manageability by making logs easier to transfer and process, ultimately streamlining the troubleshooting process. Additionally, file rotation enhances performance by reducing the risk of excessive disk usage. It also facilitates log retention, allowing older logs to be archived efficiently.

Use the `filecount` attribute to define the maximum number of log files, and the `filesize` attribute to set the size limit for each file.

The following snippet provides an example command to enable GC logging, while configuring file rotation. It sets a maximum of five log files, each with a maximum size of 10 MB:

```
java -Xlog:gc*:file=logs.txt:time,uptime,level,tags:
   filecount=5,filesize=10M -jar app.jar
```

Using these parameters, the GC will automatically create a new log file whenever the current file reaches the specified size limit (10 MB in our case). Each new file will be assigned an index, starting from 0, and subsequent logs will be stored in newly created files. Once the maximum number of log files is reached, the oldest file will be overwritten, ensuring efficient log management without excessive disk usage.

If you need to search for logs within a specific time, you can filter log files based on their creation or modification timestamps. For example, you can use the `find` command in a Linux environment or `Get-ChildItem` in PowerShell on Windows. By identifying and collecting only the relevant log files, you can focus your investigation more efficiently. This approach streamlines troubleshooting and simplifies log analysis using tools such as GCEasy or an AI assistant, as discussed in section 11.2.

Another strategy to reduce the volume of logged messages is to store only logs at specific levels of severity. You don't always need to retain every log entry. GC logs use standard logging levels, which we discussed in chapter 4. The following list ranks these levels in descending order of criticality:

1 *Error*—Logs only critical failures that may impact application stability
2 *Warning*—Captures potential problems that could lead to errors
3 *Info*—Provides general operational details about the GC process
4 *Debug*—Includes additional diagnostic information useful for troubleshooting
5 *Trace*—Produces the most detailed logs, capturing in-depth GC activity

Selecting a specific logging level is straightforward—simply include the desired level(s) in the parameter used to enable GC logging (the same one we've been using extensively throughout this chapter). The following snippet provides an example of how to enable logging for error messages only:

```
java -Xlog:gc=error:file=gc.log:filecount=5,filesize=10M -jar app.jar
```

Remember that each log level automatically includes messages from the more critical levels preceding it. This means that if you enable warning-level logging, as shown in the next snippet, it will also capture error messages since they are of higher priority:

```
java -Xlog:gc=warning:file=gc.log:filecount=5,filesize=10M -jar app.jar
```

At this point, you're probably thinking, "Alright, but what's the best choice? Do I stick with just errors, or do I go all in and log everything from trace up, drowning in a sea of GC details?"

Great question! The answer depends on what you're troubleshooting. In the following sections, you'll find some practical recommendations to help you decide which logging level to enable when debugging a problem. Because—let's be honest—too little logging, and you're flying blind; too much, and you might as well be trying to read the Matrix.

First and foremost, if you're working in a production environment, it's always best to log only errors and warnings. Production systems are performance-sensitive, and excessive GC logging can introduce unnecessary overhead, potentially affecting application efficiency.

If you encounter a problem that requires more detailed logs, the best approach is to first reproduce the problem in a staging environment rather than flooding production with verbose logging. In most cases, the info level provides sufficient details for monitoring and basic troubleshooting. This is precisely why info is the default logging level, so if you were wondering why you didn't see any trace messages in previous examples, now you know!

If you determine through info-level logging that there's a problem but still don't have enough details to piece together the puzzle, it's time to dig deeper with debug and trace levels:

- The debug level provides insights into GC behavior, pause times, and potential optimizations, helping you better understand what's happening under the hood.
- The trace level? Well, that's the "give me everything" mode—it logs every possible detail the GC collects, making it ideal for exhaustive analysis.

I usually turn to these levels in development mode when fine-tuning GC performance—or when I'm feeling completely desperate and willing to wade through an ocean of logs just to find that elusive culprit.

In summary, choosing the right GC log level is all about balancing detail and performance—log too little, and you might miss key insights; log too much, and you'll be drowning in data. By applying these recommendations, you can efficiently capture the information you need without unnecessary overhead.

Now that we've covered how to configure GC logging, let's move on to the next section, where we'll dive into real-world strategies for investigating GC logs. Here, we'll explore practical troubleshooting techniques, helping you make sense of the data and pinpoint performance problems effectively.

11.4 Analyzing GC logs

Now that we know how to obtain proper log messages and understand the possibilities of using them, let's explore real-world scenarios and how logs help us troubleshoot problems. We'll discuss common situations that can arise in applications and where to look in the logs when suspecting these problems. However, having logs is not enough—you must also know how to search through them effectively and identify potential problems they reveal.

11.4.1 Troubleshooting performance lags with GC pause times

Garbage collection is essential for memory management in Java applications, but excessive or prolonged GC pauses can significantly affect performance, leading to noticeable lags. Identifying and analyzing GC-related performance problems using logs is crucial for maintaining application responsiveness.

When an application experiences unexpected slowdowns, one common cause is excessive GC activity. Symptoms may include

- Increased response times in request processing
- High CPU usage with little actual work being done (Remember we discussed in chapter 5 how to observe the usage using a profiler.)
- Periodic application freezes or spikes in latency

To diagnose GC-related performance lags, start by reviewing the GC logs. These logs provide insights into the frequency and duration of GC pauses. If GC runs too frequently or for extended periods, it may be causing performance degradation.

Here are the main points in the GC logs you should consider when investigating a potential lag problem:

- *GC pause duration*—Look for messages indicating the time taken by each GC cycle.
- *GC frequency*—Excessive minor or full GCs in short time intervals may indicate a memory leak or poor tuning.
- *Heap utilization before and after GC*—If a full GC reclaims little memory, objects may be lingering longer than expected.
- *Stop-the-world (STW) events*—Prolonged STW pauses indicate GC is interfering with application performance.

The first step I recommend is looking for logs that indicate a longer time taken to release memory space. The next snippet shows an example of such a message:

```
[GC pause (G1 Evacuation Pause) (young), 0.0456780 secs]
    [Parallel Time: 43.5 ms, GC Workers: 8]
    [Code Root Fixup: 0.0 ms]
    [Code Root Purge: 0.0 ms]
    [Clear CSet: 0.5 ms]
```

Typically, GC pause times between 0 and 50 milliseconds are considered normal and within expected behavior. However, if pauses exceed 50 milliseconds, it could indicate a potential performance problem that requires further investigation. It's essential to verify whether this is a recurring pattern by checking multiple log entries. If only one or two exceptions appear among 1,000 log messages, it may not necessarily indicate a problem.

To conclude that the problem is genuine, you should observe frequent GC events with consistently high pause times. When this occurs, it usually means the application is experiencing memory pressure, which can lead to degraded performance and latency spikes.

Let's consider a practical example. Suppose you're analyzing the GC logs of your application due to unexplained latency problems. As you review the logs, you come across a fragment as the one shown in the next snippet.

Would this indicate a potential problem? Let's examine it together:

```
[2024-02-01T12:00:01.123+0000] GC(45)
    Pause Young (G1 Evacuation Pause) 0.025s
[2024-02-01T12:00:02.456+0000] GC(46)
    Pause Young (G1 Evacuation Pause) 0.027s
[2024-02-01T12:00:05.789+0000] GC(47)
    Pause Young (G1 Evacuation Pause) 0.026s
[2024-02-01T12:00:10.012+0000]
    GC(48) Pause Young (G1 Evacuation Pause) 0.110s
[2024-02-01T12:00:20.345+0000]
    GC(49) Pause Young (G1 Evacuation Pause) 0.250s
[2024-02-01T12:00:35.678+0000]
```

```
   GC(50) Pause Full (System.gc()) 2.567s
[2024-02-01T12:00:50.901+0000]
   GC(51) Pause Young (G1 Evacuation Pause) 0.180s
[2024-02-01T12:01:10.234+0000]
   GC(52) Pause Full (Allocation Failure) 5.321s
```

The first few GC events are minor and relatively fast (around 25–27 ms), which is within normal behavior. However, at 12:00:10, an unusual pattern emerges—the pause time jumps to 110 milliseconds, which could be an early warning sign of performance degradation.

By 12:00:20, the situation worsens with a pause of 250 milliseconds, indicating increasing memory pressure. Then, at 12:00:35, a major red flag appears—a full GC lasting 2.5 seconds, severely affecting application responsiveness. This is followed by yet another full GC at 12:01:10, signaling a serious memory management problem that requires immediate attention.

If GC pauses are impacting performance, consider the following adjustments:

- Experiment with different GC algorithms (e.g., G1GC, ZGC, Shenandoah) to find the best fit for your workload.
- Adjust heap size settings (`-Xms` and `-Xmx`) to prevent excessive GC activity.
- Optimize Eden, Survivor, and Old Generation sizes based on application behavior.
- If possible, change your application design to minimize object creation and encourage object reuse.
- If the application requires low-latency performance, consider using ZGC or Shenandoah GC, which minimize pause times.

11.4.2 *Identifying memory leaks with heap usage logs*

Memory leaks in Java applications can be subtle yet devastating, leading to degraded performance, excessive garbage collection, and eventually `OutOfMemoryError` crashes. While profiling tools such as VisualVM and Eclipse MAT offer powerful ways to analyze memory usage, sometimes a more lightweight and continuous approach is needed—this is where heap usage logs come in.

Heap usage logs provide a historical view of memory consumption over time, allowing developers to detect gradual memory growth patterns that may indicate a leak. These logs can be captured using JVM options, GC logs, or JMX monitoring tools, offering valuable insights into how objects are allocated and retained.

Let me tell you a story. It seemed to be a quiet night. Matilda woke up to the sound of her phone buzzing. Half-asleep, she grabbed it and saw a flood of messages.

"App crashed. Users are stuck. Fix ASAP!"

Sighing, she got out of bed, made a quick coffee, and opened her laptop. Logging in, she noticed that several Kubernetes pods responsible for managing the app's containers were repeatedly restarting.

With her eyes still half-closed, she knew the GC logs might hold some clues. Fortunately, the app always stored error logs on a persistent volume, making it easy to retrieve crash details.

She opened the latest log file from one of the failing containers and found the following entries:

```
[GC (Allocation Failure) [PSYoungGen: 512M->128M(1024M)] 1024M->900M(2048M),
0.250s]
[GC (Allocation Failure)
  [PSYoungGen: 640M->200M(1024M)] 1100M->980M(2048M), 0.270s]
[GC (Allocation Failure)
  [PSYoungGen: 700M->250M(1024M)] 1200M->1050M(2048M), 0.280s]
[Full GC (Ergonomics)
  [PSYoungGen: 900M->0M(1024M)] [ParOldGen: 1148M->1148M(2048M)]
     2048M->1148M(2048M), 1.200s]
```

"The memory usage keeps growing," she thought. "The first GC event freed 900 MB, the second only 980 MB, and the third 1050 MB. Instead of reclaiming more space, each cycle is leaving behind more memory. Then, the GC panicked and triggered a full collection—but even that barely made a difference. This isn't just normal memory usage—it's a leak."

Fortunately, Matilda knew how to analyze heap dumps to pinpoint the exact source of the leak (see chapter 10). As she dug into the data, she noticed that session references were lingering in a collection—one that wasn't being cleared. The culprit? A recent code deployment just hours before the crash had introduced the problem.

Realizing this wasn't a quick fix, she made the practical decision to roll back the release, ensuring the app would remain stable until the team could properly address the problem with fresh minds in the morning.

She checked the clock—3:48 AM.

"Damn," she muttered. "I need to get back to sleep."

GC logs can be a powerful tool for identifying potential memory leaks. While they won't always pinpoint the exact cause, they provide valuable clues on how to proceed with your investigation.

A key warning sign is GC struggling to free up memory, especially after an application crash. If you open the logs and see multiple GC events making little progress in reclaiming space, a memory leak is likely at play. Even more telling are full GC events that have minimal or no effect—strongly reinforcing the suspicion of a leak. If you have access to a profiler, you can also confirm the presence of a memory leak by analyzing memory allocation graphs, as discussed in chapter 5. Figure 11.5 is a reminder on how to distinguish between an application that is consuming memory as expected and one that is experiencing a memory leak.

11.4.3   *Identifying insufficient memory with full GC events*

Insufficient memory is not the same as memory leak. Section 11.4.2 discussed how GC logs can indicate a potential memory leak. A memory leak is typically caused by a flaw

Normal behavior

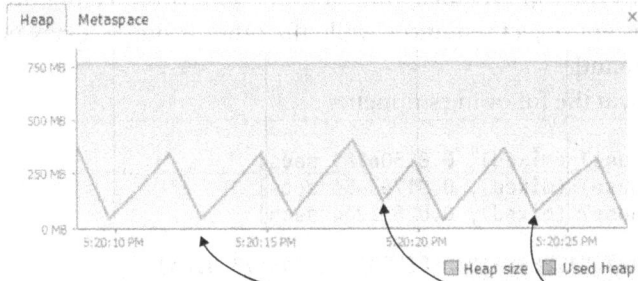

In an app that behaves normally, you will observe a pattern as presented in this visual. The memory fills and at a certain point the GC cleans the unneeded data freeing up the memory.

These are moments where the GC cleaned the unneeded data, making space for new data to be added in memory.

Abnormal behavior

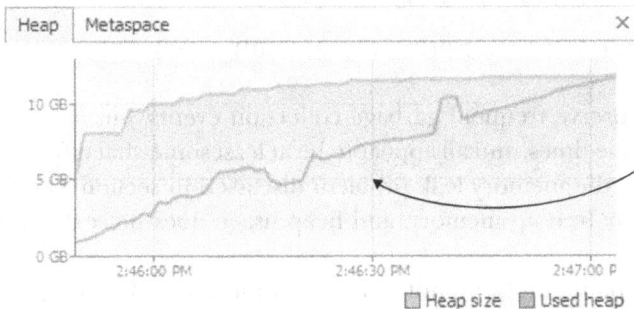

When an app has a memory leak, you will observe the used memory grows continuously. The GC makes efforts to free the memory but can't deallocate enough objects since the app holds the references for most of them.

Figure 11.5 A comparison between the memory consumption graph of an application with normal memory usage and one affected by a memory leak.

in the application's logic, where objects are continuously allocated but never properly released.

In such cases, even though the application has sufficient allocated memory, certain references persist indefinitely due to improper resource management, eventually leading to heap exhaustion. This gradual accumulation prevents the GC from reclaiming memory, ultimately causing OutOfMemoryError or performance degradation.

In this section, we discuss insufficient memory allocation. In this scenario, the application simply does not have enough memory to process the given workload. Unlike a memory leak, where memory is improperly retained, the application is genuinely under-provisioned for the data it needs to handle.

Addressing insufficient memory can involve several approaches, depending on the situation. Solutions may range from redesigning the application to improve memory efficiency, enabling horizontal scaling to distribute the load across multiple instances, or—in the simplest case—increasing the allocated heap size to better accommodate the workload.

Differentiating between a memory leak and insufficient memory can sometimes be challenging because, in both cases, the GC logs will show intensive garbage collection activity as the JVM struggles to free up memory. However, the underlying causes are different—one is due to persistent object retention, while the other is simply a lack of allocated memory to meet demand.

To illustrate this, take a look at the following snippet:

```
[GC pause (G1 Evacuation Pause) (mixed), 0.01506789 secs]
[GC pause (G1 Evacuation Pause) (mixed), 0.01783456 secs]
[GC pause (G1 Evacuation Pause) (mixed), 0.02021234 secs]

[Full GC (Allocation Failure) 8192M->6100M(8192M), 2.345678 secs]
[GC pause (G1 Evacuation Pause) (mixed), 0.01901234 secs]
[GC pause (G1 Evacuation Pause) (mixed), 0.02115678 secs]

[Full GC (Allocation Failure) 8192M->5800M(8192M), 2.678901 secs]
[GC pause (G1 Evacuation Pause) (mixed), 0.0987654 secs]
[GC pause (G1 Evacuation Pause) (mixed), 0.02254321 secs]

[Full GC (Allocation Failure) 8192M->5600M(8192M), 2.789012 secs]
```

In the previous snippet, we observe frequent garbage collection events, but none of them have excessively long pause times, and all appear to be at least somewhat effective in reclaiming memory. Unlike the memory leak problem discussed in section 11.4.2, the GC events here successfully free up memory, and heap usage does not exhibit a steady increase over time.

Additionally, the short GC pause times do not indicate an untuned GC configuration or similar inefficiencies discussed in section 11.4.1. More importantly, the fact that memory is continuously being reclaimed suggests that this is not a memory leak, since objects are eventually being collected rather than retained indefinitely.

However, the high frequency of GC events, combined with the presence of full GC occurrences, is still a concerning pattern. It indicates that the allocated heap memory is insufficient to handle the application's workload. In such cases, the JVM is forced to perform garbage collection too often, leading to performance degradation. While GC is able to keep the application running, the excessive overhead suggests that increasing the available memory would likely improve efficiency and stability.

You can also use the memory consumption graph here as confirmation (figure 11.5). If the application is affected by a memory leak, the graph will show a steady increase in memory usage until the heap is completely full. However, if the problem is simply insufficient memory allocation, the graph will display peaks and valleys, indicating that the GC is actively reclaiming memory and keeping the application running. However, if the allocation is too close to the maximum, performance may degrade, and the risk of out-of-memory errors increases.

In such cases, a short-term solution may be to increase the allocated heap memory using the -Xmx and -Xms parameters. This approach can provide immediate relief by allowing the application to handle more objects before triggering garbage collection.

However, relying solely on vertical scalability (i.e., increasing heap size) is often a temporary fix. While it may delay memory pressure problems, it does not address the root cause. A more sustainable approach involves optimizing memory usage by improving application logic to reduce unnecessary allocations and ensuring objects are properly deallocated.

In the long run, redesigning the application for horizontal scalability—distributing the workload across multiple instances instead of depending on a single, large heap—can lead to better performance, resilience, and scalability.

11.4.4 *Tuning parallelism in GC*

Garbage collection in Java is like cleaning up after a party. If done right, everything stays neat, and your application runs smoothly. But if not, your CPU gets stuck dealing with the mess while your application slows down.

Modern Java garbage collectors can use multiple threads to speed up the cleanup process, but if they aren't tuned properly, they might either work too hard—wasting CPU power—or too little, leaving memory cluttered. In this section, we focus on the G1 GC, which has been the default collector in recent Java versions. You'll also learn about key JVM settings such as -XX:ParallelGCThreads and -XX:ConcGCThreads, which control how many threads GC can use. By the end, you'll know how to fine-tune GC parallelism, so your application spends less time cleaning and more time doing what it was built for.

We'll take a few examples of different log messages patterns and discuss them. Say you frequently observe log messages such as

```
[GC pause (G1 Evacuation Pause) (young), 0.124567 secs]
    Parallel Time: 115.2 ms, Workers: 2 (out of 8 available)
    Eden: 256M->0M(1024M), Survivors: 32M->64M, Heap: 2048M->1024M(4096M)
```

As we learned earlier in this chapter, a GC event lasting longer than 50 milliseconds, especially if it occurs frequently, is a red flag for performance problems. In this case, the logs provide additional information indicating that only two out of eight available worker threads are being used for the cleanup process. This suggests that the GC is underutilizing the CPU, potentially leading to inefficient memory management and longer pause times.

To address this matter, you can experiment with increasing the number of parallel GC threads to distribute the workload across available CPU cores better. This adjustment may help reduce pause times and improve overall application performance.

You can add the following flags to your VM parameters to change:

```
-XX:ParallelGCThreads=6
-XX:ConcGCThreads=4
```

The -XX:ParallelGCThreads=6 option controls the number of threads used for parallel garbage collection during stop-the-world (STW) phases. In this case, the JVM will use six threads to perform STW garbage collection tasks, such as young generation evacuation:

- If the value is too low, GC may underutilize the CPU, leading to longer pause times.
- If the value is too high, it may cause excessive CPU usage, potentially slowing down the application by consuming resources needed for other tasks.

Similarly, the -XX:ConcGCThreads=4 setting controls the number of threads used for concurrent (background) garbage collection phases. The JVM will use four threads for non-STW GC tasks, such as marking and reclaiming memory in the background, without interrupting application execution:

- If set too low, the concurrent phases might not keep up, causing frequent stop-the-world pauses as GC struggles to clean memory in time.
- If set too high, it might consume too many CPU resources, negatively affecting overall application performance.

For example, if G1 GC logs show long concurrent phases, increasing the ConcGCThreads flag can help speed up background GC work.

However, GC tuning isn't an exact science—it requires careful observation of your application's behavior over time. Making changes without monitoring their effect can lead to unexpected problems. Personally, I prefer experimenting with these settings over an extended period to ensure that the adjustments truly optimize performance in real-world execution.

Another problem could be caused by allocating too many threads. Take a look at the following snippet:

```
[GC (Allocation Failure) [ParallelGC (workers: 16)]
  1536M->768M(3072M), 0.310456 secs]
```

We observe a long GC pause time (about 310 ms) and notice that 16 worker threads were used. This number suggests CPU contention, where too many threads are competing for CPU resources, causing inefficiencies rather than improving performance.

It's similar to a race condition, but instead of threads fighting over shared memory, GC threads are fighting over CPU time, ultimately slowing down execution instead of speeding it up.

A good approach in such cases is to reduce the number of worker threads using the -XX:ParallelGCThreads parameter. Lowering this value can help reduce CPU contention and lead to smoother, more efficient garbage collection.

Tuning -XX:ParallelGCThreads is a bit like making the perfect cup of coffee—too little, and your GC runs sluggishly, dragging your application down; too much, and suddenly your CPU is jittery, over-caffeinated, and struggling to keep up.

The key takeaway? Start small, observe, adjust, and repeat. Don't just throw more threads at the problem and hope for the best—unless, of course, you enjoy watching your CPU have a meltdown.

So, go forth and experiment! Just remember: Garbage collection should clean up your application, not your patience.

Summary

- Garbage collector logs are crucial for troubleshooting JVM memory management problems. They provide insights into memory allocation, garbage collection pauses, and heap utilization.

- Enabling GC logs is the first step in analyzing JVM memory behavior. The `-Xlog:gc*` VM option enables GC logging, helping developers track GC activity in real-time or store logs for later analysis.

- Understanding the GC log structure is essential. Logs include details on GC events, pause times, heap size changes, and memory allocation patterns.

- GC logs help diagnose excessive GC pauses. Long GC pause times (typically above 50 ms) can indicate performance problems, while frequent full GC events suggest memory pressure.

- Heap memory organization affects GC performance. Objects move through Eden, Survivor, and Old Generation memory regions. Inefficient memory usage can cause frequent GC interruptions.

- Frequent full GC events may indicate insufficient memory or a memory leak. Logs showing frequent full GC events with minimal memory reclamation suggest a leak, while effective but frequent full GCs indicate an under-provisioned heap.

- Storing GC logs in files is recommended for deeper analysis. Use `-Xlog:gc*:file =gc.log:time,uptime,level,tags` to redirect logs to a file for structured storage and easier troubleshooting.

- Log rotation prevents excessive storage use. Configuring file count and file size limits ensures logs do not consume excessive disk space.

- Choosing the right logging level improves troubleshooting efficiency. Error logs capture critical failures, while info and debug levels provide additional insights into memory management.

- Tuning GC parallelism can reduce pause times. Adjusting `-XX:ParallelGC-Threads` and `-XX:ConcGCThreads` optimizes CPU usage for better performance.

- AI tools and third-party services can simplify GC log analysis. Uploading logs to tools such as GCEasy or using AI assistants can speed up troubleshooting.

Part 4

Finding problems in large systems

So far, we've focused on diagnosing problems inside a single application. But in the real world, most systems are made up of many services, databases, and queues—all talking to each other across networks. In this environment, problems don't just live in one place. They can hide in the gaps between services, in unexpected data mismatches, or in the way the system reacts as a whole under stress.

This part is about troubleshooting at system scale. We'll learn how to uncover failures that happen only when services interact, how to measure and verify data consistency across boundaries, and how to trace multistep operations that cross multiple components. We'll also look at strategies for catching drift between systems before it becomes a serious outage.

By the end of this part, you'll be equipped to investigate problems that span entire architectures—not just single apps—using the right combination of logs, traces, metrics, and detective work to keep complex systems healthy.

Uncovering system-level failures and service communication problems

This chapter covers

- Troubleshooting failures in multiservice Java systems
- Investigating common pitfalls in REST, gRPC, and messaging
- Unfolding serialization and versioning problems between services
- Investigating cascading failures, retries, and timeout problems

"Why is the payment service down?"

"Because the email service is slow."

"What?"

In a system of services, failure is a team sport, and you may not even be invited to the game. One service times out, another starts retrying furiously, and suddenly, your logs are full of errors from a completely unrelated module. The challenge is that problems rarely stay local; they echo through the system, bouncing off APIs, queues, and unsuspecting services that were just minding their own business. By the time you join the debugging party, half the system is on fire, and no one remembers who lit the match.

Let me tell you about the time the user profile service refused to start. After extensive digging, we discovered that the service was waiting on a downstream dependency that had nothing to do with user profiles. That dependency was, in turn, waiting on a message from a service that had problems deploying. This was the software equivalent of a group of friends refusing to order pizza until someone who wasn't even invited to the party showed up.

This chapter talks about about those moments. It's about the mysterious slowdown that starts in a service you didn't even know existed—the gRPC call that fails because someone cleaned up an an enum field that seemed unused, or the cascade of retries that turns a minor hiccup into a full-on distributed meltdown.

In section 12.1, we start examining how to troubleshoot common communication patterns, such as REST, gRPC, and messaging, and the types of problems they can introduce—from unclear contracts to delivery failures. In section 12.2, we dive into serialization mismatches and versioning problems, looking at how subtle schema changes can break integrations silently.

Finally, in section 12.3, we explore systemic failure modes, such as cascading failures, retry storms, and timeout mismatches, and how to detect and investigate them using logs, metrics, thread dumps, and distributed tracing. The goal is to give you practical techniques and real-world strategies for understanding and resolving complex problems that emerge not from a single bug, but from the way services interact.

12.1 Troubleshooting communication patterns: RPC and messaging

In distributed systems, the reliability of applications no longer depends solely on their own correctness, but also on how they communicate with others. In a distributed system, services interact through various communication mechanisms such as Remote Procedure Calls (RPCs)—including REST and gRPC—or asynchronous messaging such as Kafka. While these patterns enable modularity and scalability, they also introduce new failure modes that can be subtle, inconsistent, and hard to diagnose. Communication between services—whether through REST APIs, gRPC calls, or asynchronous message queues—can introduce subtle and difficult-to-trace failures.

Each communication pattern comes with tradeoffs. REST offers simplicity and widespread adoption but can suffer from unclear contracts and weak typing. gRPC provides performance and structure, yet brings its own challenges around compatibility and tooling. Messaging enables loose coupling and asynchronous workflows, but it can introduce problems with ordering, duplication, and delivery guarantees.

This section examines how these communication mechanisms commonly fail, how to detect when they do, and what practices can help prevent outages caused by miscommunication between services. For each pattern, we'll focus on the kinds of failures that occur and the tools you can use to trace, diagnose, and resolve them. From structured logs and distributed tracing (e.g., OpenTelemetry, Jaeger, Zipkin) to protocol-specific debuggers (e.g., grpcurl, Postman, and message brokers' dashboards), we'll explore how to move from symptoms to root cause in a complex, connected system.

12.1.1 Working with trace IDs and spans

This section talks about two of the most common troubleshooting tools for distributed systems: trace IDs and spans. Let's consider the following scenario to better understand how a problem could look like and what tool is useful for untangling the case.

Suppose your company runs a Java-based e-commerce platform built as a set of microservices. One day, the customer support team reported that some users were completing checkouts, but the orders never showed up in the admin dashboard. Payments are processed, confirmation emails are sent, but what about the actual orders? Gone.

Your services look like as shown in figure 12.1:

- Checkout service (REST) → calls Order service
- Order service → publishes an event to Kafka
- Fulfillment service → consumes from Kafka and stores orders

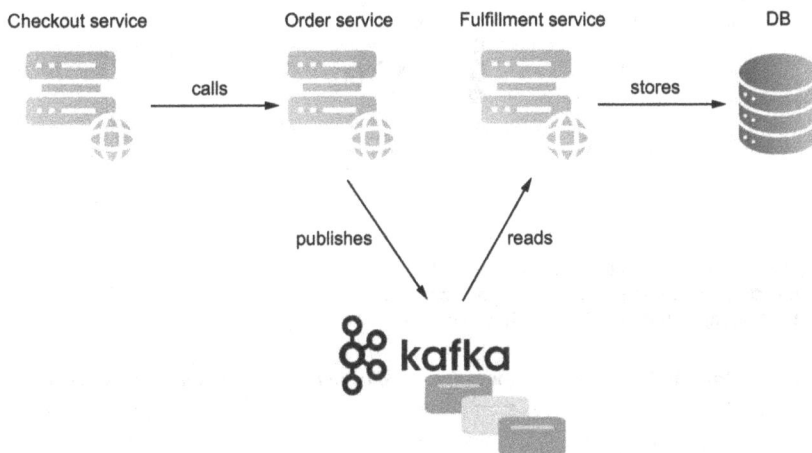

Figure 12.1 An overview of the system for our scenario. The checkout service calls the order service via REST, while the order service asynchronously talks to the fulfillment service through a Kafka topic. The fulfillment service stores details in a database.

Naturally, we first go digging through the logs. You first tail the logs of the checkout service. It shows a successful REST call to the order service. You're looking for the trace ID: it's present, the response code is 200, and the payload seems correct.

What is a trace ID? When dealing with a single Java application, a stack trace or log file is often enough to understand what went wrong. However, those traditional tools fall short quickly once you move to a distributed system, where one request may bounce between a dozen services. That's where the trace ID comes in.

DEFINITION   A trace ID is a unique identifier assigned to a request as it enters the system.

Think of a trace ID as a passport that travels with the request, stamped at every border it crosses. As the request flows through different services—via HTTP, gRPC, or message queues—each participating service logs its part of the journey, tagging the logs and telemetry data with the same trace ID. This characteristic allows you to stitch together the entire story of a request across system boundaries (figure 12.2).

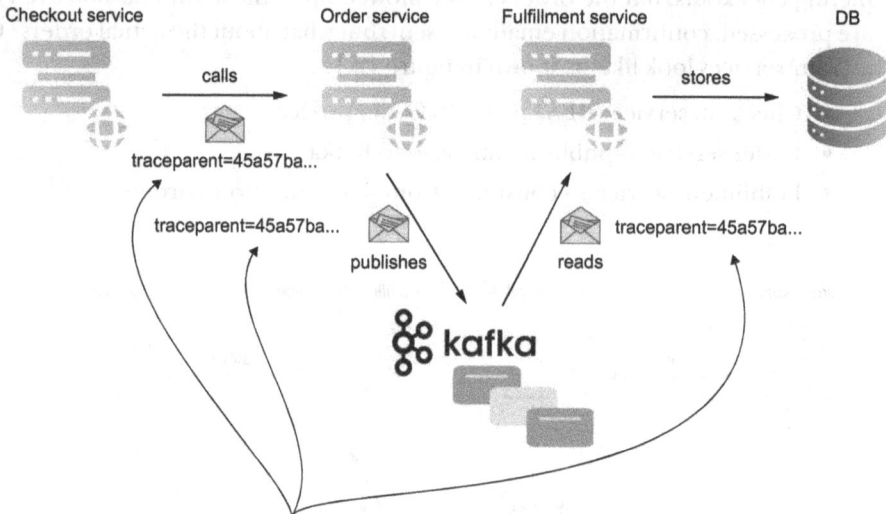

The message has an unique trace ID that identifies the message. This way, you can follow the message on its road throughout the flow.

Figure 12.2   A trace ID identifies each message so you can follow it throughout its road between multiple services.

Trace IDs are central to distributed tracing systems such as Jaeger and Zipkin (discussed later in the chapter), or commercial platforms such as Datadog and Honeycomb. These tools collect spans (individual units of work done by each service), and group them under the same trace ID to form a complete picture of how long each step took, what errors occurred, and where delays originated.

In practice, trace IDs are often propagated through HTTP headers (e.g., `traceparent` or `x-b3-traceid`) or metadata in message payloads. Ensuring consistent propagation across all your services is crucial—if just one service drops the trace ID, the chain breaks, and you're left with fragments instead of a full picture.

Going back to our scenario. You decide to continue with the next service. You check the order service logs. It receives the request, creates the order object, and publishes an event to Kafka. No errors, no exceptions. Still, the fulfillment service doesn't show any trace of the order.

When logs don't give you the full picture, and you suspect the problem spans multiple services, it's time to change your approach. This is where distributed tracing comes in, and tools such as Jaeger become invaluable.

Jaeger (https://www.jaegertracing.io/) is an open source distributed tracing system that helps visualize these traces. It collects *spans* from your instrumented services and presents them as a timeline. The following listing gives you an idea of how such a timeline (trace tree) looks like. Using the trace ID, Jaeger aggregates the information and shows how each service called another and how long each operation took.

Listing 12.1 An example of a trace timeline also called a trace tree

```
Trace ID: 6f98c1e2b3a24f59

└── [api-gateway] POST /checkout                    [950ms]
    ├── [checkout-service] Validate cart            [40ms]
    ├── [checkout-service] Call OrderService        [780ms]
    │   └── [order-service] Create order record     [100ms]
    │       ├── [order-service] Check inventory     [60ms]
    │       └── [order-service] Save to database    [30ms]
    ├── [checkout-service] Call PaymentService      [100ms]
    │   └── [payment-service] Process payment       [90ms]
    └── [checkout-service] Send confirmation email  [30ms]
```

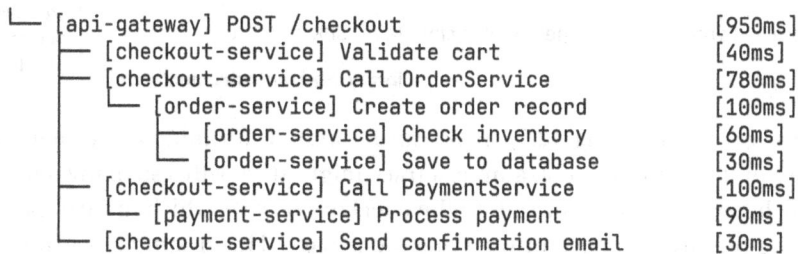

A span is the fundamental building block of a distributed trace. It represents a single unit of work done within a service, such as handling an HTTP request, querying a database, calling another service, or processing a message.

An alternative to Jaeger is Zipkin (https://zipkin.io/). Zipkin is a distributed tracing system originally developed by Twitter, designed to help users collect and visualize timing data for requests across service boundaries. Like Jaeger, it allows tracing a request as it moves through multiple services, displaying each step as a span in a timeline.

Think of a trace as the full story of a request moving through your system. Each span is a chapter in that story. It includes

- A name (e.g., `"POST /checkout"`, `"Call to OrderService"`)
- A start timestamp and duration
- The service name that produced it
- Tags (metadata such as status codes, error messages, or custom fields)
- Logs/events that occurred during the span's lifetime
- A reference to its parent span, if it's part of a larger operation

The next snippet shows a tree representation of a span, which is how you'd see it in a tool such as Jaeger or Zipkin.

```
└── [api-gateway] GET /products  [42ms]
```

For the span, the tool usually provides you a detailed view separately, such as the one presented in the next listing.

Listing 12.2   Details of a span

```
Trace ID              bf12ec184a2b48d0a28a1f07c748f6e3   ◄──   Uses the trace ID to
                                                               debug the tree of calls
Span ID               d6f0fdee62ef3c6a                         Useful to identify the
Parent Span ID        null (this is the root span)    ◄──      operation in code
Span Name             GET /products                   ◄──      Useful to identify the
Service Name          api-gateway                     ◄──      operation in code
Start Time            2025-04-17T13:42:10.512Z                 Identifies the service
End Time              2025-04-17T13:42:10.554Z                 executing the span
Duration              42ms                            ◄──
Status                OK                                        Useful when
Instrumentation       OpenTelemetry Java SDK 1.30.0   ◄──       troubleshooting
                                                                performance
              Library used for instrumentation                 problems
```

As shown earlier in listing 12.1, spans can be nested, forming a tree that shows the structure of the request. For example, a trace might start with a span in your API Gateway, which has child spans for calls to the checkout service, which in turn spawns spans for calling the order service or querying a database. This nesting lets you see exactly which part of the system slowed down or failed. The following listing shows the span for our fictive scenario.

Listing 12.3   The span tree for our fictive case

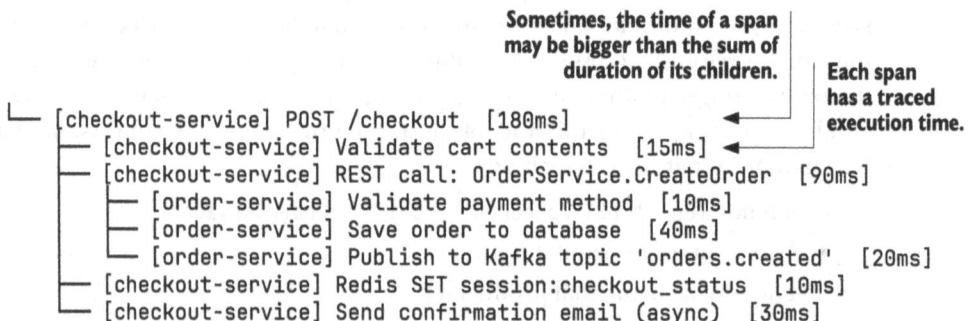

```
                                          Sometimes, the time of a span
                                          may be bigger than the sum of
                                          duration of its children.        Each span
                                                                           has a traced
   └─ [checkout-service] POST /checkout  [180ms]              ◄──          execution time.
       ├─ [checkout-service] Validate cart contents  [15ms]  ◄──
       ├─ [checkout-service] REST call: OrderService.CreateOrder  [90ms]
       │   ├─ [order-service] Validate payment method  [10ms]
       │   ├─ [order-service] Save order to database  [40ms]
       │   └─ [order-service] Publish to Kafka topic 'orders.created'  [20ms]
       ├─ [checkout-service] Redis SET session:checkout_status  [10ms]
       └─ [checkout-service] Send confirmation email (async)  [30ms]
```

Each span shows metadata such as duration, operation name, service name, and logs or tags. This makes it easy to spot bottlenecks, failures, or missing links in the flow. Sometimes, the time of a span may be bigger than the sum of duration of its children due to its own logic. Order is there, as is the order service's internal processing. But there is nothing from fulfillment. It never consumed the message. You suspect a problem in the Kafka pipeline.

You fire up Kafka's UI dashboard and inspect the topic `orders.created`. The event is there, sitting in the topic. Not consumed. Now you check fulfillment service logs. Hidden between harmless info messages, you find

```
[WARN] Failed to deserialize message from topic orders.created - Unknown enum
value: SHIPPING_METHOD_DRONE
```

Aha! Yesterday, a new enum value, `SHIPPING_METHOD_DRONE`, was added to the order service. The team deployed it, but the fulfillment service wasn't updated and still uses the old schema version. You solved another case, but things might get more complex. Of course, we cannot always understand the problem until we also learn about the business the app implements. In some simple scenarios, you can deduce what the app wants to do and why the user needs that. In more complex cases, you need to dig a bit deeper to understand the why solved by the implemented use case you troubleshoot.

Let's talk a bit more in section 12.1.2 about the tools we just mentioned we used to solve this case. Then, we'll analyze in more detail the serialization mismatch in section 12.2, and what other troubleshooting tactics we can apply in other scenarios.

12.1.2 OpenTelemetry, Jaeger, Zipkin, and other utilities

In section 12.1.1. we used a few tools to troubleshoot a fictive scenario and talk about techniques using trace IDs and spans. Let's now discuss a bit more about these tools and how they work.

To make distributed tracing work in a real system, you need to install and integrate several components into the runtime environment where your services are deployed. These tools aren't just developer-side utilities but part of the infrastructure that supports observability at system scale.

At the core of tracing is OpenTelemetry (https://opentelemetry.io/), responsible for generating telemetry data from your Java services. It can be added to your application either through manual instrumentation (writing code that creates spans) or through automatic instrumentation using the OpenTelemetry Java agent. In the latter case, you don't need to modify your code—just attach the agent to your application at startup, and it will capture spans for popular frameworks such as Spring, gRPC, JDBC, and HTTP clients out of the box.

Once spans are generated, they need to be collected and visualized. This is where Jaeger or Zipkin come into play. These are observability backends that you deploy alongside your application stack, typically in the same Kubernetes cluster or as Docker containers. Your services send trace data to them using OpenTelemetry's export protocols (e.g., OTLP or gRPC), and the backend provides a web UI for searching and exploring traces across your system. Figure 12.3 illustrates the relationship between a service, OpenTelemetry, and Jaeger or Zipkin.

Although developers may interact with traces by instrumenting code or viewing trace data during development or incident response, the actual tracing infrastructure

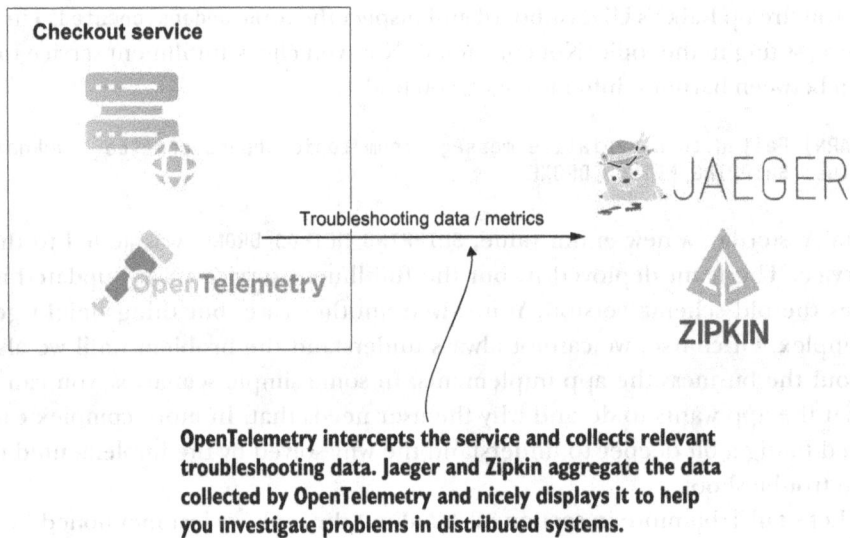

OpenTelemetry intercepts the service and collects relevant troubleshooting data. Jaeger and Zipkin aggregate the data collected by OpenTelemetry and nicely displays it to help you investigate problems in distributed systems.

Figure 12.3   OpenTelemetry collects relevant data from the running service. Jaeger and Zipkin are tools that aggregate and display nicely this data to help you easily troubleshoot the system.

is managed and operated at the system level. Platform or DevOps teams must install and configure it as part of the environment. With this setup in place, tracing becomes a powerful tool for debugging, monitoring system health, analyzing performance, and understanding how requests flow through complex architectures.

In our case, we've used distributed tracing to investigate a missing order. But tools such as OpenTelemetry, Jaeger, and Zipkin do much more than help you chase down elusive bugs. They're the foundation of system-scale observability. Let me mention some other use cases you can quicky find these tools useful:

- *Performance optimization*—Use tracing to analyze where your system is spending time. With it you can answer question such as, Which calls are slow? Is a particular DB query holding things up? Which services contribute most to request latency?

- *Dependency mapping*—Traces reveal how your services talk to each other. You can generate real-time service maps, showing which components are upstream/ downstream, and which ones may be overburdened.

- *Error isolation*—When a user reports a failure, tracing can show exactly which service or operation failed—especially valuable in asynchronous or retry-heavy flows where logs don't tell the whole story.

- *Monitoring cold starts and resource spikes*—A cold start is a delay that occurs when a system component, such as a serverless function, thread, or service instance, is invoked after being idle or uninitialized, requiring setup time that slows response. By visualizing slow or blocked spans in distributed traces, you can detect cold starts, long garbage collection (GC) pauses, or thread pool starvation. These patterns often escape traditional metrics, but tracing can reveal them clearly through latency spikes and span timing anomalies.

- *Sampling and trend analysis*—You don't need to trace every request. You can sample a small percentage (1%–5%) and still get valuable insights into the health and behavior of the system over time.

- *Combining traces with logs and metrics*—Modern observability platforms (such as Grafana, Datadog, or OpenTelemetry Collector) allow you to correlate traces with logs and metrics. For example, trace latency spikes back to a CPU/memory event or a new deployment.

While distributed tracing tools such as Jaeger and Zipkin provide you with a timeline of events and latency insights across services, they don't always capture the full details of what went wrong when a request fails. That's where tools such as Sentry (https://sentry.io/) come in.

Sentry is a real-time error monitoring platform that collects and organizes unhandled exceptions, stack traces, and runtime errors from your services. It integrates with many Java frameworks and can automatically capture contextual information such as the failed line of code, user identifiers, HTTP request details, and even tags indicating which version of the code was running. This feature makes it especially useful when debugging problems such as failed gRPC calls, bad deserialization, or unexpected response types, situations where the trace alone may show you where the problem happened, but not what the underlying error was.

Sentry is not a replacement for tracing, but a powerful complement. When used alongside OpenTelemetry-based systems, it gives you a complete view: tracing shows the flow, and Sentry shows the failure in full detail. In many setups, Sentry errors can even include the corresponding trace ID, helping you correlate between tools and move seamlessly from high-level trace data to the specific exception that triggered it.

In our scenario, the fulfillment service failed to deserialize a message from Kafka (section 2.1) due to an unrecognized enum value (`SHIPPING_METHOD_DRONE`). The service didn't crash, but it silently failed to process the message.

Had Sentry been integrated into that service, it would have captured the exception thrown during deserialization. The Sentry dashboard would show stack traces, message payload metadata, and error frequency, highlighting that this problem was recurring for specific message types. It might have even pointed to the exact line of code or class failing during deserialization. This would have accelerated discovery of the schema/version mismatch without relying solely on log grepping or deep trace analysis.

Figure 12.4 shows a sample of a Sentry dashboard giving details on a particular exception that happened in an app.

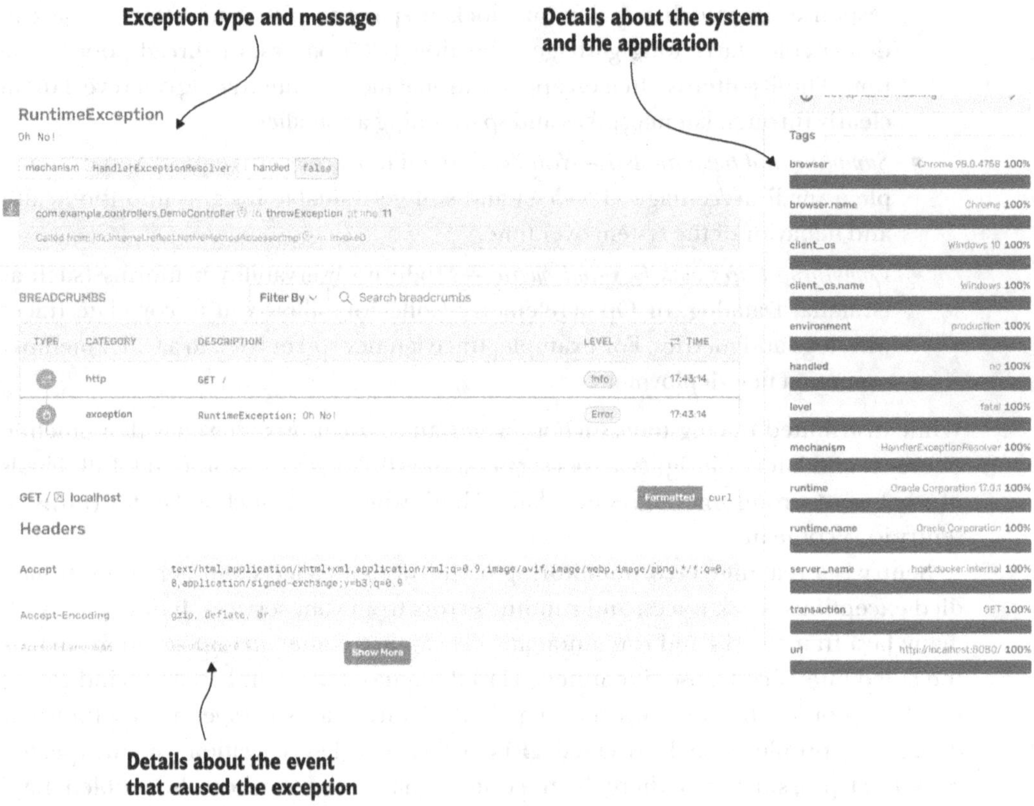

Exception type and message

Details about the system
and the application

RuntimeException
Oh No!

mechanism HandlerExceptionResolver handled false

com.example.controllers.DemoController throwException at line 11
Called from: jdk.internal.reflect.NativeMethodAccessorImpl invoke0

BREADCRUMBS   Filter By ⌄   Q Search breadcrumbs

TYPE	CATEGORY	DESCRIPTION	LEVEL	TIME
http	GET /		Info	17:43:14
exception	RuntimeException: Oh No!		Error	17:43:14

GET / ☐ localhost   Formatted curl

Headers

Accept   text/html,application/xhtml+xml,application/xml;q=0.9,image/avif,image/webp,image/apng,*/*;q=0.
8,application/signed-exchange;v=b3;q=0.9

Accept-Encoding   gzip, deflate, br

Accept-Language   Show More

Tags

browser	Chrome 99.0.4758 100%
browser.name	Chrome 100%
client_os	Windows 10 100%
client_os.name	Windows 100%
environment	production 100%
handled	no 100%
level	fatal 100%
mechanism	HandlerExceptionResolver 100%
runtime	Oracle Corporation 17.0.1 100%
runtime.name	Oracle Corporation 100%
server_name	host.docker.internal 100%
transaction	GET 100%
url	http://localhost:8080/ 100%

Details about the event
that caused the exception

Figure 12.4   Sentry aggregates and shows events such as exceptions providing a large field of details for each of these.

12.2 Serialization mismatches and versioning problems

When two services exchange data, they need to speak the same language—not just at the protocol level (such as HTTP or gRPC), but in terms of how they structure and interpret the data itself. That's where serialization comes in: transforming complex in-memory objects into a stream of bytes that can be sent over the network, and back again on the receiving end.

Unfortunately, serialization is also one of the easiest places for things to go subtly, silently wrong. What happens when one service adds a new field to a JSON payload, and another service—still using the old model—silently ignores it? What if someone renames a Protobuf enum or forgets to make a field optional? What if a Java object is serialized with a specific version UID, but deserialized with a different class entirely?

Remember our examples in section 12.1? These mismatches don't always trigger obvious failures. Sometimes they result in dropped data, default values, or deserialization errors that only appear under specific circumstances.

In this section, we explore how serialization and versioning problems show up in real systems, what to watch for when evolving data contracts, and how to build in forward and backward compatibility so your services can evolve independently without accidentally breaking each other.

Protobufs and gRPC

Protocol Buffers, or Protobuf for short, is a language-neutral, platform-neutral serialization format developed by Google. It's used to define structured data and efficiently serialize it for communication between services or for storage. Think of it as a faster, smaller, and more strictly typed alternative to JSON or XML.

With a Protobuf, you define your data structures in .proto files using a simple declarative syntax:

```
message Order {
  int64 id = 1;
  string customer_id = 2;
  repeated string items = 3;
  optional string notes = 4;
}
```

From this schema, Protobuf automatically generates Java (or other language) classes that handle both serialization (converting the object into a compact binary format) and deserialization (reading it back into structured data).

Protobuf is commonly used in systems that require high performance and strong contracts between services—especially in combination with gRPC, which uses Protobuf to define request/response messages and service APIs. While Protobuf's efficiency and schema-based design are strengths, they also introduce challenges when services evolve independently. If one service adds a new field or changes an enum, and another service hasn't been updated to understand that change, mismatches are possible. This makes versioning discipline and compatibility guarantees critical—especially in Java systems, where strict typing and deserialization behavior can turn small changes into big problems.

When debugging a serialization problem, especially in a distributed system, there's often no substitute for seeing the actual data exchanged between services. Logging the raw payload can help you confirm whether a field was missing, defaulted, or misformatted. It can also expose subtle problems such as trailing null bytes, encoding mismatches, or unexpected enum values.

However, logging raw payloads comes with real risks. Payloads can be large, and dumping entire serialized blobs (especially in binary formats such as Protobuf or Avro) can flood your logs, overwhelm log ingestion systems, or consume excessive disk space. Worse, many payloads contain sensitive information, user data, authentication tokens, and payment details, that should never appear in plain text logs, especially in production.

The key is to balance visibility and safety. Selectively logging decoded payloads (rather than raw binary) is often sufficient in development or staging environments. In production, consider

- Sampling only a subset of requests
- Filtering or redacting sensitive fields before logging
- Capping the size of logged content (e.g., log the first N characters or fields)
- Using structured logging to log fields with metadata, rather than dumping the whole object

Tools such as structured log appenders (e.g., Logback with JSON output—for a refresher, check chapter 4) can help you emit only what you need. Also, always tag logs with the trace ID so that even minimal payload data can be correlated with a full trace when needed.

One of the most effective ways to prevent serialization and versioning problems is to validate your schemas before they ever reach production. In a distributed system, where services evolve independently, schema mismatches can easily occur when teams make changes without coordination. Automated schema validation, either during service startup or as part of the continuous integration (CI) pipeline, acts as a safety net.

In a CI pipeline, schema validation is a simple but powerful way to catch breaking changes before they affect anyone. The idea is to compare your current schema, such as a .proto, Avro, or JSON Schema file, with a previous version, usually from your main branch or a shared schema registry. This approach helps make sure that the changes you've made won't break consumers that rely on older versions.

When your pipeline runs, it pulls in both the current and previous schemas and uses tools such as Buf (for Protobuf) or avro-tools (for Avro) to check for compatibility. If you've added a new optional field, you're probably fine as older clients will just ignore it. But if you've removed a field, renamed something, or changed a type (like going from a string to an int), those are usually flagged as breaking changes. In those cases, the CI job fails, informing you early that something needs fixing. The goal is to enforce backward and/or forward compatibility. For example,

- Adding an optional field is usually safe.
- Renaming or removing a field may break existing consumers.
- Changing a field's type (e.g., from string to int) is almost always a breaking change.

Tools such as Buf (for Protobuf) or avro-tools (for Avro) can perform compatibility checks automatically.

At runtime, some systems take this further by registering schemas in a central registry (e.g., Confluent Schema Registry for Kafka) and validating each message on publish or consume. This can catch serialization problems caused by misaligned versions, but at the cost of some latency and added complexity.

Whether in CI or at runtime, schema validation helps enforce a contract between services. It's not just about preventing crashes but about ensuring predictable behavior when services communicate, even as they evolve. Schema validation is one of the most reliable ways to avoid serialization-related outages when combined with clear versioning practices and good documentation.

When something goes wrong between services, especially with structured or binary payloads, it's essential to understand what was actually sent and received. Tools such as protoc, grpcurl, and jq allow you to inspect messages independently of your application code, making them ideal for debugging serialization problems.

12.3 Understanding systemic failure modes

In a distributed system, failures rarely stay in one place. What starts as a slow database query or a delayed service response can ripple outward, triggering timeouts, retries, and blocked threads across other services. These aren't just bugs, they're systemic failure modes, and they require a different kind of thinking to detect and troubleshoot.

Unlike exceptions in your local Java stack trace, systemic failures often don't show up clearly. You might see elevated latency, CPU spikes, increased error rates, or worse, everything appears to be working, just poorly. The system feels off, and debugging it feels like chasing shadows.

This section focuses on how small problems become big ones in distributed Java systems. We'll explore failure modes such as

- *Cascading failures*—When one overloaded service causes upstream services to back up, creating a domino effect
- *Retry storms*—When multiple services simultaneously retry failed requests, amplifying the load and worsening the situation.
- *Timeout mismatches*—Subtle configuration problems that break communication logic under pressure.
- *Circuit breaker misbehavior*—Incorrect settings that either trip too early or too late, or never recover.

We'll also look at how to spot the symptoms, use tools such as thread dumps, distributed traces, and metrics to understand the deeper cause, and implement resiliency patterns to prevent these problems from escalating.

12.3.1 Cascading failures

When one service becomes slow or unresponsive, it can cause upstream services to accumulate blocked threads, fill connection pools, and eventually crash, not because they're broken, but because they're waiting. This is a cascading failure: a localized problem that escalates into a system-wide outage (see figure 12.5).

One of the clearest signs of a cascading failure is thread pool exhaustion. A thread pool is a collection of pre-created worker threads that handle tasks such as processing requests, running jobs, or handling I/O in a controlled and efficient way. Instead of

During the flow, the fulfillment service
encounters a problem (such as not having
enough connections in the connection pool
when connecting to the DB).

Checkout service   Order service   Fulfillment service   DB

calls   calls   stores

The checkout service might
get stuck or bottlenecked
because one of the downstream
services faces a problem.

Other services involved
might also face instability.

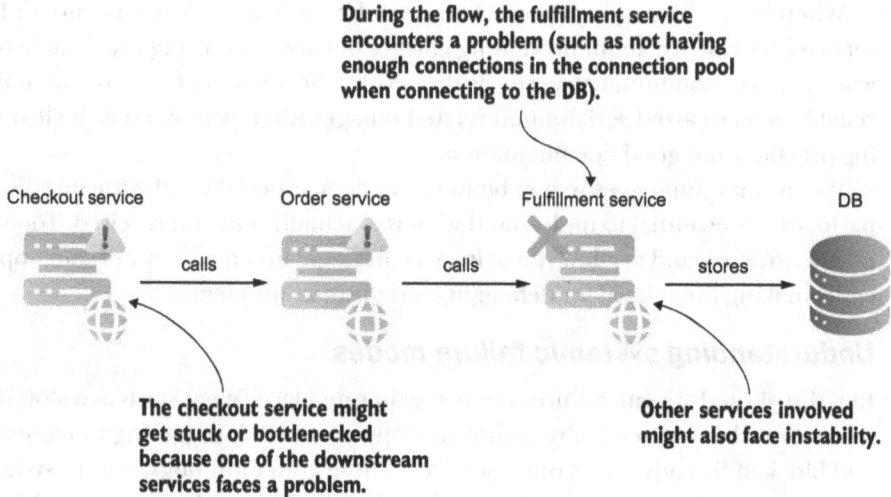

Figure 12.5   A failure or slowdown in one service (e.g., due to high latency, blocked resources, or an
overloaded dependency) can propagate through the system. Upstream services that rely on it may begin
to stall, exhaust thread pools, or trigger retries—eventually causing multiple services to degrade or fail,
even if they were functioning correctly on their own.

creating a new thread for every task, which can be expensive and risky, applications
use thread pools to reuse threads and limit the number of concurrent operations. This
helps protect the system from being overwhelmed. But when all threads in the pool are
busy, and new tasks keep coming in, the pool gets exhausted. At that point, incoming
tasks are either blocked, queued, or dropped entirely, leading to increased latency,
timeouts, and in worst cases, cascading failures as dependent services also start to pile
up while waiting for responses.

Each incoming request occupies a thread in Java applications, especially those using
servlet containers or blocking I/O. If a downstream call blocks or becomes slow, those
threads pile up and wait. You can detect this through thread dumps, which will often
show dozens or hundreds of threads in a WAITING or TIMED_WAITING state, all blocked on
the same HTTP client, socket read, or remote service call.

In thread dumps (see chapter 9 for a refresher), look for repeating stack traces that
involve remote calls such as HttpClient.send(), RestTemplate.exchange(), WebClient
.retrieve(), or gRPC stub invocations. If many threads are stuck in similar call paths,
especially in connection pools (HttpClientConnectionManager, OkHttp, etc.) or IO
reads—it's a sign that something downstream is taking too long.

Take a look at listing 12.4. This kind of thread dump is classic evidence of a cascading failure in progress. One downstream service (e.g., payment gateway) is slow.
Multiple upstream threads block while waiting for a response. Eventually, your thread
pool becomes saturated, and your service starts failing, even though the root problem
is downstream.

```
"http-nio-8080-exec-134" #217 daemon prio=5 os_prio=0 tid=0x00007f3c6809a000
nid=0x2f23 waiting on condition [0x00007f3c2ddfc000]
java.lang.Thread.State: WAITING (parking)
  at sun.misc.Unsafe.park(Native Method)
 - parking to wait for  <0x00000000f0123456> (a
        java.util.concurrent.CompletableFuture)
  at java.util.concurrent.locks.LockSupport.park(LockSupport.java:175)
  at java.util.concurrent.CompletableFuture
    .get(CompletableFuture.java:2027)
  at
    org.springframework.web.client.RestTemplate
     .doExecute(RestTemplate.java:780)
       at org.springframework.web.client.RestTemplate
     .exchange(RestTemplate.java:700)
       at com.example.service.PaymentService
     .callPaymentGateway(PaymentService.java:87)
        ...

"http-nio-8080-exec-135" #218 daemon prio=5 os_prio=0
 tid=0x00007f3c6809b000 nid=0x2f24
waiting on condition [0x00007f3c2defc000]

java.lang.Thread.State: WAITING (parking)
  at sun.misc.Unsafe.park(Native Method)
   - parking to wait for  <0x00000000f0123456>
   (a java.util.concurrent.CompletableFuture)
  at java.util.concurrent.locks.LockSupport
       .park(LockSupport.java:175)
  at java.util.concurrent.CompletableFuture
       .get(CompletableFuture.java:2027)
  at org.springframework.web.client.RestTemplate
       .doExecute(RestTemplate.java:780)
  at org.springframework.web.client.RestTemplate.exchange
(RestTemplate.java:700)
  at com.example.service.PaymentService
       .callPaymentGateway(PaymentService.java:87)
        ...
```

Waiting for an HTTP response

Calling the payment gateway

First, you observe that multiple (only two for brevity here) threads are doing the same thing (calling the callPaymentGateway() method). All threads seem to be executing a HTTP call (observe the RestTemplate), but they are waiting for a response.

Service metrics—created inside the application, either manually by developers (e.g., counters, timers) or automatically by a framework—offer another early warning. Watch for

- Thread pool utilization (approaching 100%)
- Request queue size (if using queuing thread pools)
- Increased latency or timeouts in outbound HTTP/gRPC calls
- Error rates spiking in otherwise healthy services

Distributed tracing (section 12.1) helps complete the picture. A trace that starts in a fast service and then spends most of its time waiting on a slower service shows up clearly in tools such as Jaeger, shown in the following listing.

Listing 12.5   Visualizing the origin of a slow operation in a span

```
Trace ID: 84ac99d3f2bc1d55

└─ [checkout-service] POST /checkout  [850ms]
     ├─ [checkout-service] Validate cart        [20ms]       Almost the entire
     ├─ [checkout-service] Call Payment Service  [790ms]      time is spent on
     │   └─ [payment-service] POST /pay          [780ms] ◀──┘ the /pay call.
     └─ [checkout-service] Store session         [10ms]
```

Once you've identified the slow or blocked service, the next step is to inspect its dependencies, resource usage, or code paths to determine why it's under pressure. Is it CPU-bound? Starving for database connections? Hitting a third-party API rate limit?

The key to troubleshooting cascading failures is to recognize that the service throwing the error is often just the messenger (this is very similar to the threads throwing an OutOfMemoryError; remember our discussion in chapter 10). The real problem lies further downstream, and your job is to follow the chain until you find the first domino that fell.

In the case of cascading failure, a tool such as Sentry can often surface the first warning signs. For example, if the fulfillment service starts failing because its database connection pool is exhausted, Sentry would capture exceptions such as SQLTransient-ConnectionException or TimeoutException. These errors might not be visible in logs, or they might be buried among less critical warnings. With Sentry's real-time error reporting and alerting, teams can be notified immediately when a known failure pattern emerges.

As the failure spreads upstream, Sentry also helps identify the ripple effect. Services such as order and checkout might begin timing out or retrying operations, generating exceptions of their own, such as HttpTimeoutException, CallNotPermittedException, or retry-related failures. Sentry groups these by error type, service, and context (e.g., user ID, request ID), making it easier to correlate which services are being affected and how frequently the errors are occurring.

Though Sentry doesn't visualize the full request path like tracing systems, it complements them by capturing the full exception stack trace, including local variables, environment details, and release metadata. When used together with a trace or correlation ID, developers can move between Sentry and tracing tools to get both the "what failed" and the "where and when it failed" perspectives, greatly speeding up root cause analysis.

No single tool tells the whole story in a distributed system. Tracing tools such as Jaeger and Zipkin help you follow the request across services and spot performance bottlenecks. Metrics expose trends and anomalies in system behavior. Logs offer raw details. Tools such as Sentry also bring critical visibility to exceptions and runtime errors that might otherwise go unnoticed. Used together, these tools provide a full picture, connecting the flow of data, the health of infrastructure, and the effect of failures. In complex systems, troubleshooting isn't about having one perfect tool. Troubleshooting is about having the right set of lenses to see the problem from every angle.

12.3.2 *Retry storms*

Retries are meant to add resilience, but they can do the opposite under pressure. Multiple services retrying the same failed operation, often with no backoff or coordination, can overload the target service, causing a feedback loop of failure.

Retries can help applications recover from transient failures, such as network glitches or temporary service unavailability, but if implemented without care, they can make things worse. When multiple clients retry failed requests simultaneously, especially without coordination or delay, they can overwhelm an already struggling service. This creates a retry storm, where the very mechanism meant to increase resilience causes a full-scale outage (figure 12.6).

A service repeatedly and uncontrollably retries a failing operation, leading to excessive resource consumption and potentially affecting other parts of the system.

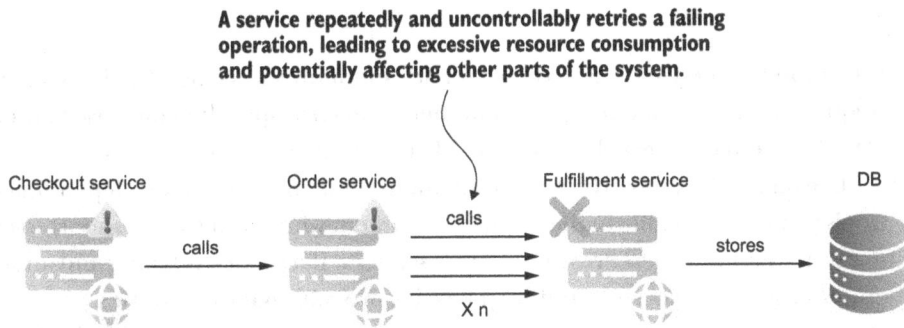

Figure 12.6 A retry storm. Due to a failing operation, an app uncontrollably retries the execution of an action, putting a larger part of the system in danger.

A misconfigured system can trigger a combination of cascading failures (see section 12.3.1) and retry storms, creating a feedback loop that amplifies the original problem. As illustrated in figure 12.7, these patterns can interact in ways that increase load, exhaust resources, and degrade the performance of otherwise healthy services.

Retry storms often hide in plain sight. From the outside, it may look like a service is under high load or is failing unexpectedly, but under the hood, it's being pummeled by hundreds or thousands of retry attempts. Your job as a troubleshooter is to recognize the signs and trace them back to their source:

- Look for elevated load without an increase in traffic.
- Inspect logs for repeated attempts.
- Trace it with spans across services.
- Check for chain reactions.

In a worst-case scenario, upstream services become affected
by cascading failures, which in turn trigger a full-scale retry
storm. As retries pile up across multiple layers, system
resources are rapidly consumed, amplifying the effects of the
original failure and increasing the risk of widespread outage.

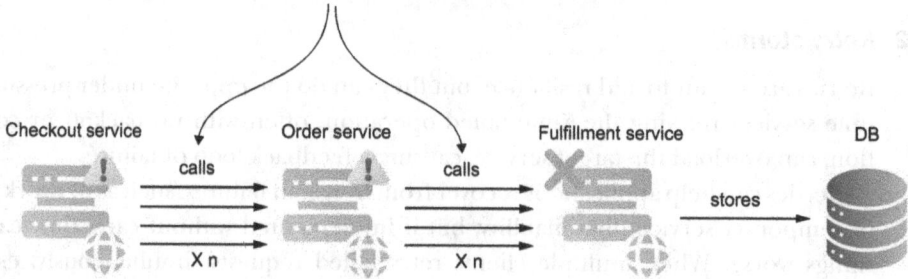

Figure 12.7   When a downstream service becomes unresponsive, upstream services may begin retrying requests excessively. This amplifies load across the system, consuming resources and potentially turning a localized failure into a widespread outage.

The most telling symptom is when a service suddenly shows high CPU usage, increased request volume, or latency spikes, but there's no corresponding increase in user traffic. That's a red flag: internal services are likely retrying failed operations.

Use metrics dashboards (e.g., Prometheus/Grafana or Datadog, depending on what tools you have available in the given environment where you troubleshoot) to correlate CPU, request rate, and error rate across services. If a service is failing and another one another suddenly sees a 5x traffic spike—it's probably handling retries.

In service logs, retry storms often show up as repeated log entries with identical or similar payloads, happening at short intervals. Look for logs such as:

```
[WARN] Timeout calling PaymentService. Retrying attempt 1...
[WARN] Timeout calling PaymentService. Retrying attempt 2...
...
Retrying POST /payment for orderId=abc123
Retrying POST /payment for orderId=abc123
```

Distributed tracing (e.g., Jaeger, Zipkin) is incredibly effective for visualizing retry storms. You'll see multiple spans with the same parent, calling the same operation repeatedly. These retry spans will usually have short durations, spaced closely together. The root service's span may show a long duration made up of several fast but failed child spans. You may see something like

```
└─ [checkout-service] POST /checkout [600ms]
     ├─ [checkout-service] Call PaymentService attempt 1 [200ms]
     ├─ [checkout-service] Call PaymentService attempt 2 [180ms]
     └─ [checkout-service] Call PaymentService attempt 3 [220ms]
```

12.3.3 Timeout mismatches

Mismatched timeout settings between clients and servers are a common and invisible source of failure. A client might give up after 2 seconds, while the server doesn't even start processing until the 3-second mark, leading to false failures and wasteful retries.

Timeout mismatches are tricky because they don't always show up clearly in logs or error messages, but they can seriously disrupt how your system behaves. They often cause strange problems: some requests fail while others work, things break randomly, or it feels like "nothing worked" even though every service seems fine on its own. This situation usually happens when a client gives up waiting too soon, while the server is still working. Consequently, retries might happen too early, or services keep doing their job, but no one is there to use the results (figure 12.8).

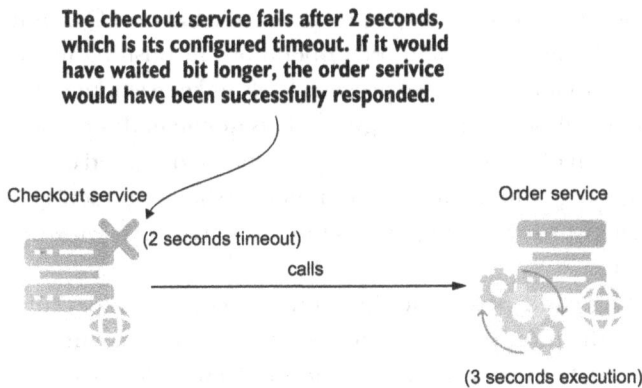

The checkout service fails after 2 seconds, which is its configured timeout. If it would have waited bit longer, the order serivice would have been successfully responded.

Checkout service

(2 seconds timeout)

calls

Order service

(3 seconds execution)

Figure 12.8 The checkout service aborts the request after 2 seconds due to its configured timeout, while the order service completes its task in 3 seconds. This mismatch results in a failed request, even though the downstream service performs correctly—highlighting the need for consistent timeout configuration across services.

In distributed tracing tools such as Jaeger or Zipkin, mismatched timeouts can be spotted by examining the span durations. Let's say your client's timeout is set to 2 seconds, but the downstream service responds in approximately 3 seconds. You'll see that the client span ends at 2 seconds, tagged as an error or timeout, but the server span continues to run, completes successfully, but has no one listening:

```
Trace ID: 7d9f3e4c9b124e91

└─ [frontend-service] Call OrderService [2,000ms] [X]          Reaches the timeout
     └─ [order-service] ProcessOrder [3,000ms]                 Ends with success
```

Sometimes the problem isn't in the code, but in the config. Make sure to check

- *Client-side timeout settings*—For example, HTTP/gRPC clients, web clients, database connection timeouts
- *Server-side processing timeouts*—For example, servlet container timeouts, controller-level timeouts, business logic delays

In Java services, common sources include

- `RestTemplate` or `WebClient` timeouts
- gRPC deadline settings (`Deadline.after(...)`)
- Tomcat/Jetty/Spring Boot server timeouts
- Third-party API limits or network proxy settings

Timeout mismatches often cause misleading log entries making you confuse them with retries. If these retries happen often but the downstream service shows no errors, that's your clue: the service is functioning, just too slowly relative to the client's patience. Moreover, check logs from the target service. If it shows "processed X successfully" but the caller logs a timeout, you have a mismatch. Additional metrics you can check to confirm this diagnostic are thread pool usage, queue buildup for message brokers (if any), request durations, timeout counts and duplicate request IDs.

In systems using asynchronous messaging (e.g., Kafka, RabbitMQ), timeout mismatches might cause upstream services to retry operations by pushing messages back into a queue. If the downstream consumers process slowly or keep working on messages that callers no longer care about, the queue grows. This queue buildup doesn't necessarily indicate high traffic. It often means retry loops are being triggered or the system is wasting resources processing stale requests. If your metrics show a sudden spike in message lag or queue size, it's worth checking whether services are retrying too aggressively or timing out too quickly.

Comparing the average and percentile durations of requests (especially P95 and P99 latencies) is one of the most direct ways to spot a mismatch. If your service has a 2-second timeout, but the 95th percentile of responses from a downstream service is 2.5 seconds, timeouts are guaranteed. Monitor the duration of both client-side requests and server-side processing time. When the client consistently gives up before the server finishes, you'll see traces or logs with premature terminations and metrics showing successful processing on the server but timeout errors on the client.

Using P95, P99, and the average for understanding metrics

When we talk about service latency, it's not enough to look at just the average (or mean) response time. Averages can be misleading. If most requests are fast but a few are extremely slow, the average hides the pain. That's where percentile-based latency metrics come in.

- *P95 latency means*—95% of requests completed in this time or faster, and the remaining 5% took longer.
- *P99 latency means*—99% of requests were faster than this value, and only 1% were slower.

Some problems such as timeout mismatches usually don't show up in the average.

Now imagine your client timeout is 2 seconds (2000 ms). The average looks fine, but 5% of users are already bumping into timeouts, and 1% are guaranteed to fail.

This is why monitoring P95 and P99 latency is essential for spotting intermittent slow-downs that might cause retries, errors, or degraded performance.

You can track these metrics using standard tools in your system environment such as distributed tracing tools or commercial platforms such as Datadog or New Relic (if available).

These percentiles give you a much sharper view of how your system behaves under pressure or at scale, and they're critical when diagnosing problems such as timeout mismatches, retry storms, and cascading failures. But you can also use them when investigating other problems, such as load-related slowdowns, resource starvation, or GC delays.

For example, if your P95 latency suddenly spikes during peak traffic hours, it may indicate your service isn't scaling properly under load, perhaps thread pools are exhausted, or database queries are getting slower. If P99 latency increases after a new deployment, it might point to a regression in a specific code path that only affects complex requests. And if you see high tail latencies (P99) correlated with GC pauses or memory pressure, it could signal JVM tuning problems.

In all these cases, percentile metrics help highlight what's happening for your slowest, most at-risk users, the ones who feel the pain first when the system begins to strain.

Figure 12.9 shows the latency distribution of a service. While the average and P90 latencies are within acceptable limits, the P95 is approaching the 2000 ms timeout threshold,

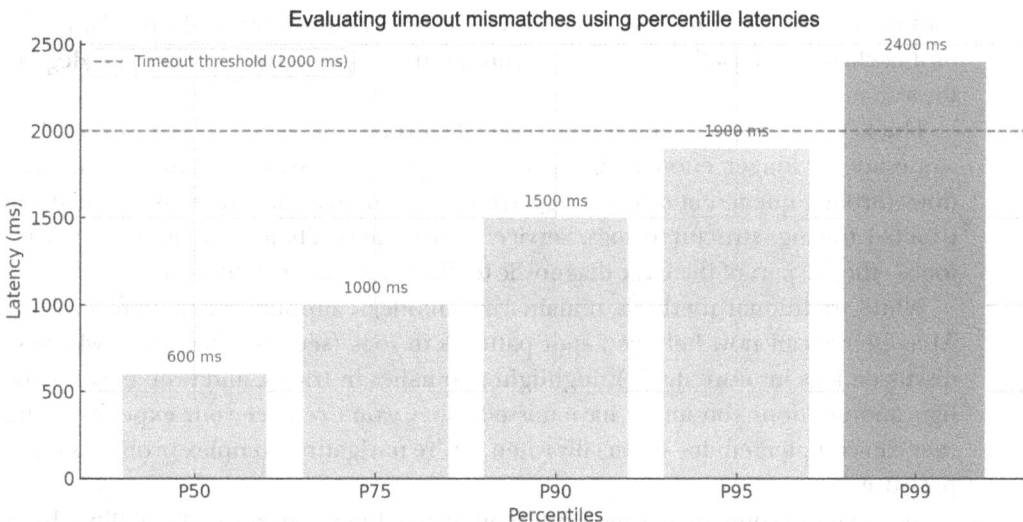

Figure 12.9 Identifying timeout mismatches using percentiles. P95 and P99 latencies approach or exceed the 2000 ms timeout threshold, revealing that some requests are likely to fail—despite the service working as expected.

and the P99 exceeds it. This indicates that a subset of requests is likely to fail due to timeouts, even though the service is functioning. Monitoring percentile latencies helps detect these edge-case failures before they escalate.

The red dashed line represents a 2000 ms timeout threshold. As shown,

- P95 latency (1900 ms) is close to the timeout.
- P99 latency (2400 ms) exceeds the timeout, indicating that a portion of requests will likely fail due to timeouts, even though the service itself may still be healthy.

As you can deduce, the average latency doesn't tell the full story. Percentile metrics are essential for tuning timeouts in distributed systems.

One subtle symptom of mismatched timeouts is the appearance of duplicate request IDs. When a client times out but the server continues working, the client may retry the same request. If your logs or traces show multiple attempts to process the same operation (same `orderId`, same `paymentId`, etc.), it's often because the client assumed the first try failed, even though it eventually succeeded. These duplicates often appear slightly offset in time and may show up in both logs and distributed tracing systems.

Many systems report timeout-specific error metrics. These can come from HTTP client libraries (such as Apache HTTP Client, `OkHttp`, or Spring's `RestTemplate`), gRPC, or even database drivers. If you start seeing an increase in timeouts without a matching spike in 500-level errors from the service you're calling, it's a clear sign of a timeout mismatch. For example, the service might be working fine, but your timeouts are too aggressive to let it respond.

Troubleshooting problems in distributed systems is rarely straightforward. Failures often begin in one place and manifest elsewhere, with symptoms disconnected from root causes. In this chapter, we've seen how slow responses, blocked threads, version mismatches, and misaligned timeouts can silently ripple across services and degrade the system.

The key takeaway is that system-level problems require system-level thinking. Logs alone are no longer enough. Understanding how services communicate, how data flows through queues, and how long each operation takes in context is essential. Distributed tracing, structured logs, service metrics, and schema validation aren't just tools—they're part of the basic diagnostic toolkit for working at this scale.

While traditional methods remain vital, modern support systems are evolving. AI assistants can now help you spot patterns in logs (see also chapter 4, where we discussed logs in more detail), highlight anomalies in traces, and even explain configuration options you might have missed. They won't replace your experience, but they can complement it—especially when you're navigating complex problems under pressure.

As systems become increasingly interconnected, the importance of visibility, observability, and structured investigation continues to grow. With the techniques in this chapter, you're better equipped to follow the evidence, ask the right questions, and find clarity in what might initially seem like chaos.

Summary

- Distributed failures often don't stay local—troubleshooting them requires system-level visibility and tools.

- Examine trace IDs and spans to reconstruct request paths, detect missing steps, and isolate problematic services in multi-hop flows. Use distributed tracing tools (such as Jaeger or Zipkin) to follow a request across services and identify where time is lost or failures originate.

- In cases of serialization problems, log decoded payloads carefully, validate schemas in CI, and use tools such as protoc, grpcurl, and jq to inspect data outside of the application.

- Detect cascading failures by analyzing thread dumps for repeating stack traces stuck on remote calls—often a sign of thread pool exhaustion.

- Identify retry storms by looking for repeating requests in logs, short retry spans in tracing tools, and sudden spikes in internal traffic without increased user load.

- Investigate timeout mismatches by comparing client and server span durations—if clients time out while servers keep processing, your configuration is misaligned.

- Watch for duplicate request IDs as they signal that clients are retrying unnecessarily due to mismatched expectations or timeouts.

- AI assistants can help analyze logs, interpret stack traces, spot anomalies in traces, or offer context on unfamiliar errors, thus accelerating troubleshooting and boosting confidence.

Measuring data consistency and transactions

This chapter covers

- Identifying and troubleshooting data inconsistencies across services
- Tracking multistep transactions using trace IDs and audit logs
- An explanation why coordination breaks down in distributed workflows
- Measuring consistency guarantees using sampling, invariants, and reconciliation

In a perfect system, data is always in sync. Every service sees the same state, updates happen atomically, and no user gets confused. In real life? Not so much.

In a distributed environment, consistency is a moving target. Services communicate over networks, store state independently, and occasionally forget to invite each other to the transaction. You'll see orders that were paid but not shipped, emails confirming things that never got saved, or records that exist in one database but not in another. The bugs are subtle, hard to reproduce, and often show up only at 2 a.m.

In this chapter, we look at how to detect and diagnose these problems before your support team finds them first. We start by identifying symptoms of inconsistency across services, then learn how to trace multistep transactions that span service boundaries, and finally cover strategies for measuring and monitoring consistency guarantees in production systems, because "it worked in staging" is not a consistency model.

This chapter focuses on the challenges of maintaining and verifying data consistency in distributed Java systems and, more importantly, on the techniques you can use to detect, trace, and monitor it effectively. In section 13.1, we begin by exploring how inconsistencies typically surface across services. You'll learn how to recognize problems such as missing records or invalid states and how to diagnose them using tools such as time-based event flow analysis and domain-level invariants. In section 13.2, we move deeper into the life cycle of distributed transactions, showing how to reconstruct transactional flows using audit logs and how to identify message loss or coordination breakdowns by replaying or inspecting event histories.

Finally, in section 13.3, we turn to measurement and long-term visibility. You'll learn how to verify data consistency using checksums, and how to detect drift in production systems through reconciliation jobs and consistency metrics. Together, these practices provide a structured approach to navigating the messy realities of distributed state, helping you not only find what went wrong, but prevent it from silently happening again.

13.1 Troubleshooting inconsistencies across services

In this section, we explore how inconsistencies can emerge across microservices, even when each service seems to function correctly on its own. These problems often manifest as missing records, duplicated data, or out-of-sync states, and it can be difficult to trace them back to a root cause. To address them, we'll walk through practical observability strategies that go beyond basic logging (discussed in chapter 4). You'll learn how to use trace correlation, business-level alerting, and other diagnostic techniques to detect and understand data mismatches across service boundaries, even when everything looks green at the surface.

13.1.1 Inspecting time-based anomalies in event flows

Time-based anomalies refer to irregularities in the timing of events that deviate from the system's expected behavior or sequence. These include delays, out-of-order operations, duplicate retries, or mismatched timestamps across services. While they might not raise immediate exceptions, such anomalies often signal deeper coordination or consistency problems.

In distributed systems, time is both a coordinating tool and a source of confusion. Services rely on timestamps to order operations, detect delays, and make assumptions about state. When those assumptions break—for example, when a request appears successful, but its effects don't materialize within the expected time window—we're most likely facing a time-based anomaly.

I'll tell you a story about an investigation case that implied time-based anomalies, but first here are a few things you need to consider when troubleshooting such problems. Can you find them applied by the team in the following story?

- Never dismiss a low-value anomaly. If the inconsistency exists at all, the same failure mode can affect higher-value or mission-critical operations.
- Use distributed tracing tools (e.g. OpenTelemetry, Zipkin) to follow the request across services. Look for missing or incomplete spans that might indicate silent failures.
- One tool alone rarely gives the full picture. Combine tracing data with Kafka topic inspection and application logs to confirm whether the message propagated through the system.
- Trace trees that end before database writes or message publishing are red flags. Investigate the last service in the trace to understand why it didn't complete downstream action.
- Query the database directly to look for missing records or gaps in sequences. These can be early indicators of deadlocks, transaction rollbacks, or unhandled write failures.
- Work with DBAs to inspect PostgreSQL deadlock logs and identify concurrency problems. Deadlock resolution might silently abort transactions if the application doesn't handle retries correctly.

In distributed systems, trouble doesn't always announce itself with alarms blaring. Sometimes, it quietly taps you on the shoulder (like a suspicious one-euro payment at a public toilet in Paris).

It all started when a friend of mine, an engineer in the payments industry, got assigned what looked like the most trivial ticket of the year:

"Investigate missing transaction. Missing one euro."

The ticket referenced a one-euro charge. For a toilet. In Paris. Naturally, jokes were made.

At first glance, it was tempting to dismiss it. After all, who's going to chase down a missing euro? But experience had taught them, and it should teach all of us, that if a system can silently lose one euro, it can just as easily lose 10,000 euros.

> **NOTE** Any small error can signal a more serious problem behind the scenes. If a system loses one euro, it can also lose much more later. Never overlook any small problem. You must troubleshoot it.

First, they checked the POS terminal logs. The device showed the customer a "Payment Approved" message, and it had indeed sent an authorization request to the payment processor. At this point, the investigation confirmed that the POS wasn't lying. The payment request was made. Next, they tried to trace the transaction through the backend payment services.

Normally, every transaction request generates a record in a processing queue and a payment audit table. But here, there was no trace of it. It was as if the request had been swallowed right after leaving the POS. Figure 13.1 briefly describes the flow. Mind that the architecture is simplified to allow you to focus on the troubleshooting rather than the system design. The system designs presented in this book might be fictional or drastically simplified. Their purpose is not to teach you practices in software architecture but to give you a picture that simplifies the teaching of troubleshooting (which is the primary focus of this book).

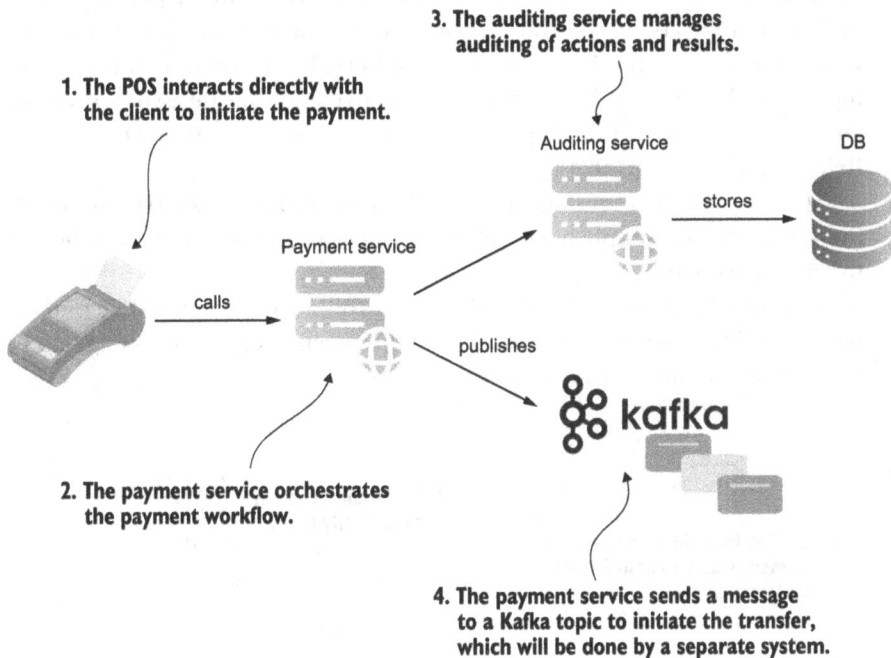

Figure 13.1 The payment system. The POS initiates a transaction that is audited and sent to execution to another system.

The first step was to check the distributed traces. Using the same tracing setup we discussed in chapter 12, based on OpenTelemetry and Jaeger, they searched for the trace ID associated with the POS device's request. In a healthy transaction, they would expect to see a full trace: POS -> API gateway -> payment processing service -> database write.

However, in this case, the trace ended abruptly at the payment-processing service, with no downstream spans recorded. The next snippet shows the idea:

```
TraceID: abc123

└── [POS Device] - initiatePayment()      (client send)
```

```
└─ [API Gateway] - forwardPayment()    (server receive / client send)
   └─ [Payment Processing Service] - processTransaction()
      ✗ No further spans recorded
```

To cross-verify, they inspected the Kafka topics where the payment processing service normally published transaction events.

Apache Kafka is a distributed event streaming platform used to build real-time data pipelines and messaging systems. In our case, services publish payment events to Kafka topics, essentially named channels, so that other systems (such as billing, reconciliation, or analytics) can consume them reliably.

Kafka ensures that messages are durable, ordered (within a partition), and scalable, making it a backbone for transactional systems where data consistency matters. We won't dive into the full Kafka architecture here, but if you're new to it, think of it as a highly durable message bus that services use to communicate asynchronously. An excellent resource covering this topic is *Kafka Streams in Action, Second Edition*, by William P. Bejeck, Jr. (Manning, 2024).

No corresponding message was found for the missing trace ID. This confirmed that the event had not simply been delayed—it had been lost somewhere before reaching the message queue.

Individually, none of these tools gave a full answer (figure 13.2). Together, they painted a clear story: the request entered the system, began processing, but never made it far enough to persist or queue any outcome.

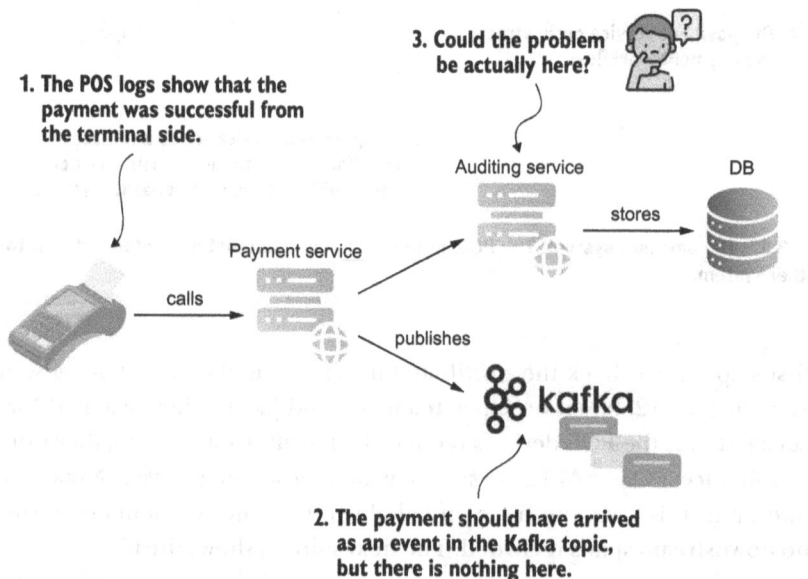

Figure 13.2   The engineer checked the POS logs followed by the Kafka topic. The clues they found revealed the possibility that the problem is in the auditing service side.

With the span tree ending inside the payment-processing service, the team knew the next place to look was the database layer—specifically, the service that should have recorded the transaction in the payment ledger.

They started by querying the transaction audit table directly, using a window around the timestamp of the POS event. As expected, there was no entry for the missing transaction. But something was off: a suspicious gap in the auto-incrementing transaction ID sequence.

To dig deeper, the team enabled and parsed database deadlock logs. Once the team suspected a database-level problem, they turned to PostgreSQL's deadlock diagnostics.

The team coordinated with the DBA to enable and collect the relevant PostgreSQL logs. They searched for error messages like the one in the following snippet:

```
ERROR:  deadlock detected
DETAIL:  Process 12345 waits for ShareLock on transaction 6789; blocked by
process 9876.
        Process 9876 waits for ShareLock on transaction 1234; blocked by
process 12345.
HINT:  See server log for query details.
```

What they found matched the missing transaction's timestamp: a deadlock between two concurrent insert operations on the same table, both competing for locks on shared indexes. The database correctly resolved the deadlock by aborting one transaction. But the application didn't retry it.

TIP Any developer should learn more than just the technology they are experts in. SQL is an indispensable skill regardless of the programming technology you are experienced with. No matter what kind of a developer you are, you will find good use for learning SQL.

They had hit a classic coordination blind spot. The payment service logged the database failure with a generic warning (something easily lost in production noise), and due to missing retry logic, it neither persisted the data nor surfaced the error downstream. The POS saw a "Success" response; the backend lost the transaction entirely.

But what if the database deadlock logs hadn't been available or had already been rotated out of existence? Teams may not have direct access to historical deadlock traces in many real-world environments, especially those with aggressive log retention policies or limited observability.

In such cases, indirect evidence becomes essential. The suspicious gap in the auto-incrementing transaction ID sequence was the first clue pointing toward a concurrency problem. Reproducing the transaction under controlled load, especially with concurrent inserts, can often reveal the same locking pattern. Additionally, examining metrics such lock wait times, transaction rollback counts, or even trace sampling anomalies can provide hints. When logs are missing, hypotheses must be validated through a mix of reasoning, simulation, and whatever breadcrumbs remain.

This investigation may have started with a trivial-looking discrepancy, but the team treated it with the rigor it deserved. By combining tracing, logs, queue inspection, and direct SQL queries, they followed the event flow across service boundaries and into the database layer. They didn't stop at the first missing record. They correlated traces with system logs, identified an invisible deadlock, and validated the root cause through controlled reproduction.

REMEMBER   Tools for distributed tracing (OpenTelemetry, Jaeger), message queue inspection (Kafka consumers), and database diagnostics (PostgreSQL logs, manual queries) are indispensable when troubleshooting complex, time-sensitive problems. But no single tool solves everything.

In practice, you often must work with whatever the environment gives you: partial logs, missing traces, or delayed access to production data. The key is to adapt, correlate, and persist. Effective troubleshooting is as much about resourcefulness as it is about tooling.

13.1.2 Applying domain invariants to identify invalid states

A QA engineer walks into a bar.
He orders one beer.
He orders zero beers.
He orders –1 beer.
He orders 99999999 beers.
He orders a lizard.
He tries to leave without paying.
Then a real customer walks in and asks,
"Hey, is this place open?"
And the bar crashes.

In any business system, some things should simply never happen, like ordering –1 beer at a bar. (Unless you're a QA engineer, in which case it's perfectly valid test input.) These are *violations of domain invariants*: fundamental rules that should always hold true, regardless of how chaotic or distributed the system gets.

NOTE   Violations of domain invariants are fundamental rules that should always be true.

When your data breaks these rules, say, by allowing a payment to complete without an order or a user to have a birthdate in the future, you're no longer just dealing with bugs. You're dealing with a broken business reality.

A *domain invariant* is like gravity in your business logic—it keeps things grounded. It's a business truth that must remain consistent even if services crash, retries happen, or messages arrive out of order. When invariants are violated, you get what we call invalid states: conditions that might technically exist in the database but make no sense in the real world.

Think of a distributed system like an airplane. Before every flight, engineers run through a checklist to ensure every component is in the right state, including fuel levels, engine sensors, and cabin pressure. Miss one item, and the consequences could be serious. Invariants play the same role: they ensure the system is in a safe, expected state before proceeding. And unlike aviation, in distributed systems, you might not even know something is missing until it's already midair. In this section, we look at how defining and validating domain invariants can help you detect inconsistencies that logs and traces often miss, and why these rules are your best defense against subtle, systemic bugs.

Violations of domain invariants typically stem from race conditions, eventual consistency delays, or a lack of defensive checks in service logic. In distributed systems, data doesn't always arrive in the expected order, messages might be delayed, retried, or processed out of sequence. For instance, a refund event might be handled before the order it references has been written to the database, simply because one message queue was temporarily faster than another.

Another common cause is insufficient transactional guarantees across service boundaries. When operations span multiple services or databases, it's easy to end up in a partially completed state. If one service fails after publishing a message but before committing its own state, consumers of that message might proceed with incomplete context. Add in weak error handling or missing idempotency controls, and you get a recipe for inconsistencies: orphaned entities, invalid references, or contradictory states that violate the core rules of your domain.

Imagine an e-commerce platform where refunds are occasionally issued for orders that, according to the database, never existed. No payment record. No order record. Just a refund floating in the system like a ghost. This is a classic case of a violated domain invariant— "a refund must always be linked to a valid, completed order."

These kinds of invalid states often creep in when workflows span multiple services. For instance, a refund microservice might consume events from a queue and process them independently. If the refund event is received before the order creation has been fully persisted, due to delays, retries, or out-of-order messaging, the refund gets processed anyway, breaking the invariant.

Now, here's some good advice that worked for me throughout the time when I had to deal with these kinds of problems:

- Define invariants explicitly in your domain model or monitoring layer. For example: `refund.orderId` *must exist AND* `refund.timestamp` > `order.timestamp`. This will help you make sure you know what you are actually looking for.
- Query the database for violations. Use SQL to find suspicious cases. Treating the database as the one source of truth for the data helps you identify when things go wrong:

```
SELECT * FROM refunds r
WHERE NOT EXISTS (
  SELECT 1 FROM orders o WHERE o.id = r.order_id
);
```

- Use trace correlation, as discussed in chapter 12, to see whether the refund flow was triggered before the corresponding order flow completed. Missing or misaligned spans can be a big clue.
- Implement reconciliation jobs or consistency checkers that regularly scan for broken relationships, such as refunds without corresponding orders. These can run as batch processes or lightweight validation services, depending on system scale and complexity.

Domain invariants are more than just validation rules. They're the sanity checks that keep your system aligned with business reality. While logs and traces tell you what happened, invariants tell you what should never happen. By encoding these rules into your system and proactively scanning for violations, you gain a powerful tool for detecting hidden inconsistencies that would otherwise go unnoticed. In a distributed architecture, you can't always control the order of events or guarantee atomicity across services, but you can hold the line on the rules that define your business.

13.2 *Tracking and correlating multistep transactions*

In this section, we'll look at two key strategies for this kind of forensic debugging: reviewing audit logs to understand what was recorded at each stage, and analyzing event logs to detect whether steps were skipped, delayed, or corrupted in transit.

Tracking and correlating multistep transactions refers to the process of observing, identifying, and linking together all the individual operations that make up a single logical business activity, even when those operations span multiple services, databases, or message queues.

In a monolith, a transaction is often a single database commit. But in distributed systems, a transaction might involve dozens of steps across loosely connected components (figure 13.3). Correlating those steps requires stitching together traces, logs, events, and audit records to recreate the full picture of what happened and where things may have gone wrong.

In section 13.2.1, we start by examining how audit logs can help reconstruct the sequence of actions that took place during a multistep transaction. These logs provide a factual timeline of what each service claims to have done, which is especially useful when transactions fail silently or partially. Then, in section 13.2.2, we shift focus to event-driven systems and explore how examining event logs, or even replaying events, can help identify missing or delayed messages that may have caused a transaction to break down. Together, these techniques give you two critical lenses: what was recorded and what was communicated.

Monolithic

T = Transaction

In a monolithic app, the transaction is managed at the realm of a single process.

Service-oriented

Auditing service

Payment service

Resolution service

Receipt service

In a service-oriented system, the transaction is managed by multiple processes. To achieve this, the system uses strategies such as distributed transactions or patterns such as Saga.

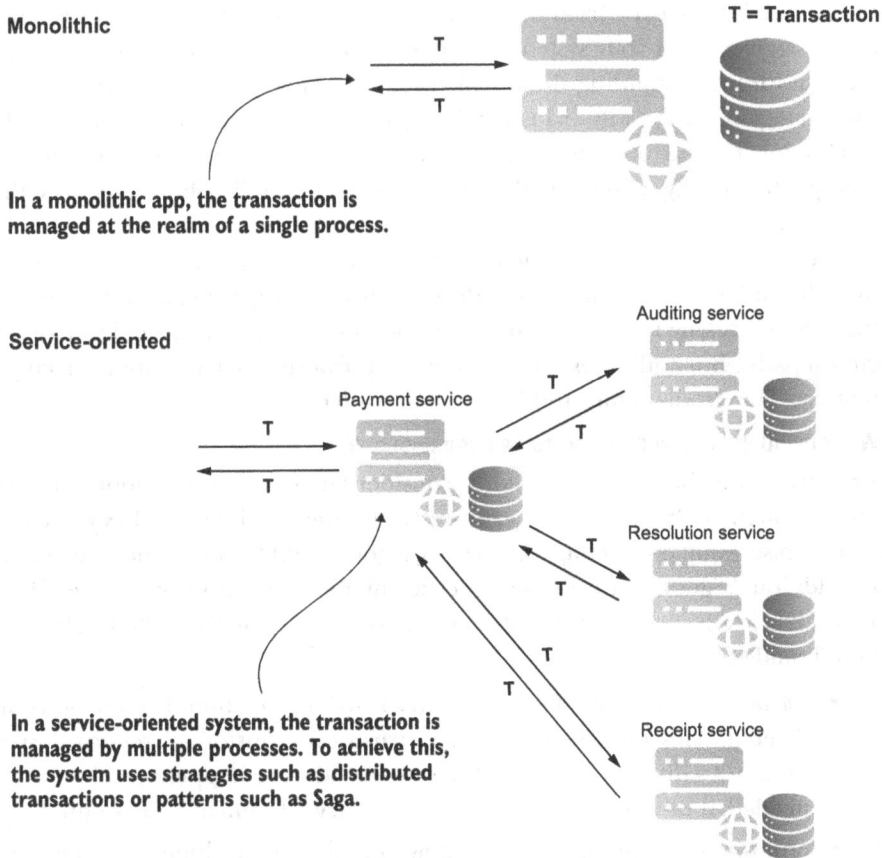

Figure 13.3 Single process transaction vs. a distributed transaction. A distributed transaction may lead to inconsistencies and domain invariants violations.

13.2.1 Reviewing audit logs to reconstruct transaction steps

Audit logs are structured records of significant actions taken by a system, such as "payment authorized," "order confirmed," or "user account created." Unlike debug or trace logs, audit logs are business focused: they're meant to answer what happened, when, and with what data. They're especially valuable in regulated or high-integrity systems, where a durable history of operations is necessary.

To reconstruct a transaction, you examine these audit entries to piece together the exact sequence of steps taken across services. It's like retracing your steps after losing your keys. You check every room you've been in, looking for clues such as an open drawer or a coat you took off. Each small detail helps rebuild the full picture of what happened and where things went wrong.

Back in chapter 4, we used the analogy of a chess game to describe good logging practices: every serious chess player writes down each move, not just to prove what happened, but to learn from it, analyze it, and explain it later. That's essentially what audit logging is. It's your system writing down its "moves," not for debugging line-by-line but for understanding the big picture. Just like a chess log helps you reconstruct the strategy behind a win or loss, audit logs let you retrace the steps of a multiservice transaction to find out where things went off course. Without that written record, you're left guessing who made the first mistake, and in distributed systems, there's no referee to ask.

In chapter 4, we focused on debug logs. We discussed how to structure them, what to include, and how to use them to understand what's happening inside a service. Debug logs are like talking to yourself: they help you think through local logic, errors, and execution paths. But audit logs serve a different purpose. They're outward-facing records that say, "Here's what I did, and here's when I did it."

WHAT DO AUDIT LOGS NEED TO DO TO BE GOOD ENOUGH?

We must remember what we need to consider keeping our logs good enough. To be good enough, audit logs should capture key business actions, not low-level implementation noise. Similar to debug log records, a good audit log entry includes a timestamp. In addition, a good audit log includes a unique transaction or business ID, a clear action label (e.g., OrderConfirmed), and the outcome (success, failed, rejected). Audit logs should be

- *Immutable*—Once an audit log entry is written, it should never be changed or deleted. This ensures the log is a trustworthy historical record, just like you wouldn't edit the minutes of a meeting after it happened. If a correction is needed, it should be recorded as a new entry referencing the original.

- *Structured*—Audit logs should follow a consistent, machine-readable format (typically JSON or a log schema), so that tools can parse and analyze them easily. Structured logs make it possible to filter by fields such as userId, transactionId, or status, rather than relying on brittle text matching.

- *Queryable*—Audit logs should be stored to allow efficient searching, filtering, and aggregation. Whether you use a log platform such as Elasticsearch, a database, or a cloud-logging service, the goal is to be able to answer questions such as "How many refunds were issued today?" or "Which transactions failed between 12:00 and 12:15?" without manual scanning.

- *Stored centrally*—Audit logs should not live only on individual service instances or local machines. They need to be collected in a centralized logging platform or storage system where all services contribute their entries. This makes it possible to reconstruct multiservice workflows, correlate events by timestamp or transaction ID, and ensure nothing is lost if a node goes down or is redeployed.

- *Retained long-term*—Audit logs aren't just for immediate troubleshooting. They're also crucial for investigating delayed failures, resolving customer disputes, or satisfying compliance requirements. That's why they should be kept for a much longer period than typical debug logs (sometimes weeks, months, or even years, depending on regulatory or business needs). Deleting audit data too early is like burning your security camera footage while the investigation is still ongoing.

Also, audit logs should be written assuming that someone else will rely on them later to understand what happened. The following listing shows an example of audit logs following the best practices mentioned earlier.

Listing 13.1 An example of an audit log record following best practices

```
{
  "timestamp": "2025-04-28T13:12:04Z",
  "event": "OrderPlaced",
  "transactionId": "TXN-324791",
  "orderId": "ORD-98231",
  "userId": "USR-49384",
  "status": "success",
  "totalAmount": 129.90,
  "currency": "EUR",
  "source": "checkout-service"
}
```

Sometimes audit logs need to provide useful context, while also masking or omitting sensitive data to comply with security and privacy standards (such as GDPR, PCI-DSS, etc.). The following listing shows how a part of the data was obfuscated to hide sensitive information.

Listing 13.2 Masking sensitive data in audit logs

```
{
  "timestamp": "2025-04-28T13:15:44Z",
  "event": "PaymentAttempted",
  "transactionId": "TXN-912378",
  "userId": "USR-20493",
  "paymentMethod": "credit_card",
  "cardNumber": "XXXX XXXX XXXX 4821",    ◀─┐ Part of the data was eliminated
  "amount": 49.99,                           │ for security reasons.
  "currency": "USD",
  "status": "success",
  "source": "checkout-service"
}
```

I always consider it important to see also an example of "don't do it this way." The next listing shows an audit log record that doesn't follow the best practices.

Listing 13.3 An example of "this way no"

```
{
  "timestamp": "2025-04-28T13:23:08Z",
  "event": "UserLogin",
  "userId": "john.doe@example.com",    ◀─┐ Sensitive secret
  "password": "hunter2",                  │ logged in plain text
```

A JWT token logged could
potentially be reused.

```
"sessionToken": "eyJhbGciOiJIUzI1NiIsInR5cCI6IkpXVCJ9...",
"ipAddress": "192.168.1.23",
"status": "success",
"source": "auth-service",
"debug": "stacktrace: NullPointerException at AuthService.java:223",
"notes": "User logged in using Chrome on Windows 10"
}
```

An IP address might reveal clues
about the networking internals.

A stack trace
may pollute
auditing.

Any data should be
structured (e.g. as JSON).

RECONSTRUCTING THE STORY

When something breaks in a distribution system like a failed transaction, a missing confirmation, or a customer complaint, audit logs should be one of the first places you check. Your initial goal is to *reconstruct the story*: what happened, when, and where. Start by searching for the audit logs for the transaction or user ID involved. You're looking for the first known action related to the incident, like a payment attempt, an order creation, or a login request.

From there, *follow the timeline.* Audit logs are typically written at major decision points: request received, payment authorized, record persisted, email sent. These give you a high-level view of which steps were attempted and whether they succeeded. Think of it like watching security footage: even if you don't see the exact problem yet, you can narrow down when and where things went off-script. Just be aware that in distributed systems, clocks may not be perfectly synchronized, so timestamps might appear slightly out of order.

As you dig deeper, *look for gaps or inconsistencies.* Was a refund issued without a matching purchase? Did the logs skip over a step that should always happen, like inventory reservation before shipment? These are signs of broken workflows, race conditions, or missing events, and audit logs can reveal them long before a customer notices.

Finally, *cross-check with other signals*: event logs, distributed traces, and system metrics. Audit logs won't show internal stack traces or memory errors, but they will tell you what the system thought it was doing, and that's often the most critical clue when hunting down silent failures. Figure 13.4 shows these four steps.

Whether you're tracing a lost transaction, debugging an incomplete workflow, or just verifying that your system behaves as expected, audit logs are one of the most trustworthy sources

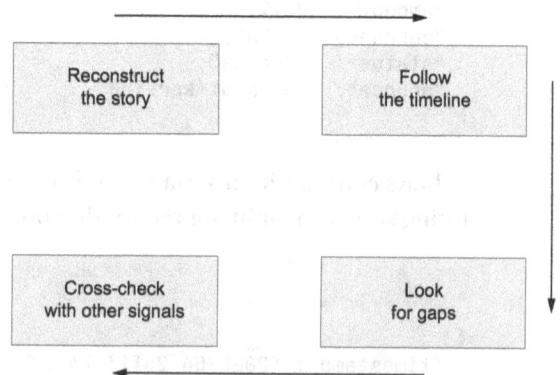

Figure 13.4 Steps for troubleshooting through story reconstruction.

of truth you have. Treat them like a flight recorder: they're not just for crashes, but they're for making sense of complexity when the path isn't clear.

13.2.2 Replaying events or examining event logs for missing messages

In many cases, we have to deal with event-driven architectures. In an event-driven architecture, services don't call each other directly, but they communicate by emitting and reacting to events. An event is a message that represents something that already happened, like `"UserRegistered"`, `"PaymentProcessed"`, or `"InventoryReserved"`. These events are usually sent through a message broker such as Kafka, RabbitMQ, or AWS SQS, and picked up by other services that react to them (figure 13.5).

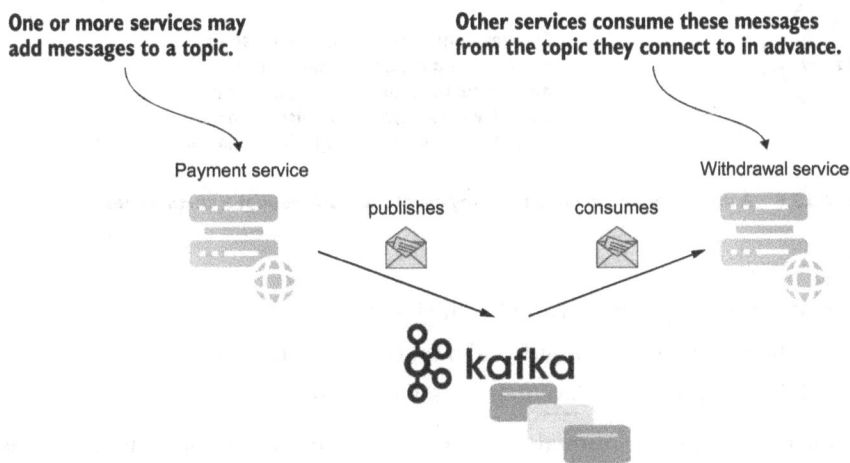

One or more services may add messages to a topic.

Other services consume these messages from the topic they connect to in advance.

Payment service   publishes   consumes   Withdrawal service

kafka

Figure 13.5 An event-driven design. A message broker manages the messages that are exchanged by several services.

A *message*, in this context, is the actual data packet that carries the event, typically in a structured format such as JSON, and includes metadata such as timestamps, IDs, and topic names. While logs tell you what an individual service did, event logs tell you what the system communicated and how services reacted to those communications.

Replaying events (figure 13.6) means taking previously recorded messages from an event log and feeding them back into the system, typically into a staging or test environment, to re-trigger workflows. This is extremely helpful for debugging missing or out-of-order behavior. For example, if a service failed to send a confirmation email, you can replay the `"UserRegistered"` event to see if the problem reproduces and whether the email service consumes it correctly.

Replaying lets you validate assumptions and isolate failure scenarios without affecting real users or data. By examining event logs, you can identify

- Whether an event was published at all

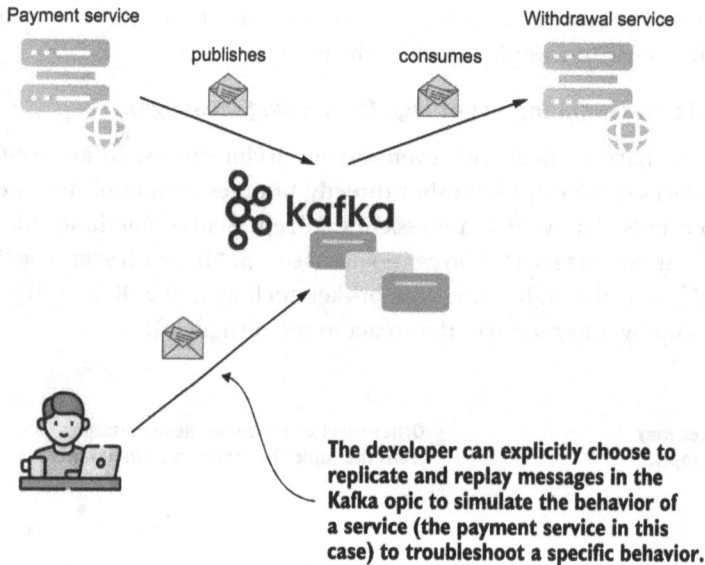

The developer can explicitly choose to replicate and replay messages in the Kafka opic to simulate the behavior of a service (the payment service in this case) to troubleshoot a specific behavior.

Figure 13.6   A developer can choose to replay events to troubleshoot a certain scenario.

- When it was published and by which service
- Whether it was consumed, and if so, by whom and when
- If it was dropped, delayed, or dead-lettered due to processing failures

Let me tell you a story. Ahmed, a developer on the user onboarding team, was investigating a puzzling bug: several users had successfully signed up for accounts, but never received their welcome emails. The "UserRegistered" events were showing up in the audit logs, and the users existed in the database, but the email service never triggered.

Rather than jumping straight into the code, Ahmed decided to start by examining the event logs from Kafka. He filtered the "user-events" topic by the user IDs involved and confirmed that the UserRegistered events were published, with the correct data. So far, everything looked normal: the event was sent, but something down the line had gone wrong.

Next, he checked the consumer group offsets for the email service. A consumer group offset is a pointer that tells Kafka how far a consumer has progressed through a topic. When a service reads messages from a Kafka topic, it does so as part of a consumer group, which is a set of consumers working together to process the same stream.

Kafka assigns each consumer in the group a portion of the topic (a partition), and as each message is read, the consumer updates its offset—essentially a bookmark saying "I've processed up to message #12345."

If the offset isn't updated, the consumer might reprocess messages (which can be good or bad, depending on your logic). If the offset is too far ahead, the consumer might miss earlier messages. If the offset is completely wrong (e.g., pointing to a different topic or partition), the consumer might see nothing at all.

Ahmed realized that the service had been misconfigured during a recent deployment to listen to the wrong Kafka topic. It had never seen the events at all. The messages weren't lost—they were just sitting there, unconsumed.

Ahmed set up a local test environment with the correct topic configuration to test and fix the problem safely. Then he replayed the missed events from the Kafka log. Ahmed knew he could do this by using specific Kafka tools: the kafka-console-consumer and kafka-console-producer tools. The Email Service picked them up as expected and sent the emails correctly. Problem confirmed. Fix validated.

> **TIP** Specific technologies often come with built-in tools that simplify troubleshooting. A best practice is to learn the technology and become familiar with the tools it provides for inspection, testing, and debugging. For example, when working with Kafka, tools such as kafka-console-producer and kafka-console-consumer are invaluable for replaying events, inspecting messages, and verifying that consumers are behaving correctly. Knowing how to use these tools can save hours of guesswork.

Ahmed wrote a postmortem describing the problem and the replay process, and added a dashboard metric to monitor lagging or idle consumer groups in the future. By understanding how event logs and replay work, Ahmed solved a real production mystery and avoided introducing a second one in the process.

> **DEFINITION** A *postmortem* is a written summary of an incident that explains what went wrong, how it was fixed, and what will be done to prevent it in the future. It's a learning tool, not a blame report.

Let's review some of the things Ahmed did well and learn from his experience with replaying messages:

- Jumping into code too early can lead to wild guesses. Always begin with observable evidence, such as audit logs or event logs.
  Ahmed began by examining the Kafka event log to see whether the UserRegistered messages had actually been published.
- Event logs can confirm whether messages were sent, when, and with what data. They are often more reliable than application logs.
  Ahmed verified that the messages were correctly published to the user-events topic.
- Use a staging or local setup to reproduce the problem and confirm the fix without touching live data.
  Ahmed reconfigured the service locally and validated that it could consume the events correctly.
- Technologies such as Kafka provide CLI tools that make it easy to inspect topics or replay events without writing extra code.

> *Ahmed used kafka-console-consumer and kafka-console-producer to replay the missing events.*

- Don't stop at theory—replay the scenario and ensure the outcome is as expected. *After replaying the messages, Ahmed confirmed the emails were sent as intended.*

13.3 *Measuring and monitoring consistency guarantees*

Consistency means that all parts of a system agree on the same data simultaneously. In simple terms, if you update something in one place, that update should show up everywhere else right away (no missing, old, or conflicting information).

For example, if you transfer money from one bank account to another, both balances should reflect the change instantly. If one shows the new amount and the other doesn't, that's a consistency problem (figure 13.7).

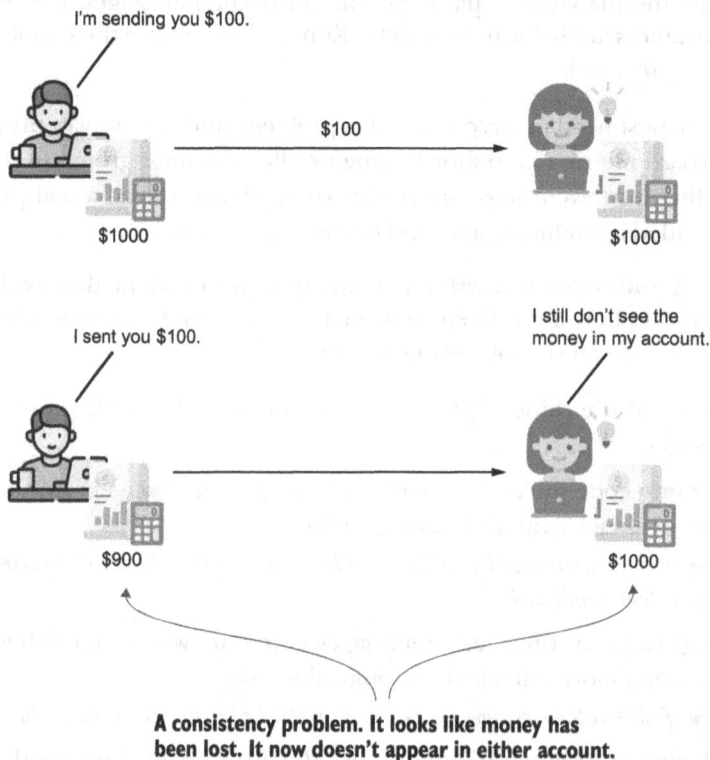

I'm sending you $100.

$100

$1000 $1000

I sent you $100.

I still don't see the money in my account.

$900 $1000

A consistency problem. It looks like money has been lost. It now doesn't appear in either account.

Figure 13.7   A consistency problem. Account balances do not reflect the correct amounts of money.

Consistency is never guaranteed by default in a distributed system. Consistency must be measured, monitored, and actively enforced. Systems that appear healthy on the surface can still suffer from silent data drift, where records that should be in sync slowly fall out of alignment across services or databases.

The challenge is that most production environments aren't designed to surface these inconsistencies automatically. You often need to build your own safety net, one that detects data mismatches, missing relationships, or eventual consistency delays before they turn into real business problems.

In this section, we explore two practical approaches to this problem. First, in section 13.3.1, I show how checksums and hashes can be used to verify data integrity between systems without transferring full datasets. Then, in section 13.3.2, we'll look at how reconciliation jobs can detect mismatches by comparing expected versus actual state across services, queues, or storage layers.

13.3.1 Verifying data integrity using checksums or hashes

Data integrity refers to the accuracy, consistency, and reliability of data over its entire life cycle. Here the "entire life cycle" refers to all the stages that data goes through, from the moment it's created until it's deleted or archived. Maintaining data integrity means ensuring the data stays accurate, consistent, and trustworthy through all these stages.

In a distributed system, it means that data stored or transmitted across services, databases, or environments remains uncorrupted, complete, and in sync with the source of truth. One way to verify data integrity efficiently (especially across system boundaries) is to use checksums or hashes.

A *checksum* is a small, fixed-size value calculated from a larger block of data using a specific algorithm. Its primary purpose is to detect accidental errors or corruption that might occur during storage, transmission, or processing. Unlike cryptographic hashes, checksums are not meant to be secure against intentional tampering; instead, they are fast and efficient tools for catching unintentional problems such as bit flips, incomplete writes, or faulty network transmissions.

Common checksum algorithms include CRC32 (Cyclic Redundancy Check) and Adler-32, which produce compact numerical representations (usually 32 bits) of the original data. These algorithms are simple and optimized for performance, making them ideal for real-time systems, file formats, and network protocols.

The basic idea is as follows: when data is first generated or transmitted, a checksum is calculated, stored, or sent along with the data. Later, the checksum is recomputed and compared with the original when the data is read or received. If the values match, the data is assumed to be intact. If they don't, it indicates that the data has likely been altered or corrupted.

You've likely seen this on many sites where you can download files such as executables you want to run. The site provides the file along with its CRC32 checksum:

```
File: file.exe
CRC32 Checksum: A12F3B4C
```

After downloading the file, your system or tool can recalculate the CRC32 checksum of the file you received. If the result matches A12F3B4C, then the file was likely downloaded correctly. If it doesn't match, it means something went wrong. Maybe a network glitch or disk error happened, and the file should be discarded or re-downloaded. Although they are not foolproof (since different data can produce the same checksum in rare cases), they provide a fast first line of defense against accidental data integrity problems.

A *hash* is a cryptographically stronger variant. It is a one-way function that converts any input (such as a record or a payload) into a fixed-size string, like a SHA-256 or MD5 digest. If two systems generate the same hash for the same input, it's a strong indication that the data is identical. If the hashes differ, you know something has changed, even if you don't yet know what. An excellent resource for understanding hash functions better is the book *Software Security for Developers* by Adib Saikali and Laurențiu Spilcă (Manning, 2025).

When you're trying to troubleshoot consistency problems across services or systems, checksums and hashes can help you quickly identify where things went wrong without having to compare full data payloads or inspect every row manually.

When data moves between services, such as from a payment processor to an accounting system, you can use checksums or hashes to verify that what was sent matches what was received. By computing a hash on both sides and comparing the results, you can quickly detect whether the data has changed in transit, even if you can't inspect every field manually. This is especially useful when dealing with large or sensitive datasets.

Hashes are also helpful when validating the consistency of replication or caching layers. If you rely on read replicas, Elasticsearch indices, or Redis caches, it's easy for those layers to fall out of sync with the primary data source. Computing hashes at both ends can give you a fast and cheap way to check whether what's being read matches what was written.

You can also include hashes in your audit logs or metadata fields. For example, when a record is first written, the application can log a hash of the key business fields. Later, during debugging or forensic analysis, you can recompute the hash and confirm whether the data was accidentally modified along the way, without having to log sensitive or bulky data (see the following snippet):

```
{
  "timestamp": "2025-04-28T15:03:41Z",
  "event": "InvoiceCreated",
  "invoiceId": "INV-842001",
  "userId": "USR-33991",
  "amount": 249.99,
  "currency": "USD",
  "hash": "f9a8d6c35d2a4e0caa8f410bcf4e7a91a18ec50b2…",    ◄─── A hash on given important fields as part of the audit log message
  "source": "billing-service"
}
```

If someone later finds a conflicting invoice record elsewhere (e.g., in a downstream system or support database), they can hash that version and compare it to the original audit log without needing to expose or compare full field-by-field data. If tampering or unexpected changes occur, a mismatch in hash values provides a clear signal that something is wrong, without storing the full, potentially sensitive content.

Finally, during incident response, hashes help you scope the blast radius of a data problem (figure 13.8). The blast radius is a way of asking, "How bad is this problem, and how far has it spread?" Imagine a small bug corrupts one record in a database—that's a small blast radius. But if the same bug affects thousands of records or multiple systems, the blast radius is much bigger.

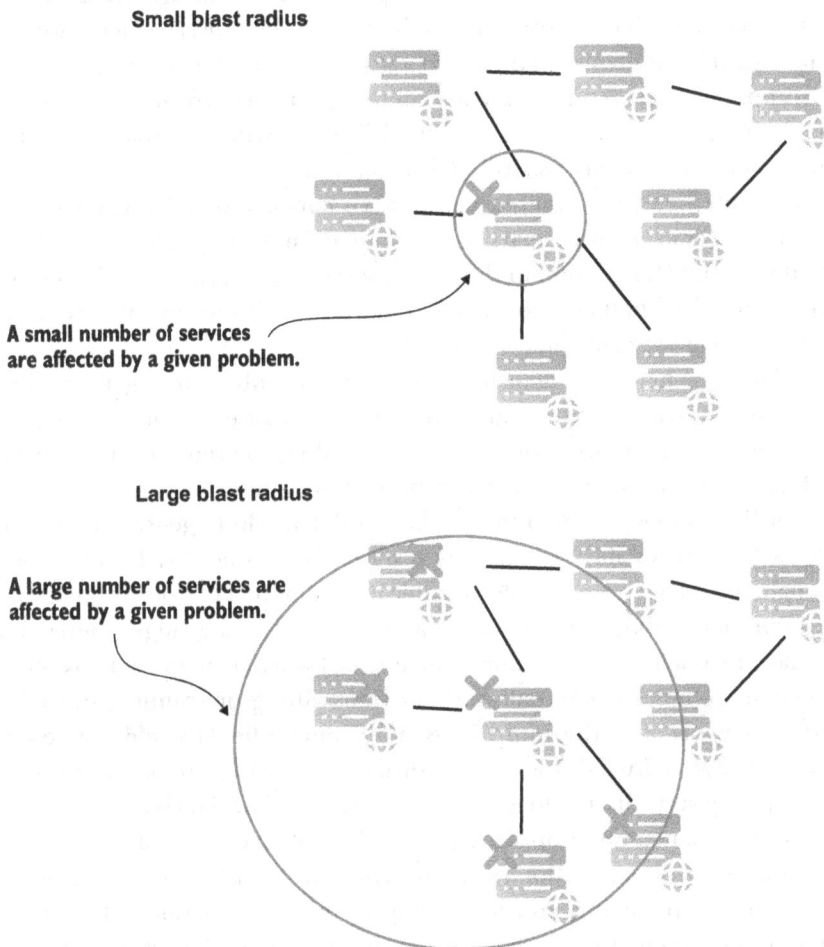

Small blast radius

A small number of services are affected by a given problem.

Large blast radius

A large number of services are affected by a given problem.

Figure 13.8 The blast radius is a way to see the effect of a problem throughout the system.

During an incident, figuring out the blast radius helps you decide how serious the problem is. Do you need a quick fix for one item or a large recovery for an entire system? Hashes help you solve that dilemma faster. By checking whether other records have the same problem, you can quickly see if the problem is just one-off, or if it's everywhere.

If you're unsure whether the inconsistency you're seeing is a single bad record or a systemic failure, spot-checking hashes across systems can quickly show whether the problem is isolated or widespread, guiding where to look next and how to respond urgently.

13.4 *Running reconciliation jobs to compare expected vs. actual state*

A *reconciliation job* is a background process that compares what should exist in systems to what is actually there. It checks whether two related systems agree, for example, whether every shipped order has a matching entry in the billing system, or whether all processed payments have corresponding invoices. When discrepancies are found, the job can flag them for manual review, alert a team, or even trigger automatic corrections.

This approach treats consistency as something you measure and verify continuously, not something you assume will always hold. Reconciliation jobs are your last line of defense against silent data loss, drift, or duplication.

For example, in an e-commerce platform, a reconciliation job might run every night to ensure that for every order marked as "shipped" in the logistics service, there's a corresponding "paid" transaction in the billing service, and a record in the customer service platform. If any of these are missing, that could indicate anything from a transient failure to a lost message or a bug in a workflow.

When discrepancies are detected, reconciliation jobs can flag them for manual investigation, send alerts to relevant teams, or in some cases, automatically attempt corrective action. It can, for example, attempt re-sending an event, regenerating a missing record, or retrying a failed step in a distributed transaction.

Reconciliation jobs are often the last line of defense in large-scale systems, catching problems that observability tools may not surface immediately and that traditional validations might miss. They are especially valuable in systems that rely on eventual consistency, where assumptions about "correct state" cannot be made at any single point in time.

To make reconciliation jobs more efficient and scalable, many systems rely on hashing to compare large sets of data without transmitting or scanning every individual record. Instead of comparing entire rows or documents field by field, a system can compute a hash (e.g., SHA-256) for each record, or even for entire partitions of data, and then compare just the hash values. If the hashes match, the data is assumed to be identical; if not, a deeper comparison is triggered to identify the exact difference.

For example, a reconciliation job might compute a hash of all invoice entries for a given day in both the billing and accounting systems. If the hashes differ, the job drills down to a finer granularity, perhaps at the per-invoice level, to isolate the mismatch. This divide-and-conquer strategy using hierarchical or chunked hashes allows reconciliation jobs to remain performant even across millions of records or across geographically distributed data centers.

Hashing also enables stateless reconciliation, where systems don't need to track previous states explicitly, because the hash itself acts as a fingerprint of current data. However, it's crucial to use stable and collision-resistant hash functions to ensure that different inputs don't mistakenly appear the same.

Summary

- Time-based inconsistencies, such as delays, out-of-order operations, or missing downstream actions, are early signs of broken coordination. By analyzing traces and timestamps, you can identify where a request silently failed or didn't propagate as expected.

- Since no single tool provides a complete picture, using multiple sources (trace spans, logs, and Kafka topics) helps confirm whether messages were successfully emitted, consumed, or lost, allowing for full event reconstruction.

- Domain invariants are business rules that must always hold true, such as "every refund must be linked to an existing order." Encoding these into your monitoring or validation layers lets you catch inconsistencies even when individual services behave correctly.

- By automating invariant checks (e.g., as batch jobs), you create an early warning system that flags data inconsistencies in production, helping to prevent minor bugs from turning into customer-facing problems.

- Audit logs act as the black box of your system, recording key business events and outcomes. They help reconstruct what happened across services, especially valuable when trying to explain partial failures or verify state transitions.

- Good audit logs include transaction IDs, clear action labels, timestamps, and outcomes. When centralized and consistently formatted (e.g., JSON), they become a powerful tool for incident analysis and compliance.

- While audit logs show what was recorded, traces show what was executed, and event logs show what was communicated. Correlating these sources helps build a full timeline and detect mismatches between intention and effect.

- Kafka topics act as durable ledgers of what happened in event-driven architectures. Examining these logs helps you confirm whether an event was sent, when, and by which producer, even if consumers missed it.

- Replaying events (e.g., with kafka-console-producer) lets you test services under controlled conditions. It's especially useful for verifying that services consume and react to events properly, or to reproduce bugs in staging.

- Hashing critical fields lets you verify that the same data exists across systems without transmitting full records. This is ideal for checking data integrity between replicas, caches, or integration points.

- Instead of comparing every record, you can hash batches or partitions to detect mismatches efficiently. This divide-and-conquer approach keeps reconciliation jobs performant, even at large scale.

appendix A
Tools you'll need

This appendix includes links to installation instructions for all the tools recommended to follow the book's examples.

To open and execute the projects provided with the book, you need to install an IDE. I used IntelliJ IDEA: https://www.jetbrains.com/idea/download/. Alternatively, you can use Eclipse IDE: https://www.eclipse.org/downloads/. Otherwise, you can use Apache Netbeans: https://netbeans.apache.org/download/index.html.

To run the Java projects provided with the book, you need to install JDK version 17 or higher. (We've tested all the book projects with Java 17, but please use the most current version as you work through them.) I recommend using the OpenJDK distribution: https://jdk.java.net/17/.

For profiling techniques and reading heap and thread dumps, we use VisualVM: https://visualvm.github.io/download.html. For some techniques we'll discuss, VisualVM will not be enough. For these, we'll use JProfiler: https://www.ej-technologies.com/jprofiler.

fastThread is a tool that will help you investigate thread dumps, which we talk about in chapter 9: https://fastthread.io/.

Throughout the book, we'll use Postman to call endpoints to demonstrate investigation techniques: https://www.postman.com/downloads/.

In chapter 12, we talk about monitoring log events with Sentry: https://sentry.io.

appendix B
Opening a project

This appendix lists the steps for opening and running an existing project. The projects provided with the book are Java apps that use Java 17. We use these projects to demonstrate the use of several techniques and tools.

First, you need to have an IDE such as IntelliJ IDEA, Eclipse, or Apache Netbeans installed. For the examples, I used IntelliJ IDEA: https://www.jetbrains.com/idea/download/.

To run the projects provided with the book, you need to install JDK version 17 or higher. You can use any Java distribution. I use the OpenJDK distribution: https://jdk.java.net/17/.

Figure B.1 shows how to open an existing project in IntelliJ IDEA. To select the project you want to open, choose File > Open.

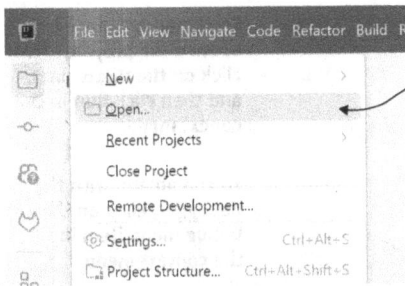

From the File menu, use the Open menu item to open an existing project.

Figure B.1 To open an existing project in IntelliJ IDEA, select Open in the File menu.

Click File > Open, and a pop-up window appears. Select the project you want to open. Figure B.2 shows this pop-up window.

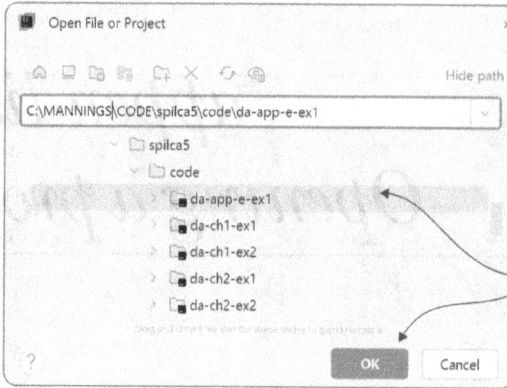

After clicking on the Open menu item in the File menu, you need to select the project you want to open. Select the project folder and click the OK button at the bottom of the dialog window.

Figure B.2   After selecting Open in the File menu, a pop-up window appears. In this window, select the project you want to open from the file system and click the OK button.

To run the application, right-click the class containing the main() method. For the projects provided with the book, the main() method is defined in a class named Main. Right-click this class, as presented in figure B.3, and select Run.

If you want to run the app with a debugger, right-click the Main class > Debug.

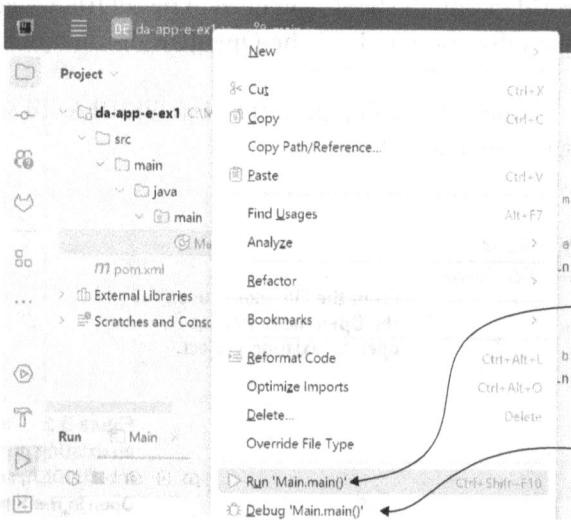

To run an app once you opened the project, right click on the Main class, and then click Run in the conext menu.

To run an app with the debugger, click on the Debug menu item in the context menu.

Figure B.3   Once you open an app, you can run it. To run the app, right-click the Main class and select the Run menu item. If you want to run the app with a debugger, click Debug.

appendix C
Recommended
further reading

This appendix lists additional readings relevant to the book's subject matter that you may find useful and interesting:

- *The Programmer's Brain* by Felienne Hermans (Manning, 2021) explores how a developer's brain works when they investigate code. Reading the code is part of understanding software, and it's something we do before applying investigation techniques. A better understanding of these aspects will also enhance your ability to analyze code effectively.

- *Monolith to Microservices* by Sam Newman (O'Reilly Media, 2019) is a recommendation I made in chapter 12 for studying microservices as an architectural style. This book focuses on the difference between a monolithic approach and microservices and where and how to use each of the two architectural styles.

- *Building Microservices: Designing Fine-Grained Systems, Second Edition* (O'Reilly Media, 2021) is another book by Sam Newman that focuses on designing systems involving fine-grained services. The author analyzes the pros and cons of the presented techniques with clear and detailed examples.

- *Microservices Patterns* by Chris Richardson (Manning, 2018) is one of the books I consider a must-read for anyone working with microservices architectures. Through clear examples, the author details the most essential techniques used in large-scale microservices and service-oriented systems.

- *Five Lines of Code* by Christian Clausen (Manning, 2021) teaches you clean coding practices. Many apps today are unstructured and challenging to understand. I designed many of the code listings available throughout the examples to be realistic, so they don't always follow clean coding principles. But once you've grasped how messy code works, you should refactor it to make it easier to understand. Developers call this principle the "Boy Scout rule." In many cases, debugging is followed by refactoring to make code easier to understand in the future.

- *Good Code, Bad Code* by Tom Long (Manning, 2021) is an excellent book that teaches high-quality code-writing principles. I also recommend reading this resource to upskill in refactoring and writing easier-to-understand apps.

- *Software Mistakes and Tradeoffs* by Tomasz Lelek and Jon Skeet (Manning, 2022) discusses using excellent examples, how to make difficult decisions, compromise, and optimize decisions in software development.

- *Refactoring: Improving the Design of Existing Code* by Martin Fowler with Kent Beck (Addison-Wesley Professional, 2018) is another must-read for any software developer wanting to improve their skills in designing and building clean and maintainable applications.

appendix D
Understanding
Java threads

This appendix discusses the basics of threads in a Java app. A thread is an independent sequential set of instructions your app runs. Operations on a given thread run concurrently with those on other threads. Modern Java applications often depend on multiple threads, which makes it inevitable to encounter situations where you need to investigate why certain threads are not behaving as expected or why they struggle to cooperate with other threads. That's why you'll find threads in several discussions throughout this book (especially chapters 7–9, but also here and there in the first half of the book when we discuss debugging). To properly understand this subject matter, you need to know some basics about threads. This appendix introduces foundational concepts essential for understanding other discussions throughout the book.

We'll start with section D.1, where I'll remind you of the threads' big picture and why we use them in apps. We continue in section D.2 with more details on how a thread executes by discussing its life cycle. Knowing the states of a thread's life cycle and the possible transitions is necessary for investigating any thread-related problems. In section D.3, we discuss thread synchronization, which is a way to control the executing threads. Faulty synchronization implementations introduce most of the problems you need to investigate and solve. In section D.4, we discuss the most common thread-related problems.

Threads are a complex subject, so I'll only focus on the topics you need to know to understand the techniques presented in this book. I can't promise to make you an expert in the subject in only a few pages, so you'll find a few resources I recommend at the end of this appendix.

D.1 What is a thread?

This section discusses what threads are and how using multiple threads helps an app. A *thread* is an independent sequence of operations in a running process. Any process can have multiple threads that run concurrently, enabling your app to solve multiple tasks, potentially, in parallel. Threads are an essential component of how a language handles concurrency.

I like to visualize a multithreaded app as a group of sequence timelines, as presented in figure D.1. Notice that the app starts with one thread (the main thread). This thread launches other threads, which can start others, and so on. Remember that each thread is independent. For example, the main thread can end its execution long before the app itself. The process stops when all its threads stop.

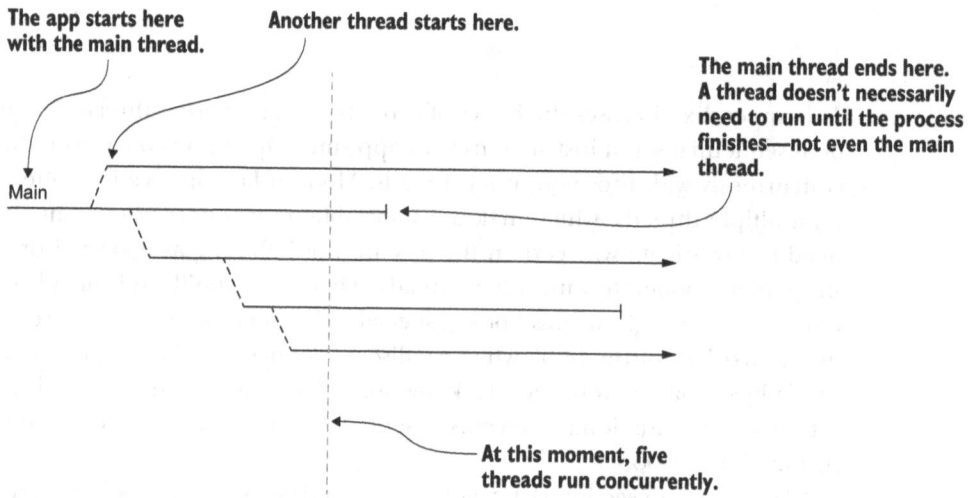

Figure D.1   A multithreaded app visualized as a group of sequence timelines. Each arrow in the figure represents the timeline of a thread. An app starts with the main thread, which can launch other threads. Some threads run until the process ends, while others stop earlier. At a given time, an app can have one or more threads running in parallel.

Instructions on a given thread are always in a defined order. You always know that A will happen before B if instruction A is before instruction B on the same thread. But since two threads are independent of one another, you can't say the same about two instructions A and B, each on a separate thread. In such a case, either A can execute before B, or vice versa (figure D.2). Sometimes, we say that one case is more probable than another, but we can't know how consistently one flow will execute.

Two instructions on the same
thread will always execute in
the order they are written.
Here, we know the app will
always print A and then B.

```
System.out.print("A");          System.out.print("B");
```

Since every thread is independent, we
can't say in which order two instructions
on two different threads will execute.
In this case, the app could print AB or BA.

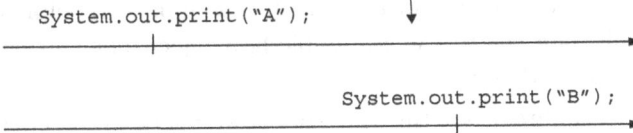

```
System.out.print("A");
```

```
System.out.print("B");
```

Figure D.2 With
two instructions
on one thread, we
can always know
the exact order
of execution.
But because
two threads are
independent, if
instructions are on
different threads,
we can't know the
order in which they
will execute. At
most, we can say
that one scenario
is more likely than
another.

In many cases, you'll see thread execution visually represented by tools as sequence timelines. Figure D.3 shows the way VisualVM (a profiler tool we use throughout the book) presents the thread execution as sequence timelines.

Thread execution seen as
sequence timelines in VisualVM

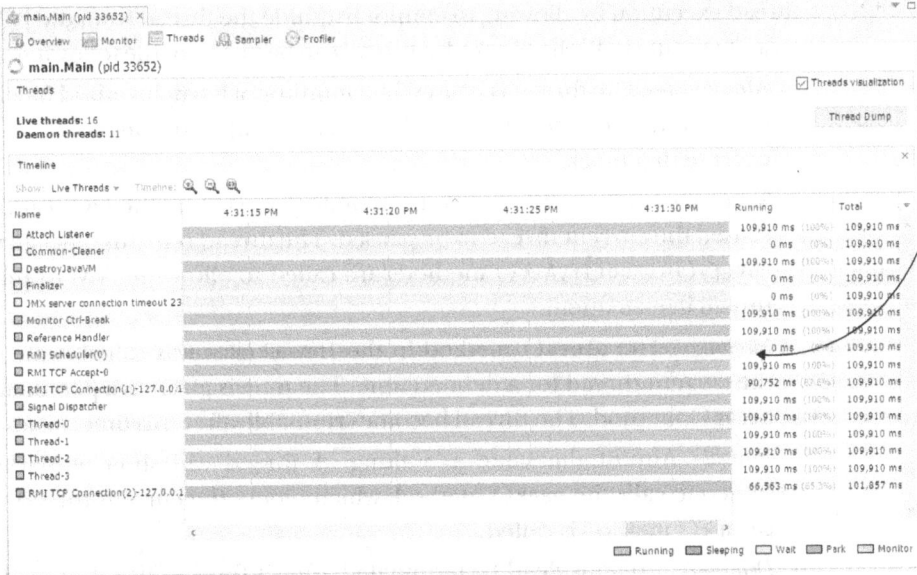

Figure D.3 VisualVM shows thread execution as sequence timelines. This visual representation makes the app's execution easier to understand and helps you to investigate possible problems.

D.2   A thread's life cycle

Once you visualize the thread execution, another essential aspect in understanding their execution is knowing the thread life cycle. Throughout its execution, a thread goes through multiple states (figure D.4). When using a profiler (as discussed in chapters 5–7) or a thread dump (as discussed in chapter 8), we'll often refer to the thread's state, which is important when trying to figure out the execution. Knowing how a thread can transition from one state to another and how the thread behaves in each state is essential to following and investigating the app's behavior.

Figure D.4 visually presents the thread states and how a thread can transition from one state to another. We can identify the following main states for a Java thread:

- *New*—The thread is in this state right after its instantiation (before being started). While in this state, the thread is a simple Java object. The app can't yet execute the instructions it defines.

- *Runnable*—The thread is in this state after its start() method has been called. In this state, the JVM can execute the instructions the thread defines. While in this state, the JVM will progressively move the thread between two substates:

- *Ready*—The thread doesn't execute, but the JVM can put it in execution at any time.

- *Running*—The thread is in execution. A CPU currently executes instructions it defines.

- *Blocked*—The thread was started, but it was temporarily taken out of the runnable state, so the JVM can't execute its instructions. This state helps us control the thread execution by allowing to temporarily hide the thread from the JVM so that it can't execute it. While blocked, a thread can be in one of the following substates:
  - *Monitored*—The thread is paused by a monitor of a synchronized block (object controlling the access to a synchronized block) and waits to be released to execute that block.
  - *Waiting*—During the execution, a monitor's wait() method was called, which caused the current thread to be paused. The thread remains blocked until the notify() or notifyAll() methods are called to allow the JVM to release the thread in execution.
  - *Sleeping*—The sleep() method in the Thread class was called, which paused the current thread for a defined time. The time is given as a parameter to the sleep() method. The thread becomes runnable after this time passes.
  - *Parked*—Almost the same as waiting. A thread will show as parked after someone calls the park() method, which blocks the current thread until the unpark() method is called.
  - *Dead*—A thread is dead or terminated after it finishes its set of instructions, an Error or Exception halted it, or it was interrupted by another thread. Once dead, a thread cannot be started again.

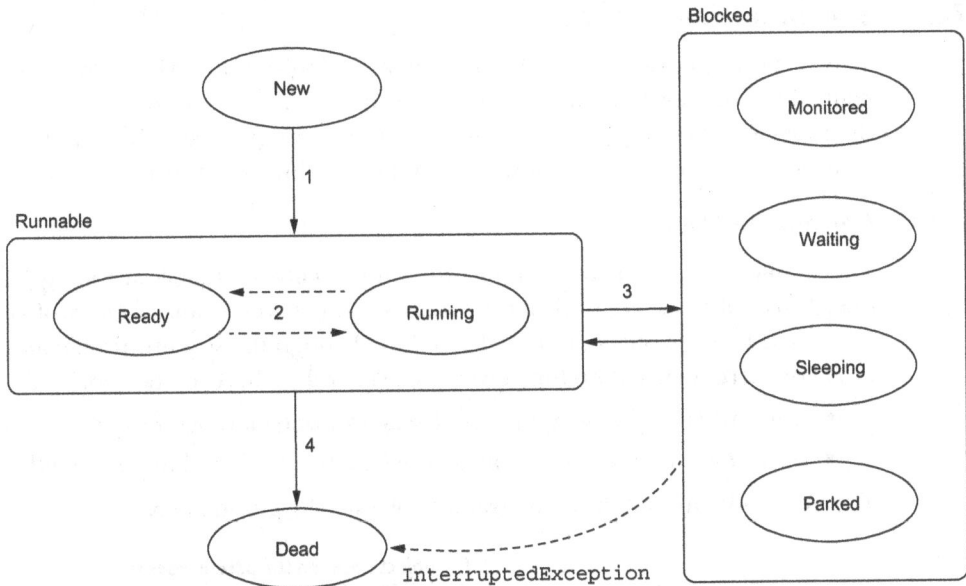

Figure D.4 A thread life cycle. During its life, a thread goes through multiple states. First, the thread is new, and the JVM cannot run the instructions it defines. After starting the thread, it becomes runnable and starts to be managed by the JVM. The thread can be temporarily blocked during its life, and at the end of its life, it goes to a dead state, from which it can't be restarted.

Figure D.4 also shows the possible transitions between thread states:

- The thread goes from new to runnable once someone calls its start() method.
- Once in the runnable state, the thread oscillates between ready and running. The JVM decides which thread is executed and when.
- Sometimes, the thread gets blocked. It can go into the blocked state in several ways:
  - The sleep() method in the Thread class is called, putting the current thread into a temporary blocked state.
  - Someone called the join() method, causing the current thread to wait for another one.
  - Someone called the wait() method of a monitor, pausing the execution of the current thread until the notify() or notifyAll() methods are called.
  - A monitor of a synchronized block paused the execution of a thread until another active thread finished the execution of the synchronized block.
- The thread can go into a dead (terminated) state either when it finishes its execution or when another thread interrupts it. The JVM considers transitioning from the blocked state to the dead state unacceptable. If a blocked thread is interrupted by another, the transition is signaled with an InterruptedException.

D.3 Synchronizing threads

This section discusses approaches to synchronizing threads, which developers use to control the threads in a multithreaded architecture. Incorrect synchronization is also the root cause of many problems you'll have to investigate and solve. We'll go through an overview of the most common ways used to synchronize threads.

D.3.1 Synchronized blocks

The simplest way to synchronize threads, and usually the first concept any Java developer learns about synchronizing threads, is using a synchronized block of code. The purpose is to allow only one thread at a time through the synchronized code—to prohibit concurrent execution for a given piece of code. There are two options:

- *Block synchronization*—Applying the synchronized modifier on a given block of code
- *Method synchronization*—Applying the synchronized modifier on a method

The next code snippet shows an example of a synchronized block:

```
synchronized (a) {          The object between the parentheses is
  // do something           the monitor of the synchronized block.
}
                            The synchronized block of instructions
                            is defined between the curly braces.
```

The next code snippet shows a method synchronization:

```
synchronized void m() {     Synchronized modifier
  // do something           applied to the method
}
                            The whole block of code of the method defined
                            between the curly braces is synchronized.
```

Both ways of using the synchronized keyword work the same, even if they look a bit different. You'll find two important components of each synchronized block:

- *The monitor*—An object managing the execution of the synchronized instructions
- *The block of instructions*—The actual instructions, which are synchronized

The method synchronization seems to be missing the monitor, but for this syntax the monitor is actually implied. For a nonstatic method, the instance "this" will be used as a monitor, while for a static method, the synchronized block will use the class's type instance.

The monitor (which cannot be null) is the object that makes a synchronized block work. It controls whether a thread can enter and run the synchronized code. The rule is simple: when a thread enters the synchronized block, it locks the monitor. No other thread can enter the block until the current thread releases the lock. For simplicity, let's say the thread releases the lock when it leaves the synchronized block. Figure D.5 shows an example. Imagine the two synchronized blocks are in different parts of the app. If both use the same monitor, M1 (the same object), only one thread can run in either block at a time. Instructions A, B, or C won't be run simultaneously from those synchronized blocks.

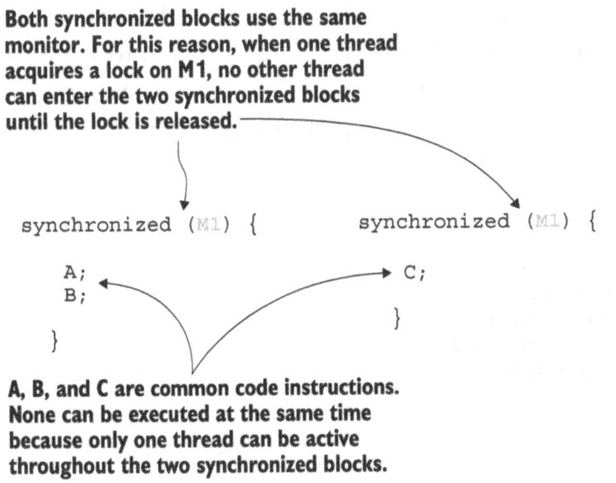

Both synchronized blocks use the same
monitor. For this reason, when one thread
acquires a lock on M1, no other thread
can enter the two synchronized blocks
until the lock is released.

```
synchronized (M1) {            synchronized (M1) {

    A;                             C;
    B;
                                   }
}
```

**A, B, and C are common code instructions.
None can be executed at the same time
because only one thread can be active
throughout the two synchronized blocks.**

**Figure D.5   An example of using
synchronized blocks. Multiple
synchronized blocks of the app
can use the same object instance
as a monitor. When this happens,
all threads are correlated so that
only one active thread executes
in all. In this image, if one thread
enters the synchronized block,
defining instructions A and B,
no other thread can enter in the
same block or in the one defining
instruction C.**

An app can have multiple synchronized blocks. The monitor connects these blocks. However, if two synchronized blocks use different monitors (figure D.6), they are not linked. In figure D.6, the first and second synchronized blocks are linked because they use the same monitor. But they are not linked to the third block. This means instruction D, in the third block, can run at the same time as any instructions in the first two blocks.

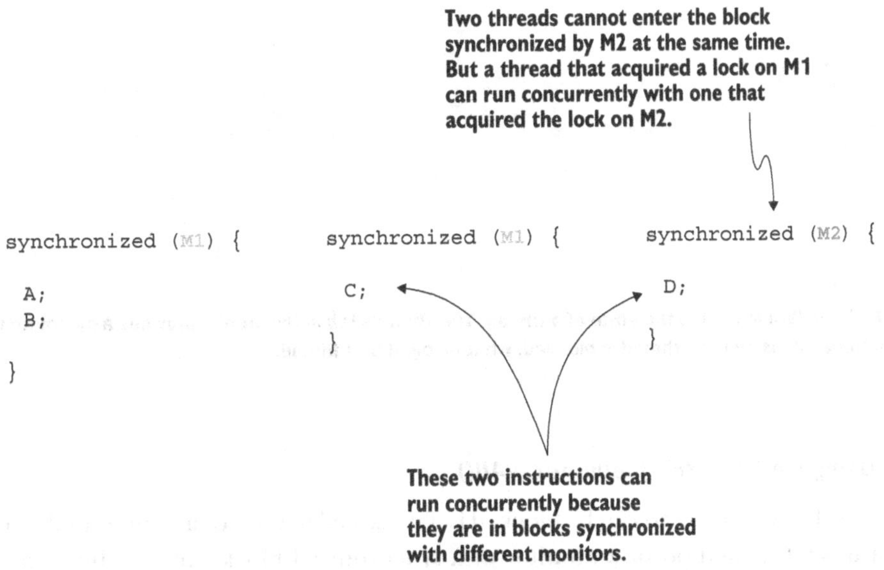

**Two threads cannot enter the block
synchronized by M2 at the same time.
But a thread that acquired a lock on M1
can run concurrently with one that
acquired the lock on M2.**

```
synchronized (M1) {      synchronized (M1) {      synchronized (M2) {

    A;                       C;                       D;
    B;
                             }                        }
}
```

**These two instructions can
run concurrently because
they are in blocks synchronized
with different monitors.**

**Figure D.6   When two synchronized blocks don't use the same object instance as the monitor, they are
not linked. In this case, the second and third synchronized blocks use different monitors. That means
instructions from these two synchronized blocks can execute simultaneously.**

When investigating problems using tools such as a profiler or a thread dump, you need to understand the way in which a thread has been blocked. This information can shed light on what happens, why, or what causes a given thread not to execute. Figure D.7 shows how VisualVM (the profiler we use in chapters 5–10) shows that the monitor of a synchronized block blocked a thread.

In this example, VisualVM shows certain threads that are blocked by a monitor of a synchronized block of code. When investigating an app's behavior, knowing what this state means helps you understand what executes and may reveal certain problems.

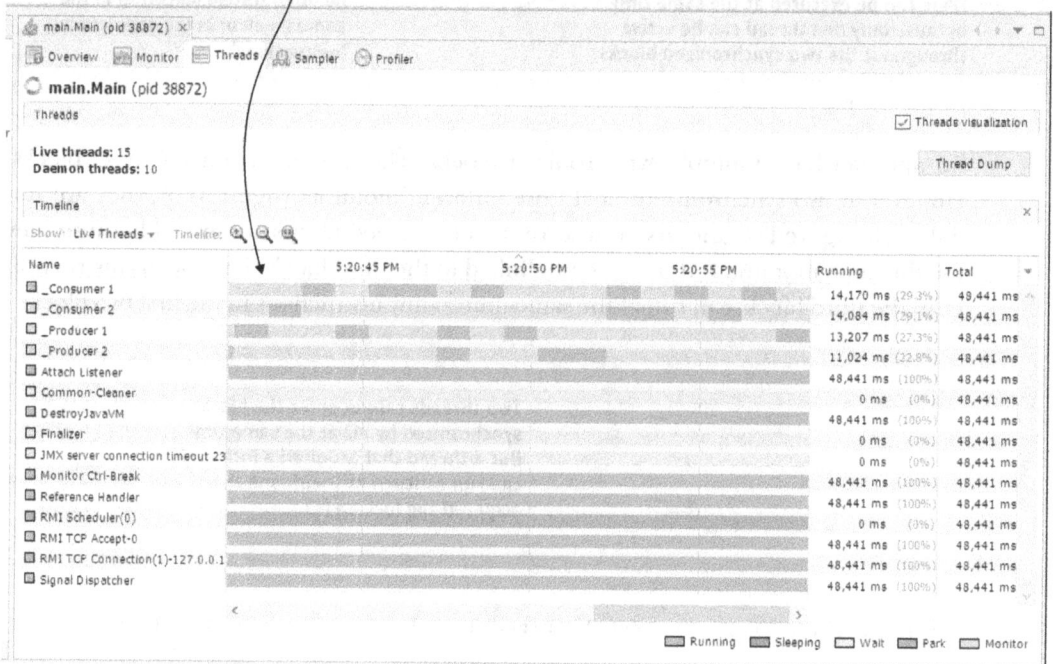

Figure D.7   VisualVM indicates the state of a thread. The Threads tab in the profiler provides a complete picture of what each thread does and, if a thread is blocked, what blocked that thread.

D.3.2   Using wait(), notify(), and notifyAll()

Another way a thread can be blocked is if it is asked to wait for an undefined time. Using the wait() method of a monitor of a synchronized block, you can instruct a thread to wait indefinitely. Some other thread can then "tell" the one that's waiting to continue its work. You can do this with the notify() or notifyAll() methods of the monitor. These methods are often used to improve an app's performance by preventing a thread from executing if it doesn't make sense to execute. Simultaneously, the wrong use of these methods can lead to deadlocks or situations where threads wait indefinitely without ever being released to execution.

Remember that `wait()`, `notify()`, and `notifyAll()` make sense only when they are used in a synchronized block. These methods are behaviors of the synchronized block's monitor, so you can't use them without having a monitor. With the `wait()`method, the monitor blocks a thread for an undefined time. When blocking the thread, it also releases the lock it acquired so that other threads can enter blocks synchronized by that monitor. When the `notify()` method is called, the thread can again be executed. Figure D.8 summarizes the `wait()` and `notify()` methods.

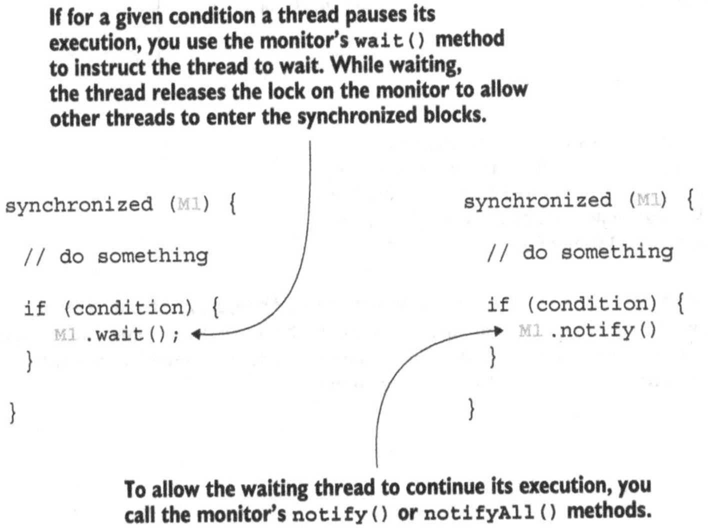

If for a given condition a thread pauses its execution, you use the monitor's `wait()` method to instruct the thread to wait. While waiting, the thread releases the lock on the monitor to allow other threads to enter the synchronized blocks.

```
synchronized (M1) {              synchronized (M1) {

// do something                  // do something

if (condition) {                 if (condition) {
   M1 .wait();                       M1 .notify()
}                                }

}                                }
```

To allow the waiting thread to continue its execution, you call the monitor's `notify()` or `notifyAll()` methods.

Figure D.8   In some cases, a thread should pause from executing and wait for something to happen. To make a thread wait, the monitor of a synchronized block can call its `wait()` behavior. When the thread becomes executable again, the monitor can call the `notify()` or `notifyAll()` methods.

Figure D.9 shows a more particular scenario. In chapter 7, we used an example of an app implementing a producer–consumer approach, in which multiple threads share a resource. The producer threads add values to the shared resource, and the consumer threads consume those values. But what happens if the shared resource no longer has value? The consumers would not benefit from executing at this time. Technically, they can still execute, but they have no value to consume, so allowing the JVM to execute them would cause unnecessary resource consumption on the system. A better approach would be to tell the consumers to wait when the shared resource has no value and to continue their execution only after a producer added a new value.

The three consumers are waiting
because the list is empty, so they
don't have a value to consume.
It doesn't make sense to execute
when the list is empty, so they should
wait to save the system's resources.

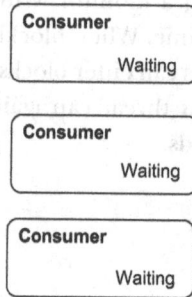

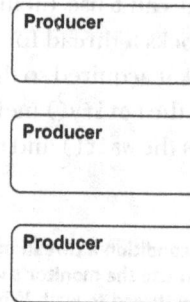

Hey, consumers,
you can continue
now!

| Consumer |
| Waiting |

| Producer |

| Consumer |
| Waiting |

| Producer |

| Consumer |
| Waiting |

| Producer |

When a producer adds an element
to the list, it notifies the consumers using
the notify() or notifyAll() methods.
The consumers enter the runnable state
again, and the JVM can execute them.

Figure D.9   A use case for wait() and notify(). When a thread brings no value by executing in the
current conditions, we can make it wait until further notice. In this case, a consumer should not execute
when it has no value to consume. We can make the consumers wait, and a producer can tell them to
continue only after it adds a new value to the shared resource.

D.3.3   Joining threads

A quite common thread synchronization approach is joining threads by making a
thread wait until another has finished its execution. What's different from the wait/
notify pattern is that the thread doesn't wait to be notified. The thread simply waits for
the other to finish its execution. Figure D.10 shows a scenario that could benefit from
this synchronization technique.

Suppose you have to implement some data processing based on data retrieved from
two different independent sources. Usually, retrieving the data from the first data
source takes about 5 seconds, and getting the data from the second data source takes
about 8 seconds. If you execute the operations sequentially, the time needed to get all
the data for processing is 5 + 8 = 13 seconds. But you know a better approach. Since
the data sources are two independent databases, you can get the data from both at
the same time if you use two threads. But then you need to make sure the thread that
processes the data waits for both threads that retrieve data to finish before it can start.
To achieve this, you make the processing thread join the threads that retrieve the data
(figure D.10).

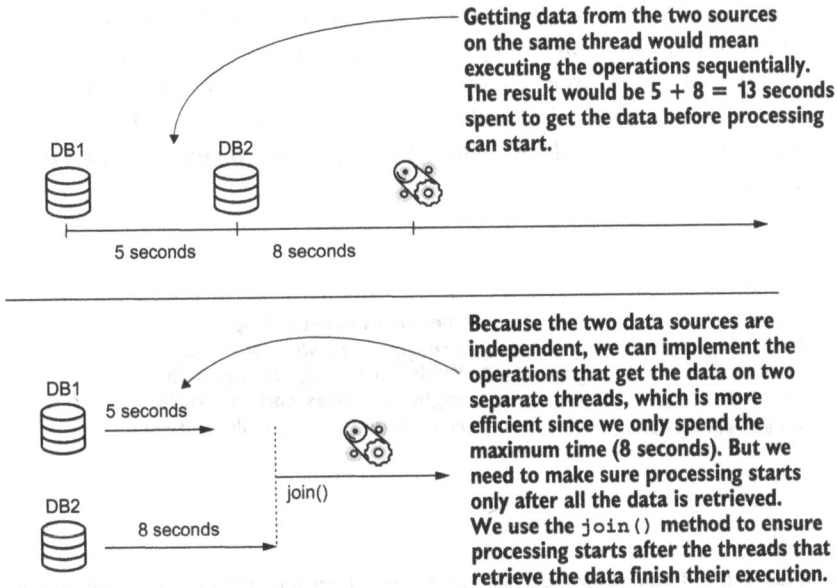

Getting data from the two sources on the same thread would mean executing the operations sequentially. The result would be 5 + 8 = 13 seconds spent to get the data before processing can start.

Because the two data sources are independent, we can implement the operations that get the data on two separate threads, which is more efficient since we only spend the maximum time (8 seconds). But we need to make sure processing starts only after all the data is retrieved. We use the join() method to ensure processing starts after the threads that retrieve the data finish their execution.

Figure D.10 In some cases, you can improve the app's performance by using multiple threads. But you need to make some threads wait for others since they depend on the execution result of those threads. You can make a thread wait for another using a join operation.

Joining threads is, in many cases, a necessary synchronization technique. But when not used well, it can also cause problems. For example, if one thread is waiting for another, is stuck, or never ends, the joining it once will never execute.

D.3.4 *Blocking threads for a defined time*

Sometimes a thread needs to wait for a given amount of time. In this case, the thread is in a "timed waiting" state or "sleeping." The following operations are the most common to cause a thread to be timed waiting:

- sleep()—You can always use the static sleep() method in the class Thread to make the thread currently executing the code wait for a fixed amount of time.

- wait(long timeout)—The wait method with a timeout parameter can be used the same as the wait() method without any parameters, as discussed in section D.3.2. However, if you provide a parameter, the thread will wait the given time if not notified earlier.

- join(long timeout)—This operation works the same as the join() method we discussed in section D.3.3, but it waits for the maximum timeout, which is given as a parameter.

A common antipattern I often find in apps is the use of sleep() to make a thread wait instead of the wait() method discussed in chapter 7. Take the producer–consumer architecture we discussed as an example. You could use `sleep()` instead of `wait()`, but how long should a consumer sleep to ensure the producer has time to run and add values to the shared resource? We don't have an answer to this question. For example, making the thread sleep for 100 milliseconds (as shown in figure D.11) can be too long or too short. In most cases, if you follow this approach, you end up not having the best performance.

```
synchronized (M1) {

    // do something

    if (condition) {
        Thread.sleep(100);
    }

}
```

Sometimes timed waiting is wrongly used instead of waiting. While functionally this approach might sometimes work, it usually is a less performant implementation.

Figure D.11   A timed waiting approach instead of `wait()` **and** `notify()` **is usually not the best strategy. Whenever your code can determine when the thread can continue its execution, use** `wait()` **and** `notify()` **instead of** `sleep()`.

D.3.5   *Synchronizing threads with blocking objects*

The JDK offers an impressive suite of tools for synchronizing threads. Out of these, a few of the best-known classes used in multithreaded architectures are

- `Semaphore`—An object you can use to limit the number of threads that can execute a given block of code
- `CyclicBarrier`—An object you can use to make sure at least a given number of threads are active to execute a given block of code
- `Lock`—An object that provides more extensive synchronization options
- `Latch`—An object you can use to make some threads wait until certain logic in other threads is performed

These objects are higher-level implementations, each deploying a defined mechanism to simplify the implementation in certain scenarios. In most cases, these objects cause trouble because of the improper way they are used, and in many cases, developers overengineer the code with them. My advice is to use the simplest solution you can find to solve a problem and, before using any of these objects, make sure you properly understand how they work.

D.4   *Common problems in multithreaded architectures*

When investigating multithreaded architectures, you'll identify common problems, which are root causes of various unexpected behavior (be it an unexpected output or a performance problem). Understanding these problems up front will help you to more quickly identify where a problem comes from and fix it. These problems are

- *Race conditions*—Two or more threads compete for modifying a shared resource.
- *Deadlocks*—Two or more threads stick while waiting for each other.
- *Livelocks*—Two or more threads fail to meet the conditions to stop and continuously run without executing any useful work.
- *Starvation*—A thread is continuously blocked while the JVM executes other threads. The thread never gets to execute the instructions it defines.

D.4.1   *Race conditions*

Race conditions happen when multiple threads try to change the same resource concurrently. When this happens, we can encounter either unexpected results or exceptions. Generally, we use synchronization techniques to avoid these situations. Figure D.12 illustrates such a case. Threads T1 and T2 simultaneously attempt to change the value of variable x. Thread T1 tries to increment the value, while thread T2 tries to decrement it. This scenario may result in different outputs for repeated executions of the app. The following scenarios are possible:

- *After the operations execute, x may be 5*—If T1 changed the value first, and T2 read the already changed value of the variable, or the other way around, the variable will still have a value of 5.
- *After the operations execute, x may be 4*—If both threads read the value of x at the same time, but T2 wrote the value last, x will be 4 (the value T2 read, 5, minus 1).
- *After the operations execute, x may be 6*—If both threads read the value of x at the same time, but T1 wrote the value last, x will be 6 (the value T1 read, 5, plus 1).

Such situations usually lead to unexpected output. With a multithreaded architecture where multiple execution flows are possible, such scenarios can be challenging to reproduce. Sometimes, they happen only in specific environments, which makes investigations difficult.

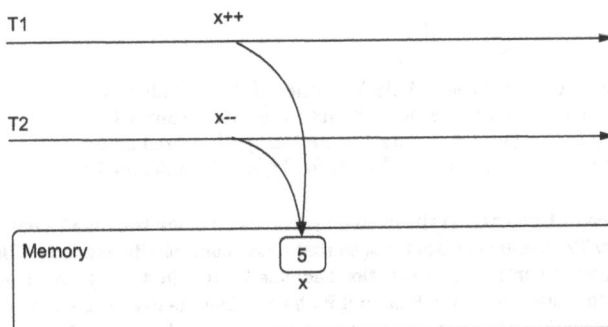

Figure D.12   A race condition. Multiple threads concurrently try to change a shared resource. In this example, threads T1 and T2 try to change the value of variable *x* simultaneously, which can result in different outputs.

D.4.2   Deadlocks

Deadlocks are situations in which two or more threads pause and then wait for something from each other to continue their execution (figure D.13). Deadlocks cause an app, or at least part of it, to freeze, preventing certain capabilities from running.

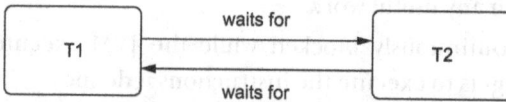

Figure D.13   Example of a deadlock. In a case in which T1 waits for T2 to continue the execution and T2 waits for T1, the threads are in a deadlock. Neither can continue because they are waiting for the other.

Figure D.14 illustrates the way a deadlock can occur with code. In this example, one thread acquired a lock on resource A, and another, on resource B. But each thread also needs the resource acquired by the other thread to continue its execution. Thread T1 waits for thread T2 to release resource A, but simultaneously, thread T2 waits for T1 to release resource B. Neither of the threads can continue since both wait for the other to release the resources they need, resulting in a deadlock.

Suppose thread T1 entered the synchronized block by acquiring resource B and now executes some instructions here.

At the same time, thread T2 entered the synchronized block by acquiring resource A and now executes some instructions here.

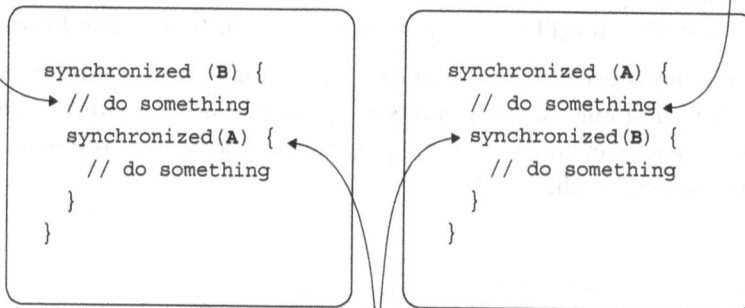

```
synchronized (B) {
    // do something
    synchronized(A) {
        // do something
    }
}
```

```
synchronized (A) {
    // do something
    synchronized(B) {
        // do something
    }
}
```

When reaching the nested synchronized block, neither of the threads can continue. T1 waits for T2 to release resource A. But to release resource A, T2 needs to first acquire resource B to enter the nested synchronized block, so T2 waits for T1 to release resource B. T1 waits for T2, and T2 waits for T1

Figure D.14   A deadlock. Thread T1 can't enter the nested synchronized block because T2 has a lock on resource A. Thread T1 waits for T2 to release resource A so that it can continue its execution. But thread T2 is in a similar situation: it cannot continue its execution because T1 acquired a lock on resource B. Thread T2 waits for thread T1 to release resource B so that it can continue its execution. Since both threads wait for each other and neither can continue its execution, the threads are in a deadlock.

The example presented in figure D.14 is simple, but it's just a didactic one. A real-world scenario is usually much more difficult to investigate and understand and can involve more than two threads. Note that synchronized blocks are not the only way threads can get stuck in a deadlock. The best way to understand such scenarios is using the investigation techniques you learned in chapters 7–9.

D.4.3 Livelocks

Livelocks are more or less the opposite of deadlocks. When threads are in a livelock, the condition always changes in such a way that the threads continue their execution even though they should stop on a given condition. The threads can't stop, and they continuously run, usually consuming the system's resources without reason. Livelocks can cause performance problems in an app's execution.

Figure D.15 demonstrates a livelock with a sequence diagram. Two threads, T1 and T2, run in a loop. To stop its execution, T1 makes a condition true before its last iteration. The next time T1 comes back to the condition, it expects it to be true and to stop. However, this doesn't happen since another thread, T2, changed it back to false. T2 finds itself in the same situation. Each thread changes the condition so that it can stop, but at the same time, each change in the condition causes the other thread to continue running.

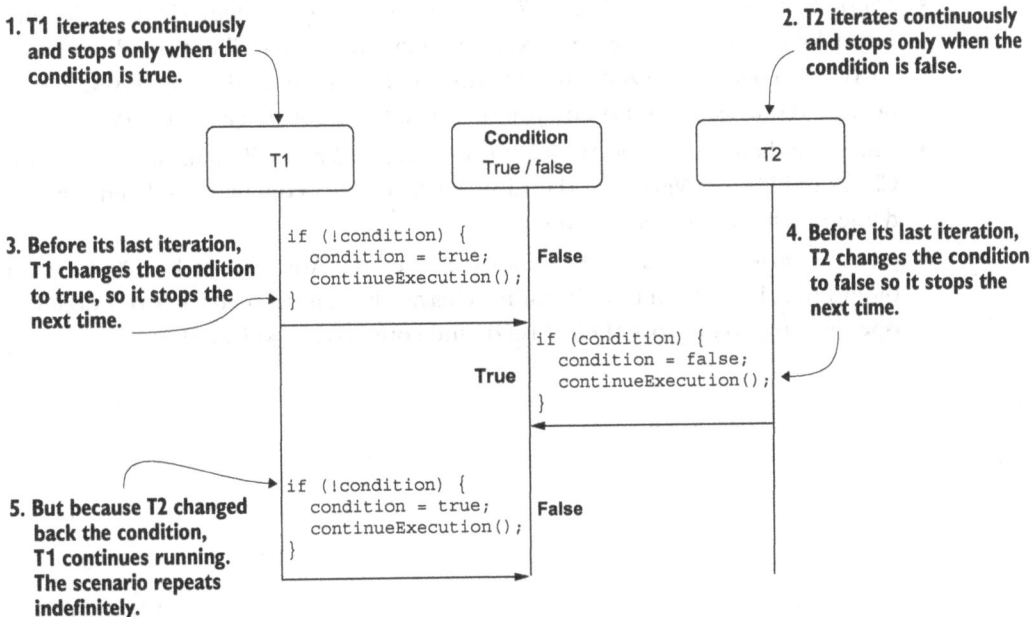

Figure D.15 An example of a livelock. Two threads rely on a condition to stop their execution. But when changing the value of the condition so that they can stop, each thread causes the other to continue running. The threads cannot stop and thus unnecessarily spend the system's resources.

Just as with the deadlock example in chapter 7, remember this is a simplified scenario. Livelocks can be caused by more complex scenarios in the real world, and more than two threads can be involved. Chapters 7–9 address several ways you can approach the investigation of such scenarios.

D.4.4   *Starvation*

Another common problem, although less likely to occur in today's apps, is starvation. Starvation is caused by a certain thread being constantly excluded from the execution even if it is runnable. The thread wants to execute its instructions, but the JVM continuously allows other threads to access the system's resources. Because the thread cannot access the system's resources and execute its defined set of instructions, we say that it is starving.

In the early JVM versions, such situations occurred when the developer set a much lower priority to a given thread. Today, the JVM implementations are much smarter in treating these cases, so (at least in my experience) starvation scenarios are less likely.

D.5   *Further reading*

Threads are complex, and in this appendix, we discussed the essential topics that will help you understand the techniques addressed throughout this book. But, for any Java developer, understanding how threads work in detail is a valuable skill. Here is a list of resources I recommend you read to learn about threads in depth:

- *Oracle Certified Professional Java SE 11 Developer Complete Study Guide* by Jeanne Boyarsky and Scott Selikoff (Sybex, 2020). Chapter 18 describes threads and concurrency, starting from zero and covering all the thread fundamentals OCP certification requires. I recommend you start with this book to learn threads.
- The second edition of *The Well-Grounded Java Developer* by Benjamin Evans, Jason Clark, and Martijn Verburg (Manning, 2022) teaches concurrency, from the fundamentals to performance tuning.
- *Java Concurrency in Practice* by Brian Goetz et al. (Addison-Wesley, 2006) is an older book, but it hasn't lost its value. This book is a must-read for any Java developer wanting to improve their threads and concurrency knowledge.

appendix E
Memory management
in Java apps

This appendix discusses how the Java Virtual Machine (JVM) manages the memory of a Java app. Some of the most challenging problems you'll have to investigate in Java apps are related to the way the apps manage memory. Fortunately, we can use several techniques to analyze such problems and find their root causes, with minimal time invested. But to benefit from those techniques, you first need to know at least some basics about how a Java app manages its memory.

An app's memory is a limited resource. Even if today's systems can offer a large amount of memory for an app to use during its execution, we still need to be careful with how an app spends this resource. No system can offer unlimited memory as a magical solution (figure E.1). Memory problems lead to performance problems (the app becomes slow, it's more costly to deploy, it starts more slowly, etc.) and sometimes can even bring the entire process to a complete stop (e.g., in the case of an OutOfMemoryError).

We'll cover the essential aspects of memory management. In section E.1, we discuss how the JVM organizes the memory for an executing process. You'll learn about three ways of allocating the app's memory: the stack, the heap, and the metaspace. In section E.2, we talk about the stack, the memory space a thread uses to store locally declared variables and their data. Section E.3 discusses the heap and the way an app stores object instances in memory. We'll end our discussion in section E.4 with the metaspace, a memory location where an app stores the object types' metadata.

Figure E.1   An app's memory is a limited resource. There's no magical solution that allows us to allocate infinite memory to an app. When building apps, we need to treat memory consumption with consideration and avoid spending it for no reason. Apps may sometimes have memory problems. If a certain capability uses too much memory, it can cause performance problems or even a complete failure. You need to be ready to find the causes of such problems and solve them properly.

Be aware that a Java app's memory management is complex. In this appendix, I'll present only the details you need to understand the discussions you'll find throughout the book.

E.1   *How the JVM organizes an app's memory*

This section discusses how the JVM organizes data in different memory locations, which are also managed differently. Understanding how the JVM manages memory is essential for investigating problems related to memory. We'll use some visuals to discuss the main aspects related to memory management, and you'll learn which data goes where in a Java app's memory. Then, we'll detail the memory management in each memory location.

For the moment (to simplify the discussion), let's assume that a Java app has two ways to manage the data it stores during its execution: the stack and the heap. Depending on how the data is defined, the app will manage it in either the stack or the heap. But before discussing which data goes where, remember one essential detail: an app has more than one thread, which allows it to concurrently process data. The heap is a singular memory location, and all the app's threads use it. However, each thread has its own memory location, called a *stack*. This can create confusion when developers first learn about memory management. Figure E.2 presents these details visually.

**The stack is not singular.
Each thread uses a different stack.**

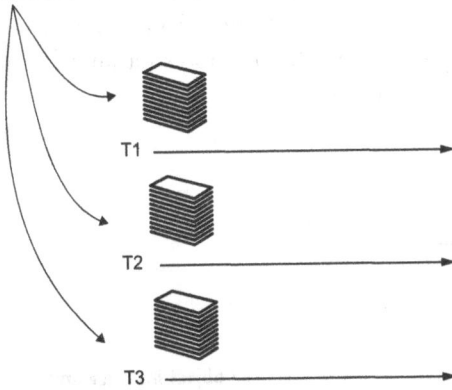

**The heap is singular. All threads
use the same heap space.**

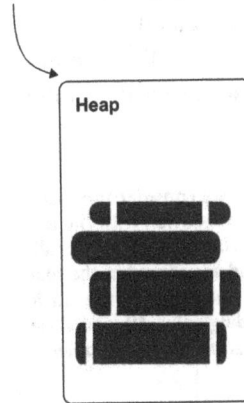

Figure E.2 T1, T2, and T3 are all threads of a Java app. All these threads use the same heap. The heap is a memory location where the app stores object instances' data. However, each thread uses its own memory location, called a stack, to store data locally declared.

The stack is a memory location owned by a thread. Each thread owns a particular stack that is not shared with other threads. The thread stores any data locally declared in a block of code and executed by that thread in this memory location. Say you have a method like the one presented in the next code snippet. The parameters x and y and the variable sum, declared inside the method's code block, are local variables. These values will be stored in the thread's stack when the method executes:

```
public int sum(int x, int y) {        Variables x, y, and sum will
    int sum = x + y;                  be stored in the stack.
    return sum;
}
```

The heap is a memory location where the app stores object instances' data. Suppose your app declares a class, Cat, such as the one shown in the next code snippet. Any time you create an instance using the class's constructor, new Cat(), the instance goes to the heap:

```
public class Cat {
}
```

If the class declares instance attributes, the JVM stores these values in the heap, too. For example, if the Cat class looks like the one in the next code snippet, the JVM will store the name and age of each instance in the heap:

```
public class Cat {
    private String name;           The object's attributes
    private int age;               are stored in the heap.

}
```

Figure E.3 visually presents an example of data allocation. Notice that the locally declared variables and their values (x and c) are stored in the thread's stack, while the Cat instance and its data go in the app's heap. A reference to the Cat instance will be stored in the thread's stack in variable c. Even the method's parameter that stores a reference to a String array will be part of the stack.

In this example, we consider the main thread, which starts its execution with the `main()` method. The variables declared locally in the `main()` method are stored in the main thread's stack. The values in the stack are variable x, holding value 10, and variable c, holding the reference of a Cat object.

The object instance and the values its attributes hold (if any) are stored in the heap.

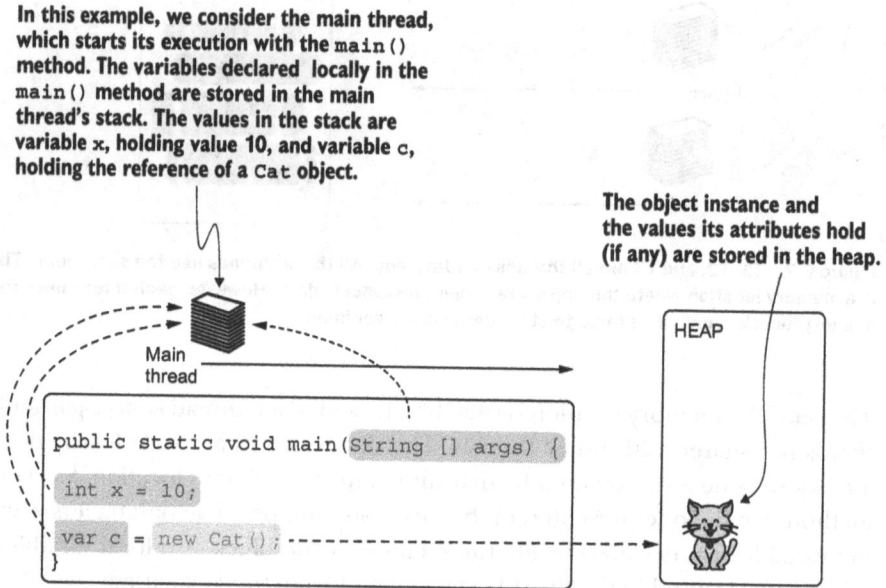

```
public static void main(String [] args) {
    int x = 10;
    var c = new Cat();
}
```

HEAP

Main thread

Figure E.3 The app reserves the locally declared variables in the thread's stack and the data defining an object instance in the heap. A variable in one thread's stack may refer to an object in the heap. In this example, variable x, holding value 10, and variable c, holding the reference to the Cat instance, are part of the thread's stack.

E.2 *The stack used by threads to store local data*

This section analyzes the mechanics behind the stack in more depth. In section E.1, you learned that local values are stored in a stack, and that each thread has its own stack location. Let's find out now how these values are stored and when the app removes them from memory. We'll use visuals to describe this process step by step with a short code example. Once we clarify the mechanics behind the stack's memory management, we'll discuss what could go wrong and cause problems related to it.

First, why is this memory location called "a stack"? A thread's stack uses the principles of a stack data structure. A *stack* is an ordered collection in which you can always remove the most recently added element. We usually visualize such a collection as a stack of layers, where each layer is stored above another. You can only add a new layer on top of all the existing ones, and you can only remove the top layer. This method of adding and removing elements is also called *last in, first out* (LIFO). Figure E.4 demonstrates how a stack works with a series of add-and-remove steps. To make the example simpler, numbers are the values in the stack.

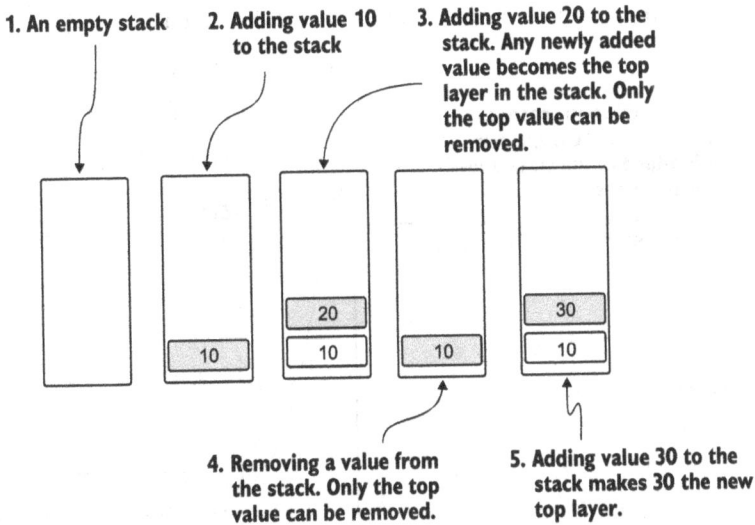

Figure E.4 Adding and removing values from a stack. The stack is an ordered collection working on the LIFO principle. When you add a value to the stack, it becomes the top layer—the only one you can remove.

You will recognize the same behavior in the way JVM running your app manages the data in a thread's stack. Whenever the execution reaches the start of a code block, it creates a new layer in the thread stack. Following a common stack principle, any new layer becomes the top layer and is the first to be removed. In figures E.5, E.6, E.7, and E.8, we follow the execution of a simple code snippet step by step to observe how the thread's stack changes:

```
public static void main(String [] args) {
  int x = 10;
  a();
  b();
}

public static void a() {
  int y = 20;
}

public static void b() {
  int y = 30;
}
```

The execution starts with the `main()` method (figure E.5). When the execution reaches the start of the `main()` method, the first layer is added to the thread's stack. This layer is a memory location where every local value declared in the code block is stored. In this case, the code block declares a variable, x, and initializes the variable with the value 10. This variable will be stored in this newly created layer of the thread's stack. This layer will be removed from the stack when the method ends its execution.

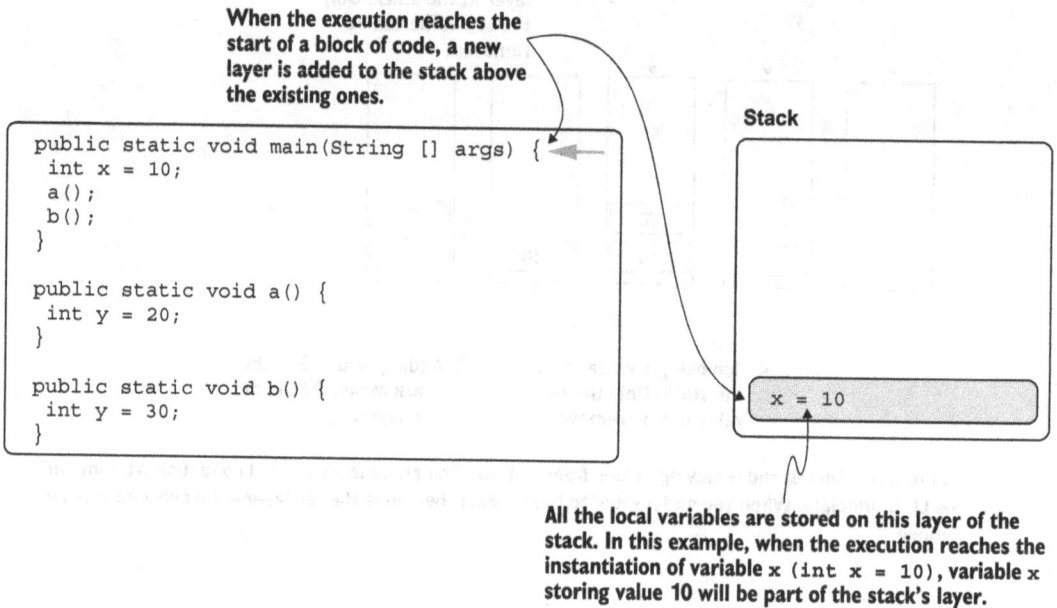

When the execution reaches the start of a block of code, a new layer is added to the stack above the existing ones.

Stack

```
public static void main(String [] args) {
  int x = 10;
  a();
  b();
}

public static void a() {
  int y = 20;
}

public static void b() {
  int y = 30;
}
```

x = 10

All the local variables are stored on this layer of the stack. In this example, when the execution reaches the instantiation of variable x (int x = 10), variable x storing value 10 will be part of the stack's layer.

Figure E.5   When the execution reaches the start of a block of code, a new layer is created in the thread's stack. All the variables the block of code defines are stored in this new layer. The layer is removed when the block of code ends. This way, we know that the values in this part of the memory are released when they're no longer needed. Besides variable x, the args parameter is also part of the stack in this case. I have simply taken it out to allow you focus on the local declared variables.

A code block can call other code blocks. For example, in this case, method `main()` calls methods `a()` and `b()`, which work similarly. When the execution reaches the start of their blocks of code, a new layer is added to the stack. That new layer is the memory location where all the data that is declared local is stored. Figure E.6 shows what happens when the execution reaches method `a()`.

When method `a()` ends its execution and returns to `main()`, the layer reserved in the thread's stack is also removed (figure E.7), meaning the data it stored is no longer in the memory. This way, the memory that is not needed is deallocated to allow space for new data to be stored. A code block ends when the execution reaches its last instruction, gives a `return` instruction, or throws an exception. Notice that when a code block ends, its layer is always the top one in the stack, fulfilling the LIFO principle.

When the execution reaches the
call to method a(), that block of
code will start to be executed.

Stack

```
public static void main(String [] args) {
  int x = 10;
  a();
  b();
}

public static void a() {
  int y = 20;
}

public static void b() {
  int y = 30;
}
```

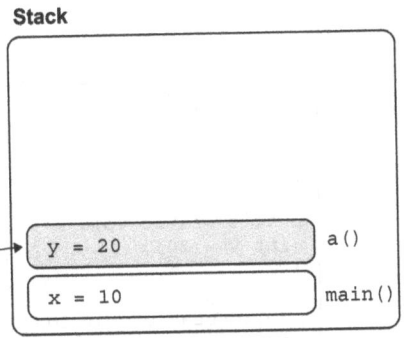

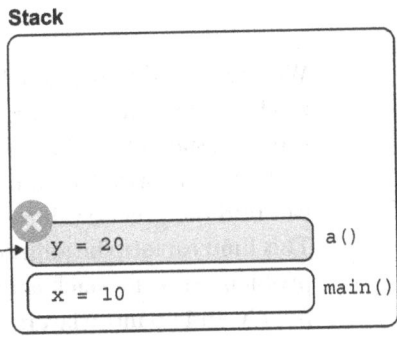

y = 20	a()
x = 10	main()

When method a()'s block of code starts
to be executed, a new layer is added to
the stack. This layer will store the local
values declared by method a().

Figure E.6 Another block of code can be called from one in execution. In this case, method main() calls method a(). Since main() didn't finish, its layer is still part of the stack. Method a() creates its own layer where the local values it defines are stored. Method names you see in the stack on the right side of the layers are used simply to map each method to the layer it produces.

Stack

```
public static void main(String [] args) {
  int x = 10;
  a();
  b();
}

public static void a() {
  int y = 20;
}

public static void b() {
  int y = 30;
}
```

y = 20	a()
x = 10	main()

When the execution reaches the end of a block of code (or if the method returns
or throws an exception), the layer in the stack and all of its content are removed.

Figure E.7 When the execution reaches the end of a block of code, the stack layer opened for that block is removed with all the data it contains. In this case, when method a() returns, its stack layer is removed. This way, we make sure the unnecessary data is removed from the memory.

Method `main()` continues its execution by calling method `b()`. Just like method `a()` did, method `b()` reserves a new layer in the stack to store the local data it declares (figure E.8).

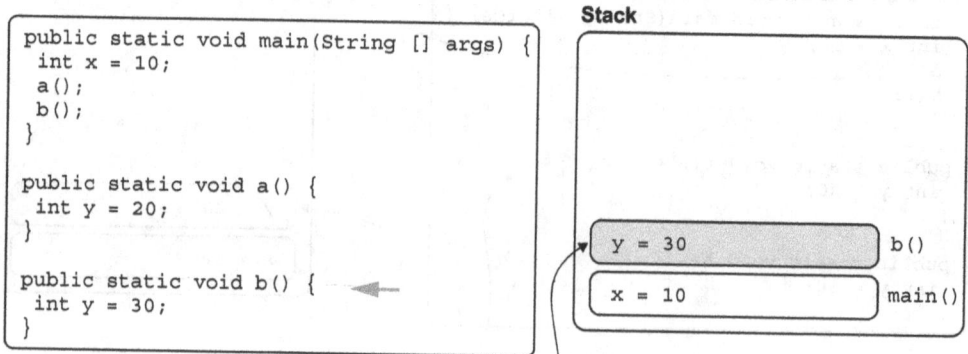

```
public static void main(String [] args) {
  int x = 10;
  a();
  b();
}

public static void a() {
  int y = 20;
}

public static void b() {
  int y = 30;
}
```

Stack

y = 30   b()

x = 10   main()

When the execution reaches `method b()`**, method** `a()`**'s stack layer no longer exists.** `Method b()` **will create its own layer in the stack and store the local values it declares in it. When** `method b()` **ends its execution, its layer in the stack will also be removed. The same will happen for** `main()`**. In the end, when the thread ends its execution, the stack will be empty.**

Figure E.8 Just like with method `a()`, when method `b()` is called and the execution reaches the start of its block of code, a new layer is added to the stack. The method can use this layer to store local data until the method returns and the layer is removed.

When method `main()` finally reaches its end, the thread ends its execution, and the stack remains empty and is completely removed. Simultaneously, the thread goes into the dead state of its life cycle, as described in appendix D.

The stack has a default memory space allocated for different CPU architectures. You can find the precise values depending on the JVM you use here: http://mng.bz/JVYp. This limit can also be adjusted, but you wouldn't be able to make it infinite. A common problem with the stack is the StackOverflowError, which means a stack is filled completely, and no more layers can be added. When this happens, the code throws a Stack-OverflowError, and the thread whose stack became full stops completely. A recursion (or recursive implementation), a method that calls itself until a given condition is filled, with a wrong stop condition usually causes such a problem. If this condition is missing or allows the method to call itself too many times, the stack may get filled with the layers the method creates every time it begins its execution. Figure E.9 visually presents the stack created by an infinite recursion caused by two methods that call one another.

Since each thread has its own stack, a StackOverflowError affects only the thread whose stack becomes full. The process can continue its execution, and other threads will not be affected. Also, a StackOverflowError produces a stack trace, which you can

Because the beginning of any new block of code execution creates a new layer in the stack, any uncontrolled recursion can cause a stack overflow: the stack fills and the app cannot allocate more layers to store the local values. In this example, method a() calls method b() and method b() calls method a(), without any condition for this cycle to stop at some point.

Stack

```
public static void main(String[] args) {
  a();
}

public static void a() {
  System.out.println("A executes");
  b();
}

public static void b() {
  System.out.println("B executes");
  a();
}
```

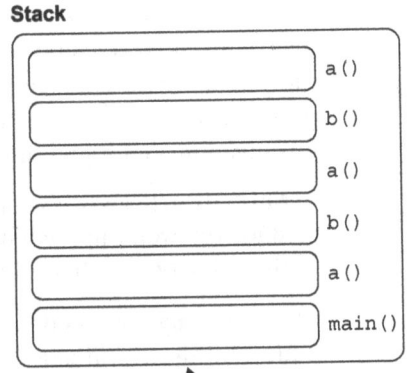

a()
b()
a()
b()
a()
main()

A stack overflow is a memory problem in which the app cannot allocate more layers in the stack.

Figure E.9 Every new execution of a method creates a new layer in the stack. In case of a recursion, a method may fill the stack if it's called too many times. When the stack gets full, the app throws a StackOverflowError, and the current thread stops.

use to identify the code that caused the problem. Figure E.10 shows an example of what this type of stack trace looks like. You can use project da-app-e-ex1 provided with the book to replicate this stack trace.

Exception in thread "main" java.lang.StackOverflowError
```
...
at main.Main.a(Main.java:11)
at main.Main.b(Main.java:16)
at main.Main.a(Main.java:11)
at main.Main.b(Main.java:16)
at main.Main.a(Main.java:11)
at main.Main.b(Main.java:16)
at main.Main.a(Main.java:11)
at main.Main.b(Main.java:16)
at main.Main.a(Main.java:11)
...
```

Whenever you get an exception stack like this one that looks like a dog chasing its tail, you are most likely facing a recursion with a wrong condition.

Figure E.10 The stack trace caused by a StackOverflowError. Usually, a StackOverflowError is easy to identify. The stack trace shows a method calling itself repeatedly or a group of methods that call each other, as in this example. You can go directly to these methods to figure out how they started infinitely calling each other.

E.3   *The heap the app uses to store object instances*

In this section, we'll discuss the heap: a memory location shared by all threads of a Java app. The heap stores object instance data. As you'll see in this section, the heap causes problems more often than the stack does. Also, the root causes of heap-related problems are more challenging to find. We'll analyze how objects are stored in the heap and who can keep references to them, which is relevant to understanding when they can be removed from the memory. Furthermore, we'll discuss the main causes of problems related to the heap. You need to know this information to understand the investigation techniques discussed in chapters 9–11.

> **NOTE**   The heap has a complex structure. We won't discuss all the heap details since you won't immediately need them. We also won't discuss details such as the string pool or heap generations.

The first thing you need to remember about the heap is that it's a memory location shared by all the threads (figure E.11). Not only does this allow for thread-related problems such as race conditions to happen (discussed in appendix D), but it also makes memory problems more challenging to investigate. Since all the threads add the object instances they create in the same memory location, one thread may affect the execution of others. If one thread suffers from a memory leak, which means it adds instances in the memory but never removes them, it affects the whole process because other threads will also suffer from the lack of memory.

In most cases, when an `OutOfMemoryError` occurs, as shown in figure E.11, the situation is signaled by a different thread than the one affected by the root cause of the

One thread might suffer from a memory leak and fill the heap space.

The heap is not unique. All threads use the same heap space.

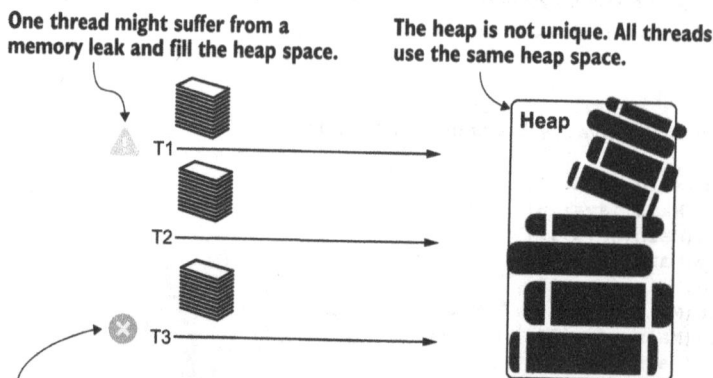

An `OutOfMemoryError` can occur on a thread that doesn't have problems, just because it was the unlucky one to try to reserve a part of the heap when no memory was left.

Figure E.11   All threads use the same heap location. If one of the threads has a problem that causes the heap to become full (memory leak), another thread may signal the problem. This scenario happens quite often because the problem will be reported by the first thread unable to store data in the heap. Because any thread can signal the problem, and it's not necessarily the one causing the problem, heap-related problems are more challenging to solve.

problem (the memory leak). The OutOfMemoryError is signaled by the first thread that tries to add something in the memory but cannot because there is no more free space.

The garbage collector (GC) is the mechanism that frees the heap by removing unnecessary data. The GC knows that an object instance is no longer needed when nothing references it. Thus, if an object isn't needed but the app fails to remove all the references, the GC won't remove that object. When an app continually fails to remove references to newly created objects until at some point they fill the memory (causing an OutOfMemoryError), we say that the app has a memory leak.

An object instance may be referred to from another object in a heap (figure E.12). A common example of a memory leak is a collection in which we continuously add object references. If these references aren't removed, then, as long as the collection is in the memory, the GC won't remove them—they become a memory leak.

> **NOTE** You should pay special attention to static objects (object instances referred to from static variables). These variables don't disappear once they are created, so unless you explicitly remove the reference, you can assume that an object referred to from a static variable will stay for the whole life of the process.

If that object is a collection that refers to other objects that are never removed, it can potentially become a memory leak.

The objects in a heap may refer to one another. In this case, the cat instance can't be removed by the garbage collector until the reference made by the person instance is removed or the person is removed.

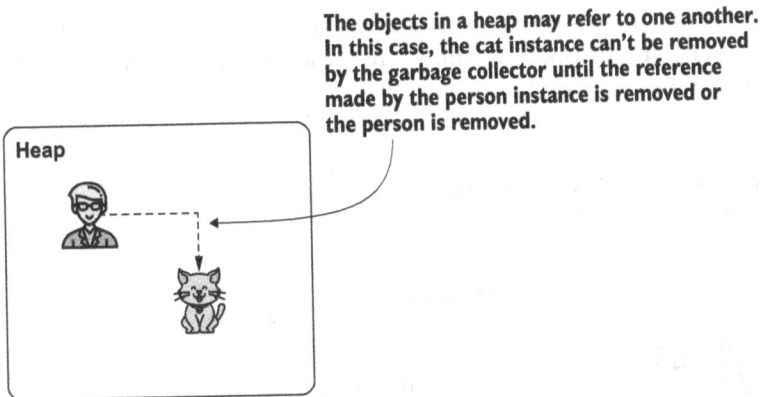

Figure E.12
Any object in the heap can keep references to other objects in the heap. The GC can remove an object only when no reference to it exists.

An object instance can also be referred to from the stack (figure E.13). Usually, references from the stack don't cause memory leaks since (as discussed in section E.2) a stack layer automatically disappears when the execution reaches the end of the code block for which the app created the layer. But in specific cases, when combined with other problems, references from the stack can also cause trouble. Imagine a deadlock that keeps the execution from running through a whole block of code. The layer in the stack won't be removed, and if it keeps references to objects, this may also become a memory leak.

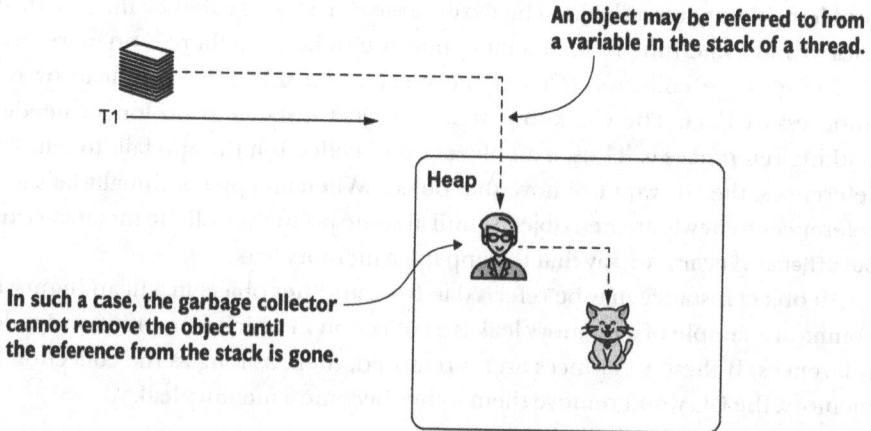

An object may be referred to from a variable in the stack of a thread.

In such a case, the garbage collector cannot remove the object until the reference from the stack is gone.

Figure E.13   A variable in the stack can also refer to an instance in the heap, which cannot be removed until all its references are gone (including the ones in the stack).

E.4   *The metaspace memory location for storing data types*

The metaspace is a memory location the JVM uses to store the data types used to create instances stored in the heap (figure E.14). The app needs this information to handle the object instances in the heap. Sometimes, in specific conditions, an OutOfMemory-Error can also affect the metaspace. If the metaspace becomes full and there's no more space for the app to store new data types, the app throws an OutOfMemoryError, announcing that the metaspace is full. In my experience, these errors are rare, but I would like you to be aware of them.

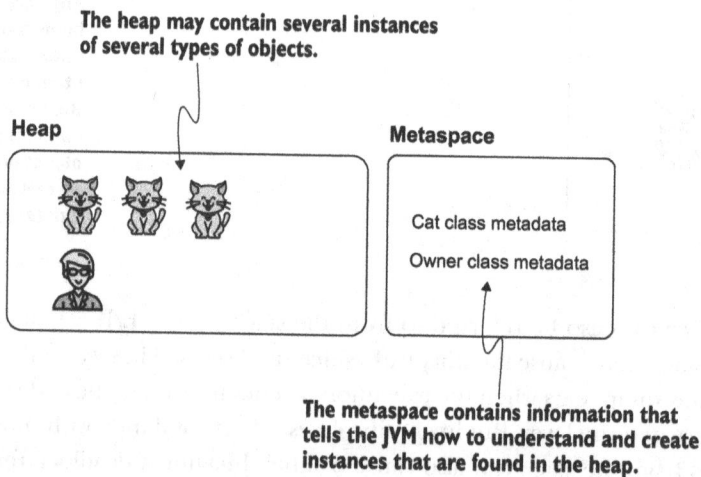

The heap may contain several instances of several types of objects.

Heap

Metaspace

Cat class metadata

Owner class metadata

The metaspace contains information that tells the JVM how to understand and create instances that are found in the heap.

Figure E.14   The metaspace is a memory location where the app stores the data types' descriptors. It holds the blueprints used to define the instances stored in the heap.

references

CHAPTER 1

Hermans, F. (2021). *The programmer's brain: What every programmer needs to know about cognition.* Manning Publications.

Hilgevoord, J., & Uffink, J. (2024). The uncertainty principle. In E. N. Zalta & U. Nodelman (Eds.), *The Stanford encyclopedia of philosophy* (Spring 2024 Edition). Stanford University. https://plato.stanford.edu/archives/spr2024/entries/qt-uncertainty/

Making Data Mistakes. (n.d.). *How to write good software faster: We spend 90% of our time debugging.* https://www.makingdatamistakes.com/how-to-write-good-software-faster-we-spend-90-of-our-time-debugging/

Martin, R. C. (2008). *Clean code: A handbook of agile software craftsmanship.* Pearson.

CHAPTER 2

Spilcă, L. (2021). *Spring start here.* Manning Publications.

Spilcă, L. (2023). *Spring Security in action* (2nd ed.). Manning Publications.

CHAPTER 4

Wilkins, P. (2022). *Logging in action.* Manning Publications.

CHAPTER 6

Bonteanu, A. M., & Tudose, C. (2024). Performance analysis and improvement for CRUD operations in relational databases from Java programs using JPA, Hibernate, Spring Data JPA. *Applied Sciences, 14*(7), 2743. https://www.mdpi.com/2076-3417/14/7/2743

Tudose, C. (2023). *Java Persistence with Spring and Hibernate.* Manning Publications.

CHAPTER 12

Bejeck, W. P., Jr. (2024). *Kafka Streams in action* (2nd ed.). Manning Publications.

APPENDIX D

Boyarsky, J., & Selikoff, S. (2020). *Oracle certified professional Java SE 11 developer complete study guide.* Sybex.

Evans, B., Clark, J., & Verburg, M. (2022). *The well-grounded Java developer.* Manning Publications.

Goetz, B., Peierls, T., Bloch, J., Bowbeer, D., Holmes, D., & Lea, D. (2006). *Java concurrency in practice.* Addison-Wesley.

index